The Ultimate Guide to Creating Custom Legal Forms

The Legal Forms Toolkit

The Ultimate Guide to Creating Custom Legal Forms

The Legal Forms Toolkit

DANIEL SITARZ, ATTORNEY-AT-LAW

Nova Publishing Company
Small Business and Consumer Legal Books
Carbondale Illinois

ISBN 13: 978-1-892949-48-6
Book w/CD-Rom   price: $39.95

Cataloging-in-Publication Data
       The legal forms toolkit / Daniel Sitarz. -- 1st ed. -- Carbondale, Ill. : Nova Publishing, c2009.
       p. ; cm. + CD-ROM
       (Legal toolkit series)
       ISBN: 978-1-892949-48-6
       Includes index.
       1. Forms (Law)--United States--Popular works. 2. Contracts--United States--Forms. 3. Inheritance and succession--United
       States--Forms. I. Title. III. Series.
            KF801.A65 S583 2009   346.7302--dc22   0907

Nova Publishing Company is dedicated to providing up-to-date and accurate legal information to the public. All Nova publications are
periodically revised to contain the latest available legal information.

1st Edition; 1st Printing / July, 2009

This publication is designed to provide accurate and authoritative information in regard to the subject matter covered. It is sold with the
understanding that the publisher and author are not engaged in rendering legal, accounting, or other professional services. If legal advice
or other expert assistance is required, the services of a competent professional person should be sought.
—From a Declaration of Principles jointly adopted by a Committee of
the American Bar Association and a Committee of Publishers

DISCLAIMER

Because of possible unanticipated changes in governing statutes and case law relating to the application of any information contained in this
book, the author, publisher, and any and all persons or entities involved in any way in the preparation, publication, sale, or distribution of this
book disclaim all responsibility for the legal effects or consequences of any document prepared or action taken in reliance upon information
contained in this book. No representations, either express or implied, are made or given regarding the legal consequences of the use of any
information contained in this book. Purchasers and persons intending to use this book for the preparation of any legal documents are advised
to check specifically on the current applicable laws in any jurisdiction in which they intend the documents to be effective.

Nova Publishing Green Business Policies
Nova Publishing Company takes seriously the impact of book publishing on the Earth and its resources. Nova Publishing
Company is committed to protecting the environment and to the responsible use of natural resources. As a book publisher, with
paper as a core part of our business, we are very concerned about the future of the world's remaining endangered forests and
the environmental impacts of paper production. We are committed to implementing policies that will support the preservation of
endangered forests globally and to advancing 'best practices' within the book and paper industries. Nova Publishing Company is
committed to preserving ancient forests and natural resources. Our company's policy is to print all of our books on 100% recycled
paper, with 100% post-consumer waste content, de-inked in a chlorine-free process. In addition, all Nova Publishing Company books
are printed using soy-based inks. As a result of these environmental policies, Nova Publishing Company has saved hundreds of
thousands of gallons of water, hundreds of thousands of kilowatts of electricity, thousand of pounds of pollution and carbon dioxide,
and thousands of trees that would otherwise have been used in the traditional manner of publishing its books. Nova Publishing
Company is very proud to be one of the first members of the Green Press Initiative, a nonprofit program dedicated to supporting
publishers in their efforts to reduce their use of fiber obtained from endangered forests. (see www.greenpressinitiative.org).
Nova Publishing Company is also proud to be an initial signatory on the Book Industry Treatise on Responsible Paper Use. In
addition, Nova Publishing Company uses all compact fluorescent lighting; recycles all office paper products, aluminum and plastic
beverage containers, and printer cartridges; uses 100% post-consumer fiber, process-chlorine-free, acid-free paper for 95% of in-house
paper use; and, when possible, uses electronic equipment that is EPA Energy Star-certified. Nova's freight shipments are coordinated
to minimize energy use whenever possible. Finally, all carbon emissions from Nova Publishing Company office energy use are offset by
the purchase of wind-energy credits that are used to subsidize the building of wind turbines on the Rosebud Sioux Reservation in South
Dakota (see www.nativeenergy.com). We strongly encourage other publishers and all partners in publishing supply chains to adopt
similar policies.

Nova Publishing Company
Small Business and Consumer Legal Books and Software
1103 West College St.
Carbondale, IL 62901
Editorial: (800) 748-1175
www.novapublishing.com

Distributed by:
National Book Network
4501 Forbes Blvd., Suite 200
Lanham, MD 20706
Orders: (800) 462-6420

Table of Contents

INTRODUCTION: Introduction to The Legal Forms Toolkit 13
    How to Use This Book 14
    State Law Appendices Provided on CD 14
    Instructions for Using Forms-on-CD 15

CHAPTER 1: Contracts 19
    Instructions 20
    General Contract 24
    Extension of Contract 25
    Modification of Contract 26
    Termination of Contract 27
    Assignment of Contract 28
    Consent to Assignment of Contract 29

CHAPTER 2: Signatures and Notary Acknowledgments 30
    Instructions 31
    Corporate Acknowledgment and Signature Line 34
    Partnership Acknowledgment and Signature Line 35
    Limited Liability Company Acknowledgment and Signature Line 36
    Sole Proprietorship Acknowledgment and Signature Line 37
    Power of Attorney Acknowledgment and Signature Line 38
    Individual Acknowledgment and Signature Line 39
    Husband and Wife Acknowledgment and Signature Line 40

CHAPTER 3: Powers of Attorney 41
    Types of Powers of Attorney 41
    General Power of Attorney 43
    Unlimited Power of Attorney 48
    Limited Power of Attorney 59
    Durable Unlimited Powers of Attorney for Financial Affairs 64
        Effective Immediately 67
        Effective on Incapacitation or Disability 71
    Durable Health Care Power of Attorney 75
    Revocation of Durable Health Care Power of Attorney 84
    Witness Affidavit of Oral Revocation of Durable Health Care Power of Attorney .86
    Revocation of Powers of Attorney 88

CHAPTER 4: Probate and Successor Trustee/Executor Information 90
Successor Trustee/Executor Duties Checklist Instructions 93
Successor Trustee/Executor Information List Instructions 96

CHAPTER 5: Wills 97
Property and Taxation Information 98
Federal and State Taxes Relating to Estates 103
Property Questionnaire Instructions 105
Beneficiary and Gift Information 106
Selecting Your Will 110
Preparing and Signing a Will 115
Safeguarding Your Will 117
Instructions for Will for Married Person with Children (Using Children's Trust) ..118
Instructions for Will For Married Person with No Children 126
Instructions for Will For Single Person with No Children 132

CHAPTER 6: Living Trusts 138
Creating a Living Trust 141
Living Trust with a Children's Trust Included....................................148
Living Trust without a Children's Trust 153
Schedule of Assets of Living Trust 158
Schedule of Beneficiaries of Living Trust 160
Assignment to Living Trust 165
Registration of Living Trust 167
New York Notice of Assignment of Property to Living Trust 167

CHAPTER 7: Living Wills 168
Typical Living Will Provisions 169
Instructions for Preparing and Signing a Living Will 171
Instructions for Revocation of Living Will 177

CHAPTER 8: Advance Health Care Directives 178
When You Should Use an Advance Health Care Directive 181
Witness and Notary Requirements 182
Instructions for Preparing Your Advance Health Care Directive 183
Instructions for Revocation of Advance Health Care Directive 185
Witness Affidavit of Oral Revocation of Advance Health Care Directive 188
Additional Information for Advance Health Care Directive 190

CHAPTER 9: Premarital Agreements 191
Instructions for Premarital Agreement 194

CHAPTER 10: Marital Settlement Agreements 197
Preliminary Questionnaire 198
Document Checklist 199
What Will be the Grounds for Your Divorce? 200
Tax Consequences of Divorce 201
Marital Settlement Agreement Instructions 204
Property Division Questionnaire 216
Property Division Worksheet 223
Financial Statement Instructions 226
Alimony, Maintenance, Spousal Support 231
Alimony Questionnaire 231
Child Custody Questionnaire 235
Child Custody and Visitation 236
Custody and Visitation Worksheet Instructions 241
Child Support 246
Child Support Worksheet and Guidelines Instructions ..249
Completing Your Marital Settlement Agreement 253

CHAPTER 11: Releases 256
Instructions for Releases 257
General Release 258
Mutual Release 259
Specific Release 260

CHAPTER 12: Receipts 261
Instructions for Receipts 261
Receipt in Full 263
Receipt on Account 264
Receipt for Goods 265

CHAPTER 13: Leases of Real Estate 266
Instructions 267
Credit/Rental Application 283
Move-in/Move-Out Checklist and Acknowledgment 285
Residential Lease 287
Month-to-Month Rental Agreement 290
Commercial Lease 292
Lease with Purchase Option 294
Amendment of Lease 297
Extension of Lease 298
Mutual Termination of Lease 299
Assignment of Lease 300

Consent to Assignment of Lease 301
Sublease 302
Consent to Sublease of Lease 303
Notice of Rent Default 304
Notice of Breach of Lease 305
Notice to Pay Rent or Vacate 306
Landlord's Notice to Terminate Lease 307
Final Notice Before Legal Action 308
Notice of Lease 309
Receipt for Lease Security Deposit 310
Rent Receipt 310

CHAPTER 14: Rental and Sale of Personal Property

CHAPTER 14: Rental and Sale of Personal Property 311
Instructions for Rental of Personal Property 311
Instructions for Sale of Personal Property 312
Personal Property Rental Agreement 315
Contract for Sale of Personal Property 317
Bill of Sale with Warranties 318
Bill of Sale without Warranties 319
Bill of Sale, Subject to Debt 320

CHAPTER 15: Sale of Real Estate

CHAPTER 15: Sale of Real Estate 321
Instructions for Sale of Real Estate 321
Agreement to Sell Real Estate 332
Contract for Deed 335
Declaration of Intent to Default and Forfeit Contract for Deed 338
Option to Buy Real Estate 339
Offer to Purchase Real Estate 340
Lead Warning Statement 341
Appraisal Report 342
Appraisal Affidavit 343
Quitclaim Deed 344
Warranty Deed 346

CHAPTER 16: Promissory Notes

CHAPTER 16: Promissory Notes 348
Promissory Note Instructions...348
Promissory Note (Installment Repayment) 352
Promissory Note (Lump Sum Repayment) 352
Promissory Note (on Demand) 353
Release of Promissory Note 354
Demand and Notice of Default on Installment Promissory Note 354

CHAPTER 17: Business Operations 355

Instructions for Business Operations Forms 358
Agreement for Sale of Business 364
Agreement for Sale of Business Assets 367
Notice of Intention to Use Fictitious Name.......................................369
Affidavit of Use of Fictitious Name 370
Partnership Agreement 371

CHAPTER 18: Employment Documents 373

Employment Document Instructions 373
General Employment Contract 376
Independent Contractor Agreement 378

INDEX 380

LIST OF FORMS ON CD

(All forms are in book and on CD as both PDF and text forms unless noted)

APPENDICES of State Laws
    Divorce (on CD only as PDF form)
    Real Estate ((on CD only as PDF form)
    Estate Planning (on CD only as PDF form)
Chapter 1: Contracts
    General Contract
    Extension of Contract
    Modification of Contract
    Termination of Contract
    Assignment of Contract
    Consent to Assignment of Contract
Chapter 2: Signatures and Notary Acknowledgments (all forms text only)
    Corporate Acknowledgment
    Corporate Signature Line
    Partnership Acknowledgment
    Partnership Signature Line
    Limited Liability Company Acknowledgment
    Limited Liability Company Signature Line
    Sole Proprietorship Acknowledgment
    Sole Proprietorship Signature Line
    Power of Attorney Acknowledgment
    Power of Attorney Signature Line

Individual Acknowledgment
Individual Signature Line
Husband and Wife Acknowledgment
Husband and Wife Signature Line

Chapter 3: Powers of Attorney
General Power of Attorney
Unlimited Power of Attorney
Limited Power of Attorney
Durable Unlimited Power of Attorney for Financial Affairs (Effective Immediately)
Durable Unlimited Power of Attorney for Financial Affairs (Effective on Incapacity or Disability)
Durable Health Care Power of Attorney
Durable Powers of Attorney - State Specific (on CD only)
Revocation of Durable Health Care Power of Attorney
Witness Affidavit of Oral Revocation of Durable Health Care Power of Attorney
Revocation of Power of Attorney

Chapter 4: Probate and Successor Trustee/Executor Information
Successor Trustee/Executor Duties Checklist
Successor Trustee/Executor Information List (on CD only)

Chapter 5: Wills
Property Questionnaire (on CD only)
Beneficiary Questionnaire (on CD only)
Will For Married Person With Children
Will For Married Person Without Children
Will For Single Person Without Children

Chapter 6: Living Trusts
Living Trust with Children's Trust
Living Trust without Children's Trust
Schedule of Assets of Living Trust
Schedule of Beneficiaries of Living Trust
Assignment to Living Trust
Registration of Living Trust (on CD only)
New York Notice of Assignment of Property to Living Trust (on CD only)

Chapter 7: Living Wills
Living Will Declaration and Directive to Physicians
Revocation of Living Will

Chapter 8: Advance Health Care Directives
Advance Health Care Directives - State-Specific (on CD only)
Revocation of Advance Health Care Directive
Witness Affidavit of Oral Revocation of Advance Health Care Directive
Additional Information for Advance Health Care Directive

Chapter 9: Premarital Agreements
Premarital Agreement

Chapter 10: Marital Settlement Agreements
Preliminary Questionnaire (on CD only as PDF form)
Document Checklist (on CD only as PDF form)
Property Questionnaire (on CD only as PDF form)
Property Division Worksheet (on CD only as PDF form)
Financial Statement (on CD only as PDF form)
Alimony Questionnaire (on CD only as PDF form)
Child Custody Questionnaire (on CD only as PDF form))
Custody and Visitation Worksheet (on CD only as PDF form)
Child Support Worksheet and Guidelines (on CD only as PDF form)
Marital Settlement Agreement

Chapter 11: Releases
General Release
Mutual Release
Specific Release

Chapter 12: Receipts
Receipt in Full
Receipt on Account
Receipt for Goods

Chapter 13: Leases of Real Estate
Credit/Rental Application
Move-in/Move-out Checklist and Acknowledgment
Residential Lease
Month-to-Month Rental Agreement
Commercial Lease
Lease with Purchase Option
Amendment of Lease
Extension of Lease
Mutual Termination of Lease
Assignment of Lease
Consent to Assignment of Lease
Sublease
Consent to Sublease
Notice of Rent Default
Notice of Breach of Lease
Notice to Pay Rent or Vacate
Landlord's Notice to Terminate Lease
Final Notice Before Legal Action
Notice of Lease
Receipt for Lease Security Deposit
Rent Receipt
Addendum to Lease (California) (on CD only)

Addendum to Lease (Chicago) (on CD only)
Chicago Heating Disclosure Form (on CD only as PDF form)
Chicago Residential Landlord and Tenant Ordinance Summary (on CD only as PDF form)

Chapter 14: Rental and Sale of Personal Property
Personal Property Rental Agreement
Contract for Sale of Personal Property
Bill of Sale, with Warranties
Bill of Sale, without Warranties
Bill of Sale, Subject to Debt

Chapter 15: Sale of Real Estate
Addendum to Contract-California
Agreement to Sell Real Estate
Contract for Deed
Declaration of Intent to Forfeit and Terminate Contract for Deed
Option to Buy Real Estate
Offer to Purchase Real Estate
Lead Warning Statement
Federal Lead Brochure (on CD only as PDF form)
Appraisal Report
Appraisal Affidavit
Quitclaim Deed
Warranty Deed

Chapter 16: Promissory Notes
Promissory Note (Installment Repayment)
Promissory Note (Lump Sum Repayment)
Promissory Note (on Demand)
Release of Promissory Note
Demand and Notice of Default on Installment Promissory Note

Chapter 17: Business Operations
Agreement for Sale of Business
Agreement for Sale of Business Assets
Notice of Intention to Use Fictitious Name
Affidavit of Use of Fictitious Business Name
Partnership Agreement

Chapter 18: Employment Documents
General Employment Contract
Independent Contractor Agreement

California Notary Acknowledgment (on CD only)
California Residents: Please see page 31 for information regarding the new California Notary Acknowledgement form that is required to be used on documents that are intended to be valid in the state of California. The new California Notary Acknowledgment form is included on the CD in a separate folder as both a text and PDF form.

Introduction to The Legal Forms Toolkit

The contracts and other various legal documents that are used in this book are written in plain English. Standard legal jargon, as used in most lawyer-prepared documents, is, for most people, totally incomprehensible. The vast majority of such legalese is absolutely unnecessary. Clarity, simplicity, and readability should be the goal in legal documents. In most contexts, "buyer" and "seller," "landlord" and "tenant," or some other straightforward term of definition of the parties involved is possible. Unfortunately, certain obscure legal terms are the only words that accurately and precisely describe some things in certain legal contexts. In those few cases, the unfamiliar legal term will be defined when first used. Generally, however, simple terms are used. Although this book will provide an overview of the uses of legal contracts in many standard situations, it is not intended to be a complete reference on the subject of contract law.

All of the legal documents contained in this book have been prepared in essentially the same manner that attorneys use to create legal forms. This book provides individuals with a set of legal forms that have been prepared with the problems and normal transactions of everyday life in mind. These forms are intended to be used in those situations that are clearly described by the specific terms of the particular form. Of course, while most transactions will fall within the bounds of these normal situations, some legal circumstances will present non-standard situations. The forms in this book are designed to be readily adaptable to most usual situations. They may be carefully altered to conform to the particular transaction that you may be confronted with. However, if you are faced with a complex or tangled legal situation, the advice of a competent lawyer is highly recommended. It may also be advisable to create your legal document for a certain legal situation and have a lawyer check it for any local legal circumstances.

The proper and cautious use of the forms provided in this book will allow the typical person to save considerable money on legal costs. Perhaps more importantly, these forms will provide a method for the person to avoid costly misunderstandings about what exactly was intended in a particular situation or transaction. By using the forms provided to clearly set out the terms and conditions of everyday personal dealings, disputes over what was really meant can be avoided.

How to Use This Book

In each chapter of this book, you will find an introductory section that will give you an overview of the types of situations in which the forms in that chapter will generally be used. Following that overview, there will be a brief explanation of the specific uses for each form. Included in the information provided for each form will be a discussion of the legal terms and conditions provided in the form. Finally, for each form, there is a listing of the information that must be compiled to complete the form.

For purposes of simplification, most of the forms in this book are set out as a form that would be used by two individuals. If businesses are parties to the contract, please identify the name and type of business entity (for example: Jackson Car Stereo, a New York sole proprietorship, etc.) in the first section of the contract. Many of the forms in this book have blanks for inserting the state or county. If you are a resident of Louisiana, substitute "parish" for "county." If you are a resident of Pennsylvania, Massachusetts, Virginia, or Kentucky, substitute "Commonwealth" for "state." If you are a resident of Washington D.C., please substitute "District of Columbia" for "state." In most cases, masculine and feminine terms have been eliminated and the generic "it" or "them" is used instead. In the few situations where this leads to awkward sentence construction, "his or her" or "he or she" may be used instead.

It is recommended that you review the table of contents of this book in order to gain a broad overview of the range and type of legal documents that are available. Then, before you prepare any of the forms for use, you should carefully read the introductory information and instructions in the chapter containing the particular form that you wish to use. Try to be as detailed and specific as possible as you fill in these forms. The more precise the description, the less likelihood that later disputes may develop over what was actually intended by the language chosen. The careful preparation and use of the legal forms in this book should provide the typical individual with most of the legal documents necessary for day-to-day life. If in doubt as to whether a particular form will work in a specific application, please consult a competent lawyer.

State Law Appendices Provided on CD

A number of Appendices that contain detailed information about specific state laws are provided on the CD that accompanied this book. These appendices provide information about the many differences in state laws regarding many of the forms in this book. Please refer to them for information regarding your particular state's laws. The following state laws are outlined in these appendices:

- Real Estate Laws
- Estate Planning Laws
- Divorce Laws

Installation Instructions for Installing Forms-on-CD

Installation Instructions for PCs

1. Insert the enclosed CD in your computer.
2. The installation program will start automatically. Follow the onscreen dialogue and make your appropriate choices.
3. If the CD installation does not start automatically, click on START, then RUN, then BROWSE, and select your CD drive, and then select the file "Install.exe." Finally, click OK to run the installation program.
4. During the installation program, you will be prompted as to whether or not you wish to install the Adobe Acrobat Reader® program. This software program is necessary to view and fill in the PDF (potable document format) forms that are included on the Forms-on-CD. If you do not already have the Adobe Acrobat Reader® program installed on your hard drive, you will need to select the full installation that will install the program on your computer.

Installation Instructions for MACs®

1. Insert the enclosed CD in your computer.
2. Copy the folder "Forms for Macs" to your hard drive. All of the PDF and text-only forms are included in this folder.
3. If you do not already have the Adobe Acrobat Reader® program installed on your hard drive, you will need to download the version of this software that is appropriate for your particular MAC operating system from www.adobe.com. Note: The latest versions of the MAC operating system (OS-X) has PDF capabilities built into it.

Instructions for Using Forms-on-CD

All of the forms that are included in this book have been provided on the Forms-on-CD for your use if you have access to a computer. If you have completed the Forms-on-CD installation program, all of the forms will have been copied to your computer's hard drive. By default, these files are installed in the C:\Legal FormsToolkit\Forms folder which is created by the installation program. (Note for MAC users: see instructions above). Opening the Forms folder will provide you with access to folders for each of the topics corresponding to chapters in the book. Within each chapter, the forms are provided in two separate formats:

Text forms may be opened, prepared, and printed from within your own word processing program (such as Microsoft Word®, or WordPerfect®). The text forms all have the file extension: .txt. These forms are located in the TEXT FORMS folders supplied for each chapter's forms. You will use the forms in this format if you will be making changes to any of the text on the forms.

PDF forms may be filled in on your computer screen and printed out on any printer. This particular format provides the most widely-used format for accessing computer files. Files in this format may be opened as images on your computer and printed out on any printer. The files in PDF format all have the file extension: .pdf. Although this format provides the easiest method for completing the forms, the forms in this format can not be altered (other than to fill in the information required on the blanks provided). To access the PDF forms, please see below. If you wish to alter the language in any of the forms, you will need to access the forms in their text-only versions.

To Access PDF Forms

1. You must have already installed the Adobe Acrobat Reader® program to your computer's hard drive. This program is installed automatically by the installation program. (MAC users will need to install this program via www.adobe.com).

2. On your computer's desktop, you will find a shortcut icon labeled "Acrobat Reader®" Using your mouse, left double- click on this icon. This will open the Acrobat Reader® program. When the Acrobat Reader® program is opened for the first time, you will need to accept the Licensing Agreement from Adobe in order to use this program. Click "Accept" when given the option to accept or decline the Agreement.

3. Once the Acrobat Reader® program is open on your computer, click on FILE (in the upper left-hand corner of the upper taskbar). Then click on OPEN in the drop down menu. Depending on which version of Windows or other operating system you are using, a box will open which will allow you to access files on your computer's hard drive. The files for estate planning forms are located on your computer's "C" drive, under the folder "Legal Forms Toolkit." In this folder, you will find a subfolder "Forms." (Note: if you installed the forms folder on a different drive, access the forms on that particular drive).

4. If you desire to work with one of the forms, you should then left double-click your mouse on the sub-folder: "Forms." A list of form topics (corresponding to the chapters in the book) will appear and you should then left double-click your mouse on the topic of your choice. This will open two folders: one for text forms and one for PDF forms. Left double click your mouse on the PDF forms folder and a list of the PDF forms for that topic should appear. Left double- click your mouse on the form of your choice. This will open the appropriate form within the Acrobat Reader® program.

To Fill in and Use PDF Forms

1. Once you have opened the appropriate form in the Acrobat Reader® program, filling in the form is a simple process. A 'hand tool' icon will be your cursor in the Acrobat Reader® program. Move the 'hand tool' cursor to the first blank space that will need to be completed on the form. A vertical line or "I-beam" should appear at the beginning of the first space on a form that you will need to fill in. You may then begin to type the necessary information in the space provided. When you have filled in the first blank space, hit the TAB key on your keyboard. This will move the 'hand' cursor to the next space which must be filled in. Please note that some of the spaces in the forms must be completed by hand, specifically the signature, witness and notary blanks.

2. Move through the form, completing each required space, and hitting TAB to move to the next space to be filled in. For details on the information required for each blank on the forms, please read the instructions in this book. When you have completed all of the fill-ins, you may print out the form on your computer's printer. (Please note: hitting TAB after the last fill-in will return you to the first page of the form.)

3. If you wish to save a completed form, you should "save as" a renamed form. This will allow you to retain a blank form on your hard drive for later use.

To Access and Complete Text Forms

For your convenience, all of the forms in this book (except certain state-specific forms) are also provided as text-only forms which may be altered and saved. To open and use any of the text forms:

1. First, open your preferred word processing program. Then click on FILE (in the upper left-hand corner of the upper taskbar). Then click on OPEN in the drop down menu. Depending on which version of Windows or other operating system you are using, a box will open which will allow you to access files on your computer's hard drive. The files for estate planning forms are located on your computer's "C" drive, under the folder "Legal Forms Toolkit." In this folder, you will find a sub-folder: "Forms."

2. If you desire to work with one of the forms, you should then left double-click your mouse on the sub-folder: "Forms." A list of form topics (corresponding to the chapters in the book) will appear and you should then left double-click your mouse on the topic of your choice. This will open two folders: one for text forms and one for PDF forms. Left double-click your mouse on the text forms folder and a list of the text forms for that topic should appear. Left double-click

your mouse on the form of your choice. This will open the appropriate form within your word processing program.

3.   You may now fill in the necessary information while the text-only file is open in your word processing program. You may need to adjust margins and/or line endings of the form to fit your particular word processing program. Note that there is an asterisk (*) in every location in these forms where information will need to be included. Replace each asterisk with the necessary information. When the form is complete, you may print out the completed form and you may save the completed form. If you wish to save the completed form, you should rename the form so that your hard drive will retain an unaltered version of the original form.

Technical Support

Please also note that Nova Publishing Company cannot provide legal advice regarding the effect or use of the forms in this book or on the CD. For questions about installing the Forms-on-CD and software, you may call Nova Technical Support at 1-800-748-1175 or access the Nova Publishing Website for support at www.novapublishing.com.

For any questions relating to Adobe Acrobat Reader®, please access Adobe Technical Support at www.adobe.com/support/main.html or you may search for assistance in the HELP area of Adobe Acrobat Reader® (located in approximately the center of the top line of the program's desktop).

Note regarding legal updates: Although business law is relatively stable and the information provided in this book is based on the most current state statutes, laws regarding business start-up are subject to constant change. In the Appendices of this book on the enclosed CD are provided internet addresses for each state's legislature and statutes. These sites may be accessed to check if any of the laws have changed since the publication of this book. In addition, the Nova Publishing website noted above also provides legal updates for information that has changed since the publication of any Nova titles.

California Residents: Please see page 31 for information regarding the new California Notary Acknowledgement form that is required to be used on documents that are intended to be valid in California. The new California Notary Acknowledgment form is included on the CD as both a text and PDF form.

Chapter 1

Contracts

The foundation of most agreements is a contract. A *contract* is merely an agreement by which two or more parties each promise to do something. This simple definition of a contract can encompass incredibly complex agreements. The objective of a good contract is to clearly set out the terms of the agreement. Once the parties have reached an oral understanding of what their agreement should be, the terms of the deal should be put in writing. Contrary to what many attorneys may tell you, the written contract should be clearly written and easily understood by both parties to the agreement. It should be written in precise and unambiguous terms. The most common causes for litigation over contracts are arguments over the meaning of the language used. Remember that both sides of the agreement should be able to understand and agree to the language being used.

A contract has to have certain prerequisites to be enforceable in court. These requirements are relatively simple and most will be present in any standard agreement. However, you should understand what the various legal requirements are before you prepare your own contracts. To be enforceable, a contract must have *consideration*. In the context of contract law, this simply means that both parties to the contract must have promised to do something or forego taking some type of action. If one of the parties has not promised to do anything or forego any action, he or she will not be able to legally force the other party to comply with the terms of the contract. There has to be some form of mutual promise for a contract to be valid. For example: Andy agrees to pay Bill if Bill paints a car. Andy's promise is to pay Bill if the job is completed. Bill's promise is to paint the car. If Bill paints the car and is not paid, Andy's promise to pay Bill can be enforced in court. Similarly, if Bill fails to paint the car, Andy can have the contract enforced in court. Andy and Bill's mutual promises are the consideration necessary to have a valid and enforceable contract.

Another requirement is that the parties to the contract be clearly identified and the terms of the contract also be clearly spelled out. The terms and description need not be complicated, but they must be spelled out in enough detail to enable the parties to the contract (and any subsequent court) to clearly determine what exactly the parties were referring to when they made the contract. In the prior example, the names and addresses of the parties must be included for the contract to be enforceable. In addition, a description of the car must be incorporated in the contract. Finally, a description of the type of paint job and the amount of money to be paid should also be contained in the contract. The following documents are included for use in situations requiring a basic contract. There are documents for assigning, modifying, extending, and terminating a basic contract. *Note*: If you are at all unsure of the correct use of any forms in this chapter, please consult a competent attorney.

General Contract: This basic document can be adapted for use in many situations. The terms of the contract that the parties agree to should be carefully spelled out and inserted where indicated. The other information that is required are the names and addresses of the parties to the contract and the date the contract is to take effect. This basic contract form is set up to accommodate an agreement between two individuals. If a business is party to the contract, please identify the name and type of business entity (for example: Jackson Car Stereo, a New York sole proprietorship, etc.) in the first section of the contract.

Instructions for General Contract

In order to complete this form, fill in the following information:
① Date of contract
② Name of first party to the contract [If a business is party to the contract, please identify the name and type of business entity (for example: Jackson Car Stereo, a New York sole proprietorship, etc.)]
③ Address of first party
④ City of first party
⑤ State of first party
⑥ Name of second party
⑦ Address of second party
⑧ City of second party
⑨ State of second party
⑩ Exact terms of the contract to which Party One agrees
⑪ Exact terms of the contract to which Party Two agrees
⑫ Any additional terms
⑬ State whose laws will govern this contract (Generally, where the contract actions will take place)
⑭ Date of contract
⑮ Signature of Party One
⑯ Printed name of Party One
⑰ Signature of Party Two
⑱ Printed name of Party Two

Extension of Contract: This document should be used to extend the effective time period during which a contract is in force. The use of this form allows the time limit to be extended without having to entirely redraft the contract. Under this document, all of the other terms of the contract will remain the same, with only the expiration date changing. You will need to fill in both the original expiration date and the new expiration date. Other information necessary will be the names and addresses of the parties to the contract and a description of the contract. A copy of the original contract should be attached to this form.

Instructions for Extension of Contract

In order to complete this form, fill in the following information:
1. Date of extension of contract
2. Name of first party to the contract [If a business is party to the contract, please identify the name and type of business entity]
3. Address of first party
4. Name of second party
5. Address of second party
6. Date that the original contract will end
7. Date that the extension will end
8. Signature of Party One
9. Printed Name of Party One
10. Signature of Party Two
11. Printed Name of Party Two

Modification of Contract: Use this form to modify any other terms of a contract (other than the expiration date). The modification can be used to change any portion of the contract. Simply note what changes are being made in the appropriate place on this form. If a portion of the contract is being deleted, make note of the deletion. If certain language is being substituted, state the substitution clearly. If additional language is being added, make this clear. For example, you may wish to use language as follows:

- "Paragraph _____ is deleted from this contract."
- "The following new paragraph is added to this contract:"

A copy of the original contract should be attached to this form.

Instructions for Modification of Contract

In order to complete this form, fill in the following information:
1. Date of modification contract

② Name of first party to the contract [If a business is party to the contract, please identify the name and type of business entity]
③ Address of first party
④ Name of second party
⑤ Address of second party
⑥ Describe the original contract
⑦ Describe what modifications are being made to the original contract
⑧ Signature of Party One
⑨ Printed Name of Party One
⑩ Signature of Party Two
⑪ Printed Name of Party Two

Termination of Contract: This document is intended to be used when both parties to a contract mutually desire to end the contract prior to its original expiration date. Under this form, both parties agree to release each other from any claims against each other based on anything in the contract. This document effectively ends any contractual arrangement between two parties. Information necessary to complete this form are the names and addresses of the parties to the contract, a description of the contract, and the effective date of the termination of the contract.

Instructions for Termination of Contract

In order to complete this form, fill in the following information:
① Date of the termination contract
② Name of first party to the contract [If a business is party to the contract, please identify the name and type of business entity]
③ Address of first party
④ Name of second party
⑤ Address of second party
⑥ Describe the original contract
⑦ Signature of Party One
⑧ Printed Name of Party One
⑨ Signature of Party Two
⑩ Printed Name of Party Two

Assignment of Contract: This form is for use if one party to a contract is assigning its full interest in the contract to another party. This effectively substitutes one party for another under a contract. This particular assignment form has both of the parties agreeing to indemnify and hold each other harmless for any failures to perform under the contract while they were the party liable under it. This *indemnify and hold harmless* clause simply means that if a claim arises for failure to perform, each party agrees to be responsible for the period of their own performance obligations. A description of the contract which is assigned should include the parties to the contract, the purpose of the contract, and the date of the contract. Other information that is necessary to complete the assignment is the name and address of the *assignor* (the party who is assigning the contract), the name and address of the *assignee* (the party to whom the contract is being assigned), and the date of the assignment. A copy of the original contract should be attached to this form. A copy of a Consent to Assignment of Contract should also be attached, if necessary.

Instructions for Assignment of Contract

In order to complete this form, fill in the following information:
1. Date of the assignment of contract
2. Name of first party to the contract [If a business is party to the contract, please identify the name and type of business entity]
3. Address of first party
4. Name of second party
5. Address of second party
6. Describe the original contract
7. Signature of Assignor
8. Printed Name of Assignor
9. Signature of Assignee
10. Printed Name of Assignee

Consent to Assignment of Contract: This form is used if the original contract states that the consent of one of the parties is necessary for the assignment of the contract to be valid. A description of the contract and the name and signature of the person giving the consent are all that is necessary for completing this form. A copy of the original contract should be attached to this form.

Instructions for Consent to Assignment of Contract

In order to complete this form, fill in the following information:
1. Date of the consent to assignment of contract
2. Name of person assigning contract interest
3. Describe the original contract
4. Signature
5. Printed Name

Contract Exhibit: This form may be used with any contract. It provides a simple method for attaching other documents to the contract and having them considered as a legal part of the contract. If you have documents, letters, forms, etc. that you feel are necessary to have as a part of a contract, use this simple form. The space after "Exhibit" in the title of this document is for placing a letter to describe this exhibit (for example: Exhibit A). In the space provided, describe clearly which particular contract the exhibit is to be attached to (for example: The Contract dated June 1, 2008, between John Smith of 111 Main St., Uptown, NY and Mary Johnson of 222 Broadway Ave., Downtown, CA).

GENERAL CONTRACT

This Contract is made on ① , between ② , Party One, of ③ , City of ④ , State of ⑤ , and ⑥ , Party Two, of ⑦ , City of ⑧ , State of ⑨ .

For valuable consideration, the parties agree to the following:

Party One agrees to: ⑩

Party Two agrees to: ⑪

Any additional terms: ⑫

No modification of this Contract will be effective unless it is in writing and is signed by both parties. This Contract binds and benefits both parties and any successors or assigns. Time is of the essence of this Contract. This document, including any attachments, is the entire agreement between the parties. This Contract is governed by the laws of the State of ⑬ .

Dated: ⑭

⑮
Signature of Party One

⑯
Printed Name of Party One

⑰
Signature of Party Two

⑱
Printed Name of Party Two

EXTENSION OF CONTRACT

This Extension of Contract is made on ① , between ② , whose address is ③ , and ④ , whose address is ⑤ .

For valuable consideration, the parties agree as follows:

1. The following described contract will end on ⑥ :

This contract is attached to this Extension and is a part of this Extension.

2. The parties agree to extend this contract for an additional period, which will begin immediately on the expiration of the original time period and will end on ⑦ .

3. The Extension of this contract will be on the same terms and conditions as the original contract. This Extension binds and benefits both parties and any successors. This document, including the attached original contract, is the entire agreement between the parties.

The parties have signed this Extension on the date specified at the beginning of this Extension of Contract.

⑧
Signature
⑨
Printed Name

⑩
Signature
⑪
Printed Name

MODIFICATION OF CONTRACT

This Modification of Contract is made on ① , between ② , whose address is ③ , and ④ , whose address is ⑤ .

For valuable consideration, the parties agree as follows:

1. The following described contract is attached to this Modification and is made a part of this Modification: ⑥

2. The parties agree to modify this contract as follows: ⑦

3. All other terms and conditions of the original contract remain in effect without modification. This Modification binds and benefits both parties and any successors. This document, including the attached contract, is the entire agreement between the parties.

The parties have signed this Modification on the date specified at the beginning of this Modification of Contract.

⑧
Signature
⑨
Printed Name

⑩
Signature
⑪
Printed Name

TERMINATION OF CONTRACT

This Termination of Contract is made on ① , between ② , whose address is ③ , and ④ , whose address is ⑤ .

For valuable consideration, the parties agree as follows:

1. The parties are currently bound under the terms of the following described contract, which is attached and is part of this Termination: ⑥

2. They agree to mutually terminate and cancel this contract effective on this date. This Termination Agreement will act as a mutual release of all obligations under this contract for both parties, as if the contract has not been entered into in the first place.

3. This Termination binds and benefits both parties and any successors. This document, including the attached contract being terminated, is the entire agreement between the parties.

The parties have signed this Termination on the date specified at the beginning of this Termination of Contract.

⑦
Signature
⑧
Printed Name

⑨
Signature
⑩
Printed Name

ASSIGNMENT OF CONTRACT

This Assignment of Contract is made on ① , between ② , whose address is ③ , and ④ , whose address is ⑤ .

For valuable consideration, the parties agree to the following terms and conditions:

1. The Assignor assigns all interest, burdens, and benefits in the following described contract to the Assignee: ⑥

   This contract is attached to this Assignment and is a part of this Assignment.

2. The Assignor warrants that this contract is in effect, has not been modified, and is fully assignable. If the consent of a third party is necessary for this Assignment to be effective, such consent is attached to this Assignment and is a part of this Assignment. Assignor agrees to indemnify and hold the Assignee harmless from any claim which may result from the Assignor's failure to perform under this contract prior to the date of this Assignment.

3. The Assignee agrees to perform all obligations of the Assignor and receive all of the benefits of the Assignor under this contract. Assignee agrees to indemnify and hold the Assignor harmless from any claim which may result from the Assignee's failure to perform under this contract after the date of this Assignment.

4. This Assignment binds and benefits both parties and any successors. This document, including any attachments, is the entire agreement between the parties.

The parties have signed this Assignment on the date specified at the beginning of this Assignment of Contract.

⑦
Signature of Assignor
⑧
Printed Name of Assignor

⑨
Signature of Assignee
⑩
Printed Name of Assignee

CONSENT TO ASSIGNMENT OF CONTRACT

Date: ①

To: ②

I am a party to the following described contract: ③

This contract is the subject of the attached Assignment of Contract.

I consent to the Assignment of this Contract as described in the attached Assignment, which provides that the Assignee is substituted for the Assignor.

④
Signature
⑤
Printed Name

Chapter 2

Signatures and Notary Acknowledgments

Signatures and notary acknowledgments for legal forms serve similar but slightly different purposes. Both are used to document the formal signing of a legal instrument, but the notarized acknowledgment also serves as a method of providing a neutral witness to the signature, and so, authenticates the signature. In addition, a notarized acknowledgment can serve an additional purpose of providing a statement under oath. For example, a notarized acknowledgment can be used to assert that a person states, under oath, that he has read the document that she or he is signing and believes that what it contains is the truth.

The use of a notary acknowledgment is not required for all legal forms. The notary acknowledgments contained in this chapter are to be used only for the purpose of providing a notarization required for recording a document. Generally, notarization is only necessary if the document is intended to be recorded with an official government office in some manner. For example, all documents which intend to convey real estate should be recorded in the county recorder's office or register of deeds office in the county (or parish) where the property is located. In virtually all jurisdictions, such documents must be notarized before they will be recorded. Similarly, some states require automobile titles and similar documents to be notarized. Check with your local county clerk to determine the requirements in your locale.

Another unofficial purpose of notarization of legal documents is to make the document seem more important to the parties. By formally having their signatures witnessed by a notary public, they are attesting to the fact that they ascribe a powerful purpose to the document. Although this type of notarization carries with it no legal value, it does serve a valid purpose in solemnizing the signing of an important business document.

For all of the notary acknowledgment forms contained in this chapter, the following information is necessary:

- The name of the state in which the document is signed
- The name of the county in which the document is signed
- The date on which the document is signed
- The name of the person who is signing the document
- The entity on whose behalf the person is signing (for example: a corporation, partnership, etc.)
- The name of the notary public (or similar official)
- The county in which the notary is registered to act
- The state in which the notary is authorized to perform
- The date on which the notary's commission will expire

In addition, many states require that the notary place an embossed seal on the document to authenticate the notarization process. The notary who completes the acknowledgment will know the correct procedure for your state.

NOTE for residents of California: The state of California requires a different notary block than other states. If you intend any of the notarized forms in this book to be valid in California, you will need to use the California notary block that is provided on the accompanying Forms-on-CD.

A simple signature line merely serves to provide a place for a party to a document to sign his or her name. However, care must be taken to be sure that the type of signature line used corresponds exactly with the person or business entity who is joining in the signing of a document. If the entity is a partnership, the signature must be set up for a partner to sign and clearly state that the signature is for the partnership. The same holds true for the signature of a corporate officer.

Instructions

The following notary acknowledgments and signature lines are intended to be used for the specific purposes outlined below. When preparing a legal document, choose the correct version of these additions carefully. You may need to use the 'text' versions of a particular form in order to add the correct notary acknowledgment and/or signature lines to the document. The following are contained in this chapter:

Corporate Acknowledgment: This clause should be used on documents where a corporation is one of the parties who is to sign the document and the document needs to be notarized. The person signing the document on behalf of the corporation must be either an officer of the corporation or be specifically authorized by a resolution of the Board of Directors of the corporation to act on its behalf.

Corporate Signature Line: This line should be inserted on all documents where a party that will sign the document is a corporation. This may be used regardless of whether the corporation is a corporation, an S-corporation, or a not-for-profit corporation. The person signing must have authority to bind the corporation. Again, it must either be an officer of the corporation or a person specifically authorized by a resolution of the Board of Directors of the corporation to act on its behalf. The state in which the corporation is registered to do business should be noted.

Partnership Acknowledgment: This clause should be used on documents where one of the parties who is to sign the document is a standard partnership and the document needs to be notarized. Any partner in a partnership may have authority to act on behalf of the corporation. However, it may be wise to request a copy of the partnership agreement which authorizes the partner to bind the partnership.

Partnership Signature Line: This line should be inserted on all documents where one of the parties that will sign the document is a partnership. This may be used if the entity is a partnership. Any partner may bind the partnership if authorized by the partnership agreement. The state in which the partnership is doing business should be noted.

Limited Liability Company Acknowledgment: This clause should be used on documents where a limited liability company is one of the parties who is to sign the document and the document needs to be notarized. Any member of a limited liability company has authority to bind the limited liability company.

Limited Liability Company Signature Line: This line should be inserted on all documents where one of the parties who will sign the document is a limited liability company. Any member may sign on behalf of a limited liability company. The state in which the limited liability company is doing business should be noted.

Sole Proprietorship Acknowledgment: This clause should be used on documents where an individual who owns a sole proprietorship is one of the parties who is to sign the document and the document needs to be notarized. Many sole proprietorships are designated as persons "doing business as." This is abbreviated as "DBA." For example: "John Washington, DBA Washington's Restaurant" indicates that John Washington is operating Washington's Restaurant as a sole proprietorship. The owner of the sole proprietorship is the person who should sign all documents for this type of business.

Sole Proprietorship Signature Line: This line should be inserted on all documents where a party that will sign the document is an individual that owns a sole proprietorship. Only the owner of a sole proprietorship has authority to bind such a business. The state in which the sole proprietorship is doing business should be noted.

Power of Attorney Acknowledgment: This clause should be used on documents where an individual acting under a power of attorney is one of the parties who is to sign the document and the document needs to be notarized. As noted in Chapter 3, an attorney-in-fact is a person who is authorized to act for another person by virtue of a document entitled a "power of attorney," also found in Chapter 3.

Power of Attorney Signature Line: This line should be inserted on all documents where a party that will sign the document is an individual acting under a power of attorney. The person signing must have the specific authority to act for another person under some form of Power of Attorney. The date of the Power of Attorney form should be noted.

Individual Acknowledgment: This clause should be used on documents where an individual is one of the parties who is to sign the document and the document needs to be notarized. However, if the document is to be signed by a husband and wife together, use the appropriate acknowledgment form which follows.

Individual Signature Line: This line should be inserted on all documents where a party that will sign the document is an individual. Again, however, if the document is to be signed by a husband and wife together, use the appropriate signature line which follows.

Husband and Wife Acknowledgment: This clause should be used on documents where both a husband and wife are to sign the document and the document needs to be notarized.

Husband and Wife Signature Line: This line should be inserted on all documents where both a husband and wife are intended to sign the document.

Corporate Signature Line

_____ (name of corporation), a(n)
_____ (state of incorporation) corporation

By:

_____
Signature of Corporate Officer

_____
Printed Name of Corporate Officer

The _____ (_title of corporate officer_) of the corporation

Corporate Acknowledgment

State of _____
County of _____

On _____, 20 _____, _____ personally came
before me and, being duly sworn, did state that he or she is the _____ of
the corporation described in the above document; that he or she signed the above document in
my presence on behalf of this corporation; and that he or she had full authority to do so.

_____
Signature of Notary Public

Notary Public, In and for the County of _____
State of _____
My commission expires: _____   Notary Seal

Partnership Acknowledgment

State of _____

County of _____

On _____ , 20 _____ , _____ personally came before me and, being duly sworn, did state that he or she is a partner of the partnership described in the above document; that he or she signed the above document in my presence on behalf of this partnership; and that he or she had full authority to do so.

_____

Signature of Notary Public

Notary Public, In and for the County of _____

State of _____

My commission expires: _____   Notary Seal

Partnership Signature Line

_____ (*name of partnership*), a(n)

_____ (*state of operation*) partnership

By:

_____

Signature of Partner

_____

Printed Name of Partner

A Partner of the Partnership

Limited Liability Company Acknowledgment

State of _____
County of _____

On _____ , 20 _____ , _____ personally came before me and, being duly sworn, did state that he or she is a member of the limited liability company described in the above document; that he or she signed the above document in my presence on behalf of this limited liability company; and that he or she had full authority to do so.

_____
Signature of Notary Public

Notary Public, In and for the County of _____
State of _____

My commission expires: _____   Notary Seal

Limited Liability Company Signature Line

_____ (*name of limited liability company*), a(n) _____
_____ (*state of operation*) limited liability company

By:

_____
Signature of Member

_____
Printed Name of Member

A Member of the Limited Liability Company

Sole Proprietorship Acknowledgment

State of _____
County of _____

On _____ , 20 _____ , _____ personally
came before me and, being duly sworn, did state that he or she is the person who owns the sole
proprietorship described in the above document and that he or she signed the above document
in my presence on behalf of the sole proprietorship and on his or her own behalf.

_____
Signature of Notary Public

Notary Public, In and for the County of _____
State of _____

My commission expires: _____   Notary Seal

Sole Proprietorship Signature Line

_____
Signature of Sole Proprietor

_____
Printed Name of Sole Proprietor

DBA _____ (name of business), a(n)
_____ (state of operation) sole proprietorship

Power of Attorney Acknowledgment

State of _____
County of _____

On _____ , 20 _____ , _____ personally came before me and, being duly sworn, did state that he or she is the attorney-in-fact of _____ _____ described in the above document; that he or she signed the above document in my presence as attorney-in-fact on behalf of this person; and that he or she had full authority to do so under Power of Attorney dated _____ , 20 _____ .

_____
Signature of Notary Public

Notary Public, In and for the County of _____
State of _____

My commission expires: _____   Notary Seal

Power of Attorney Signature Line

_____
Signature of Person Holding Power of Attorney

_____
Printed Name of Person Holding Power of Attorney

As attorney-in-fact for _____
(name of person granting power of attorney)

Under Power of Attorney dated _____ , 20 _____

Individual Acknowledgment

State of _____

County of _____

On _____ , 20 _____ , _____ personally came before me and, being duly sworn, did state that he or she is the person described in the above document and that he or she signed the above document in my presence as a free and voluntary act for the purposes stated.

_____

Signature of Notary Public

Notary Public, In and for the County of _____

State of _____

My commission expires: _____   Notary Seal

Individual Signature Line

_____

Signature

_____

Printed Name

Husband and Wife Acknowledgment

State of _____

County of _____

On _____ , 20 _____ , _____ and _____
_____ personally came before me and, being duly sworn, did state that
they are the husband and wife described in the above document and that they signed the above
document in my presence as a free and voluntary act for the purposes stated.

_____
Signature of Notary Public

Notary Public, In and for the County of _____
State of _____

My commission expires: _____   Notary Seal

Husband and Wife Signature Line

_____
Signature of Husband

_____
Printed Name of Husband

_____
Signature of Wife

_____
Printed Name of Wife

Chapter 3

Powers of Attorney

A power of attorney is simply a document that is used to allow one person to give authority to another person to act on their behalf. The person signing the power of attorney (generally referred to as the *principal*) grants legal authority to another to "stand in their shoes" and act legally for them. The person who receives the such authority is called an *attorney-in-fact*. This title and the power of attorney form *does not* mean that the person receiving the power has to be a lawyer. If you appoint your spouse or a trusted relative or friend, then that person is your "attorney-in-fact". Think of the term "attorney-in-fact" as actually meaning "agent." Using a power of attorney, you will be appointing an "agent" to act in your place for some activities, perhaps relating to financial actions or perhaps relating to health care decisions, or any of a number of other possible actions that your "agent" may perform. The word 'attorney' in the context of a power of attorney or an attorney-in-fact is *not* related to the generally accepted notion of an 'attorney' as a lawyer.

Types of Powers of Attorney

Let's take a look at the various different types of powers of attorney. (Note that the plural for power of attorney is "powers of attorney" and not "power of attorneys." That is because the legal document is actually creating a "power," the ability for someone else to act on your behalf. The legal document provides them with the "power" to do so.) The following will be a very brief explanation of the types of powers of attorney. Each specific section of this chapter will contain a more detailed description of each type of power of attorney. You should read through this list carefully to determine which type of power of attorney is most appropriate in your particular circumstances. Here are the various types of powers of attorney that are included in this book:

General Power of Attorney: A basic power of attorney allows you to authorize your agent (your "attorney in fact") to handle a few or all of your financial and/or business transactions. This power of attorney is not valid if you become disabled or incapacitated. You must use a 'durable' power of attorney for that purpose (see below). It also can *not* be used for health care decisions.

Unlimited Power of Attorney: This is a power of attorney that grants your agent (your "attorney in fact") full and complete power to handle all of your business and financial affairs. This power of attorney is not valid if you become disabled or incapacitated. You must use a 'durable' power of attorney for that purpose (see below). It also can *not* be used for health care decisions.

Limited Power of Attorney: A Limited Power of Attorney is one that grants your agent (your "attorney in fact") only the exact power to handle the matter that you specifically spell out in the document. This power of attorney is not valid if you become disabled or incapacitated. You must use a 'durable' power of attorney for that purpose (see below). It also can *not* be used for health care decisions.

Durable Unlimited Power of Attorney for Financial Affairs (effective immediately): There are two different durable powers of attorney. The term "durable" means that this type of power of attorney is not affected by your health. In other words, a durable power of attorney remains in effect even if you become disabled and/or incapacitated. A durable unlimited power of attorney for financial affairs allows you to appoint someone to handle your financial affairs during a period that you are unable to handle them yourself. This particular durable power of attorney is effective immediately (as opposed to a durable power of attorney that *only* becomes effective upon your disability—see below). This type of power of attorney, however, can *not* be used for health care decisions. You must use a 'durable health care power of attorney' for that purpose.

Durable Unlimited Power of Attorney for Financial Affairs (effective on disability): Another type of durable power of attorney is a power of attorney that grants your agent (your "attorney in fact") full and complete power to handle all of your business and financial affairs, but only when and if you become incapacitated and unable to handle your own affairs. This power of attorney is effective *only* upon your disability (as opposed to a durable power of attorney that becomes effective immediately and remains in effect regardless of your disability or incapacity—see above).

Durable Health Care Power of Attorney: This is a specialized type of power of attorney that has been developed to allow you to authorize another person to make all of your health care decisions for you in the event that you become disabled or incapacitated and unable to make such decisions for yourself. This document allows the person you designate to make health care decisions whenever you are unable to communicate your own desires. As such, it is much more powerful than a living will (which generally provides a statement of your wishes should you be terminally ill or in a persistent vegetative state). Note that this is also a type of "durable" power of attorney in that it is effective even if you incapacitated and are unable to communicate your wishes and desires regarding your health care choices.

State Specific Durable Powers of Attorney: The CD which accompanies this book provides state-specific versions of durable powers of attorney for financial affairs. While the two generic forms provided in this chapter (durable unlimited powers of attorney for financial affairs--effective immediately and effective on disability) are legally-valid in all states, some states provide their own particular form for a durable power of attorney. You may choose to use one of the generic forms provided in this chapter or you may choose to use the state-specific forms provided on the CD. Please check the Estate Planning Appendix for your state listing to determine if your state has a state-specific form for this purpose.

General Power of Attorney

A general power of attorney allows you to authorize your agent (your "attorney in fact") to handle a few or all of your financial and/or business transactions. With this form, you are giving another person the right to manage your financial and/or business matters on your behalf. They are given the power to act exactly as you could. This, of course, is a very powerful grant of authority to someone else to act on your behalf. The person appointed must be someone that you fully trust to handle your affairs. The authority granted by this power of attorney may be revoked by you at any time and is automatically revoked if you die or become incapacitated or incompetent. If there is anything about this form that you do not understand, you should ask a lawyer to explain it to you. This power of attorney contains an important notice prior to the form itself. Please read this notice carefully before you complete this form.

When You Should Use a General Power of Attorney

A general power of attorney allows you to select any or all of a range of powers that you wish for your agent (attorney-in-fact) to have. This type of power of attorney can be used to authorize someone else to sign certain documents if you can not be present when the signatures are necessary. They can be used to authorize someone to handle any or all of the following possible matters:

> Real estate transactions; Goods and services transactions; Stock, bond, share and Commodity transactions; Banking transactions; Business operating transactions; Insurance transactions; Estate transactions; Legal claims and litigation; Personal relationships and affairs; Benefits from military service; Records, reports and statements; Retirement benefit transactions; Making gifts to a spouse, children, parents and other descendants; Tax matters.

Additionally, you may also authorize your attorney-in-fact to delegate any or all of the above powers to someone that your appointed attorney-in-fact selects. This option should only be taken if you trust your appointed attorney-in-fact totally to make such a decision only with your best interests in mind.

A general power of attorney is most useful if you wish to grant your agent some, but not all of the possible powers available to an agent. If you wish to grant full and complete authority to your agent, you should use an *unlimited power of attorney* instead. An unlimited power of attorney provides that your agent will have total authority to act on your behalf for all financial and/or business matters (but not for health care decisions). If you wish to provide a very limited power to your agent, you may wish to use a *limited power of attorney* instead of a general power of attorney. A limited power of attorney allows you to limit the power granted to a specific action or a specific date range. A general power of attorney is not valid if you become disabled or incapacitated. You must use a *'durable'* *power of attorney* for that purpose. In addition, a general power of attorney also can *not* be used for health care decisions. You must use a *durable health care power of attorney* for that purpose.

To complete your general power of attorney, please follow the instructions below. To use the form on the enclosed CD, simply fill in the required information in either the text or PDF versions of this form.

Instructions for General Power of Attorney

① Name and address of person granting power (principal)
② Name and address of person granted power (attorney-in-fact)
③ Initial each of the specific powers that you wish your attorney-in-fact to have. If you wish your attorney-in-fact to have full authority to do anything that you yourself could do, simply initial line (q). (Note: if you wish to have your attorney-in-fact to have full authority, you may wish to use the *unlimited power of attorney* form instead).
④ Name and address of successor to person originally granted power (successor attorney-in-fact) (optional-if not used, write n/a in this space)
⑤ Date
⑥ Printed name of principal, date of signing of power of attorney, and signature of principal (signed in front of notary public)
⑦ Printed names and signatures of witnesses (signed in front of notary public)
⑧ Notary acknowledgement should be completed by the notary public
⑨ Printed name, date, and signature of attorney-in-fact (need not be witnessed or notarized)
⑩ Printed name, date, and signature of successor attorney-in-fact (optional-if not used, write N/A in this space)(need not be witnessed or notarized)

General Power of Attorney

Notice: This is an important document. Before signing this document, you should know these important facts. By signing this document, you are not giving up any powers or rights to control your finances and property yourself. In addition to your own powers and rights, you may be giving another person, your attorney-in-fact, broad powers to handle your finances and property. This general power of attorney may give the person whom you designate (your "attorney-in-fact") broad powers to handle your finances and property, which may include powers to encumber, sell or otherwise dispose of any real or personal property without advance notice to you or approval by you. THE POWERS GRANTED WILL NOT EXIST AFTER YOU BECOME DISABLED, OR INCAPACITATED. This document does not authorize anyone to make medical or other health care decisions for you. If you own complex or special assets such as a business, or if there is anything about this form that you do not understand, you should ask a lawyer to explain this form to you before you sign it. If you wish to change your general power of attorney, you must complete a new document and revoke this one. You may revoke this document at any time by destroying it, by directing another person to destroy it in your presence or by signing a written and dated statement expressing your intent to revoke this document. If you revoke this document, you should notify your attorney-in-fact and any other person to whom you have given a copy of the form. You also should notify all parties having custody of your assets. These parties have no responsibility to you unless you actually notify them of the revocation. If your attorney-in-fact is your spouse and your marriage is annulled, or you are divorced after signing this document, this document is invalid. Since some 3rd parties or some transactions may not permit use of this document, it is advisable to check in advance, if possible, for any special requirements that may be imposed. You should sign this form only if the attorney-in-fact you name is reliable, trustworthy and competent to manage your affairs. This form must be signed by the Principal (the person appointing the attorneyin-fact), witnessed by two persons other than the notary public, and acknowledged by a notary public.

①I, _____ (printed name) ,
of (address)_____,
as principal, to grant a general power of attorney to, and do hereby appoint:
②_____ (printed name),
of (address)_____,
my attorney-in-fact to act in my name, place and stead in any way which I myself could do, if I were personally present, with respect to the following matters to the extent that I am permitted by law to act through an agent:
③
_____ (a) real estate transactions;
_____ (b) goods and services transactions;
_____ (c) bond, share and commodity transactions;
_____ (d) banking transactions;
_____ (e) business operating transactions;
_____ (f) insurance transactions;
_____ (g) estate transactions;
_____ (h) claims and litigation;

_____ (i) personal relationships and affairs;

_____ (j) benefits from military service;

_____ (k) records, reports and statements;

_____ (l) retirement benefit transactions;

_____ (m) making gifts to my spouse, children and more remote descendants, and parents;

_____ (n) tax matters;

_____ (o) all other matters;

_____ (p) full and unqualified authority to my attorney-in-fact to delegate any or all of the foregoing powers to any person or persons whom my attorney-in-fact shall select;

_____ (q) unlimited power and authority to act in all of the above situations (a) through (p)

If the attorney-in-fact named above is unable or unwilling to serve, I appoint

④ _____ (printed name),

of (address) _____ ,

to be my attorney-in-fact for all purposes hereunder.

To induce any third party to rely upon this power of attorney, I agree that any third party receiving a signed copy or facsimile of this power of attorney may rely upon such copy, and that revocation or termination of this power of attorney shall be ineffective as to such third party until actual notice or knowledge of such revocation or termination shall have been received by such third party. I, for myself and for my heirs, executors, legal representatives and assigns, agree to indemnify and hold harmless any such third party from any and all claims that may arise against such third party by reason of such third party having relied on the provisions of this power of attorney. This power of attorney shall not be effective in the event of my future disability or incapacity. This power of attorney may be revoked by me at any time and is automatically revoked upon my death. My attorney-in-fact shall no be compensated for his or her services nor shall my attorney-in-fact be liable to me, my estate, heirs, successors, or assigns for acting or refraining from acting under this document, except for willful misconduct or gross negligence.

⑤ Dated: _____

⑥ Signature and Declaration of Principal

I, _____ (printed name) , the principal, sign my name to this power of attorney this _____ day of _____ and, being first duly sworn, do declare to the undersigned authority that I sign and execute this instrument as my power of attorney and that I sign it willingly, or willingly direct another to sign for me, that I execute it as my free and voluntary act for the purposes expressed in the power of attorney and that I am eighteen years of age or older, of sound mind and under no constraint or undue influence.

_____

Signature of Principal

⑦ Witness Attestation

I, _____ (printed name), the first witness,

and I, _____ (printed name), the second witness, sign my name to the foregoing power of attorney being first duly sworn and do declare to the undersigned authority that the principal signs and executes this instrument as his/her power of attorney and that he\she signs it willingly, or willingly directs another to sign for him/her, and that I, in the presence and hearing of the principal, sign this power of attorney as witness to the principal's signing and that to the best of my knowledge the principal is eighteen years of age or older, of sound mind and under no constraint or undue influence.

_____
Signature of First Witness

_____
Signature of Second Witness

⑧ **Notary Acknowledgment**

State of _____ County of _____
Subscribed, sworn to and acknowledged before me by _____,
the Principal, and subscribed and sworn to before me by _____
and _____, the witnesses, this _____ day of
_____ .

_____
Notary Signature
Notary Public,
In and for the County of _____ State of _____
My commission expires: _____ Seal

⑨ **Acknowledgment and Acceptance of Appointment as Attorney-in-Fact**

I, _____, (printed name) have read the attached power of attorney and am the person identified as the attorney-in-fact for the principal. I hereby acknowledge that I accept my appointment as attorney-in-fact and that when I act as agent I shall exercise the powers for the benefit of the principal; I shall keep the assets of the principal separate from my assets; I shall exercise reasonable caution and prudence; and I shall keep a full and accurate record of all actions, receipts and disbursements on behalf of the principal.

_____   _____
Signature of Attorney-in-Fact   Date

⑩ **Acknowledgment and Acceptance of Appointment as Successor Attorney-in-Fact**

I, _____, (printed name) have read the attached power of attorney and am the person identified as the successor attorney-in-fact for the principal. I hereby acknowledge that I accept my appointment as successor attorney-in-fact and that, in the absence of a specific provision to the contrary in the power of attorney, when I act as agent I shall exercise the powers for the benefit of the principal; I shall keep the assets of the principal separate from my assets; I shall exercise reasonable caution and prudence; and I shall keep a full and accurate record of all actions, receipts and disbursements on behalf of the principal.

_____   _____
Signature of Successor Attorney-in-Fact   Date

Unlimited Power of Attorney

An unlimited power of attorney should be used only in situations where you desire to authorize another person to act for you in *any and all* transactions. The grant of power under this document is unlimited. However, the powers you grant with this document cease to be effective should you become disabled or incompetent. This form gives the person whom you designate as your "attorney-in-fact" extremely broad powers to handle your property during your lifetime, which may include powers to mortgage, sell, or otherwise dispose of any real or personal property without advance notice to you or approval by you. This document does not authorize anyone to make medical or other health care decisions. You must execute a durable health care power of attorney to do this. The authority granted by this power of attorney may be revoked by you at any time and is automatically revoked if you die or become incapacitated or incompetent. If there is anything about this form that you do not understand, you should ask a lawyer to explain it to you. This power of attorney contains an important notice prior to the form itself.

When You Should Use an Unlimited Power of Attorney

An unlimited power of attorney authorizes your agent to handle *any and all* of your financial and business affairs, including all of the following possible matters:

> Real estate transactions; Personal property and goods and services transactions; Stock, bond, share and commodity transactions; Banking and financial institution transactions; Business operating transactions; Insurance and annuity transactions; Estate, trust, and other transactions where the principal is a beneficiary; Legal claims and litigation; Personal and family maintenance; Benefits from social security, medicare, medicaid, or civil or military service; Records, reports and statements; Retirement benefit transactions; Tax matters; Delegation of the agent's authority to others; and any and all other matters.

All of the above mentioned powers that are granted to your agent are spelled out in great detail in this particular power of attorney form. This is the most extensive and detailed power of attorney form that is provided. It should only be used if you are absolutely certain that the agent you choose is fully and totally trustworthy and able to exercise these broad powers in your best interest. The detailed powers that are listed in this form are taken from the Uniform Power of Attorney Act that has been legislatively adopted by many states. Please note that the "delegation of the agent's authority to others" provision in this document grants your chosen agent the power to delegate any of his or her powers to another person of his or her own choosing. If you do not wish your agent to have this authority, or you wish to limit your agent's power under any of the other powers which are enumerated in this document, you should use instead a *general power of attorney*. A general power of attorney will allow you to pick and choose which of these powers you wish to grant to your agent.

If you wish to provide a very limited power to your agent, you may wish to use a *limited power of attorney* instead of an unlimited power of attorney. A limited power of attorney allows you to limit the power granted to a specific action or a specific date range. An unlimited power of attorney is not valid if you become disabled or incapacitated. You must use a *'durable' power of attorney* for that purpose. In addition, an unlimited power of attorney also can *not* be used for health care decisions. You must use a *durable health care power of attorney* for that purpose.

To complete your unlimited power of attorney, please follow the instructions below. To use the form on the enclosed CD, simply fill in the required information in either the text or PDF versions of this form.

Instructions for Unlimited Power of Attorney

① Name and address of person granting power (principal)
② Name and address of person granted power (attorney-in-fact)
③ Name and address of successor to person originally granted power (successor attorney-in-fact) (optional-if not used, write N/A in this space)
④ Date
⑤ Printed name of principal, date of signing of power of attorney, and signature of principal (signed in front of notary public)
⑥ Printed names and signatures of witnesses (signed in front of notary public)
⑦ Notary acknowledgement should be completed by the notary public
⑧ Printed name, date, and signature of attorney-in-fact (need not be witnessed or notarized)
⑨ Printed name, date, and signature of successor attorney-in-fact (optional-if not used, write N/A in this space) (need not be witnessed or notarized)

Unlimited Power of Attorney

Notice: This is an important document. Before signing this document, you should know these important facts. By signing this document, you are not giving up any powers or rights to control your finances and property yourself. In addition to your own powers and rights, you are giving another person, your attorney-in-fact, broad powers to handle your finances and property. This unlimited power of attorney will give the person whom you designate (your "attorney-in-fact") broad powers to handle your finances and property, which includes powers to encumber, sell or otherwise dispose of any real or personal property without advance notice to you or approval by you. THE POWERS GRANTED WILL NOT EXIST AFTER YOU BECOME DISABLED, OR INCAPACITATED. This document does not authorize anyone to make medical or other health care decisions for you. If you own complex or special assets such as a business, or if there is anything about this form that you do not understand, you should ask a lawyer to explain this form to you before you sign it. If you wish to change your unlimited power of attorney, you must complete a new document and revoke this one. You may revoke this document at any time by destroying it, by directing another person to destroy it in your presence or by signing a written and dated statement expressing your intent to revoke this document. If you revoke this document, you should notify your attorney-in-fact and any other person to whom you have given a copy of the form. You also should notify all parties having custody of your assets. These parties have no responsibility to you unless you actually notify them of the revocation. If your attorney-in-fact is your spouse and your marriage is annulled, or you are divorced after signing this document, this document is invalid. Since some 3rd parties or some transactions may not permit use of this document, it is advisable to check in advance, if possible, for any special requirements that may be imposed. You should sign this form only if the attorney-in-fact you name is reliable, trustworthy and competent to manage your affairs. This form must be signed by the Principal (the person appointing the attorney-in-fact), witnessed by two persons other than the notary public, and acknowledged by a notary public.

①I, _____ (printed name),
of (address)_____,
as principal, do grant an unlimited power of attorney to, and do hereby appoint:
②_____ (printed name),
of (address)_____,
my attorney-in-fact and do grant him or her unlimited power and authority to act in my name, place and stead in any way which I myself could do, if I were personally present, with respect to all of the following matters to the extent that I am permitted by law to act through an agent:

IN GENERAL, the principal authorizes the agent to: (1) demand, receive, and obtain by litigation or otherwise, money or other thing of value to which the principal is, may become, or claims to be entitled, and conserve, invest, disburse, or use anything so received for the purposes intended; (2) contract in any manner with any person, on terms agreeable to the agent, to accomplish a purpose of a transaction, and perform, rescind, reform, release, or modify the contract or another contract made by or on behalf of the principal; (3) execute, acknowledge, seal, and deliver a deed, revocation, mortgage, security agreement, lease, notice, check, promissory note, electronic funds transfer, release, or other instrument or communication the agent considers desirable to accomplish a purpose of a transaction, including creating a schedule of the principal's property and attaching it to the power of attorney; (4) prosecute, defend, submit to arbitration or mediation, settle, and propose or accept a compromise with respect to, a claim existing in favor of or against the principal or intervene in litigation relating to the claim; (5) seek on the principal's behalf the assistance of a court to carry out an act authorized by the principal in the power of attorney; (6) engage, compensate, and discharge an attorney, accountant, expert witness, or other assistant; (7) keep appropriate records of each transaction, including an accounting of receipts and disbursements; (8) prepare, execute, and file a record, report, or other document the agent considers desirable to safeguard or promote the principal's interest under a statute or governmental regulation; (9) reimburse the agent for expenditures properly made by the agent in exercising the powers granted by the power of attorney; and (10) in general, do any other lawful act with respect to the power and all property related to the power.

WITH RESPECT TO REAL PROPERTY, the principal authorizes the agent to: (1) accept as a gift or as security for an extension of credit, reject, demand, buy, lease, receive, or otherwise acquire, an interest in real property or a right incident to real property; (2) sell, exchange, convey with or without covenants, quitclaim, release, surrender, mortgage, retain title for security, encumber, partition, consent to partitioning, subdivide, apply for zoning, rezoning, or other governmental permits, plat or consent to platting, develop, grant options concerning, lease, sublease, or otherwise dispose of, an interest in real property or a right incident to real property; (3) release, assign, satisfy, or enforce by litigation or otherwise, a mortgage, deed of trust, conditional sale contract, encumbrance, lien, or other claim to real property which exists or is asserted; (4) manage or conserve an interest in real property or a right incident to real property, owned or claimed to be owned by the principal, including: (a) insuring against a casualty, liability, or loss; (b) obtaining or regaining possession, or protecting the interest or right, by litigation or otherwise; (c) paying, compromising, or contesting taxes or assessments, or applying for and receiving refunds in connection with them; and (d) purchasing supplies, hiring assistance or labor, and making repairs or alterations to the real property; (5) use, develop, alter, replace, remove, erect, or install structures or other improvements upon real property in or incident to which the principal has, or claims to have, an interest or right; (6) participate in a reorganization with respect to real property or a legal entity that owns an interest in or right incident to real property and receive and hold, directly or indirectly, shares of stock or obligations, or other evidences of ownership or debt, received in a plan of reorganization, and act with respect to them, including: (a) selling or otherwise disposing of them; (b) exercising or selling an option, conversion, or similar right with respect to them; and (c) voting them in person or by proxy; (7) change the form of title of an interest in or right incident to real property, and (8) dedicate to public use, with or without consideration, easements or other real property in which the principal has, or claims to have, an interest.

WITH RESPECT TO TANGIBLE PERSONAL PROPERTY, the principal authorizes the agent to: (1) accept as a gift or as security for an extension of credit, reject, demand, buy, receive, or otherwise acquire ownership or possession of tangible personal property or an interest in tangible personal property; (2) sell, exchange, convey with or without covenants, release, surrender, create a security interest in, grant options concerning, lease, sublease to others, or otherwise dispose of tangible personal property or an interest in tangible personal property; (3) release, assign, satisfy, or enforce by litigation or otherwise, a security interest, lien, or other claim on behalf of the principal, with respect to tangible personal property or an interest in tangible personal property; (4) manage or conserve tangible personal property or an interest in tangible personal property on behalf of the principal, including: (a) insuring against casualty, liability, or loss; (b) obtaining or regaining possession, or protecting the property or interest, by litigation or otherwise; (c) paying, compromising, or contesting taxes or assessments or applying for and receiving refunds in connection with taxes or assessments; (d) moving from place to place; (e) storing for hire or on a gratuitous bailment; and (f) using, altering, and making repairs or alterations; and (5) change the form of title of an interest in tangible personal property.

WITH RESPECT TO TRANSACTIONS CONCERNING STOCKS AND BONDS, the principal authorizes the agent to: (1) buy, sell, and exchange stocks, bonds, mutual funds, and all other types of securities and financial instruments, whether held directly or indirectly, except commodity futures contracts and call and put options on stocks and stock indexes, (2) receive certificates and other evidences of ownership with respect to securities, (3) exercise voting rights with respect to securities in person or by proxy, enter into voting trusts, and consent to limitations on the right to vote.

WITH RESPECT TO TRANSACTIONS CONCERNING COMMODITIES AND OPTIONS, the principal authorizes the agent to: (1) buy, sell, exchange, assign, settle, and exercise commodity futures contracts and call and put options on stocks and stock indexes traded on a regulated option exchange, and (2) establish, continue, modify, and terminate option accounts with a broker.

WITH RESPECT TO TRANSACTIONS CONCERNING BANKS AND OTHER FINANCIAL INSTITUTIONS, the principal authorizes the agent to: (1) continue, modify, and terminate an account or other banking arrangement made by or on behalf of the principal; (2) establish, modify, and terminate an account or other banking arrangement with a bank, trust company, savings and loan association, credit union, thrift company, brokerage firm, or other financial institution selected by the agent; (3) rent a safe deposit box or space in a vault; (4) contract for other services available from a financial institution as the agent considers desirable; (5) withdraw by check, order, or otherwise money or property of the principal deposited with or left in the custody of a financial institution; 6) receive bank statements, vouchers, notices, and similar documents from a financial institution and act with respect to them; (7) enter a safe deposit box or vault and withdraw or add to the contents; (8) borrow money at an interest rate agreeable to the agent and pledge as security personal property of the principal necessary in order to borrow, pay, renew, or extend the time of payment of a debt of the principal; (9) make, assign, draw, endorse, discount, guarantee, and negotiate promissory notes, checks, drafts, and other negotiable or nonnegotiable paper of the principal, or payable to the principal or the principal's order, transfer money, receive the cash or other proceeds of those transactions, accept a draft drawn by a person upon the principal, and pay it when due; (10) receive for the principal and act upon a sight draft, warehouse receipt, or other negotiable or nonnegotiable instrument; (11) apply for, receive, and use letters of credit, credit and debit cards, and traveler's checks from a financial institution and give an indemnity or other agreement in connection with letters of credit; and (12) consent to an extension of the time of payment with respect to commercial paper or a financial transaction with a financial institution.

WITH RESPECT TO OPERATING A BUSINESS, the principal authorizes the agent to: (1) operate, buy, sell, enlarge, reduce, and terminate a business interest; (2) act for a principal, subject to the terms of a partnership agreement or operating agreement, to: (a) perform a duty or discharge a liability and exercise a right, power, privilege, or option that the principal has, may have, or claims to have, under the partnership agreement or operating agreement, whether or not the principal is a partner in a partnership or member of a limited liability company; (b) enforce the terms of the partnership agreement or operating agreement by litigation or otherwise; and (c) defend, submit to arbitration, settle, or compromise litigation to which the principal is a party because of membership in a partnership or limited liability company; (3) exercise in person or by proxy, or enforce by litigation or otherwise, a right, power, privilege, or option the principal has or claims to have as the holder of a bond, share, or other instrument of similar character and defend, submit to arbitration or mediation, settle, or compromise litigation to which the principal is a party because of a bond, share, or similar instrument; (4) with respect to a business controlled by the principal: (a) continue, modify, renegotiate, extend, and terminate a contract made by or on behalf of the principal with respect to the business before execution of the power of attorney; (b) determine: (i) the location of its operation; (ii) the nature and extent of its business; (iii) the methods of manufacturing, selling, merchandising, financing, accounting, and advertising employed in its operation; (iv) the amount and types of insurance carried; and (v) the mode of engaging, compensating, and dealing with its accountants, attorneys, other agents, and employees; (c) change the name or form of organization under which the business is operated and enter into a partnership agreement or operating agreement with other persons or organize a corporation or other business entity to take over all or part of the operation of the business; and (d) demand and receive money due or claimed by the principal or on the principal's behalf in the operation of the business, and control and disburse the money in the operation of the business; (5) put additional capital into a business in which the principal has an interest; (6) join in a plan of reorganization, consolidation, or merger of the business; (7) sell or liquidate a business or part of it at the time and upon the terms the agent considers desirable; (8) establish the value of a business under a buy-out agreement to which the principal is a party; (9) prepare, sign, file, and deliver reports, compilations of information, returns, or other papers with respect to a business which are required by a governmental agency or instrumentality or which the agent considers desirable, and make related payments; and (10) pay, compromise, or contest taxes or assessments and perform any other act that the agent considers desirable to protect the principal from illegal or unnecessary taxation, fines, penalties, or assessments with respect to a business, including attempts to recover, in any manner permitted by law, money paid before or after the execution of the power of attorney.

WITH RESPECT TO INSURANCE AND ANNUITIES, the principal authorizes the agent to: (1) continue, pay the premium or assessment on, modify, rescind, release, or terminate a contract procured by or on behalf of the principal which insures or provides an annuity to either the principal or another person, whether or not the principal is a beneficiary under the contract; (2) procure new, different, and additional contracts of insurance and annuities for the principal and the principal's spouse, children, and other dependents, and select the amount, type of insurance or annuity, and mode of payment; (3) pay the premium or assessment on, modify, rescind, release, or terminate a contract of insurance or annuity procured by the agent; (4) apply for and receive a loan on the security of a contract of insurance or annuity; (5) surrender and receive the cash surrender value; (6)

exercise an election; (7) change the manner of paying premiums; (8) change or convert the type of insurance or annuity, with respect to which the principal has or claims to have a power described in this section; (9) apply for and procure government aid to guarantee or pay premiums of a contract of insurance on the life of the principal; (10) collect, sell, assign, hypothecate, borrow upon, or pledge the interest of the principal in a contract of insurance or annuity; and (11) pay from proceeds or otherwise, compromise or contest, and apply for refunds in connection with, a tax or assessment levied by a taxing authority with respect to a contract of insurance or annuity or its proceeds or liability accruing by reason of the tax or assessment.

WITH RESPECT TO ESTATES, TRUSTS, AND OTHER RELATIONSHIPS IN WHICH THE PRINCIPAL IS A BENEFICIARY, the principal authorizes the agent to act for the principal in all matters that affect a trust, probate estate, guardianship, conservatorship, escrow, custodianship, or other fund from which the principal is, may become, or claims to be entitled, as a beneficiary, to a share or payment, including to: (1) accept, reject, disclaim, receive, receipt for, sell, assign, release, pledge, exchange, or consent to a reduction in or modification of a share in or payment from the fund; (2) demand or obtain by litigation or otherwise money or other thing of value to which the principal is, may become, or claims to be entitled by reason of the fund; (3) initiate, participate in, and oppose litigation to ascertain the meaning, validity, or effect of a deed, will, declaration of trust, or other instrument or transaction affecting the interest of the principal; (4) initiate, participate in, and oppose litigation to remove, substitute, or surcharge a fiduciary; (5) conserve, invest, disburse, and use anything received for an authorized purpose; and (6) transfer an interest of the principal in real property, stocks, bonds, accounts with financial institutions or securities intermediaries, insurance, annuities, and other property, to the trustee of a revocable trust created by the principal as settlor.

WITH RESPECT TO CLAIMS AND LITIGATION, the principal authorizes the agent to: (1) assert and prosecute before a court or administrative agency a claim, a claim for relief, cause of action, counterclaim, offset, or defense against an individual, organization, or government, including actions to recover property or other thing of value, to recover damages sustained by the principal, to eliminate or modify tax liability, or to seek an injunction, specific performance, or other relief; (2) bring an action to determine adverse claims, intervene in litigation, and act as amicus curiae; (3) in connection with litigation, procure an attachment, garnishment, libel, order of arrest, or other preliminary, provisional, or intermediate relief and use an available procedure to effect or satisfy a judgment, order, or decree; (4) in connection with litigation, perform any lawful act, including acceptance of tender, offer of judgment, admission of facts, submission of a controversy on an agreed statement of facts, consent to examination before trial, and binding the principal in litigation; (5) submit to arbitration or mediation, settle, and propose or accept a compromise with respect to a claim or litigation; (6) waive the issuance and service of process upon the principal, accept service of process, appear for the principal, designate persons upon whom process directed to the principal may be served, execute and file or deliver stipulations on the principal's behalf, verify pleadings, seek appellate review, procure and give surety and indemnity bonds, contract and pay for the preparation and printing of records and briefs, receive and execute and file or deliver a consent, waiver, release, confession of judgment, satisfaction of judgment, notice, agreement, or other instrument in connection with the prosecution, settlement, or defense of a claim or litigation; (7) act for the principal with respect to bankruptcy or insolvency, whether voluntary or involuntary, concerning the principal or some other person, or with respect to a reorganization, receivership, or application for the appointment of a receiver or trustee which affects an interest of the principal in property or other thing of value; and (8) pay a judgment against the principal or a settlement made in connection with litigation and receive and conserve money or other thing of value paid in settlement of or as proceeds of a claim or litigation.

WITH RESPECT TO PERSONAL AND FAMILY MAINTENANCE, the principal authorizes the agent to: (1) perform the acts necessary to maintain the customary standard of living of the principal, the principal's spouse, children, and other individuals customarily or legally entitled to be supported by the principal, including providing living quarters by purchase, lease, or other contract, or paying the operating costs, including interest, amortization payments, repairs, and taxes, on premises owned by the principal and occupied by those individuals; (2) provide for the individuals described under (1) normal domestic help, usual vacations and travel expenses, and funds for shelter, clothing, food, appropriate education, and other current living costs; (3) pay on behalf of the individuals described under (1) expenses for necessary medical, dental, and surgical care, hospitalization, and custodial care; (4) act as the principal's personal representative pursuant to sections 1171 through 1179 of the Social Security Act, 42 U.S.C. Section 1320d (sections 262 and 264 of Public Law 104-191) [or successor provisions] and applicable regulations, in making decisions related to the past, present, or future payment for the provision of health care consented to by the principal or anyone authorized under the law of this state to consent to health care on behalf of the principal; (5) continue any provision made by the principal, for the individuals described under (1), for automobiles or other means of transportation, including registering, licensing, insuring, and replacing them; (6) maintain or open charge accounts for the convenience of the individuals described under (1) and open new accounts the agent considers desirable to accomplish a lawful purpose; and (7) continue payments incidental to the membership or affiliation of the principal in a church, club, society, order, or other organization or to continue contributions to those organizations.

WITH RESPECT TO BENEFITS FROM SOCIAL SECURITY, MEDICARE, MEDICAID, OTHER GOVERNMENTAL PROGRAMS, OR CIVIL OR MILITARY SERVICE, the principal authorizes the agent to: (1) execute vouchers in the name of the principal for allowances and reimbursements payable by the United States or a foreign government or by a state or subdivision of a state to the principal, including allowances and reimbursements for transportation of the individuals described in Section 212(1), and for shipment of their household effects; (2) take possession and order the removal and shipment of property of the principal from a post, warehouse, depot, dock, or other place of storage or safekeeping, either governmental or private, and execute and deliver a release, voucher, receipt, bill of lading, shipping ticket, certificate, or other instrument for that purpose; (3) prepare, file, and prosecute a claim of the principal to a benefit or assistance, financial or otherwise, to which the principal claims to be entitled under a statute or governmental regulation; (4) prosecute, defend, submit to arbitration or mediation, settle, and propose or accept a compromise with respect to any benefit or assistance the principal may be entitled to receive under a statute or governmental regulation; and (5) receive the financial proceeds of a claim of the type described in paragraph (3) and conserve, invest, disburse, or use anything so received for a lawful purpose.

WITH RESPECT TO RETIREMENT PLANS, the principal authorizes the agent to: (1) select a payment option under a retirement plan in which the principal participates, including a plan for a self-employed individual; (2) make voluntary contributions to those plans; (3) exercise the investment powers available under a self-directed retirement plan; (4) make a rollover of benefits into another retirement plan; (5) if authorized by the plan, borrow from, sell assets to, purchase assets from, or request distributions from the plan; and (6) waive the right of the principal to be a beneficiary of a joint or survivor annuity if the principal is a spouse who is not employed.

WITH RESPECT TO TAX MATTERS, the principal authorizes the agent to: (1) prepare, sign, and file federal, state, local, and foreign income, gift, payroll, Federal Insurance Contributions Act, and other tax returns, claims for refunds, requests for extension of time, petitions regarding tax matters, and any other tax-related documents, including receipts, offers, waivers, consents, including consents and agreements under the Internal Revenue Code, 26 U.S.C. Section 2032A [or successor provisions], closing agreements, and any power of attorney required by the Internal Revenue Service or other taxing authority with respect to a tax year upon which the statute of limitations has not run and the following 25 tax years; (2) pay taxes due, collect refunds, post bonds, receive confidential information, and contest deficiencies determined by the Internal Revenue Service or other taxing authority; (3) exercise any election available to the principal under federal, state, local, or foreign tax law; and (4) act for the principal in all tax matters for all periods before the Internal Revenue Service, and any other taxing authority.

WITH RESPECT TO GIFTS, the principal authorizes the agent to make gifts of any of the principal's property to individuals or organizations within the limits of the annual exclusion under the Internal Revenue Code, 26 U.S.C. Section 2503(b) [or successor provisions], as the agent determines to be in the principal's best interest based on all relevant factors, including: (1) the value and nature of the principal's property; (2) the principal's foreseeable obligations and need for maintenance; 3) minimization of income, estate, inheritance, generation-skipping transfer or gift taxes; (4) eligibility for public benefits or assistance under a statute or governmental regulation; and (5) the principal's personal history of making or joining in making gifts.

WITH RESPECT TO DELEGATION OF AGENCY AUTHORITY, the principal authorizes the agent to delegate revocably by writing or other record to one or more persons a power granted to the agent by the principal.

If the attorney-in-fact named above is unable or unwilling to serve, I appoint
③_____ (printed name),
of (address) _____ ,
to be my attorney-in-fact for all purposes hereunder.

To induce any third party to rely upon this power of attorney, I agree that any third party receiving a signed copy or facsimile of this power of attorney may rely upon such copy, and that revocation or termination of this power of attorney shall be ineffective as to such third party until actual notice or knowledge of such revocation or termination shall have been received by such third party. I, for myself and for my heirs, executors, legal representatives and assigns, agree to indemnify and hold harmless any such third party from any and all claims that may arise against such third party by reason of such third party having relied on the provisions of this power of attorney. This power of attorney shall not be effective in the event of my future disability or incapacity. This power of attorney may be revoked by me at any time and is automatically revoked upon my death. My attorney-in-fact shall no be compensated for his or her services nor shall my attorney-in-fact be liable to me, my estate, heirs, successors, or assigns for acting or refraining from acting under this document, except for willful misconduct or gross negligence.

④ Dated: _____

Signature and Declaration of Principal

⑤
I, _____ (printed name), the principal, sign my name to this power of attorney this _____ day of _____ and, being first duly sworn, do declare to the undersigned authority that I sign and execute this instrument as my power of attorney and that I sign it willingly, or willingly direct another to sign for me, that I execute it as my free and voluntary act for the purposes expressed in the power of attorney and that I am eighteen years of age or older, of sound mind and under no constraint or undue influence.

_____

Signature of Principal

Witness Attestation

⑥
I, _____ (printed name), the first witness, and I, _____ (printed name), the second witness, sign my name to the foregoing power of attorney being first duly sworn and do declare to the undersigned authority that the principal signs and executes this instrument as his/her power of attorney and that he\she signs it willingly, or willingly directs another to sign for him/her, and that I, in the presence and hearing of the principal, sign this power of attorney as witness to the principal's signing and that to the best of my knowledge the principal is eighteen years of age or older, of sound mind and under no constraint or undue influence.

_____

Signature of First Witness

_____

Signature of Second Witness

Notary Acknowledgment

⑦
State of _____ County of _____
Subscribed, sworn to and acknowledged before me by _____,
the Principal, and subscribed and sworn to before me by _____,
and _____, the witnesses, this _____ day of

_____ .

_____

Notary Signature
Notary Public,
In and for the County of _____ State of _____
My commission expires: _____ Seal

Acknowledgment and Acceptance of Appointment as Attorney-in-Fact

⑧

I, _____, (printed name) have read the attached power of attorney and am the person identified as the attorney-in-fact for the principal. I hereby acknowledge that I accept my appointment as attorney-in-fact and that when I act as agent I shall exercise the powers for the benefit of the principal; I shall keep the assets of the principal separate from my assets; I shall exercise reasonable caution and prudence; and I shall keep a full and accurate record of all actions, receipts and disbursements on behalf of the principal.

_____   _____

Signature of Attorney-in-Fact   Date

Acknowledgment and Acceptance of Appointment as Successor Attorney-in-Fact

⑨

I, _____, (printed name) have read the attached power of attorney and am the person identified as the successor attorney-in-fact for the principal. I hereby acknowledge that I accept my appointment as successor attorney-in-fact and that, in the absence of a specific provision to the contrary in the power of attorney, when I act as agent I shall exercise the powers for the benefit of the principal; I shall keep the assets of the principal separate from my assets; I shall exercise reasonable caution and prudence; and I shall keep a full and accurate record of all actions, receipts and disbursements on behalf of the principal.

_____   _____

Signature of Successor Attorney-in-Fact   Date

Limited Power of Attorney

This document provides for a *limited* grant of authority to another person. It should be used in those situations when you need to authorize another person to act for you in a specific transaction or transactions. The type of acts that you authorize the other person to perform should be spelled out in detail to avoid confusion (for example, to sign any necessary forms to open a bank account). If desired, the dates when the power of attorney will be valid may also be specified. The authority that you grant with a limited power of attorney may be revoked by you at any time and is automatically revoked if you die or become incapacitated or incompetent. This document does not authorize the appointed attorney-in-fact to make any decisions relating to medical or health care. If there is anything about these forms that you do not understand, you should ask a lawyer to explain it to you. These powers of attorney contain an important notice prior to the form itself.

When You Should Use a Limited Power of Attorney

A limited power of attorney allows you to select a specific power that you wish for your agent (attorney-in-fact) to have. This type of power of attorney can be used to authorize someone else to sign certain documents if you can not be present when the signatures are necessary. They can be used to authorize someone to handle any of the following possible matters:

> Real estate transactions; goods and services transactions; stock, bond, share and commodity transactions; banking transactions; business operating transactions; insurance transactions; estate transactions; legal claims and litigation; personal relationships and affairs; benefits from military service; records, reports and statements; retirement benefit transactions; making gifts to a spouse, children, parents and other descendants; tax matters; and certain child care decisions, such as consent to emergency medical care.

A limited power of attorney is most useful if you wish to grant your agent only some, but not all of the possible powers available to an agent. If you wish to grant full and complete authority to your agent, you may wish to use an *unlimited power of attorney* instead. An unlimited power of attorney provides that your agent will have total authority to act on your behalf for all financial and/or business matters (but not for health care decisions). If you wish to provide a range of powers to your agent, you may wish to use a *general power of attorney* instead of a limited power of attorney. A limited power of attorney allows you to limit the power granted to a specific action or a specific date range. A limited power of attorney is not valid if you become disabled or incapacitated. You must use a *'durable' power of attorney* for that purpose (Note: you can prepare a *'durable' limited power of attorney*). In addition, a limited power of attorney also can *not* be used for health care decisions. You must use a *durable health care power of attorney* for that purpose.

To complete a limited power of attorney, please follow the instructions below. To use the form on the enclosed CD, simply fill in the required information in either the text or PDF versions of this form.

Instructions for Limited Power of Attorney

① Name and address of person granting power (principal)
② Name and address of person granted power (attorney-in-fact)
③ List specific acts that you want your attorney-in-fact to perform (be as detailed as possible)
④ Name and address of successor to person originally granted power (successor attorney-in-fact) (optional-if not used, write N/A in this space.)
⑤ Date
⑥ Printed name of principal, date of signing of power of attorney, and signature of principal (signed in front of notary public)
⑦ Printed names and signatures of witnesses (signed in front of notary public)
⑧ Notary acknowledgement should be completed by the notary public
⑨ Printed name, date, and signature of attorney-in-fact (need not be witnessed or notarized)
⑩ Printed name, date, and signature of successor attorney-in-fact (optional-if not used, write N/A in this space) (need not be witnessed or notarized)

Limited Power of Attorney

Notice: This is an important document. Before signing this document, you should know these important facts. By signing this document, you are not giving up any powers or rights to control your finances and property yourself. In addition to your own powers and rights, you may be giving another person, your attorney-in-fact, broad powers to handle your finances and property. This limited power of attorney may give the person whom you designate (your "attorney-in-fact") broad powers to handle your finances and property, which may include powers to encumber, sell or otherwise dispose of any real or personal property without advance notice to you or approval by you. THE POWERS GRANTED WILL NOT EXIST AFTER YOU BECOME DISABLED, OR INCAPACITATED. This document does not authorize anyone to make medical or other health care decisions for you. If you own complex or special assets such as a business, or if there is anything about this form that you do not understand, you should ask a lawyer to explain this form to you before you sign it. If you wish to change your limited power of attorney, you must complete a new document and revoke this one. You may revoke this document at any time by destroying it, by directing another person to destroy it in your presence or by signing a written and dated statement expressing your intent to revoke this document. If you revoke this document, you should notify your attorney-in-fact and any other person to whom you have given a copy of the form. You also should notify all parties having custody of your assets. These parties have no responsibility to you unless you actually notify them of the revocation. If your attorney-in-fact is your spouse and your marriage is annulled, or you are divorced after signing this document, this document is invalid. Since some 3rd parties or some transactions may not permit use of this document, it is advisable to check in advance, if possible, for any special requirements that may be imposed. You should sign this form only if the attorney-in-fact that you appoint is reliable, trustworthy and competent to manage your affairs. This form must be signed by the Principal (the person appointing the attorney-in-fact), witnessed by two persons other than the notary public, and acknowledged by a notary public.

① I, _____ (printed name),
of (address)_____,
as principal, do grant a limited and specific power of attorney to, and do hereby appoint
② _____ (printed name),
of (address)_____,
to act as my attorney-in-fact and to have the full power and authority to perform only the following acts on my behalf to the same extent that I could do so personally if I were personally present, with respect to the following matter to the extent that I am permitted by law to act through an agent: (list specific acts) ③

If the attorney-in-fact named above is unable or unwilling to serve, I appoint
④_____ (printed name),
of (address) _____ ,
to be my attorney-in-fact for all purposes hereunder.

To induce any third party to rely upon this power of attorney, I agree that any third party receiving a signed copy or facsimile of this power of attorney may rely upon such copy, and that revocation or termination of this power of attorney shall be ineffective as to such third party until actual notice or knowledge of such revocation or termination shall have been received by such third party. I, for myself and for my heirs, executors, legal representatives and assigns, agree to indemnify and hold harmless any such third party from any and all claims that may arise against such third party by reason of such third party having relied on the provisions of this power of attorney.

This power of attorney shall not be effective in the event of my future disability or incapacity. This limited grant of authority does not authorize my attorney-in-fact to make any decisions regarding my medical or health care. This power of attorney may be revoked by me at any time and is automatically revoked upon my death. My attorney-in-fact shall not be compensated for his or her services nor shall my attorney-in-fact be liable to me, my estate, heirs, successors, or assigns for acting or refraining from acting under this document, except for willful misconduct or gross negligence. My attorney-in-fact accepts this appointment and agrees to act in my best interest as he or she considers advisable. This grant of authority shall include the power and authority to perform any incidental acts which may be reasonably required in order to perform the specific acts stated above.

⑤
Dated: _____

Signature and Declaration of Principal

⑥
I, _____ (printed name), the principal, sign my name to this power of attorney this _____ day of _____ and, being first duly sworn, do declare to the undersigned authority that I sign and execute this instrument as my power of attorney and that I sign it willingly, or willingly direct another to sign for me, that I execute it as my free and voluntary act for the purposes expressed in the power of attorney and that I am eighteen years of age or older, of sound mind and under no constraint or undue influence.

_____
Signature of Principal

Witness Attestation

⑦
I, _____ (printed name), the first witness,
and I, _____ (printed name), the second witness,
sign my name to the foregoing power of attorney being first duly sworn and do declare to the undersigned authority that the principal signs and executes this instrument as his/her power of attorney and that he\she signs it willingly, or willingly directs another to sign for him/her, and that I, in the presence and hearing of the principal, sign this power of attorney as witness to the

principal's signing and that to the best of my knowledge the principal is eighteen years of age or older, of sound mind and under no constraint or undue influence.

_____
Signature of First Witness

_____
Signature of Second Witness

Notary Acknowledgment
⑧
State of _____ County of _____
Subscribed, sworn to and acknowledged before me by _____,
the Principal, and subscribed and sworn to before me by _____,
and _____, the witnesses, this _____ day of
_____ .

_____
Notary Signature
Notary Public,
In and for the County of _____ State of _____
My commission expires: _____ Seal

Acknowledgment and Acceptance of Appointment as Attorney-in-Fact
⑨
I, _____, (printed name) have read the attached power of attorney and am the person identified as the attorney-in-fact for the principal. I hereby acknowledge that I accept my appointment as attorney-in-fact and that when I act as agent I shall exercise the powers for the benefit of the principal; I shall keep the assets of the principal separate from my assets; I shall exercise reasonable caution and prudence; and I shall keep a full and accurate record of all actions, receipts and disbursements on behalf of the principal.

_____   _____
Signature of Attorney-in-Fact   Date

Acknowledgment and Acceptance of Appointment as Successor Attorney-in-Fact
⑩
I, _____, (printed name) have read the attached power of attorney and am the person identified as the successor attorney-in-fact for the principal. I hereby acknowledge that I accept my appointment as successor attorney-in-fact and that, in the absence of a specific provision to the contrary in the power of attorney, when I act as agent I shall exercise the powers for the benefit of the principal; I shall keep the assets of the principal separate from my assets; I shall exercise reasonable caution and prudence; and I shall keep a full and accurate record of all actions, receipts and disbursements on behalf of the principal.

_____   _____
Signature of Successor Attorney-in-Fact   Date

Durable Unlimited Powers of Attorney For Financial Affairs

A *durable power of attorney* is a specific type of power of attorney that gives another person the authority to sign legal papers, transact business, buy or sell property, etc., and is only effective in one of two scenarios: (1) it may be written so that it *remains* in effect *even* if a person becomes disabled or incompetent, or (2) it may be written so that it *only* goes into effect *if and when* a person becomes disabled or incompetent. A durable power of attorney does not confer authority on another person to make health care decisions on someone else's behalf. Only a *durable health care power of attorney* can do that. There are two durable power of attorney forms contained in this book: one is written for the (1) scenario above (remains in effect if a person becomes incapacitated) and the other is written for the (2) scenario (it will only go into effect when and if a person becomes incapacitated). Note that a durable limited power of attorney for financial affairs is also possible to create for granting authority to act in specific situation or for particular transactions. However, because of its limited scope, this type of power of attorney is not as practical in situations when a durable power of attorney is generally used. If you wish to limit the powers that you grant in your durable power of attorney, please consult an attorney.

A *durable unlimited power of attorney for financial affairs* allows you to appoint an agent (who is then referred to as an 'attorney-in-fact') to handle your financial affairs during a period that you are unable to handle them yourself. With this form, you are giving another person the right to manage your financial and business matters on your behalf. They are given the power to act as you could, if you were able. If there is someone available who can be trusted implicitly to act on your behalf, the appointment of such a person can eliminate many problems that may arise if you are unable to handle your own affairs. The appointment of an agent for your financial affairs allows for the paying of bills, writing of checks, etc. while you are unable to do so yourself. You should appoint someone whom you trust completely. With the forms in this book, you are granting the appointed agent very broad powers to handle your affairs. You will give your agent the maximum power under law to perform any and all acts relating to any and all of your financial and/or business affairs Your attorney-in-fact (agent) is granted full power to act on your behalf in the same manner as if you were personally present.

The first durable unlimited power of attorney for financial affairs that is provided immediately appoints your chosen attorney-in-fact and provides that such appointment will remain in effect *even if* you become incapacitated. The second durable unlimited power of attorney for financial affairs that is provided will become effective *only* upon your incapacitation, as certified by your primary physician or, if your primary physician is not available, by any other attending physician. Neither power of attorney grants any power or authority to your designated attorney-in-fact regarding health care decisions. Only the *durable health care power of attorney* can confer those powers. You may, of course, choose to select the very same person to act as both your health care representative and your agent for financial affairs.

By accepting their appointment, your agent agrees to act in your best interest as he or she considers advisable. A durable unlimited power of attorney for financial matters may be revoked at any time and is automatically revoked on your death. The durable unlimited powers of attorney included in this chapter are intended to be used to confer a very powerful authority to another person. You will be providing another person with the power to handle all of your affairs (other than health care decisions). This is not a power that should be conferred lightly. Very serious thought should be given to both who you appoint as your attorney-in-fact (the person you authorize to act on your behalf) and to any specific directions that you may want to give to that person regarding financial decisions. You do not have to appoint anyone to handle your financial affairs, but it is often very useful to do so.

At the beginning of each of the documents are notices regarding the use of a durable power of attorney. They clearly explain the importance of caution in the use of this form and are applicable to all states. Please read each carefully to decide which of these forms are appropriate for your situation. Please note that this form provides a release for your attorney-in-fact to receive your medical records under the federal HIPAA regulations relating to the privacy of health care records. This does not confer any authority for your attorney-in-fact to make health care decisions on your behalf. The HIPAA release is for the purpose of allowing your attorney-in-fact to have access to your medical files for the purpose of paying or examining medical bills and charges.

Please also note that the state-specific advance health care directives that are explained in Chapter 8 *do not* contain a durable power of attorney for financial affairs. If you wish to have this type of document as part of your advance health care plans, you will need to complete one of the two types of forms that are contained in this chapter.

When You Should Use a Durable Power of Attorney for Financial Affairs

A *durable unlimited power of attorney* allows you to authorize someone to handle all of the following possible matters when you are incapacitated and unable to handle such matters yourself: real estate transactions; goods and services transactions; stock, bond, share and commodity transactions; banking transactions; business operating transactions; insurance transactions; estate transactions; legal claims and litigation; personal relationships and affairs; benefits from military service; records, reports and statements; retirement benefit transactions; making gifts to a spouse, children, parents and other descendants (if any); and tax matters.

A *durable unlimited power of attorney* provides that your agent will have total authority to act on your behalf for all financial and/or business matters (but not for health care decisions). If you wish to provide a very limited power to your agent, you may wish to use a *limited power of attorney* instead of a durable unlimited power of attorney. In addition, a durable unlimited power of attorney for financial affairs can *not* be used for health care decisions. You must use a *durable health care power of attorney* for that purpose.

State-Specific Durable Power of Attorney for Financial Affairs

Although, the forms provided in this chapter (durable unlimited powers of attorney for financial affairs) are legally-valid in all states, some states provide their own particular form for a durable power of attorney. You may choose to use one of the generic forms provided in this chapter or you may choose to use the state-specific forms provided on the CD.

A 'state-specific statutory form' is a form that has been taken directly from the laws of your particular state. The legal effects of the language in such a document have been approved by the legislature of the state. This provides an advantage in that the legal language in such a 'statutory' form is generally familiar to most financial institutions in the particular state and they know that such language has been approved. This does not mean, however, that other 'non-statutory' forms are not legally valid in the state as well. All states specifically provide, in their legislation regarding powers of attorney, that power of attorney forms other than those contained in the statute itself are legally valid. Anyone may use a 'non-statutory' legal form with language that they find appropriate to their own situation, as long as the document meets certain minimum legal standards for a particular state. All of the forms in this book meet such required legal standards. The following states have developed state-specific statutory forms for durable powers of attorney:

> Alaska, Arkansas, California, Colorado, Connecticut, District of Columia, Georgia, Illinois, Montana, Nebraska, New Hampshire, New Mexico, New York, North Carolina, Oklahoma, Pennsylvania, Rhode Island, Texas

In all other states, the legislatures have not developed specific forms for durable powers of attorney. In such situations, you may use the individual durable unlimited power of attorney forms in this chapter. The generic forms in this chapter have been prepared following any guidelines or requirements set out by the particular state's legislature.

When You Should Use a State-Specific Durable Power of Attorney for Finanacial Affairs

You should use the form for your specific state if, after reading through the form, you feel that it meets your particular needs. The state-specific forms on the CD have been taken directly from each state's statutes and, thus, are well known to financial institutions in the particular state. This makes these forms more readily acceptable to some institutions. However, if the forms on the CD do not fit your particular needs, you should read through the two durable power of attorney forms in this chapter and determine if either of those forms will be more acceptable in your situation.

Instructions for Durable Unlimited Power of Attorney for Financial Affairs (effective immediately)

(1) Goes into effect immediately and remains in effect even upon your incapacitation

This form should be used only in situations where you desire to authorize another person to act for you in *all* transactions immediately and you wish the power to remain in effect in the event that you become incapacitated and unable to handle your own affairs. The grant of power under this document is unlimited (except for health care decisions). This form gives the person whom you designate as your "attorney-in-fact" broad powers to handle your property during your lifetime, which may include powers to mortgage, sell, or otherwise dispose of any real or personal property without advance notice to you or approval by you. This document does not authorize anyone to make medical or other health care decisions. You must execute a health care power of attorney to accomplish this. This form does provide a HIPPA medical records privacy release that will allow the person that you appoint to access any hospital or medical bills or records on your behalf. This form also provides that you will also name a successor attorney-in-fact who will have the same powers as the original person appointed, but who will only have the powers if the original person appointed is unable to perform the necessary tasks required by the power of attorney. The authority granted by this power of attorney may be revoked by you at any time and is automatically revoked if you die. If there is anything about this form that you do not understand, you should ask a lawyer to explain it to you. To complete this form, fill in the following:

① Name and address of person granting power (principal)

② Name and address of person granted power (attorney-in-fact)

③ Name and address of successor to person originally granted power (successor attorney-in-fact) (optional-if not used, write N/A in this space)

④ Printed name of principal, date of signature, and signature of principal (signed in front of notary public)

⑤ Witnesses printed names and signatures (signed in front of notary public)

⑥ Notary acknowledgement should be completed by the notary public

⑦ Printed name and signature of attorney-in-fact and successor attorney-in-fact (need not be witnessed or notarized)

⑧ Printed name and signature of attorney-in-fact and successor attorney-in-fact (optional-if not used, write N/A in this space) (need not be witnessed or notarized)

Durable Unlimited Power of Attorney For Financial Affairs

Effective Immediately

Notice to Adult Signing this Document: This is an important document. Before signing this document, you should know these important facts. By signing this document, you are not giving up any powers or rights to control your finances and property yourself. In addition to your own powers and rights, you are giving another person, your attorney-in-fact, broad powers to handle your finances and property, which may include powers to encumber, sell or otherwise dispose of any real or personal property without advance notice to you or approval by you. THE POWERS GRANTED UNDER THIS DOCUMENT ARE EFFECTIVE IMMEDIATELY AND WILL REMAIN IN EFFECT IF YOU BECOME DISABLED OR INCAPACITATED. This document does not authorize anyone to make medical or other health care decisions for you. If you own complex or special assets such as a business, or if there is anything about this form that you do not understand, you should ask a lawyer to explain this form to you before you sign it. If you wish to change your durable unlimited power of attorney, you must complete a new document and revoke this one. You have the right to revoke the designation of the attorney-in-fact and the right to revoke this entire document at any time and in any manner. You may revoke this document at any time by destroying it, by directing another person to destroy it in your presence or by signing a written and dated statement expressing your intent to revoke this document. If you revoke this document, you should notify your attorney-in-fact and any other person to whom you have given a copy of the form. You also should notify all parties having custody of your assets. These parties have no responsibility to you unless you actually notify them of the revocation. If your attorney-in-fact is your spouse and your marriage is annulled, or you are divorced after signing this document, this document may become invalid. Since some third parties or some transactions may not permit use of this document, it is advisable to check in advance, if possible, for any special requirements that may be imposed. You should sign this form only if the attorney-in- fact you name is reliable, trustworthy and competent to manage your affairs. Generally, you may designate any competent adult as the attorney-in-fact under this document.

① I; _____ (printed name),
of (address) _____, as
principal, ② do appoint _____ (printed name),
of (address) _____, as my
attorney-in- fact to act in my name, place and stead in any way which I myself could do, if I were personally present, with respect to all of the following matters to the extent that I am permitted by law to act through an agent: I grant my attorney-in-fact the maximum power under law to perform any act on my behalf that I could do personally, including but not limited to, all acts relating to any and all of my financial transactions and/or business affairs including all banking and financial institution transactions, all real estate or personal property transactions, all insurance

or annuity transactions, all claims and litigation, and any and all business transactions. **This power of attorney shall become effective immediately and shall remain in full effect upon my disability or incapacitation.** This power of attorney grants no power or authority regarding healthcare decisions to my designated attorney-in-fact.

③

If the attorney-in-fact named above is unable or unwilling to serve, then I appoint
_____(printed name),
of _____ (address),
to be my successor attorney-in-fact for all purposes hereunder.

My attorney-in-fact is granted full and unlimited power to act on my behalf in the same manner as if I were personally present. My attorney-in-fact accepts this appointment and agrees to act in my best interest as he or she considers advisable. To induce any third party to rely upon this power of attorney, I agree that any third party receiving a signed copy or facsimile of this power of attorney may rely upon such copy, and that revocation or termination of this power of attorney shall be ineffective as to such third party until actual notice or knowledge of such revocation or termination shall have been received by such third party. I, for myself and for my heirs, executors, legal representatives and assigns, agree to indemnify and hold harmless any such third party from any and all claims that may arise against such third party by reason of such third party having relied on the provisions of this power of attorney. This power of attorney may be revoked by me at any time and is automatically revoked upon my death. My attorney-in-fact shall not be compensated for his or her services nor shall my attorney-in-fact be liable to me, my estate, heirs, successors, or assigns for acting or refraining from acting under this document, except for willful misconduct or gross negligence. Revocation of this document is not effective unless a third party has actual knowledge of such revocation. I intend for my attorney-in-fact under this Power of Attorney to be treated as I would be with respect to my rights regarding the use and disclosure of my individually identifiable health information or other medical records. This release authority applies to any information governed by the Health Insurance Portability and Accountability Act of 1996 (aka HIPAA), 42 USC 1320d and 45 CFR 160-164.

④

Signature and Declaration of Principal

I, _____(printed name), the principal, sign my name to this power of attorney this _____ day of _____and, being first duly sworn, do declare to the undersigned authority that I sign and execute this instrument as my power of attorney and that I sign it willingly, or willingly direct another to sign for me, that I execute it as my free and voluntary act for the purposes expressed in the power of attorney and that I am eighteen years of age or older, of sound mind and under no constraint or undue influence ,and that I have read and understand the contents of the notice at the beginning of this document.

_____
Signature of Principal

⑤ **Witness Attestation**

I, _____ (printed name), the first witness, and I, _____ (printed name), the second witness, sign my name to the foregoing power of attorney being first duly sworn and do declare to the undersigned authority that the principal signs and executes this instrument as his/her power of attorney and that he/she signs it willingly, or willingly directs another to sign for him/her, and that I, in the presence and hearing of the principal, sign this power of attorney as witness to the principal's signing and that to the best of my knowledge the principal is eighteen years of age or older, of sound mind and under no constraint or undue influence.

_____
Signature of First Witness

_____
Signature of Second Witness

⑥ **Notary Acknowledgment**
The State of _____
County of _____
Subscribed, sworn to and acknowledged before me by _____, the principal, and subscribed and sworn to before me by _____, the first witness, and _____, the second witness on this date _____.

_____

Notary Public Signature
Notary Public, In and for the County of _____ State of _____
My commission expires: _____   Notary Seal

⑦ **Acknowledgment and Acceptance of Appointment as Attorney-in-Fact**
I, _____, (printed name) have read the attached power of attorney and am the person identified as the attorney-in-fact for the principal. I hereby acknowledge that I accept my appointment as attorney-in-fact and that when I act as agent I shall exercise the powers for the benefit of the principal; I shall keep the assets of the principal separate from my assets; I shall exercise reasonable caution and prudence; and I shall keep a full and accurate record of all actions, receipts and disbursements on behalf of the principal.

_____   _____
Signature of Attorney-in-Fact   Date

⑧ **Acknowledgment and Acceptance of Appointment as Successor Attorney-in-Fact**
I, _____, (printed name) have read the attached power of attorney and am the person identified as the successor attorney-in-fact for the principal. I hereby acknowledge that I accept my appointment as successor attorney-in-fact and that, in the absence of a specific provision to the contrary in the power of attorney, when I act as agent I shall exercise the powers for the benefit of the principal; I shall keep the assets of the principal separate from my assets; I shall exercise reasonable caution and prudence; and I shall keep a full and accurate record of all actions, receipts and disbursements on behalf of the principal.

_____   _____
Signature of Successor Attorney-in-Fact   Date

Instructions for Durable Unlimited Power of Attorney for Financial Affairs (effective on incapacitation or disability)

(2) Goes into effect only upon your incapacitation as certified by your primary physician, or another physician, if your primary physician is not available.

This form should be used only in situations where you desire to authorize another person to act for you in *all* transactions but you desire that the powers granted will not take effect until you become incapacitated and unable to handle your own affairs. This documents also provides that your incapacitation must be certified by your primary physician, or another attending physician if your primary physician is not available. The grant of power under this document is unlimited (except for health care decisions). This form gives the person whom you designate as your "attorney-in-fact" broad powers to handle your property during your incapacitation, which may include powers to mortgage, sell, or otherwise dispose of any real or personal property without advance notice to you or approval by you. This document does not authorize anyone to make medical or other health care decisions. You must execute a durable health care power of attorney to accomplish this. This form does provide a HIPPA medical records privacy release that will allow the person that you appoint to access any hospital or medical bills or records on you behalf. This form also provides that you will also name a successor attorney-in-fact who will have the same powers as the original person appointed, but who will only have the powers if the original person appointed is unable to perform the necessary tasks required by the power of attorney. The authority granted by this power of attorney may be revoked by you at any time and is automatically revoked if you die. If there is anything about this form that you do not understand, you should ask a lawyer to explain it to you. Please note that this form provides a release for your attorney-in-fact to receive your medical records under the federal HIPAA regulations relating to the privacy of health care records.

To complete this form, fill in the following:

① Name and address of person granting power (principal)
② Name and address of person granted power (attorney-in-fact)
③ Name and address of successor to person originally granted power (successor attorney-in-fact) (optional-if not used, write N/A in this space)
④ Printed name of principal, date of signature, and signature of principal (signed in front of notary public)
⑤ Witnesses printed names and signatures (signed in front of notary public)
⑥ Notary acknowledgement should be completed by the notary public
⑦ Printed name and signature of attorney-in-fact and successor attorney-in-fact (need not be witnessed or notarized)
⑧ Printed name and signature of attorney-in-fact and successor attorney-in-fact (optional-if not used, write N/A in this space) (need not be witnessed or notarized)

Durable Unlimited Power of Attorney
For Financial Affairs
Effective Only Upon Incapacitation or Disability

Notice to Adult Signing this Document: This is an important document. Before signing this document, you should know these important facts. By signing this document, you are not giving up any powers or rights to control your finances and property yourself. In addition to your own powers and rights, you are giving another person, your attorney-in-fact, broad powers to handle your finances and property, which may include powers to encumber, sell or otherwise dispose of any real or personal property without advance notice to you or approval by you. THE POWERS GRANTED UNDER THIS DOCUMENT WILL ONLY GO INTO EFFECT IF YOU BECOME DISABLED OR INCAPACITATED, AS CERTIFIED BY YOUR PRIMARY PHYSICIAN, OR BY ANOTHER ATTENDING PHYSICIAN, IF YOUR PRIMARY PHYSICIAN IS NOT AVAILABLE. This document does not authorize anyone to make medical or other health care decisions for you. If you own complex or special assets such as a business, or if there is anything about this form that you do not understand, you should ask a lawyer to explain this form to you before you sign it. If you wish to change your durable unlimited power of attorney, you must complete a new document and revoke this one. You have the right to revoke the designation of the attorney-in-fact and the right to revoke this entire document at any time and in any manner. You may revoke this document at any time by destroying it, by directing another person to destroy it in your presence or by signing a written and dated statement expressing your intent to revoke this document. If you revoke this document, you should notify your attorney-in-fact and any other person to whom you have given a copy of the form. You also should notify all parties having custody of your assets. These parties have no responsibility to you unless you actually notify them of the revocation. If your attorney-in-fact is your spouse and your marriage is annulled, or you are divorced after signing this document, this document may become invalid. Since some third parties or some transactions may not permit use of this document, it is advisable to check in advance, if possible, for any special requirements that may be imposed. You should sign this form only if the attorney-in-fact you name is reliable, trustworthy and competent to manage your affairs. Generally, you may designate any competent adult as the attorney-in-fact under this document.

① I, _____(printed name),
of (address) _____, as principal,
② do appoint _____(printed name),
of (address) _____, as my
attorney-in-fact to act in my name, place and stead in any way which I myself could do, if I were personally present, with respect to all of the following matters to the extent that I am permitted by law to act through an agent: I grant my attorney-in-fact the maximum power under law to perform any act on my behalf that I could do personally, including but not limited to, all acts relating to any and all of my financial transactions and/or business affairs including all banking and financial institution transactions, all real estate or personal property transactions, all insurance or annuity

transactions, all claims and litigation, and any and all business transactions. This power of attorney shall only become effective upon my disability or incapacitation, as certified by my primary physician, or if my primary physician is not available, by any other attending physician. This power of attorney grants no power or authority regarding healthcare decisions to my designated attorney-in-fact.

③

If the attorney-in-fact named above is unable or unwilling to serve, then I appoint

_____(printed name),

of_____(address),

to be my successor attorney-in-fact for all purposes hereunder.

My attorney-in-fact is granted full and unlimited power to act on my behalf in the same manner as if I were personally present. My attorney-in-fact accepts this appointment and agrees to act in my best interest as he or she considers advisable. To induce any third party to rely upon this power of attorney, I agree that any third party receiving a signed copy or facsimile of this power of attorney may rely upon such copy, and that revocation or termination of this power of attorney shall be ineffective as to such third party until actual notice or knowledge of such revocation or termination shall have been received by such third party. I, for myself and for my heirs, executors, legal representatives and assigns, agree to indemnify and hold harmless any such third party from any and all claims that may arise against such third party by reason of such third party having relied on the provisions of this power of attorney. This power of attorney may be revoked by me at any time and is automatically revoked upon my death. My attorney-in-fact shall not be compensated for his or her services nor shall my attorney-in-fact be liable to me, my estate, heirs, successors, or assigns for acting or refraining from acting under this document, except for willful misconduct or gross negligence. Revocation of this document is not effective unless a third party has actual knowledge of such revocation.

I intend for my attorney-in-fact under this Power of Attorney to be treated as I would be with respect to my rights regarding the use and disclosure of my individually identifiable health information or other medical records. This release authority applies to any information governed by the Health Insurance Portability and Accountability Act of 1996 (aka HIPAA), 42 USC 1320d and 45 CFR 160-164.

④

Signature and Declaration of Principal

I, _____ (printed name), the principal, sign my name to this power of attorney this _____day of _____and, being first duly sworn, do declare to the undersigned authority that I sign and execute this instrument as my power of attorney and that I sign it willingly, or willingly direct another to sign for me, that I execute it as my free and voluntary act for the purposes expressed in the power of attorney and that I am eighteen years of age or older, of sound mind and under no constraint or undue influence ,and that I have read and understand the contents of the notice at the beginning of this document.

_____

Signature of Principal

⑤ Witness Attestation

I, _____ (printed name), the first witness, and I, _____ (printed name), the second witness, sign my name to the foregoing power of attorney being first duly sworn and do declare to the undersigned authority that the principal signs and executes this instrument as his/her power of attorney and that he/she signs it willingly, or willingly directs another to sign for him/her, and that I, in the presence and hearing of the principal, sign this power of attorney as witness to the principal's signing and that to the best of my knowledge the principal is eighteen years of age or older, of sound mind and under no constraint or undue influence.

_____   _____
Signature of First Witness   Signature of Second Witness

⑥ Notary Acknowledgment

The State of _____
County of _____
Subscribed, sworn to and acknowledged before me by _____,the principal, and subscribed and sworn to before me by _____ , the first witness, and _____,the second witness on this date _____.

_____
Notary Public Signature
Notary Public, In and for the County of _____State of _____
My commission expires: _____ Notary Seal

⑦ Acknowledgment and Acceptance of Appointment as Attorney-in-Fact

I, _____ (printed name) have read the attached power of attorney and am the person identified as the attorney-in-fact for the principal. I hereby acknowledge that I accept my appointment as attorney-in-fact and that when I act as agent I shall exercise the powers for the benefit of the principal; I shall keep the assets of the principal separate from my assets; I shall exercise reasonable caution and prudence; and I shall keep a full and accurate record of all actions, receipts and disbursements on behalf of the principal.

_____   _____
Signature of Attorney-in-Fact   Date

⑧ Acknowledgment and Acceptance of Appointment as Successor Attorney-in-Fact

I, _____ (printed name) have read the attached power of attorney and am the person identified as the successor attorney-in-fact for the principal. I hereby acknowledge that I accept my appointment as successor attorney-in-fact and that, in the absence of a specific provision to the contrary in the power of attorney, when I act as agent I shall exercise the powers for the benefit of the principal; I shall keep the assets of the principal separate from my assets; I shall exercise reasonable caution and prudence; and I shall keep a full and accurate record of all actions, receipts and disbursements on behalf of the principal.

_____   _____
Signature of Successor Attorney-in-Fact   Date

Durable Health Care Power of Attorney

A *power of attorney* is a document that is used to allow one person to give authority to another person to act on their behalf. The person signing the power of attorney grants legal authority to another to "stand in their shoes" and act legally for them. The person who receives the power of attorney is called an *attorney-in-fact*. This title and the power of attorney form does not mean that the person receiving the power has to be a lawyer. Power of attorney forms are useful documents for many occasions. They can be used to authorize someone else to sign certain documents if you can not be present when the signatures are necessary. Traditionally, financial and property matters were the type of actions handled with powers of attorney. Increasingly, however, people are using a specific type of power of attorney to authorize other persons to make health care decisions on their behalf in the event of a disability which makes the person unable to communicate their wishes to doctors or other health care providers. This broad type of power of attorney is called a *durable health care power of attorney*. It is different from *durable power of attorney for financial affairs*, which gives another person the authority to sign legal papers, transact business, buy or sell property, etc. but is intended to remain in effect even if a person becomes disabled or incompetent. A *durable power of attorney for financial affairs* does not confer authority on another person to make health care decisions on someone else's behalf. Only a *durable health care power of attorney* can do that.

When You Should Use a Durable Health Care Power of Attorney

Durable health care powers of attorney are useful documents that go beyond the provisions of a living will. They provide for health care options that living wills do not cover, and are important additions to the use of a living will. Basically, a durable health care power of attorney allows you to appoint someone to act for you in making health care decisions when you are unable to make them for yourself. A living will does not provide for this. Also, a durable health care power of attorney generally applies to all medical decisions (unless you specifically limit the power). Most living wills only apply to certain decisions regarding life support at the end of your life and are most useful in "terminal illness" or "permanent unconsciousness" situations.

Additionally, a durable health care power of attorney can provide your chosen agent with a valuable flexibility in making decisions regarding medical choices that may arise. Often, during the course of medical treatment, unforeseen situations may occur that require immediate decision-making. If you are unable to communicate your desires regarding such choices, the appointment of a *health care representative* for you (appointed with a durable health care power of attorney) will allow such decisions to be made on your behalf by a trusted person.

Finally, a durable health care power of attorney can provide specific detailed instructions regarding what you would like done by your attending physician in specific circumstances. Generally, living wills are limited to options for the withholding of life support. In order to be certain that you have made provisions for most potential health care situations, it is recommended you prepare both a living will and a durable health care power of attorney. Not everyone, however, has a trusted person available to serve as their health care representative. In these situations, the use of a living will alone will be necessary. It is, of course, possible to add additional instructions to any living will to clearly and specifically indicate your desires. (Note: living wills are explained in Chapter 7 and are contained on the enclosed CD).

Your health care representative can be a relative or close friend. It should be someone who knows you very well and whom you trust completely. Your representative should be someone who is not afraid to ask questions of health care providers and is able to make difficult decisions. Your representative may need to be assertive on your behalf. You should discuss your choice with your representative and make certain that he or she understands the responsibilities involved.

All states have enacted legislation regarding this type of form and recognize the validity of this type of legal document. In some states, they are called Appointment of Health Care Agent; in others, they are referred to as a Health Care Proxy. The form included in this book is officially titled Durable Health Care Power of Attorney and Appointment of Health Care Agent and Proxy, and is designed to be legally valid in all states. Information regarding each state's provisions are included in the Appendix.

The durable health care power of attorney included in this chapter is intended to be used to confer a very powerful authority to another person. In some cases, this may actually mean that you are giving that other person the power of life or death over you. This is not a power that should be conferred lightly. Very serious thought should be given to both who you appoint as your health care attorney-in-fact (the person you authorize to act on your behalf) and to any specific directions that you may want to give to that person regarding health care decisions. You may, of course, revoke your durable health care power of attorney at any time prior to your incapacitation (and even during any incapacitation if you are able to make your desire to revoke the power known). Remember, however, that should you become disabled or incapacitated and unable to communicate your wishes to anyone, you may be unable to communicate your desire to revoke your durable health care power of attorney.

Please note that this form provides a release for your health care representative to receive your medical records under the federal HIPAA regulations relating to the privacy of health care records. Also, at the beginning of the form is a notice that clearly explains the importance of caution in the use of this form and is applicable to all states. Please read it carefully before you sign your durable health care power of attorney.

This is a general, standardized durable health care power of attorney. The CD also contains state-specific health care powers of attorney as part of the state-specific advance health care directives (explained in Chapter 8) that have been taken directly from the most recent legislation regarding health care powers of attorney in each state. A few states do not currently have specific legislation providing express statutory recognition of health care powers of attorney. For those states, the durable health care power of attorney in this chapter has been prepared by legal professionals to comply with the basic requirements that courts in that state or other states have found important. In such states, be assured that courts, health care professionals, and physicians will be guided by this expression of your desires concerning life support as expressed in the durable health care power of attorney prepared using this book. You may use either the general durable health care power of attorney form in this chapter or the state-specific advance health care directive form for your state (explained in Chapter 8). Please compare your state's form (in your state's advance health care directive found on the CD) with the standardized form in this chapter and select the appropriate form that you feel best expresses your wishes regarding the appointment of a health care agent to make your health care decisions for you if you are unable to make those decisions for yourself.

The Federal Patient Self-Determination Act encourages all people to make their own decisions about the type of medical care they wish to receive. This act also requires all health care agencies (hospitals, long-term care facilities, and home health agencies) receiving Medicare and Medicaid reimbursement to recognize a living will and/or health care power of attorney as advance directives. Under this Act, all health care agencies must ask you if you have advance directives and must give you materials with information about your rights under state law. The durable health care power of attorney included in this chapter and/or the state-specific health care power of attorney (included as part of the state-specific advance health care directives on the CD) must be recognized by all health care agencies.

Revoking Your Durable Health Care Power of Attorney

All states have provided methods for the easy revocation of durable health care powers of attorney. Since such forms provide authority to medical personnel to withhold life-support technology that will likely result in death to the patient, great care must be taken to insure that a change of mind by the patient is heeded. For the revocation of a durable power of attorney for health care, any one of the following methods of revocation is generally acceptable:

- Physical destruction of the durable power of attorney for health care, such as tearing, burning, or mutilating the document.

- A written revocation of the durable power of attorney for health care by you or by a person acting at your direction. A form for this is provided later in this chapter and on the CD.

- An oral revocation in the presence of a witness who signs and dates an affidavit confirming a revocation. This oral declaration may take in any manner (verbal or non-verbal). Most states allow for a person to revoke such a document by any indication (even non-verbal) of the intent to revoke a durable power of attorney for health care, regardless of his or her physical or mental condition. A form for this (Witness Affidavit of Oral Revocation of Durable Health Care Power of Attorney) is included later in this chapter and on the CD.

If you use the revocation forms in this chapter or if you physically destroy your health care power of attorney, make sure that you provide a copy (or notice) of this revocation to anyone or any health care facility that has a copy or original of the durable power of attorney for health care that you are revoking.

Instructions for Durable Health Care Power of Attorney

This form should be used for preparing a durable health care power of attorney that appoints another person whom you chose to have the authority to make health care decisions for you in the event that you become incapacitated.

To complete this form, you will need the following information:

① Name and address of person granting power of attorney
② Name and address of person appointed as the "health care representative" (same as the "attorney-in-fact for health care decisions")
③ State whose laws will govern the powers granted
④ Signature of person granting power of attorney. IMPORTANT NOTE: You should only sign this section if you have carefully read and agree with the statement that grants your health care representative the authority to order the withholding of nutrition, hydration, and any other medical care when you are diagnosed as being in a persistent vegetative state.
⑤ Any additional terms or conditions that you wish to add
⑥ Date of signing of durable health care power of attorney
⑦ Your signature and printed name (do not sign unless in front of a notary public and witnesses)
⑧ Signature and printed name of witnesses (signed in front of a notary)
⑨ The notary acknowledgment section (to be completed by notary public)
⑩ Signature and printed name of person appointed as health care representative (This signature need not be witnessed or notarized)

Durable Health Care Power of Attorney and Appointment of Health Care Agent and Proxy

NOTICE TO ADULT SIGNING THIS DOCUMENT: This is an important legal document. Before executing this document, you should know these facts: This document gives the person you designate (the attorney-in-fact) the power to make MOST health care decisions for you if you lose the capacity to make informed health care decisions for yourself. This power is effective only when your attending physician determines that you have lost the capacity to make informed health care decisions for yourself. Regardless of this document, as long as you have the capacity to make informed health care decisions for yourself, you retain the right to make all medical and other health care decisions for yourself. You may include specific limitations in this document on the authority of the attorney-in-fact to make health care decisions for you. Subject to any specific limitations you include in this document, if your attending physician determines that you have lost the capacity to make an informed decision on a health care matter, the attorney-in-fact GENERALLY will be authorized by this document to make health care decisions for you to the same extent as you could make those decisions yourself, if you had the capacity to do so. The authority of the attorney-in-fact to make health care decisions for you GENERALLY will include the authority to give informed consent, to refuse to give informed consent, or to withdraw informed consent to any care, treatment, service, or procedure to maintain, diagnose, or treat a physical or mental condition. Additionally, when exercising authority to make health care decisions for you, the attorney-in-fact will have to act consistently with your desires or, if your desires are unknown, to act in your best interest. You may express your desires to the attorney-in-fact by including them in this document or by making them known to the attorney-in-fact in another manner. When acting pursuant to this document, the attorney-in-fact GENERALLY will have the same rights that you have to receive information about proposed health care, to review health care records, and to consent to the disclosure of health care records. You can limit that right in this document if you so choose. GENERALLY, you may designate any competent adult as the attorney-in-fact under this document. You have the right to revoke the designation of the attorney-in-fact and the right to revoke this entire document at any time and in any manner. Any such revocation generally will be effective when you express your intention to make the revocation. However, if you made your attending physician aware of this document, any such revocation will be effective only when you communicate it to your attending physician, or when a witness to the revocation or other health care personnel to whom the revocation is communicated by such a witness communicates it to your attending physician. If you execute this document and create a valid Health Care Power of Attorney with it, this will revoke any prior, valid power of attorney for health care that you created, unless you indicate otherwise in this document. This document is not valid as a Health Care Power of Attorney unless it is acknowledged before a notary public or is signed by at least two adult witnesses who are present when you sign or acknowledge your signature. No person who is related to you by blood, marriage, or adoption may be a witness. The attorney-in-fact, your attending physician, and the administrator of any nursing home in which you are receiving care also are ineligible to be witnesses. If there is anything in this document that you do not understand, you should ask a lawyer to explain it to you.

① I, _____ (printed name) ,
residing at _____,
appoint the following person as my attorney-in-fact for health care decisions, my health care agent, and confer upon this person my health care proxy. This person shall hereafter referred to as my "health care representative":
② _____ (printed name) ,
residing at _____.

③ I grant my health care representative the maximum power under law to perform any acts on my behalf regarding health care matters that I could do personally under the laws of the State of _____, including specifically the power to make any health decisions on my behalf, upon the terms and conditions set forth below. My health care representative accepts this appointment and agrees to act in my best interest as he or she considers advisable. This health care power of attorney and appointment of health care agent and proxy may be revoked by me at any time and is automatically revoked on my death. However, this power of attorney shall not be affected by my present or future disability or incapacity.

This health care power of attorney and appointment of health care agent and proxy has the following terms and conditions:

If I have signed a Living Will or Directive to Physicians, and it is still in effect, I direct that my health care representative abide by the directions that I have set out in that document. If at any time I should have an incurable injury, disease, or illness which has been certified as a terminal condition by my attending physician and one additional physician, both of whom have personally examined me, and such physicians have determined that there can be no recovery from such condition and my death is imminent, and where the application of life prolonging procedures would serve only to artificially prolong the dying process, then:

I direct my health care representative to assure that such procedures be withheld or withdrawn, and that I be permitted to die naturally with only the administration of medication, the administration of nutrition and/or hydration, or the performance of any medical procedure deemed necessary to provide me with comfort, care, or to alleviate pain. If at any time I should have been diagnosed as being in a persistent vegetative state which has been certified as incurable by my attending physician and one additional physician, both of whom have personally examined me, and such physicians have determined that there can be no recovery from such condition, and where the application of life prolonging procedures would serve only to artificially prolong the dying process, then: I direct that my health care representative assure that such procedures be withheld or withdrawn, and that I be permitted to die naturally with only the administration of medication, the administration of nutrition and/or hydration, or the performance of any medical procedure deemed necessary to provide me with comfort, care, or to alleviate pain.

④ **THE FOLLOWING INSTRUCTIONS (IN BOLDFACE TYPE) ONLY APPLY IF I HAVE SIGNED MY NAME IN THIS SPACE:** _____

However, if at any time I should have been diagnosed as being in a persistent vegetative state which has been certified as incurable by my attending physician and one additional physician, both of whom have personally examined me, and such physicians have determined that there can be no recovery from such condition, I also direct that my health care representative have sole authority to order the withholding of any aid, including the administration of nutrition, hydration, and any other medical procedure deemed necessary to provide me with comfort, care, or to alleviate pain.

If I am able to communicate in any manner, including even blinking my eyes, I direct that my health care representative try and discuss with me the specifics of any proposed health care decision.

⑤ If I have any further terms or conditions, I state them here:

I have discussed my health care wishes with the person whom I have herein appointed as my health care representative, I am fully satisfied that the person who I have herein appointed as my health care representative will know my wishes with respect to my health care and I have full faith and confidence in their good judgement.

I further direct that my health care representative shall have full authority to do the following, should I lack the capacity to make such a decision myself, provided however, that this listing shall in no way limit the full authority that I give my health care representative to make health care decisions on my behalf:

    a. to give informed consent to any health care procedure;

    b. to sign any documents necessary to carry out or withhold any health care procedures on my behalf, including any waivers or releases of liabilities required by any health care provider;

    c. to give or withhold consent for any health care or treatment;

    d. to revoke or change any consent previously given or implied by law for any health care treatment;

    e. to arrange for or authorize my placement or removal from any health care facility or institution;

    f. to require that any procedures be discontinued, including the withholding of any medical treatment and/or aid, including the administration of nutrition, hydration, and any other medical procedure deemed necessary to provide me with comfort, care, or to alleviate pain, subject to the conditions earlier provided in this document;

    g. to authorize the administration of pain-relieving drugs, even if they may shorten my life.

I desire that my wishes with respect to all health care matters be carried out through the authority that I have herein provided to my health care representative, despite any contrary wishes, beliefs, or opinions of any members of my family, relatives, or friends. I have read the Notice that precedes this document. I understand the full importance of this appointment, and I am emotionally and mentally competent to make this appointment of health care representative. I intend for my health care representative to be treated as I would be with respect to my rights regarding the use and disclosure of my individually identifiable health information or other medical records. This release authority applies to any information governed by the Health Insurance Portability and Accountability Act of 1996 (aka HIPAA), 42 USC 1320d and 45 CFR 160-164.

I declare to the undersigned authority that I sign and execute this instrument as my health care power of attorney and that I sign it willingly, or willingly direct another to sign for me, that I execute it as my free and voluntary act for the purposes expressed in this document and that I am nineteen years of age or older, of sound mind and under no constraint or undue influence ,and that I have read and understand the contents of the notice at the beginning of this document, and .that I understand the purpose and effect of this document.

⑥ Dated _____ , 20_____

⑦ _____
Signature of person granting health care power of attorney and appointing health care representative

_____
Printed name of person granting health care power of attorney and appointing health care representative

⑧ **Witness Attestation**
I, _____(printed name), the first witness,
and I, _____(printed name), the second witness, sign my name to the foregoing power of attorney being first duly sworn and do declare to the undersigned authority that the principal signs and executes this instrument as his/her power of attorney and that he/she signs it willingly, or willingly directs another to sign for him/her, and that I, in the presence and hearing of the principal, sign this power of attorney as witness to the principal's signing and that to the best of my knowledge the principal is nineteen years of age or older, of sound mind and under no constraint or undue influence. I am nineteen years of age or older. I am not appointed as the health care representative or attorney-in-fact by this document. I am not related to the principal by blood, adoption or marriage, nor am I entitled to any portion of the principal's estate under the laws of intestate succession or under any will or codicil of the principal. I also do not provide health care services to the principal, nor an employee of any health care facility in which the principal is a patient and am not financially responsible for the principal's health care.

_____   _____
Signature of First Witness   Address of First Witness

_____   _____
Signature of Second Witness   Address of Second Witness

⑨ Notary Acknowledgment

State of _____ County of _____

Subscribed, sworn to and acknowledged before me on this date _____ , 20_____ by _____ , the principal, who came before me personally, and under oath, stated that he or she is the person described in the above document and he or she signed the above document in my presence, or willingly directed another to sign for him or her. I declare under penalty of perjury that the person whose name is subscribed to this instrument appears to be of sound mind and under no duress, fraud, or undue influence. This document was also subscribed and sworn to before me on this date by _____ , the first witness, and _____ ,the second witness .

_____

Notary Signature
Notary Public
In and for the County of _____ State of _____
My commission expires: _____ Notary Seal

In California, Delaware, Georgia, and Vermont, the following statement is required to be signed by a patient advocate, ombudsman (in California, Delaware and Vermont) or facility director (in Georgia or Vermont, if the principal is a patient in a skilled nursing facility:

Statement of Patient Advocate or Ombudsman: I declare under penalty of perjury under the laws of the State of _____ that I am a patient advocate or ombudsman (or medical facility director) and am serving as a witness required by the laws of this state and that the principal appeared to be of sound mind and under no duress, fraud, or undue influence. Dated _____

_____ _____
Signature of Patient Advocate or Ombudsman Printed name and title of witness

Acceptance of Appointment as Health Care Attorney-in-Fact and Health Care Representative

I have read the attached durable health care power of attorney and am the person identified as the attorney-in-fact and health care representative for the principal. I hereby acknowledge that I accept my appointment as health care attorney-in-fact and health care representative and that when I act as agent I shall exercise the powers in the best interests of the principal.

⑩_____

Signature of person granted health care power of attorney and appointed as health care representative

_____

Printed name of person granted health care power of attorney and appointed as health care representative

Instructions for Revocation of a Durable Health Care Power of Attorney

On the following page, there is included a revocation of health care power of attorney. You have the right at any time to revoke your health care power of attorney. Remember, however, that should you become disabled or incapacitated and unable to communicate your wishes to anyone, you may be unable to communicate your desire to revoke your health care power of attorney. In any event, if you choose to revoke your health care power of attorney, a copy of this revocation should be provided to the person to whom the power was originally given. Copies should also be given to any party that may have had dealings with the attorney-in-fact before the revocation and to any party with whom the attorney-in-fact may be expected to attempt to deal with after the revocation, for example, your family physician.

Also note that you may also revoke a health care power of attorney by an oral revocation that takes place in the presence of a witness who then signs and date a written statement that confirms the revocation. Your oral declaration may take any manner, even a non-verbal indication (such as nodding your head or blinking your eyes) that signifies your intent to revoke the health care power of attorney. Such revocation can take place regardless of your physical or mental condition, as long as you are able to communicate, in some recognizable manner, your clear intent to revoke the power that was granted. For an oral revocation, use the Witness Affidavit of Oral Revocation of Durable Health Care Power of Attorney.

If you are able to, this form should be filled out and signed by the person revoking the health care power of attorney. It should also be notarized.

①   Name and address of person granting original health care power of attorney
②   Date of original durable health care power of attorney (that is now being revoked)
③   Name and address of person originally appointed as the "health care representative"
④   Date of signing of Revocation of Durable Health Care Power of Attorney
⑤   Your signature and printed name

Revocation of Durable Health Care Power of Attorney

① I, _____ (printed name),
of (address) _____

② do revoke the Durable Health Care Power of Attorney dated _____ , 20_____ ,

③ which was granted to _____ (printed name),
of (address) _____ ,
to act as my attorney-in-fact for health care decisions and I revoke any appointment of the above person as my health care agent, health care representative, or health care proxy.

④ Dated _____ , 20_____

⑤ _____
Signature of person revoking power of attorney

_____
Printed name of person revoking power of attorney

Instructions for Witness Affidavit of Oral Revocation of Durable Health Care Power of Attorney

If it is necessary to use the Witness Affidavit of Oral Revocation of Durable Health Care Power Of Attorney form, the witness should actually observe your indication of an intention to revoke your durable health care power of attorney. This may take the form of any verbal or non-verbal direction, as long as your intent to revoke is clearly and unmistakably evident to the witness. This form does not need to be notarized to be effective. Make sure that you provide a copy of this revocation to anyone or any health care facility that has a copy or original of the durable health care power of attorney that you are revoking.

To complete this document, fill in the following information:

① Name and address of person who originally signed health care power of attorney (principal)
② Date of original health care power of attorney
③ State in which health care power of attorney was originally signed
④ Printed name of witness to act of revocation
⑤ Date of act of revocation
⑥ Witness signature
⑦ Date of witness signature
⑧ Printed name of witness

Witness Affidavit of Oral Revocation of Durable Health Care Power of Attorney

The following person ① _____,
referred to as the Principal, was the maker and signatory of a Durable Health Care Power of Attorney which was dated ② _____ , and which was executed by him or her for use in the State of ③ _____ .

By this written affidavit, I, ④ _____ , the witness, hereby affirm that on the date of ⑤ _____ , I personally witnessed the above-named declarant make known to me, through verbal and/or non-verbal methods, their clear and unmistakable intent to entirely revoke such Durable Health Care Power of Attorney, or any other appointment or designation of a person to make any health care decisions on his or her behalf. It is my belief that the above-named principal fully intended that all of the above-mentioned documents no longer have any force or effect whatsoever.

Witness Acknowledgment

The declarant is personally known to me and I believe him or her to be of sound mind and under no duress, fraud, or undue influence.

Witness Signature ⑥ _____   Date ⑦ _____

Printed Name of Witness ⑧ _____

Revocation of Powers of Attorney

This document may be used with any of the previous power of attorney forms. The revocation is used to terminate the original authority that was granted to the other person in the first place. Some limited powers of attorney specifiy that the powers that are granted will end on a specific date. If that is the case, you will not need a revocation unless you wish the powers to end sooner than the date specified. If the grant of power was for a limited purpose and that purpose is complete but no date for the power to end was specified, this revocation should be used as soon after the transaction as possible. In any event, if you choose to revoke a power of attorney, a copy of this revocation should be provided to the person to whom the power was given. Copies should also be given to any party that may have had dealings with the attorney-in-fact before the revocation and to any party with whom the attorney-in-fact may be expected to attempt to deal with after the revocation. If you feel that it is important to verify the revocation of your power of attorney, you should have any third party that you supply with a copy of the revocation sign another copy for you to keep. If that is not possible, you should mail a copy of the revocation to that person or institution by first class mail, with a return receipt requested that requires a signature to verify delivery.

Although this revocation may be used to revoke a health care power of attorney, please also note that there are other acceptable methods to revoke a health care power of attorney.

To complete this document, fill in the following information:

① Printed name and address of person who originally granted power (principal)
② Date of original power of attorney
③ Printed name and address of person granted power (attorney-in-fact)
④ Date of revocation of power of attorney
⑤ Signature of person revoking power of attorney (principal) (signed in front of notary)
⑥ Notary to complete the notary acknowledgment

Revocation of Power of Attorney

① I, _____ (printed name) ,
address: _____

② do revoke the power of attorney dated _____ , 20 _____ ,
③ which was granted to _____ (printed name),
address:_____ ,

to act as my attorney-in-fact.

④ This Revocation is dated _____ , 20 _____

⑤ _____
Signature of Person Revoking Power of Attorney

⑥ **Notary Acknowledgement**

State of _____
County of _____

On _____ , 20 _____ , _____ personally
came before me and, being duly sworn, did state that he or she is the person described in the
above document and that he or she signed the above document in my presence.

_____
Signature of Notary Public

Notary Public, In and for the County of _____
State of _____

My commission expires: _____   Notary Seal

Chapter 4

Probate and Successor Trustee/Executor Information

In this chapter, various information relating to the probate process is provided. In addition, information relating to the executor of your will (or successor trustee of your living trust) is also outlined. For a living trust, you will need to select someone to distribute your trust assets to your chosen beneficiaries after your death. This person is referred to as your *successor trustee*. For a will, the person appointed in the will to administer your estate upon your death is referred to an *executor*. (Note that in some states an executor is referred to as a *personal representative*). Before actually preparing a will or living trust, an overview of how the legal system operates after a person's death may be useful to keep in mind. The system of court administration of the estates of deceased parties is generally entitled *probate*. How to avoid the probate court was the subject of one of the first self-help law books to challenge the legal establishment's monopoly on law. Probate, however, despite what many lawyers would have you believe, is not all that mysterious a matter.

Overview of a Typical Probate Proceeding

If the bulk of your assets is placed in a living trust, your chosen successor trustee is authorized by the terms of the trust to distribute the assets to the chosen beneficiaries upon your death without notice to any court and without any court supervision. Additionally, if you have assets that have chosen beneficiaries, such as a life insurance policy or a payable-on-death bank account, the beneficiary will automatically become the owner of the property upon your death (although the beneficiary will have to provide the holder of the assets with proof of the death). Finally, if you have assets that are held as joint tenants with survivorship or community property assets in a community property state, those assets will automatically become the property of the joint owner or spouse upon your death. These situations all take place outside of a probate proceeding.

If, however, there is a will, upon a person's death, in most states there is a general sequence of events which takes place. First, if there is a will, the *executor* appointed in the will (who, hopefully, has been notified of her or his duties in advance) locates the will and files it with the proper authority. If necessary, the executor arranges for the funeral and burial. If the estate is complicated or very large, it may be prudent for the executor to hire a lawyer to handle the probate proceeding. Upon presenting the will to the probate court, the will is *proved*, which means that it is determined whether or not the document presented is actually the deceased's will. This may be done in most states with a *self-proving affidavit* that is prepared and notarized at the time your will is signed. The wills in this book are designed to be self-proving when completed and signed as indicated.

Upon proof that the will is valid, the executor is officially given legal authority to gather together all of the estate's property. This authority for the executor to administer the estate is generally referred to as *letters testamentary*. The probate court also officially appoints any trustees and also the parties who are designated as guardians of any minor children.

If no executor was chosen in the will, or if the one chosen cannot serve, the probate court will appoint one. The order of preference for appointment is commonly as follows: surviving spouse, next of kin, and then a person having an interest in the estate or claims against the estate.

If the will is shown to be invalid, or if there is no will, the same sequence of events generally is followed. When a person dies without a will this is referred to as dying *intestate*. However, in this case, the party appointed to administer the estate is usually titled an *administrator* of the estate rather than an executor. The court orders granting authority to an administrator are generally referred to as *letters of administration*. The probate court will then use state law to determine how a person's assets are distributed. Please refer to the Appendix of estate planning laws on the included CD for details regarding how your particular state handles distribution of estates of intestate persons.

After the executor or administrator is given authority, he or she handles the collection of assets, management of the estate, and payment of any debts and taxes until such time as all creditors' claims have been satisfied and other business of the estate completed. An inventory of all of the assets is typically the first official act of an executor. Creditors, by the way, only have a certain time period in which to make a claim against an estate. The same holds true for any *contests* (challenging the validity) of the will. Contesting a will is a fairly rare occurrence and is most difficult if the will was properly prepared and signed by a competent, sane adult.

The executor generally will also be empowered under state law to provide an allowance for the surviving spouse and children until such time as all affairs of the deceased person are completed and the estate is closed.

Upon completion of all business and payment of all outstanding charges against the estate, an accounting and inventory of the estate's assets are then presented to the probate court by the executor. At this time, if everything appears to be in order, the executor is generally empowered to distribute all of the remaining property to the persons or organizations named in the will and probate is officially closed. The entire probate process generally takes from four to 12 months to complete.

The distribution of your property and money is usually handled solely by the executor (possibly with a lawyer's help to be certain that all legal requirements are fulfilled). Normally, this is done without further court approval of the disbursement.

Simplified Probate Procedures

Although, in the past, probate used to be a very expensive and time-consuming process, all states (except Georgia and Louisiana) now provide various methods for streamlined and simplified probate procedures for smaller estates. These simplified procedures generally take two forms: probate methods that consist of using affidavits to complete all of the distribution of an estate's assets and/or procedures that greatly simplify the probate process. These probate simplification procedures are generally available for estates that have limited assets, although in some states the cut-off amounts can be as high as several hundred thousand dollars. These simplified probate procedures have, in some cases, made estate planning issues for the sole purpose of probate avoidance somewhat less important. You may wish, however, to use your state's maximum limits for simplified probate to plan your estate in such a way as to make certain that you have removed enough property from probate to qualify for use of the simplified probate procedures for the remaining property. For example, let's say you have an estate consisting of a $200,000.00 home, $50,000.00 in a bank account, a $10,000.00 car, and $15,000.00 in personal property for a total estate of $275,000.00. This amount is over the simplified probate cutoff level for nearly all states. But you could put your home into a living trust and change your bank account to a payable-on-death account, leaving only $25,000.00 in property that is subject to probate, which you could then leave to your beneficiaries by way of a will. This amount of property left by will would then qualify for simplified probate procedures in most states. Please check the Estate Planning Appendix on the CD for an explanation of the simplified probate procedures in your state.

Choosing a Successor Trustee or Executor

Your choice of who should be your successor trustee or executor is a personal decision. A spouse, sibling, or other trusted party is usually chosen to act as successor trustee/executor, although a bank officer, accountant, or attorney can also be chosen. The person chosen should be someone you trust and whom you feel can handle or at least efficiently delegate the complicated tasks of making an inventory of all of your property and distributing it to your chosen beneficiaries. The person chosen should, generally, be a resident of the state in which you currently reside (See warning box below left). In addition, all states require that successor trustee/executors be competent, of legal age (generally, over 18) and a citizen of the United States. Although it is possible, it is generally not wise to appoint two or more persons as co-successor trustee/executors. It is preferable to appoint your first choice as primary successor trustee/executor and the other person as alternate successor trustee/executor. Note that if you will be using both a will and a living trust in your estate plan, you may select different people to serve as executor and successor trustee. It may, however, be more prudent to select the same person to act in each capacity in order to simplify the coordination of the distribution of your estate's assets. If you do choose to select different people to serve in these roles, you will need to specify which person you expect to handle the non-legal duties (these duties are outlined later in this chapter) that a successor trustee/executor may be expected to carry out. Generally, it is the executor of an estate that handles these various duties, but there is no legal requirement that would prevent a successor trustee from being requested to handle these duties.

In your will or living trust, you will grant the successor trustee/executor broad powers to manage your estate and will also provide that he or she is not required to post a bond in order to be appointed to serve as successor trustee/executor. This provision can save your estate considerable money, depending upon the estate's size. The fees for executor bonds are based upon the size of the estate and can amount to hundreds of dollars for every year that your estate is being managed. By waiving this bond requirement, these potential bond fees can be eliminated and the money saved can be passed on to your beneficiaries.

You should discuss your choice with the person chosen to be certain that he or she is willing to act as successor trustee/executor. In addition, it is wise to provide your successor trustee/executor, in advance, with a copy of your will, living trust, living will and any other estate planning documents; a copy of any organ-donation desires, a copy of your property and beneficiary questionnaires, and a copy of the information contained in this chapter.

Successor Trustee/Executor Duties Checklist Instructions

Provided on the following pages is a checklist of items that your successor trustee/executor may have to deal with after your death. Although this list is extensive, there may be other personal tasks that are not included. Scanning this list can give you an idea of the scope and range of the successor trustee/executor's duties. You can provide invaluable assistance to your successor trustee/executor by being aware of his or her duties and providing the successor trustee/executor with information to help him or her complete them. This checklist is divided into immediate and first-month time periods. These time periods are approximations and many of the duties may be required to be performed either before or after the exact time specified. Also included in the checklist are a number of financial duties. These duties cannot be delegated (except to an attorney or accountant specifically hired by the executor for that purpose). Following this list, a section is provided for listing such information for your successor trustee/executor. Please note that these checklists are also included on the Forms-on-CD.

Successor Trustee/Executor Duties Checklist

Immediate Duties

- ☐ Contact mortuary or funeral home regarding services
- ☐ Contact cemetery regarding burial or cremation
- ☐ Contact local newspaper with obituary information
- ☐ Contact relatives and close friends
- ☐ Contact employer and business associates
- ☐ Contact lawyer and accountant
- ☐ Arrange for Pallbearers
- ☐ Contact guardians or trustees named in will
- ☐ Arrange for immediate care of decedent's minor children
- ☐ Arrange for living expenses for decedent's spouse
- ☐ Contact veteran's organizations

Duties within First Month

- ☐ Contact insurance agent and report death
- ☐ Contact general insurance agent
- ☐ Contact medical and health insurance companies
- ☐ Contact Medicare
- ☐ Contact employer regarding pensions and death benefits
- ☐ Contact unions regarding pensions and death benefits

☐ Contact military regarding pensions and death benefits

☐ Contact Social Security Administration

☐ Obtain death certificates from attending physician

☐ Contact IRA or KEOGH account trustees

☐ Contact county recorder

☐ Contact post office

☐ Contact department of motor vehicles

☐ Arrange for management of business or real estate holdings

☐ Review all of decedent's records and legal documents

☐ Contact gas, telephone, cable, electric, trash and water companies

☐ Contact newspaper and magazine subscription departments

☐ Contact credit card companies

Financial Duties
Cannot be delegated

☐ Begin inventory of assets

☐ Arrange for appraisal of assets

☐ Begin collection of assets

☐ Contact banks, savings and loans, and credit unions

☐ Contact mortgage companies

☐ Contact stockbroker and investment counselor

☐ Open bank accounts for estate

☐ Open decedent's safe deposit box

☐ File the will with probate court (Executor duty only)

☐ Inventory all estate assets

☐ Collect all monies and property due to decedent

☐ Pay all taxes due and file all necessary tax returns

☐ Provide notice to all creditors of the time limit for claims

☐ Pay all debts and expenses of decedent, including funeral expenses

☐ Arrange for sale of estate assets, if necessary

☐ Distribute all remaining assets according to will

☐ Submit final accounting and receipts to probate court

☐ Close estate books and affairs

Successor Trustee/Executor Information List Instructions

This listing will provide your successor trustee/executor with valuable information that will make performing his or her difficult task much easier. Included in this questionnaire is information relating to the location of your records, any funeral or burial arrangements that you have made, lists of important persons, businesses, or organizations whom the successor trustee/executor will need to contact after your death, and information that will assist your successor trustee/executor in preparing any obituary listing. It may be very difficult to confront your own mortality and the need for this information. Please take the time to provide this valuable record of information for your successor trustee/executor. After your death, he or she may be under tremendous emotional stress and this information will help him or her perform the successor trustee/executor's necessary duties with the least difficulty. You will probably wish to give this information list and a copy of your will and/or living trust to the person whom you have chosen as your successor trustee/executor. Please note that this information list is ONLY included on the Forms-on-CD.

Note: You may also wish to leave a letter for your executor or successor trustee that explains any of your reasons for particular actions that you have taken in preparing your will, trust, or other estate planning devices. This letter will have no legal effect, but may go a long way in providing your beneficiaries with clear reasons why certain actions were taken, such as why (or why not) some gifts were made, or why there may be differences in the amounts or types of property that were left to siblings. A letter of this type may also be a good place to express your sentiments regarding friends or family. You may also wish to use such a letter to leave instructions for the care of pets.

Chapter 5

Wills

A will is a legal document that, when accepted by the probate court, is proof of an intent to transfer property to the person(s) or organization(s) named in the will upon the death of the maker of the will. The maker of the will is known as the *testator*. A will is effective for the transfer of property that is owned by the testator on the date of his or her death. A will can be changed, modified, or revoked at any time by the testator prior to death.

It is equally important to understand that for a will to be valid, it must generally be prepared, witnessed, and signed according to certain technical legal procedures. Although a will is perfectly valid if it is written in plain English and does not use technical legal language, it *must* be prepared, witnessed, and signed in the manner outlined in this book. This cannot be overemphasized. You cannot take any shortcuts when following the instructions as they relate to the procedures necessary for completing and signing your will. These procedures are not at all difficult and consist generally of carefully typing (or printing on a computer) your will in the manner outlined later, signing it in the manner specified, and having three witnesses and a notary public also sign the document. (Although not a legal requirement, the notarization of your will can aid in its proof in court later, if necessary).

In the past, it was possible to simply write down your wishes, sign the paper, and be confident that your wishes would be followed upon your death. Unfortunately, this is, in most cases, no longer possible. *Holographic* (or handwritten and unwitnessed) wills are no longer accepted as valid in most jurisdictions. *Nuncupative* (or oral) wills are also not admissible in most probate courts to prove a person's intent to dispose of property on death. For this reason, a valid, typewritten (or computer printed) will that is prepared, signed, and witnessed according to formal legal requirements is necessary. This type of will is now essentially the only secure method to ensure the desired disposition of your property, possessions, and money after your death and to assure that your loved ones are taken care of according to your final wishes.

To prepare a will, please read the following sections on property, beneficiaries and probate. Then follow the instructions to select and prepare your own will.

Property and Taxation Information

The methods and manners of disposition of your property using an estate plan are discussed in this chapter. Your estate consists of different types of property. They may be personal property, real estate, "community" property, stocks, bonds, cash, heirlooms, or keepsakes. Regardless of the type of property you own, there are certain general rules that must be kept in mind as you prepare your estate plan.

Later in this chapter, there is also a discussion of federal and state estate, inheritance and income taxes as they relate to estate plans. Recent changes in federal law have made the tax consequences of estate planning relevant mainly for people whose estates are valued at $3.5 million or more.

In addition, in this chapter you will also prepare an inventory of all of your assets and liabilities. This will allow you to have before you a complete listing of all of the property that you own as you begin to consider which beneficiaries should receive which property in your estate plan.

What Property May be Disposed of With Your Estate Plan?

In general, you may dispose of any property that you own at the time of your death. This simple fact, however, contains certain factors which require further explanation. There are forms of property which you may "own," but which may not be transferred by way of a living trust or will. In addition, you may own only a percentage or share of certain other property. In such situations, only that share or percentage which you actually own may be left to others via your estate plan. Finally, there are types of property ownership which are automatically transferred to another party at your death, regardless of the presence of a will or trust in your estate plan.

In the first category of property which cannot be transferred by will or trust are properties that have a designated beneficiary outside of the provisions of your will or living trust. These types of properties include:

- Life insurance policies
- Retirement plans
- IRAs and KEOGHs
- Pension plans
- Trust bank accounts
- Payable-on-death bank accounts
- U.S. Savings Bonds, with payable-on-death beneficiaries

In general, if there is already a valid determination of who will receive the property upon your death (as there is, for example, in the choice of a life insurance beneficiary), you may not alter this choice of beneficiary through the use of your will or trust. If you wish to alter your choice of beneficiary in any of these cases, you must alter the choice directly with the holder of the particular property (for instance, the life insurance company, bank, or pension plan). Note also that property that is included in a living trust may not be left by will, since it already (presumably) has a named beneficiary under the terms of the living trust. In a similar vein, property that is already promised to another under a contract cannot be left to another by will.

The next category of property that may have certain restrictions regarding its transfer by will or trust is property in which you may only own a certain share or percentage. Examples of this might be a partnership interest in a company or jointly-held property. Using a will or trust, you may only leave that percentage or fraction of the ownership of the property that is actually yours. For business interests, it is generally advisable to pass the interest that you own to a beneficiary intact. The forced sale of the share of a business for estate distribution purposes often results in a lower value being placed on the share. Of course, certain partnership and other business ownership agreements require the sale of a partner's or owner's interest upon death. These buy-out provisions will be contained in any ownership or partnership documents that you may have. Review such documentation carefully to determine both the exact share of your ownership and any post-death arrangements that are specified in the business documents. If your business situation is complex or if you are unsure of how your estate plan will impact your business upon your death, you should consult an attorney knowledgeable in business matters.

The ownership rights and shares of property owned jointly must also be considered. This is discussed below under common-law property states, although most joint ownership laws also apply in community property states as well. Another example of property in which only a certain share is actually able to be transferred by will or trust is a spouse's share of marital property in states that follow community property designation of certain jointly-owned property. The following is a discussion of the basic property law rules in both community property and common-law property states. The rules regarding community property only apply to married persons in those states that follow this type of property designation. If you are single, please disregard this section and use the common-law property states rules below to determine your ownership rights.

Note for residents of Louisiana: Louisiana law is derived from French law and has slightly differing rules. Differences in Louisiana law will be highlighted in the text when applicable, but please check the Estate Planning Appendix listing for details of Louisiana laws relating to estate planning issues.

Community Property States

Several states, mostly in the western United States, follow the community property type of marital property system. Please refer to the Appendix to see if your state has this type of system. The system itself is derived from ancient Spanish law. It is a relatively simple concept. All property owned by either spouse during a marriage is divided into two types: separate property and community property.

Separate property consists of all property considered owned entirely by one spouse. Separate property, essentially, is all property owned by the spouse prior to the marriage and kept separate during the marriage; and all property received individually by the spouse by gift or inheritance during the marriage. All other property is considered community property. In other words, all property acquired during the marriage by either spouse, unless by gift or inheritance, is community property. Community property is considered to be owned in equal shares by each spouse, regardless of whose efforts actually went into acquiring the property. (Major exceptions to this general rule are Social Security and Railroad retirement benefits, which are considered to be separate property by federal law).

Specifically, separate property generally consists of:

- All property owned by a spouse prior to a marriage (if kept separate)
- All property a spouse receives by gift or inheritance during a marriage (if kept separate)
- All income derived from separate property (if kept separate). Note: in Texas and Idaho, income from separate property is considered community property

Community property generally consists of:

- All property acquired by either spouse during the course of a marriage, unless it is separate property (thus it is community property unless it is acquired by gift or inheritance or is income from separate property)
- All pensions and retirement benefits earned during a marriage (except Social Security and Railroad retirement benefits)
- All employment income of either spouse acquired during the marriage
- All separate property which is mixed or co-mingled with community property during the marriage

Thus, if you are a married resident of a community property state, the property that you may dispose of by will or living trust consists of all of your separate property and one-half of your jointly-owned marital community property. The other half of the community property automatically becomes your spouse's sole property upon your death. A spouse in a community property state may disinherit the other spouse from receiving any of their separate property. However, a surviving spouse will still receive the deceased spouse's share of marital property. In addition, residents of most community property states may also generally own property jointly as tenant-in-common or as joint tenants. These forms of ownership are discussed below.

Common-Law Property States

Residents of all other states are governed by a common-law property system, which was derived from English law. Under this system, there is no rule that gives fifty percent ownership of the property acquired during marriage to each spouse.

In common-law states, the property that you may dispose of with your will or living trust consists of all the property held by title in your name, any property that you have earned or purchased with your own money, and any property that you may have been given as a gift or have inherited, either before or during your marriage.

If your name alone is on a title document in these states (for instance, a deed or automobile title), then you own the property solely. If your name and your spouse's name is on the document, you both generally own the property as tenants-in-common, unless the title specifically states that your ownership is to be as joint tenants with right of survivorship, or if your state allows, as a tenancy-by-the-entireties (a form of joint tenancy between married persons). There is an important difference between these types of joint ownership: namely, survivorship. (Note: a few common law states provide that when spouses acquire property jointly, the property is assumed to be held as joint tenants). With property owned as tenants-in-common, the percentage or fraction that each tenant-in-common owns is property that may be disposed of under a will or trust. If the property is held as joint tenants with right of survivorship or as tenants-by-the entireties, the survivor automatically receives the deceased party's share. Thus, in your will or trust, you may not dispose of any property held in joint tenancy or tenancy-by-the entirety since it already has an automatic legal disposition upon your death. For example: if two persons own a parcel of real estate as equal tenants-in-common, each person may leave a one-half interest in the property to the beneficiary of their choice by their will or living trust. By contrast, if the property is owned as joint tenants with right of survivorship, the one-half interest that a person owns will automatically become the surviving owner's property upon death.

In common-law states, you may dispose of any property that has your name on the title in whatever share that the title gives you, unless the title is held specifically as joint tenants with right of survivorship or tenants-by-the-entireties. You may also dispose of any property that you earned or purchased with your own money, and any property that you have been given as a gift or have inherited. If you are married, however, there is a further restriction on your right to dispose of property by will or trust.

All common-law states protect spouses from total disinheritance by providing a statutory scheme under which a spouse may choose to take a minimum share of the deceased spouse's estate, regardless of what the deceased spouse's will or living trust states. This effectively prevents any spouse from being entirely disinherited through the use of the common law rules of property: name on the title equals ownership of property. In most states, the spouse has a right to a one-third share of the deceased spouse's estate, regardless of what the deceased spouse's will or living trust states. However, all states are slightly different in how they apply this type of law and some allow a spouse to take as much as one-half of the estate. Please check your particular state's laws on this aspect in the Estate Planning Appendix on the CD. The effect of these statutory provisions is to make it impossible to disinherit a spouse entirely in common law states (recall that you can't really disinherit a spouse in community property states either as the spouse has a legal right to one-half of the marital property in such states). If you choose to leave nothing to your spouse under your will or by other means (such as life insurance or joint tenancies), he or she may take it anyway, generally from any property that you tried to leave to others. The details of each state's spousal statutory share are outlined in the Appendix on the CD under the listing "Spouses Right to Property Regardless of Will."

You may, however, disinherit anyone else, even your children (except in the state of Louisiana in certain circumstances). To disinherit children, you will need to specifically name them in your will or living trust in order to effectively disinherit them. For anyone else, merely leaving them out of your estate plan effectively disinherits them.

Some states also allow a certain family allowance and/or homestead allowance to the spouse or children to insure that they are not abruptly cut off from their support by any terms of a will or living trust. These allowances are generally of short duration for relatively minor amounts of money and differ greatly from state to state. Thus, the property that you may dispose of by will or living trust is as follows:

- In community property states: For married couples, all separate property (property that was brought into a marriage and held separately, or obtained by gift or inheritance during the marriage) and one-half of the community property (all other property acquired during the marriage by either spouse). If you are single, follow the common-law state rules below.

- In common-law states: Your share of all property where your name is on the title document, unless the property is held as joint tenants or tenants-by-the-entireties. Also your share of all other property that you own, earned, or purchased in your own name. An exception to this is property for which a beneficiary has already been chosen by the terms of the owner-ship of the property itself (for example: life insurance or payable-on-death bank accounts). In addition, please check the Appendix for information relating to the spouse's minimum statutory share of an estate in your state.

Finally, if you live in a common-law state, but own property in a community property state, your estate will be probated in the state in which you reside (the common-law state). Generally, probate courts will treat out-of-state property in the same manner that it would be treated in the state where it is located. Thus, the common-law state probate court will, generally, treat the community prop-erty state asset as if it were a community property asset. The same would hold true if you live in a community property state, but own property in a common-law state. The community property state probate court would generally treat the common-law state asset as common-law property. If you are in this situation, however, it may be a good idea to consult with an attorney to be certain about how your property will be treated by different states.

Federal and State Taxes Relating to Estates

Various taxes may apply to property transfers upon death. In general, there are two main type of taxes: estate taxes and inheritance taxes. An estate tax is a government tax on the privilege of being allowed to transfer property to others upon your death. This tax is assessed against the estate itself and is paid out of the estate before the assets are distributed to the beneficiaries. An inheritance tax is a tax on property received and is paid by the person who has actually inherited the property. The federal government assesses an estate tax. Various states impose additional estate taxes and inheritance taxes. Additionally, the federal government and a few states apply a gift tax on property transfers during a person's life. There are a number of states that do not impose any estate, inheritance, or gift taxes. Basic information regarding each state's tax situation is provided in the Appendix under the listing "State Gift, Estate or Inheritance Taxes".

Federal Estate Taxes

With regard to federal estate taxes, recent changes in the federal Income Tax Code, as it relates to estate taxes, have released an estimated 97 percent of the American public from any federal estate tax liability on their death. The current Internal Revenue Service rules provide for the equivalent of an exemption from all estate tax for the first $3.5 million of a person's assets. If you are married, both you and your spouse are entitled to separate $3.5 million exemptions. The $3.5 million figure is current in 2009. In 2010, the estate tax is scheduled to be repealed altogether, although only for one year. Congress will undoubtedly tinker with the federal estate tax again as we approach 2010.

In addition, all of the value of a person's estate that is left to a spouse who is a U.S. citizen (or to a tax-exempt charity) is exempt from any federal estate tax. Even if your particular assets are over this minimum exemption, there are still methods to lessen or eliminate your tax liability. One such method for couples is referred to as an AB trust. A QDOT trust may be used to leave property to a non-citizen spouse. These methods, however, are beyond the scope of this book. Note also that the $3.5 million exemption includes any substantial gifts that you have made during your lifetime. See the discussion of gift taxes below. From a planning standpoint, the changes in the federal estate tax have virtually eliminated any consideration of tax consequences from the preparation of a estate plan for most Americans. However, if your assets (or your joint assets, if married) total over approximately $3.5 million, it is recommended that you consult a tax professional prior to preparing your estate plan. The estate tax rate for assets over the $3.5 million limit is very high: 45% of all taxable assets for the tax year 2009.

State Estate Taxes

State estate taxes are, as a rule, also very minimal or even non-existent until the value of your estate is over $3.5 million. Most state's estate tax laws were previously tied directly to the federal estate tax regulations and allowed for the same level of exemption equivalent from state estate taxes on death if the estate property totaled under the federal exemption level. This changed in 2006 and now some states may impose an additional level of estate tax. However, unless your estate is very large, any such state estate taxes will be minimal. The details of each state's estate tax situation are outlined in the Appendix. If your estate is large (over $3.5 million), you are urged to consult a tax professional for assistance in lessening the potential estate tax bite on your estate.

State Inheritance Taxes

Estate taxes are levied on the estate itself, prior to its distribution to any beneficiaries. Inheritance taxes, on the other hand, are taxes levied on the person that actually inherits property. There is no federal inheritance tax and less than half of the states impose an inheritance tax on the receipt of property resulting from someone's death. There are generally relatively high exemptions allowed and the inheritance taxes are usually scaled such that spouses, children, and close relatives pay much lower rates than more distant relatives or unrelated persons. If your estate is over $3.5 million, you are advised to consult with a tax planning specialist prior to preparing your estate plan.

Federal Gift Tax

Besides estate and inheritance taxes, the federal gift tax may also apply to distributions under your estate plan. This tax is levied on the giver of the gift, not on the recipient. Its purpose is to prevent people from avoiding the federal estate tax by giving away large amounts of property during their lifetimes. From 2006 through 2010, the lifetime federal gift tax exemption is $1 million. You are also allowed under current rules to give a gift of up to $13,000.00 to an individual each year without incurring any gift tax. The amount of gifts over this yearly minimum exclusion is the amount that is subject to the federal gift tax. However, you do not actually pay the federal gift tax when you make a large gift. The amount of the gift that is subject to the gift tax is deducted from the amount of your personal exemption from the federal estate tax. For example, if in tax year 2009, you make a gift to your daughter of $63,000.00, the first $13,000.00 is exempt from any gift tax and the additional $50,000.00 (the amount that is subject to a gift tax) is deducted from your estate tax exemption ($3.5 million minus $50,000.00), leaving an estate tax exemption of $1,950,000.00. Two final notes regarding gift taxes: First, any gifts between spouses are totally exempt from any gift taxes (unless one spouse is not an American citizen, in which case the exclusion amount is $133,000.00, rather than the $13,000.00 limit that applies to all other gifts). Finally, any gifts that are made directly to a school or health care provider to pay for educational or health care expenses, and any gifts that are made to tax-exempt charities are exempt from the federal gift tax. As with all situations where an estate is large enough for tax consequences to be important, you are advised to seek additional professional assistance if you anticipate making gifts of over $13,000.00 per year to any individual.

Income Tax on Inheritances

Under current federal law, there are no income or capital gains taxes on inherited property. Inherited property is valued at its "fair market value" at the time of death of the property's owner. Thus, any increase in the value of the property during the life of the deceased owner escapes any capital gains tax. This can provide a substantial tax savings for the recipient of an inheritance of property that has increased in value during the life of the owner. (Note that this tax rule is scheduled to change in 2010). Any income that the inherited property earns after the inheritance will be subject to income tax, however.

Property Questionnaire Instructions

Before you begin to actually prepare your will, you must understand what your assets are, who your beneficiaries are to be, and what your personal desires are as to how those assets should be distributed among your beneficiaries. Since you may only give away property that you actually own, before you prepare your plan it is helpful to gather all of the information regarding your personal financial situation together in one place. The Property Questionnaire will assist you in that task. Determining who your dependents are, what their financial circumstances are, what gifts you wish to leave them, and whether you wish to make other persons or organizations beneficiaries under your estate plan are questions that will be answered as you complete the Beneficiary Questionnaire in the next section.

Together, these two questionnaires should provide you with all of the necessary information to make the actual preparation of your estate plan a relatively easy task. In addition, the actual process of filling out these questions will gently force you to think about and make the important decisions that must be made in the planning and preparation of your will. When you have finished completing this Questionnaire, have it in front of you as you complete your will. It may also be prudent to leave a photocopy of these questionnaires with the original of your will and provide a copy to your executor, in order to provide a readily-accessible inventory of your assets and list of your beneficiaries for use by your executor in managing your estate.

Please note that copies of both the Property Questionnaire and the Beneficiary Questionnaire are **ONLY** included on the Forms-on-CD. They are included as text forms that may be filled in on your computer or as PDF forms that may be printed out and filled in by hand.

Please complete the Property Questionnaire on the CD now.

Beneficiary and Gift Information

In this section you will determine both whom you would like your beneficiaries to be and what specific property you will leave each beneficiary under your estate plan. First, there is a brief discussion regarding who may be a beneficiary. Next, there is an explanation of the various methods that you may use to leave gifts to your beneficiaries. Finally, there is a Beneficiary Questionnaire that you will use to actually make the decisions regarding which beneficiaries will receive which property.

Who May Be a Beneficiary?

Any person or organization who receives property under a will or trust is termed a beneficiary. Just as there are certain requirements that the person signing the will or trust must meet, there are certain requirements relating to who may receive property under a will. These generally, however, are in the form of negative requirements. Stated in another way, this means that any person or organization may receive property under a will or living trust unless they fall into certain narrow categories of disqualification.

Besides these few exceptions noted below, any person or organization you choose may receive property under your will or living trust. This includes any family members, the named executor (or successor trustee), illegitimate children (if named specifically), corporations, charities (but see below on possible restrictions), creditors, debtors, friends, acquaintances, or even strangers.
The few categories of disqualified beneficiaries are as follows:

- An attorney who drafts the will or living trust is generally assumed to have used undue influence if he or she is made a beneficiary.
- Many states disqualify any witnesses to the signing (execution) of the will. Check the Estate Planning Appendix on the CD to see if your state has this restriction. However, to be safe, it is recommended that none of your witnesses be beneficiaries under your will or living trust.
- A person who murders a testator is universally disqualified from receiving any property under the murdered person's will (even if they are named as a beneficiary).
- An unincorporated association is typically not allowed to receive property under a will or living trust. This particular disqualification stems from the fact that such associations generally have no legal right to hold property.

A few states also have restrictions on the right to leave property to charitable organizations and churches. These restrictions are usually in two forms: a time limit prior to death when changes to a will that leave large amounts of money or property to a charitable organization are disallowed or a percentage limit on the amount of a person's estate that may be left to a charitable organization (often a limit of 50 percent). The reasoning behind this rule is to prevent abuse of a dying person's desire to be forgiven. There have been, in the past, unscrupulous individuals or organizations who have obtained last-minute changes in a will in an attempt to have the bulk of a person's estate left to them or their group. If you intend to leave large sums of money or property to a charitable organization or church, please consult an attorney for further assistance to see if there are any restrictions of this type in force in your state.

Under this same category as to who may be a beneficiary under your will or living trust are several points related to marriage, divorce, and children. First and foremost, you are advised to review your estate plan periodically and make any necessary changes as your marital or family situation may dictate. If you are divorced, married, remarried, or widowed, or adopt or have a child, there may be unforeseen consequences based on the way you have prepared your estate plan. Each state has differing laws on the effect of marriage and divorce on a person's will. In some states, divorce entirely revokes a will as it pertains to the divorced spouse. In other states, divorce has no effect and your divorced spouse may inherit your estate if you do not change your will. Marriage and the birth of children are also treated somewhat differently by each state. You are advised to review the Appendix as it relates to these aspects of your life and prepare your estate plan accordingly.

Your estate plan should be prepared with regard to how your life is presently arranged. It should, however, always be reviewed and updated each time there is a substantial change in your life.

What Type of Gifts May You Make?

There are various standard terms and phrases that may be employed when making gifts under your estate plan. The wills and living trusts that are used in this book incorporate these standard terms. Using these standard phrases, you may make a gift of any property that you will own at your death to any beneficiary whom you choose (remembering the few disqualified types of beneficiaries).

A few types of gifts are possible but are not addressed in the wills or living trusts that may be prepared using this book. Simple shared gifts (for example: I give all my property to my children, Alice, Bill, and Carl, in equal shares) are possible using this book. However, any complex shared gift arrangements will require the assistance of an attorney. In addition, you may impose simple conditions on any gifts in wills or living trusts prepared using this book. However, complex conditional gifts that impose detailed requirements that the beneficiary must comply with in order to receive the gift are also beyond the scope of this book. Finally, although it is possible to leave any gifts through your estate plan in many types of trusts, a living trust and a simple trust for leaving gifts to children are the only trusts available in estate plans prepared using this book. If you desire to leave property in trust to an adult or in a complex trust arrangement, you are advised to seek professional legal advice.

The terms that you use to make a gift can be any that you desire, as long as the gift is made in a clear and understandable manner. Someone reading the document at a later date, perhaps even a stranger appointed by a court, must be able to determine exactly what property you intended to be a gift and exactly who it is you intended to receive it. If you follow the few rules that follow regarding how to identify your gifts and beneficiaries, your intentions will be clear to whomever may need to interpret your estate plan documents in the future:

Always describe the property in as detailed and clear a manner as possible. For example: do not simply state "my car;" instead state, for example, "my 2002 Honda Accord Sedan, Serial #123456789." Describe exactly what it is you wish for each beneficiary to receive. You may make any type of gift that you wish, either a cash gift, a gift of a specific piece of personal property or real estate, or a specific share of your total estate. If you wish to give some of your estate in the form of portions of the total, it is recommended to use fractional portions. For example, if you wish to leave your estate in equal shares to two persons, use "I give one-half of my total estate to …" for each party.

In your description of the property, you should be as specific and precise as possible. For land, it is suggested that you use the description exactly as shown on the deed to the property. For personal property, be certain that your description clearly differentiates your gift from any other property.

Always describe the beneficiaries in as precise and clear a manner as is possible. For example: do not simply state "my son;" instead state "my son, Robert Edward Smith, of Houston Texas." This is particularly important if the beneficiary is an adopted child.

Never provide a gift to a group or class of people without specifically stating their individual names. For example: do not simply state "my sisters;" instead state "my sister Katherine Mary Jones, and my sister Elizabeth Anne Jones, and my sister Annette Josephine Jones."

You may put simple conditions on the gift if they are reasonable and not immoral or illegal. For example: you may say "This gift is to be used to purchase daycare equipment for the church nursery;" but you may not say "I give this gift to my sister only if she divorces her deadbeat husband Ralph Edwards."

You should always provide for an alternate beneficiary for the purpose of allowing you to designate someone to receive the gift if your first choice to receive the gift dies before you do (or, in the case of an organization chosen as primary beneficiary, is no longer in business). Your choice for alternate beneficiary may be one or more persons or an organization. In addition, you may delete the alternate beneficiary choice and substitute the words "the residue" instead. The result of this change will be that if your primary beneficiary dies before you do, your gift will pass under your residuary clause. Although not a technical legal requirement, a residuary clause should be included in every will (and living trust) in this book. With this clause, you will choose the person, persons, or organization to receive anything not covered by other clauses of your will or living trust. Even if you feel that you have given away everything that you own under other clauses of your will or living trust, this can be a very important clause.

If, for any reason, any other gifts under your will or living trust are not able to be completed, this clause takes effect. For example, if a beneficiary refuses to accept your gift or the chosen beneficiary has died and no alternate was selected or both the beneficiary and alternate have died, the gift will be returned to your estate and would pass under the "residuary clause." If there is no "residuary clause" included in your will, any property not disposed of under your will is treated as though you did not have a will and could potentially be forfeited to the state. Note that if there is no residuary clause in your living trust, any property not disposed of under your living trust will then be disposed of under the terms of your will, if you have one.

A survivorship clause also should be included in every will and living trust. This provides for a period of survival for any beneficiary. For wills and living trusts prepared using this book, the period is set at 30 days. The practical effect of this is to be certain that your property passes under your will (or living trust) and not that of a beneficiary who dies shortly after receiving your gift. Without this clause in your will or trust, it would be possible that property would momentarily pass to a beneficiary under your will or trust. When that person dies (possibly immediately if a result of a common accident or disaster), your property could wind up being left to the person whom your beneficiary designated, rather than to your alternate beneficiary.

To disinherit anyone from receiving property under your will, you should specifically name the person to be disinherited, rather than rely upon simply not mentioning them in your will. To disinherit children and grandchildren of deceased children, they must be mentioned specifically. In the case of children born after a will is executed and of spouses of a marriage that takes place after a will is executed, there are differing provisions in many states as to the effect of their not being mentioned in a will.

Please also note that although one may choose to leave nothing to a spouse in a will, all states provide rules that allow a spouse the right to a certain share of the other spouse's property on death. Please also see the Appendix for information regarding the laws in your particular state. The safest method of disinheritance, however, is to specifically mention anyone to be disinherited. Be sure to clearly identify the person being disinherited by full name. (Also note, in Louisiana, in order to disinherit children or grandchildren, specific and just reasons must be stated in the will). Another legal method to achieve approximately the same result as disinheritance is to leave the person a very small amount (at least $1.00) as a gift in your will. Also, be sure to review your estate plan each time there is a change in your family circumstances. Please see later in this chapter for a discussion regarding changing your will. Finally, property may be left to your children in trust using the children's trust that is included in the appropriate wills and living trusts in this book.

If you state your gifts simply, clearly, and accurately, you can be assured that they will be able to be carried out after your death regardless of who may be required to interpret the language in your will or living trust. The beneficiary questionnaire (on CD ONLY) will help you determine who you wish to leave gifts and what those gifts may be.

Please complete the Property Questionnaire on the CD now.

Selecting Your Will

There are three separate wills that have been prepared for the purpose of allowing persons whose situations fall into certain standard formats to prepare their wills quickly and easily on pre-assembled forms. Generally, the wills are for a single person without children and for a married person with or without children. Please read the description prior to each will to be certain that the will you choose is appropriate for your particular situation. Please note that each of the wills in this book is intended to be a *self-proving* will. This means that the signatures of the witnesses and the *testator* (the person whose will it is) will be verified by a notary public and thus, the witnesses' testimony will not be needed in probate court at a later date in order to authenticate their signatures.

Instructions for Selecting Your Will

These pre-assembled will forms are intended to be used as simplified worksheets for preparing your own personal will. The forms should be filled-in by hand and then retyped or printed out according to the following instructions and the instructions contained in later in this chapter. These pre-assembled wills are not intended to be filled-in and used "as is" as an original will. Such use would most likely result in an invalid will. The forms *must* be either retyped or completed on a computer and printed out. Be certain to carefully follow all of the instructions for use of these forms. They are not difficult to fill out, but must be prepared properly to be legally valid. In order to prepare any of the wills in this chapter, you should follow these simple steps:

1. Carefully read through all of the clauses in the blank pre-assembled will to determine if the clauses provided are suitable in your situation. Choose the will that is most appropriate. Make a photocopy or print out a copy of the will that you select to use as a worksheet . If you wish, you may use this book itself as a worksheet (unless it is a library book!).

2. Using your Property and Beneficiary Questionnaires, fill in the appropriate information where necessary on these forms.

3. After you have filled in all of the appropriate information, carefully reread your entire will. Be certain that it contains all of the correct information that you desire. Then, starting at the beginning of the will, cross out all of the words and phrases in the pre-assembled will that do not apply in your situation.

4. When you have completed all of your will clauses, see page 115 for instructions on the final preparation of your will.

As you fill in the information for each clause, keep in mind the following instructions:

Title Clause: The title clause is mandatory for all wills and must be included. Fill in the name blank with your full legal name. If you have been known by more than one name, use your principal name.

Identification Clause: The identification clause is mandatory and must be included in all wills. In the first blank, include any other names that you are known by. Do this by adding the phrase: "also known as" after your principal full name. For example:

John James Smith, also known as Jimmy John Smith.

In the spaces provided for your residence, use the location of your principal residence; that is, the place where you currently live permanently.

Marital Status Clause: Each of the pre-assembled wills in this chapter is either for a married or single person. Select the proper will and if you are married, fill in the appropriate information. If you have previously been married, please add and complete the following sentence:

I was previously married to [name of your former spouse], and that marriage ended by [select either death, divorce, or annulment].

Identification of Children Clause: This clause will only be present in the pre-assembled wills that relate to children. In this clause, you should specifically identify all of your children, indicating their full names, current addresses, and dates of birth. Cross out those spaces that are not used.

Identification of Grandchildren Clause: This clause will only be used in the two pre-assembled wills that relate to grandchildren. If you do not have grandchildren, cross out this entire clause. If you do have grandchildren, you should specifically identify all of your grandchildren in this clause, indicating their full names, current addresses, and dates of birth. Cross out those spaces that are not used.

Specific Gifts Clause: For making specific gifts, use as many of the "I give …" paragraphs as is necessary to complete your chosen gifts. In these paragraphs, you may make any type of gift that you wish; either a cash gift, a gift of a specific piece of personal property or real estate, or a specific share of your total estate. If you wish to give some of your estate in the form of portions of the total, it is recommended to use fractional portions. For example, if you wish to leave your estate in equal shares to two persons, use "I give one-half of my total estate to…" for each party. Although none of the wills in this chapter contain a specific clause that states that you give one person your entire estate, you may make such a gift using this clause by simply stating:

"I give my entire estate to…."

Be sure that you do not attempt to give any other gifts. However, you should still include the residuary clause in your will, which is explained on the next page.

In your description of the property, you should be as specific and precise as possible. For land, it is suggested that you use the description exactly as shown on the deed to the property. For personal property, be certain that your description clearly differentiates your gift from any other property. For example: "I give my blue velvet coat which was a gift from my brother John to…." Use serial numbers, colors, or any other descriptive words to clearly indicate the exact nature of the gift. For cash gifts, specifically indicate the amount of the gift. For gifts of securities, state the amount of shares and the name of the company. You may add simple conditions to the gifts that you make, if you desire. For example, you may state "I give $1,000.00 to the Centerville Church for use in purchasing a new roof for the church." Complex conditions, however, are not possible in this clause, and immoral or illegal conditions are not acceptable.

Be sure to clearly identify the beneficiary and alternate beneficiary by full name. You can also name joint beneficiaries, such as several children, if you choose. The space provided for an identification of the relationship of the beneficiary can simply be a descriptive phrase like "my wife," "my brother-in-law," or "my best friend." It does not mean that the beneficiary must be related to you personally.

The choice of alternate beneficiary is for the purpose of allowing you to designate someone to receive the gift if your first choice to receive the gift dies before you do (or, in the case of an organization chosen as primary beneficiary, is no longer in business). In this or any of the other gift clauses, your choice for alternate beneficiary may be one or more persons or an organization. It is recommended to always specifically name your beneficiary(ies), rather than using a description only, such as "my children." In addition, you may delete the alternate beneficiary choice and substitute the words "the residue" instead. The result of this change will be that if your primary beneficiary dies before you do, your gift will pass under your residuary clause, which is discussed below. If additional gifts are desired, simply photocopy an additional page to use as a worksheet.

Residuary Clause: Although not a technical legal requirement, it is strongly recommended that you include the residuary clause in every will. With this clause, you will choose the person(s) or organization(s) to receive anything not covered by other clauses of your will. Even if you feel that you have given away everything that you own under other clauses of your will, this can be a very important clause. If, for any reason, any gifts under your will are not able to be completed, this clause goes into effect. For example, if a beneficiary refuses to accept your gift, the chosen beneficiary has died and no alternate was selected, or both the beneficiary and alternate has died, the gift is put back into your estate and would *pass under* (be distributed under the terms of) the residuary clause. If there is no residuary clause included in your will, any property not disposed of under your will is treated as though you did not have a will and could potentially be forfeited to the state. To avoid this, it is strongly recommended that you make this clause mandatory in your will.

In addition, you may use this clause to give all of your estate (except your specific gifts) to one or more persons. For example: you make specific gifts of $1,000.00 to a sister and a car to a friend. By then naming your spouse as the residuary clause beneficiary, you will have gifted everything in your estate to your spouse—except the $1,000.00 and the car. You could then name your children, in equal shares, as the alternate residuary beneficiaries. In this manner, if your spouse were to die first, your children would then equally share your entire estate—except the $1,000.00 and the car.

As with naming the beneficiary under any other clause, you should always be sure to clearly identify the beneficiary by full name and a description of their relationship to you (need not be a relative).

Survivorship Clause: This clause is included in every will. This clause provides for two possibilities. First, it provides for a required period of survival for any beneficiary to receive a gift under your will. The practical effect of this is to be certain that your property passes under your will and not under that of a beneficiary who dies shortly after receiving your gift. The second portion of this clause provides for a determination of how your property should pass in the eventuality that both you and a beneficiary (most likely your spouse) should die in a manner that makes it impossible to determine who died first. Without this clause in your will, it would be possible that property could momentarily pass to a beneficiary under your will. When that person dies (possibly immediately if a result of a common accident or disaster), your property could wind up being left to the person whom your beneficiary designated, rather than to your alternate beneficiary. If you and your spouse are both preparing wills, it is a good idea to be certain that each of your wills contains identical survivorship clauses. If you are each other's primary beneficiary, it is also wise to attempt to coordinate who your alternate beneficiaries may be in the event of simultaneous deaths.

Executor Clause: The executor clause must be included in every will. With this clause, you will make your choice of executor, the person who will administer and distribute your estate, and an alternate choice if your first choice is unable to serve. A spouse, sibling, or other trusted party is usually chosen to act as executor. The person chosen should be a resident of the state in which you currently reside. Please refer to Chapter 4 for more information on executors. Note that you allow your executor to seek independent administration of your estate. Where allowed by state law, this enables your executor to manage your estate with minimal court supervision and can save your estate extensive court costs and legal fees. Additionally, you grant the executor broad powers to manage your estate and also provide that he or she not be required to post a bond in order to be appointed to serve as executor. Be sure to clearly identify the executor and alternate executor by full name. The space provided for an identification of the relationship of the executor can simply be a descriptive phrase like "my wife," "my brother-in-law," or "my best friend." It does not mean that the executor must be related to you personally.

Child Guardianship Clause: This clause will only be present in the pre-assembled wills that relate to children. With this clause you may designate your choice as to whom you wish to care for any of your minor children after you are gone. If none of your children are minors, you may delete this clause.

Who you choose to be the guardian of your children is an important matter. If you are married, your spouse is generally appointed by the probate or family court, regardless of your designation in a will. However, even if you are married, it is a good idea to choose your spouse as first choice and then provide a second choice. This will cover the contingency in which both you and your spouse die in a single accident. Your choice should obviously be a trusted person whom you feel would provide the best care for your children in your absence. Be aware, however, that the court is guided, but not bound, by this particular choice in your will. The court's decision in appointing a child's guardian is based upon what would be in the best interests of the child. In most situations, however, a parent's choice as to who should be their child's guardian is almost universally followed by the courts. Additionally, you grant the guardian broad power to care for and manage your children's property and also provide that the appointed guardian not be required to post a bond in order to be appointed. Be sure to clearly identify the guardian and alternate guardian by full name. The space provided for an identification of the relationship of the guardian can simply be a descriptive phrase like "my wife," "my brother-in-law," or "my best friend." It does not mean that the guardian must be related to you personally.

Children's Trust Fund Clause: This clause will only be present in the pre-assembled wills that relate to children. It is with this clause that you may set up a trust fund for any gifts you have made to your minor children. You also may delay the time when they will actually have unrestricted control over your gift. It is not recommended, however, to attempt to delay receipt of control beyond the age of 30. If you have left assets to more than one child, this clause provides that individual trusts be set up for each child. If none of your children are minors, you may delete this clause.

The choice for trustee under a children's trust should generally be the same person whom you have chosen to be the children's guardian. This is not, however, a requirement. The choice of trustee is generally a spouse if alive, with the alternate being a trusted friend or family member. Be sure to clearly identify the trustee and alternate trustee by full name. The space provided for an identification of the relationship of the trustee can simply be a descriptive phrase like "my wife," "my brother-in-law," or "my best friend." It does not mean that the trustee must be related to you personally. The terms of the trust provide that the trustee may distribute any or all of the income or principal to the children as he or she deems necessary to provide for the children's health, support, and education. The trust will terminate when either the specific age is reached, all of the money is spent prior to that age, or the child dies prematurely. Upon termination, any remaining trust funds will be distributed to the child (beneficiary) if surviving; if not surviving, to the heirs of the beneficiary (if any); or if there are no heirs of the beneficiary, to the residue of your estate. Additionally, you grant the trustee broad power to manage the trust and also provide that he or she not be required to post a bond in order to be appointed.

Organ Donation Clause: The use of this clause is optional. If you do not wish to make any organ donations, simply delete this clause. If you choose not to use this clause, you may delete it from your will. Use this clause to provide for any use of your body after death. You may, if you so desire, limit your donation to certain parts; for example, your eyes. If so desired, simply delete "any of my body parts and/or organs" from the following provision and insert your chosen donation. A copy of your will or instructions regarding this donation should be kept in a place that is readily-accessible by your executor and spouse. Be sure that if you use a will clause for organ donation and a separate document that the terms of each are identical.

Funeral Arrangements Clause: The use of this clause is optional. If you choose not to use this clause, you may delete it from your will. Use this clause to make known your wishes as to funeral and burial arrangements. Since it may be difficult to obtain your will quickly in an emergency, it is also a good idea to leave information regarding these desires with your executor, your spouse, a close friend, or a relative.

Signature, Witness, and Notary Clauses: The signature lines and final paragraph of this clause must be included in your will. You will fill in the number of pages and the appropriate dates where indicated after you have properly typed or printed out your will. The use of the notary acknowledgment, although not a strict legal necessity, is strongly recommended. This allows the will to become "self-proving" and the witnesses need not be called upon to testify in court at a later date (after your death) that they, indeed, signed the will as witnesses. Although a few states have not enacted legislation to allow for the use of this type of sworn and acknowledged testimony to be used in court, the current trend is to allow for its use in probate courts. This saves time, money, and trouble in having your will admitted to probate when necessary.

Preparing and Signing a Will

This section will explain how to prepare your will and have it readied for your signature. Using your Property and Beneficiary Questionnaires as guides, you should already have selected and filled in the necessary information on the appropriate will worksheet.

Below are instructions for preparing the final version of your will. As you go about preparing your will, take your time and be very careful to proofread the original will before you sign it, to be certain that it states your desires exactly.

Instructions for Preparing Your Will

1. You should have before you a completed and filled-in photocopy or printed-out worksheet of the will that you have chosen. Then, carefully reread the entire worksheet version of your will to be certain that it is exactly as you wish.

2. After making any necessary changes, type or print-out the entire will on good quality 8-½" x 11" paper.

3. After you have completed typing or printing out your will, fill in the total number of pages in the Signature paragraph. At the bottom of each page, also fill in the page number and the total number of pages. Do not yet sign your will, fill in the date, or initial the spaces on each page.

4. Again, very carefully proofread your entire will. Be certain that there are no errors. If there are any

errors, retype or reprint the particular page containing the error. *Do not* attempt to correct any errors with type-correcting fluid or tape, or with erasures of any kind. *Do not* cross-out or add anything to the typewritten words using a pen or pencil. Doing so will generally invalidate the will.

5. When you have a perfect original of your will, with no corrections and no additions, staple all of the pages together in the upper left-hand corner. You are now ready to prepare for the *execution* (signing) of your will.

Do not sign your will until you have read this section and have all of the necessary witnesses and Notary Public present. The legal requirements listed in this section regarding the proper signing of your will are extremely important and must not be deviated from in any manner in order for your will to be legally valid. These requirements are not at all difficult to follow, but they must be followed precisely. These formal requirements are what transform your will from a mere piece of paper outlining your wishes to a legal document that grants the power to dispose of your property under court order after your death.

The reasons for the formality of these requirements are twofold: first, by requiring a ceremonial-type signing of the document, it is hoped that the testator is made fully aware of the importance of what he or she is doing; and second, by requiring a formal signing witnessed by other adults, it is hoped that any instances of forgery, fraud, and coercion will be avoided, or at least minimized. Again, these legal formalities must be observed strictly. *Do not* deviate from these instructions in any way. The formal execution or signing of your will makes it legally valid and failure to properly sign your will renders it invalid.

Instructions for Signing Your Will

To properly execute your will, follow these few simple steps:

1. Select three (3) witnesses who will be available to assist you in witnessing your will. These persons may be any adults who are not mentioned in the will either as a beneficiary, executor, trustee, or guardian. The witnesses can be friends, neighbors, co-workers, or even strangers. However, it is prudent to choose persons who have been stable members of your community, since they may be called upon to testify in court someday.

2. Arrange for all of your witnesses to meet you at the office or home of a local Notary Public. Many banks, real estate offices, and government offices have notary services and most will be glad to assist you. (The Notary Public may *not* be one of the required three (3) witnesses.)

3. In front of all of the witnesses and the Notary Public, the following should take place in the order shown:

(a) You should state: "This is my Last Will and Testament, which I am about to sign. I ask that each of you witness my signature." There is no requirement that the witnesses know any of the terms of your will or that they read any of your will. All that is necessary is that they hear you state that it is your will, that you request them to be witnesses, that they observe you sign your will, and that they also sign the will as witnesses in each other's presence.

(b) You will then sign your will in ink, using a pen, at the end of the will in the place indicated, exactly as your name is typewritten on your will. You should also sign your initials on the bottom of each page of your will at this time.

(c) After you have signed, pass your will to the first witness, who should sign in the place indicated and fill in his or her address.

(d) After the first witness has signed, have the will passed to the second witness, who should also sign in the place indicated and fill in his or her address.

(e) After the second witness has signed, have the will passed to the third and final witness, who also signs in the place indicated and fills in his or her address. Throughout this ceremony, you and all of the witnesses must remain together. It is easier if you are all seated around a table or desk.

(f) For the final step, the Notary Public completes the notary acknowledgment section of the will and signs in the space indicated. When this step is completed, your will is a valid legal document and you can be assured that your wishes will be carried out upon the presentation of your will to a probate court upon your death.

Safeguarding Your Will

Please note that you should *never* under any circumstances sign a duplicate of your will. Once your will has been properly executed following the steps above, you may make photocopies of it. It is a good idea to label any of these photocopies as "COPIES."

Having completed your will according to the instructions above, it is now time to place your will in a safe place. Many people keep their important papers in a safe deposit box at a local bank. Although this is an acceptable place for storing a will, be advised that there are certain drawbacks. Your will should be in a place that is readily accessible at a moment's notice to your executor. Often there are certain unavoidable delays in gaining access to a safe deposit box in an emergency situation. If you are married, and your safe deposit box is jointly held, many of these delays can be avoided. However, even in this situation, some states prevent immediate access to the safe deposit box of a deceased married person. If you decide to keep the original will in your safe deposit box, it is a good idea to keep a copy of your will clearly marked "COPY" at home in a safe but easily-located place, with a note as to where the original will can be found.

If in the future you should decide to make any changes to your will, make certain that your executor is informed of the changes and that the changes are kept with the original will. For more information regarding changing your will, please refer to the next section.

An acceptable alternative to a safe deposit box is a home file box or desk that is used for home storage of your important papers. If possible, this storage place should be fireproof and under lock and key. Wherever you decide to store your will, you will need to inform your chosen executor of its location. The executor will need to obtain the original of your will shortly after your demise to determine if there are any necessary duties that must be looked after without delay; for example, funeral plans or organ donations.

It is also a good practice to store any life insurance policies and a copy of your birth certificate in the same location as your original will. Additionally, it is also prudent to store a copy of your Property Questionnaire, Beneficiary Questionnaire, and Successor Trustee/Executor Information List with your will in order to provide your executor with an inventory and location list of your assets and a list of information regarding your heirs and beneficiaries. Any title documents or deeds relating to property that will be transferred under your will may also be stored with your will for the convenience of your executor. One final precaution: If you wish, allow the executor whom you have named to keep a copy of your will. Be careful, however, to be certain that you immediately inform him or her of any new will that you prepare, of any *codicils* (formal changes to your will) you make to your will, or of any decision to *revoke* (cancel) your will.

Instructions for Will for Married Person with Children (Using Children's Trust)

This will is appropriate for use by a married person with one or more children. There are also provisions in this will for use if the parent has minor children and desires to place the property and assets that may be left to the children into a trust fund. In addition, this will allows a parent to choose a person to act as guardian for any minor children. In most cases, a married person may desire to choose the other spouse as both trustee and guardian for any of their children, although this is not a legal requirement. If the parent has no minor children, the will clauses relating to the children's trust and to guardianship of the children may be deleted. Each spouse/parent must prepare his or her own will. Do not attempt to prepare a joint will for both you and your spouse together.

This will contains the following standard clauses:

- Title Clause
- Identification Clause
- Marital Status Clause
- Children Identification Clause
- Grandchildren Identification Clause
- Specific Gifts Clause

- Residuary Clause
- Survivorship Clause
- Executor Clause
- Guardianship Clause
- Children's Trust Fund Clause
- Organ Donation Clause
- Funeral Arrangements Clause
- Signature and Witness Clause

Fill in each of the appropriate blanks in this will using the information that you included in your Property and Beneficiary Questionnaires. Cross out any information that is not appropriate to your situation. The necessary information to be filled-in is noted below and should be written into the place where the corresponding number appears in the following will form.

① Full name of testator
② Full name of testator (and any other names that you are known by)
③ Full address of testator

④ Spouse's full name (insert information on previous marriage, if necessary [see earlier instructions on this point])
⑤ Number of children
⑥ Child's name (repeat for each child)
⑦ Child's address (repeat for each child)
⑧ Child's date of birth (repeat for each child)

⑨ Number of grandchildren (if applicable)
⑩ Grandchild's name (repeat for each grandchild)
⑪ Grandchild's address (repeat for each grandchild)
⑫ Grandchild's date of birth (repeat for each grandchild)

⑬ Complete description of specific gift (repeat for each specific gift)
⑭ Full name of beneficiary (repeat for each specific gift)
⑮ Relationship of beneficiary to testator (repeat for each specific gift)
⑯ Full name of alternate beneficiary (repeat for each specific gift)
⑰ Relationship of alternate beneficiary to testator (repeat for each specific gift)

⑱ Full name of residual beneficiary
⑲ Relationship of residual beneficiary to testator
⑳ Full name of alternate residual beneficiary
㉑ Relationship of alternate residual beneficiary to testator

㉒ Full name of executor

㉓　Relationship of executor to testator
㉔　Full address of executor
㉕　Full name of alternate executor
㉖　Relationship of alternate executor to testator
㉗　Full address of alternate executor

㉘　Full name of guardian of children
㉙　Relationship of guardian of children to testator
㉚　Full address of guardian of children
㉛　Full name of alternate guardian of children
㉜　Relationship of alternate guardian of children to testator
㉝　Full address of alternate guardian of children

㉞　Children's age to be subject to children's trust
㉟　Children's age for end of children's trust (21, 25, or 30 years old or other age)
㊱　Full name of trustee of children's trust
㊲　Relationship of trustee of children's trust to testator
㊳　Full address of trustee of children's trust
㊴　Full name of alternate trustee of children's trust
㊵　Relationship of alternate trustee of children's trust to testator
㊶　Full address of alternate trustee of children's trust

㊷　Name of funeral home
㊸　Address of funeral home
㊹　Name of cemetery
㊺　Address of cemetery

Number of total pages of will (fill in when will is typed or printed)
Date of signing of will (DO NOT FILL IN YET)
Signature of testator (DO NOT FILL IN YET)
Printed name of testator
Date of witnessing of will (DO NOT FILL IN YET)
Signature of witness (repeat for each witness) [DO NOT FILL IN YET]
Printed name of witness (repeat for each witness) [DO NOT FILL IN YET]
Address of witness (repeat for each witness) [DO NOT FILL IN YET]

㊻　Notary Acknowledgment (to be filled in by Notary Public)

Will for Married Person with Children (Using Children's Trust)

Last Will and Testament of ①

I, ② ,
whose address is ③ ,
declare that this is my Last Will and Testament and I revoke all previous wills.

I am married to ④ .

I have ⑤ child(ren) living. His/Her/Their name(s), address(es), and date(s) of birth is/are as follows:

⑥
⑦
⑧

⑥
⑦
⑧

⑥
⑦
⑧

I have ⑨ grandchild(ren) living. His/Her/Their name(s), address(es), and date(s) of birth is/are as follows:

⑩
⑪
⑫

⑩
⑪
⑫

⑩
⑪
⑫

Page ___ of ___ pages   Testator's initials _____

I make the following specific gifts:
I give ⑬ ,
to ⑭ ,
my ⑮ ,
or if not surviving, then to ⑯ ,
my ⑰ .

I give ⑬ ,
to ⑭ ,
my ⑮ ,
or if not surviving, then to ⑯ ,
my ⑰ .

I give ⑬ ,
to ⑭ ,
my ⑮ ,
or if not surviving, then to ⑯ ,
my ⑰ .

I give ⑬ ,
to ⑭ ,
my ⑮ ,
or if not surviving, then to ⑯ ,
my ⑰ .

I give ⑬ ,
to ⑭ ,
my ⑮ ,
or if not surviving, then to ⑯ ,
my ⑰ .

I give ⑬ ,
to ⑭ ,
my ⑮ ,
or if not surviving, then to ⑯ ,
my ⑰ .

Page ___ of ___ pages

Testator's initials _____

I give all the rest of my property, whether real or personal, wherever located,
to ⑱ ,
my ⑲ ,
or if not surviving, to ⑳ ,
my ㉑ .

All beneficiaries named in this will must survive me by thirty (30) days to receive any gift under this will. If any beneficiary and I should die simultaneously, I shall be conclusively presumed to have survived that beneficiary for purposes of this will.

I appoint ㉒ ,
my ㉓ ,
of ㉔ ,
as Executor, to serve without bond. If not surviving or otherwise unable to serve,
I appoint ㉕ ,
my ㉖ ,
of ㉗ ,
as Alternate Executor, also to serve without bond. In addition to any powers, authority, and discretion granted by law, I grant such Executor or Alternate Executor any and all powers to perform any acts, in his/her sole discretion and without court approval, for the management and distribution of my estate, including independent administration of my estate.

If a Guardian is needed for any of my minor child(ren),
I appoint ㉘ ,
my ㉙ ,
of ㉚ ,
as Guardian of the person and property of any of my minor child(ren), to serve without bond. If not surviving, or unable to serve,
I appoint ㉛ ,
my ㉜ ,
of ㉝ ,
as Alternate Guardian, also to serve without bond. In addition to any powers, authority, and discretion granted by law, I grant such Guardian or Alternate Guardian any and all powers to perform any acts, in his/her sole discretion and without court approval, for the management and distribution of the property of any of my minor child(ren).

If any of my child(ren) are under ㉞ years of age, upon my death, I direct that any property that I give each child under this will be held in an individual trust for each child(ren), under the following terms, until each shall reach ㉟ years of age.

Page ___ of ___ pages   Testator's initials _____

In addition, I appoint ㊱ ,
my ㊲ ,
of ㊳ ,
as trustee of any and all required trusts, to serve without bond. If not surviving, or otherwise unable to serve, then I appoint ㊴ ,
my ㊵ ,
of ㊶ ,
as Alternate Trustee, also to serve without bond. In addition to all powers, authority, and discretion granted by law, I grant such trustee or alternate trustee full power to perform any act, in his/her sole discretion and without court approval, to distribute and manage the assets of any such trust.

In the trustee's sole discretion, the trustee may distribute any or all of the principal, income, or both, of any such trust as deemed necessary for the beneficiary's health, support, welfare, and education. Any income not distributed shall be added to the trust principal.

Any such trust shall terminate when the beneficiary reaches the required age, when the beneficiary dies prior to reaching the required age, or when all trust funds have been distributed. Upon termination, any remaining undistributed principal and income shall pass to the beneficiary; or if not surviving, to the beneficiary's heirs; or if none, to the residue of my estate.

I also declare that, pursuant to the Uniform Anatomical Gift Act, I donate any of my body parts and/or organs to any medical institution willing to accept and use them, and I direct my executor to carry out such donation.

Funeral arrangements have been made with the ㊷ ,
of ㊸ ,
for burial at ㊹ ,
located in ㊺ ,
and I direct my Executor to carry out such arrangements.

I publish and sign this Last Will and Testament, consisting of _____ typewritten pages,
on _____ , and declare that I do so freely, for the purposes expressed, under no constraint or undue influence, and that I am of sound mind and of legal age.

_____   _____
Signature of Testator   Printed Name of Testator

Page ___ of ___ pages   Testator's initials _____

We, the undersigned, being first sworn on oath and under penalty of perjury, state that:

On _____ , in the presence of all of us, the above-named Testator published and signed this Last Will and Testament, and then at Testator's request, and in Testator's presence, and in each other's presence, we all signed below as witnesses, and we declare that, to the best of our knowledge, the Testator signed this instrument freely, under no constraint or undue influence, and is of sound mind and legal age.

_____
Signature of Witness

_____
Printed Name of Witness

_____
Address of Witness

_____
Signature of Witness

_____
Printed Name of Witness

_____
Address of Witness

_____
Signature of Witness

_____
Printed Name of Witness

_____
Address of Witness

Notary Acknowledgment
State of _____
County of _____

On _____ , _____ the testator, and
_____ , _____ , and
_____ , the witnesses, personally came before me and, being duly sworn, did state that they are the persons described in the above document and that they signed the above document in my presence as a free and voluntary act for the purposes stated.

_____
Signature of Notary Public
Notary Public, In and for the County of _____State of _____
My commission expires: _____   Notary Seal

Instructions for Will for Married Person with No Children

This will is appropriate for use by a married person with no children or grandchildren. Each spouse must prepare his or her own will. Do not attempt to prepare a joint will for both you and your spouse together.

This will contains the following standard clauses:

- Title Clause
- Identification Clause
- Marital Status Clause
- Specific Gifts Clause
- Residuary Clause
- Survivorship Clause
- Executor Clause
- Organ Donation Clause
- Funeral Arrangements Clause
- Signature and Witness Clause

Fill in each of the appropriate blanks in this will using the information that you included in your Property and Beneficiary Questionnaires. Cross out any information that is not appropriate to your situation. The necessary information to be filled-in is noted below and should be written into the place where the corresponding number appears in the following will form.

①　Full name of testator
②　Full name of testator (and any other names that you are known by)
③　Full address of testator

④　Spouse's full name (insert information on previous marriage, if necessary [see earlier instructions])

⑤　Complete description of specific gift (repeat for each specific gift)
⑥　Full name of beneficiary (repeat for each specific gift)
⑦　Relationship of beneficiary to testator (repeat for each specific gift)
⑧　Full name of alternate beneficiary (repeat for each specific gift)
⑨　Relationship of alternate beneficiary to testator (repeat for each specific gift)

⑩　Full name of residual beneficiary
⑪　Relationship of residual beneficiary to testator
⑫　Full name of alternate residual beneficiary
⑬　Relationship of alternate residual beneficiary to testator

⑭   Full name of executor
⑮   Relationship of executor to testator
⑯   Full address of executor
⑰   Full name of alternate executor
⑱   Relationship of alternate executor to testator
⑲   Full address of alternate executor

⑳   Name of funeral home
㉑   Address of funeral home
㉒   Name of cemetery
㉓   Address of cemetery

Number of total pages of will (fill in when will is typed or printed)
Date of signing of will (DO NOT FILL IN YET)
Signature of testator (DO NOT FILL IN YET)
Printed name of testator
Date of witnessing of will (DO NOT FILL IN YET)
Signature of witness (repeat for each witness) [DO NOT FILL IN YET]
Printed name of witness (repeat for each witness) [DO NOT FILL IN YET]
Address of witness (repeat for each witness) [DO NOT FILL IN YET]

㉔   Notary Acknowledgment (to be filled in by Notary Public)

Will for Married Person with No Children

Last Will and Testament of ①

I, ② ,
whose address is ③ ,
declare that this is my Last Will and Testament and I revoke all previous wills.

I am married to ④ .

I have no children or grandchildren living.

I make the following specific gifts:

I give ⑤ ,
to ⑥ ,
my ⑦ ,
or if not surviving, then to ⑧ ,
my ⑨ .

I give ⑤ ,
to ⑥ ,
my ⑦ ,
or if not surviving, then to ⑧ ,
my ⑨

I give ⑤ ,
to ⑥ ,
my ⑦ ,
or if not surviving, then to ⑧ ,
my ⑨

I give ⑤ ,
to ⑥ ,
my ⑦ ,
or if not surviving, then to ⑧ ,
my ⑨

Page ___ of ___ pages   Testator's initials _____

I give ⑤ ,
to ⑥ , .
my ⑦ ,
or if not surviving, then to ⑧ ,
my ⑨

I give ⑤ ,
to ⑥ ,
my ⑦ ,
or if not surviving, then to ⑧ ,
my ⑨

I give ⑤ ,
to ⑥ ,
my ⑦ ,
or if not surviving, then to ⑧ ,
my ⑨

I give ⑤ ,
to ⑥ ,
my ⑦ ,
or if not surviving, then to ⑧ ,
my ⑨

I give ⑤ ,
to ⑥ ,
my ⑦ ,
or if not surviving, then to ⑧ ,
my ⑨

I give all the rest of my property, whether real or personal, wherever located,
to ⑩ ,
my ⑪ ,
or if not surviving, to ⑫ ,
my ⑬ .

All beneficiaries named in this will must survive me by thirty (30) days to receive any gift under this will. If any beneficiary and I should die simultaneously, I shall be conclusively presumed to have survived that beneficiary for purposes of this will.

Page ___ of ___ pages   Testator's initials _____

I appoint ⑭ ,
my ⑮ ,
of ⑯ ,
as Executor, to serve without bond. If not surviving or otherwise unable to serve,
I appoint ⑰ ,
my ⑱ ,
of ⑲ ,
as Alternate Executor, also to serve without bond. In addition to any powers, authority, and discretion granted by law, I grant such Executor or Alternate Executor any and all powers to perform any acts, in his/her sole discretion and without court approval, for the management and distribution of my estate, including independent administration of my estate.

I also declare that, pursuant to the Uniform Anatomical Gift Act, I donate any of my body parts and/or organs to any medical institution willing to accept and use them, and I direct my executor to carry out such donation.

Funeral arrangements have been made with the ⑳ ,
of ㉑ ,
for burial at ㉒ ,
located in ㉓ ,
and I direct my Executor to carry out such arrangements.

I publish and sign this Last Will and Testament, consisting of _____ typewritten pages,
on _____ , and declare that I do so freely, for the purposes expressed, under no constraint or undue influence, and that I am of sound mind and of legal age.

_____   _____
Signature of Testator   Printed Name of Testator

Page ___ of ___ pages   Testator's initials _____

We, the undersigned, being first sworn on oath and under penalty of perjury, state that:

On _____ , in the presence of all of us, the above-named Testator published and signed this Last Will and Testament, and then at Testator's request, and in Testator's presence, and in each other's presence, we all signed below as witnesses, and we declare that, to the best of our knowledge, the Testator signed this instrument freely, under no constraint or undue influence, and is of sound mind and legal age.

_____
Signature of Witness

_____
Printed Name of Witness

_____
Address of Witness

_____
Signature of Witness

_____
Printed Name of Witness

_____
Address of Witness

_____
Signature of Witness

_____
Printed Name of Witness

_____
Address of Witness

㉔ Notary Acknowledgment
State of _____
County of _____

On _____ , _____ the testator, and
_____ , _____ , and
_____ , the witnesses, personally came before me and, being duly sworn, did state that they are the persons described in the above document and that they signed the above document in my presence as a free and voluntary act for the purposes stated.

_____
Signature of Notary Public

Notary Public, In and for the County of _____
State of _____
My commission expires: _____   Notary Seal

Instructions for Will for Single Person with No Children

This will is appropriate for use by a single person with no children or grandchildren. This will contains the following standard clauses:

- Title Clause
- Identification Clause
- Marital Status Clause
- Specific Gifts Clause
- Residuary Clause
- Survivorship Clause
- Executor Clause
- Organ Donation Clause
- Funeral Arrangements Clause
- Signature and Witness Clause

Fill in each of the appropriate blanks in this will using the information that you included in your Property and Beneficiary Questionnaires. Cross out any information that is not appropriate to your situation. The necessary information to be filled-in is noted below and should be written into the place where the corresponding number appears in the following will form.

① Full name of testator
② Full name of testator (and any other names that you are known by)
③ Full address of testator

(Insert information on previous marriage, if necessary [see earlier instructions])

④ Complete description of specific gift (repeat for each specific gift)
⑤ Full name of beneficiary (repeat for each specific gift)
⑥ Relationship of beneficiary to testator (repeat for each specific gift)
⑦ Full name of alternate beneficiary (repeat for each specific gift)
⑧ Relationship of alternate beneficiary to testator (repeat for each specific gift)

⑨ Full name of residual beneficiary
⑩ Relationship of residual beneficiary to testator
⑪ Full name of alternate residual beneficiary
⑫ Relationship of alternate residual beneficiary to testator

⑬ Full name of executor
⑭ Relationship of executor to testator
⑮ Full address of executor

132

⑯ Full name of alternate executor
⑰ Relationship of alternate executor to testator
⑱ Full address of alternate executor

⑲ Name of funeral home
⑳ Address of funeral home
㉑ Name of cemetery
㉒ Address of cemetery

Number of total pages of will (fill in when will is typed or printed)
Date of signing of will (DO NOT FILL IN YET)
Signature of testator (DO NOT FILL IN YET)
Printed name of testator
Date of witnessing of will (DO NOT FILL IN YET)
Signature of witness (repeat for each witness) [DO NOT FILL IN YET]
Printed name of witness (repeat for each witness) [DO NOT FILL IN YET]
Address of witness (repeat for each witness) [DO NOT FILL IN YET]

㉓ Notary Acknowledgment (to be filled in by Notary Public)

Will for Single Person with No Children

Last Will and Testament of ①

I, ② ,
whose address is ③ ,
declare that this is my Last Will and Testament and I revoke all previous wills.

I am not currently married.

I have no children or grandchildren living.

I make the following specific gifts:

I give ④ ,
to ⑤ ,
my ⑥ ,
or if not surviving, then to ⑦ ,
my ⑧ .

I give ④ ,
to ⑤ ,
my ⑥ ,
or if not surviving, then to ⑦ ,
my ⑧ .

I give ④ ,
to ⑤ ,
my ⑥ ,
or if not surviving, then to ⑦ ,
my ⑧ .

I give ④ ,
to ⑤ ,
my ⑥ ,
or if not surviving, then to ⑦ ,
my ⑧ .

Page ___ of ___ pages   Testator's initials _____

I give ④ ,
to ⑤ ,
my ⑥ ,
or if not surviving, then to ⑦ ,
my ⑧ .

I give ④ ,
to ⑤ ,
my ⑥ ,
or if not surviving, then to ⑦ ,
my ⑧ .

I give ④ ,
to ⑤ ,
my ⑥ ,
or if not surviving, then to ⑦ ,
my ⑧ .

I give ④ ,
to ⑤ ,
my ⑥ ,
or if not surviving, then to ⑦ ,
my ⑧ .

I give ④ ,
to ⑤ ,
my ⑥ ,
or if not surviving, then to ⑦ ,
my ⑧ .

I give ④ ,
to ⑤ ,
my ⑥ ,
or if not surviving, then to ⑦ ,
my ⑧ .

Page ___ of ___ pages

Testator's initials _____

I give all the rest of my property, whether real or personal, wherever located,
to ⑨ ,
my ⑩ ,
or if not surviving, to ⑪ ,
my ⑫ .

All beneficiaries named in this will must survive me by thirty (30) days to receive any gift under this will. If any beneficiary and I should die simultaneously, I shall be conclusively presumed to have survived that beneficiary for purposes of this will.

I appoint ⑬ ,
my ⑭ ,
of ⑮ ,
as Executor, to serve without bond. If not surviving or otherwise unable to serve,
I appoint ⑯ ,
my ⑰ ,
of ⑱ ,
as Alternate Executor, also to serve without bond. In addition to any powers, authority, and discretion granted by law, I grant such Executor or Alternate Executor any and all powers to perform any acts, in his/her sole discretion and without court approval, for the management and distribution of my estate, including independent administration of my estate.

I also declare that, pursuant to the Uniform Anatomical Gift Act, I donate any of my body parts and/or organs to any medical institution willing to accept and use them, and I direct my executor to carry out such donation.

Funeral arrangements have been made with the ⑲ ,
of ⑳ ,
for burial at ㉑ ,
located in ㉒ ,
and I direct my Executor to carry out such arrangements.

I publish and sign this Last Will and Testament, consisting of _____ typewritten pages,
on _____ , and declare that I do so freely, for the purposes expressed, under no constraint or undue influence, and that I am of sound mind and of legal age.

_____   _____
Signature of Testator   Printed Name of Testator

We, the undersigned, being first sworn on oath and under penalty of perjury, state that:

On _____ , in the presence of all of us, the above-named Testator published and signed this Last Will and Testament, and then at Testator's request, and in Testator's presence, and in each other's presence, we all signed below as witnesses, and we declare that, to the best of our knowledge, the Testator signed this instrument freely, under no constraint or undue influence, and is of sound mind and legal age.

_____
Signature of Witness

_____
Signature of Witness

_____
Printed Name of Witness

_____
Printed Name of Witness

_____
Address of Witness

_____
Address of Witness

_____
Signature of Witness

_____
Printed Name of Witness

_____
Address of Witness

㉓ Notary Acknowledgment
State of _____
County of _____

On _____ , _____ the testator, and
_____ , _____ , and
_____ , the witnesses, personally came before me and, being duly sworn, did state that they are the persons described in the above document and that they signed the above document in my presence as a free and voluntary act for the purposes stated.

_____
Signature of Notary Public
Notary Public, In and for the County of _____
State of _____
My commission expires: _____   Notary Seal

Chapter 6

Living Trusts

A living trust or *revocable trust* is a legal document that is used to pass on your assets to your beneficiaries upon your death. Thus, it accomplishes much the same results as a will. Like a will, it is revocable at any time during your life. Also, like a will, it allows you to retain control over your assets during your life and affords no direct tax advantages. A trust consists of assets of a *grantor* (the person who creates the trust) which are managed and distributed by a *trustee* to benefit one or more *beneficiaries* (those persons or organizations who will receive property under the trust). A living trust provides for all three of these designations to be held by the same person. You are the grantor, trustee, and beneficiary of your living trust while you are still alive. Upon your death, your chosen *successor trustee* succeeds you in the management of the trust and the distribution of your trust assets to your chosen beneficiaries.

A living trust is a legal document that allows for the transfer of property to the persons or organizations named in the living trust upon the death of the maker of the living trust. A living trust is only effective for the on-death distribution of property that has been previously transferred to the living trust. A living trust can be changed, modified, or revoked at any time by the grantor prior to death. A living trust may also be called a *revocable trust*, because during your lifetime you may *revoke*, or cancel the trust at any time. Upon your death, however, your living trust becomes irrevocable and its terms can no longer be altered in any way.

An increasingly popular estate planning tool, living or revocable trusts can be effectively used to avoid *probate*. As explained in Chapter 4, probate is an official series of court proceedings which begin with either proving a will is valid or determining that no will existed and then continuing with the distribution of the deceased person's property. To avoid probate, a living trust generally provides that all or most of a person's property be transferred to trust ownership. The owner of the property generally retains full control and management of the trust as trustee. In the trust document, beneficiaries are chosen, much the same as in a will. The terms of the trust can actually parallel the terms of a will.

The difference is that, upon the death of the creator (grantor) of the trust, all of the property that has been transferred to trust ownership passes immediately and automatically to the beneficiaries without any court intervention or supervision and without an official probate proceeding. The owner of the property (who is the creator or the trust) retains full control over the property until death and the creator of the trust can terminate this type of trust at any time prior to death. After the trust itself is prepared, all of the property that a person wishes placed in the living trust (stocks, bonds, bank accounts, real estate deeds, car titles, etc.) is actually transferred to the living trust. It is equally important to understand that for a living trust to be valid, it must generally be prepared, signed, and notarized carefully. Although a living trust is perfectly valid if it is written in plain English and does not use technical legal language, it must be prepared, signed, and notarized in the manner outlined in this book. These procedures are not at all difficult and consist generally of carefully typing your living trust in the manner outlined later, and signing it in the manner specified.

In some cases (for example, those involving extremely complicated business or personal financial holdings or the desire to create a complex trust arrangement) it is clearly advisable to consult an attorney for the preparation of your living trust. However, in most circumstances and for most people, the terms of a living trust that can provide for the necessary protection are relatively routine and may safely be prepared without the added expense of consulting a lawyer.

Why You Still Need a Will

Although it can be short and simple, a living trust is an important document which can accomplish many tasks. The proper use of a living trust can eliminate much confusion for those left behind. Since it provides a clear and legal record of your wishes, it can avoid feuding and squabbles among your family members. Perhaps most importantly, it can make your last wishes come true. The main advantage to using a living trust instead of a will is that it allows your assets to be passed to your beneficiaries automatically upon your death, without any delay, probate, court intervention, or lawyer's fees. To many people, this very important advantage outweighs any disadvantages.

Even if you have used a living trust and the various other estate planning tools outlined in this book to attempt to have your estate avoid probate, a will is still highly recommended. There may be assets that you have neglected, forgotten about, or that will not be uncovered until your death. Even if you decide to use a living trust to pass your assets to your beneficiaries, you will also need to prepare a will. This is because regardless of your best efforts, generally, you will not be able to name each and every item of property that you own. Without a will as a backup, any property not named in the living trust will pass to your closest relatives, or if there are none, the property may be forfeited to the state. If you have a will as a backup to a living trust, you will retain the ability to be certain that all of your property will pass to those who you personally choose to receive it. In addition, a will is necessary to name a personal guardian for any minor children that you may have. Finally, if you wish to disinherit a child (or a spouse in a community property state), you must use a will to accomplish this. Chapter 5 provides basic wills for you to create to supplement your living trust.

Additional Types of Trusts

Please note that there are many, many other types of trusts that are available for estate planning purposes. A brief explanation of some of these type of trusts is below. As this book is an effort at simplifying the estate planning process, none of these more complex trust arrangements are covered in this book. If you feel that your situation may benefit from the use of one or more of these more complex trusts, please consult an attorney.

Support Trust: Authorizes the trustee to spend the principal and/or income of a trust for the health care, education, and general support of a beneficiary. The children's trust included in one of the living trusts in this chapter is one type of 'support trust".

Discretionary Trust: Authorizes the trustee to spend the principal and/or income of a trust in different amounts to various beneficiaries of a trust, in the sole discretion of the trustee.

Charitable Lead Trust: An irrevocable trust set up to support a charitable purpose for a set period of time, after which the trust assets revert to the grantor or beneficiaries.

Charitable Remainder Trust: An irrevocable trust with a beneficiary who receives the income for a certain period of time and then has a charity named as the final beneficiary.

Spendthrift Trust: Set up to provide for a person whom the grantor does not feel has the ability to manage their own affairs or for a person who may need protection from creditors.

Insurance Trust: This type of trust is used to purchase life insurance to benefit the beneficiaries or to pay any expected estate taxes.

Medicaid Trust: Set up to help one qualify for Medicaid benefits.

AB Trust: This type of trust is for estate tax avoidance purposes and provides that after the death of a first spouse, the surviving spouse is the beneficiary of the trust (but not the owner of the trust assets). This trust, thus, bypasses the surviving spouse and can save on estate taxes if the spouses combined assets are over $3.5 million in 2009.

QTIP Trust: For estate tax avoidance purposes, this trust provides that a surviving spouse becomes the beneficiary of the trust for his or her life. On the death of the surviving spouse, the remaining trust property passes to the beneficiaries named by the first spouse to die.

QDOT Trust: Also for estate tax avoidance. Provides a method that allows estate assets to be left to a non-U.S. citizen spouse and receive the estate tax marital deduction (which is normally limited for non-citizen spouses).

Creating a Living Trust

To create a living trust, you will first need to decide what property you wish to place in trust. To do this, you may use the property questionnaire that is provided in Chapter 5: Assets that are subject to being sold or discarded regularly should not be put in the trust. Next, you will need to decide who is to receive your assets upon your death. Again, you may use the beneficiary questionnaire that is included in Chapter 5. Finally, you will need to decide if you wish to retain all control over the trust. To achieve this end, you will name yourself as trustee.

Once you have created your living trust, you will need to actually transfer the ownership of all of the assets selected to the trust. This transfer may include obtaining a new title to your car, new bank accounts, and a new deed to any real estate. The new ownership will be in the name of the trust itself, with the name of the trustee specified; for example, *The Jane Smith Revocable Living Trust; Jane Smith, Trustee* might be the name on the deed or title. *Note*: In order to transfer property into your trust, you may need to use an Assignment to Living Trust form for personal property (see below) or a Quitclaim Deed for real estate.

Living Trust: This is the main legal document that establishes your trust. Two versions of this main trust document are included: one for use by an individual with no minor children and one for use by an individual with minor children who wishes to set up a children's trust to handle any gifts to the minor children until they are of an age to be able to handle their own affairs.

Schedule of Assets of Living Trust: On this form, you will include a listing of all of the property that you wish to transfer into the trust. This document should be attached to the living trust when completed. This form needs to be notarized.

Schedule of Beneficiaries of Living Trust: On this form, you will include a list of all of your chosen beneficiaries, alternate beneficiaries, and the trust property that you wish them to receive. You will also choose a residual beneficiary. (For more information on beneficiary choices, refer to Chapter 5). This form must be notarized.

Assignment to Living Trust: This form is used to transfer personal property to the trust. On this form, you will provide a full description of the property transferred. This form should also be notarized.

Registration of Living Trust: This form is used in those states (10 as of the date of printing this book) that require that a trust be registered with a county clerk. Please check the Estate Planning Appendix listing for "Additional Trust Requirement" to see if your state requires this registration. (Form and instructions on CD only)

New York Notice of Assignment of Property to a Living Trust: This form is required in the state of New York for any assignments of property to a living trust. (Form and instructions on CD only)

Note Regarding Individual State Requirements

A number of states have special requirements regarding the use of living trusts, generally involving the registration of the living trust in the county where the grantor is a resident or in which the trust itself will hold title to any real estate. A Registration of Living Trust is supplied for those states on the CD. In addition, New York state requires a Notice of Assignment of Property to a Living Trust form and this form and instructions are also included on the CD. Some states also require notification of beneficiaries when the grantor dies and the trust thus become irrevocable. Please check your state's requirements in the Estate Planning Appendix on the CD under the listing "Additional Trust Requirements".

Preparing Your Living Trust Declaration

Carefully read through all of the clauses in the appropriate blank living trust. Make a photocopy or print out a copy of the living trust form to use as a worksheet. If you wish, you may use this book itself as a worksheet (unless it is a library book!). The first set of instructions given apply to both trust declaration forms that are supplied with this book. Following these general instructions are the specific instructions for each of the two trust forms.

If you are at all unsure of the correct use of these forms, please consult a competent attorney. As you fill in the information for each clause, keep in mind the following instructions:

Title Clause: The title is mandatory for all living trusts. Fill in the name blank with your full legal name (such as the "Andrea Ann Doria Living Trust"). If you have been known under more than one name, use only your principal name.

Identification and Date Clause: The identification clause is mandatory and must be included in all living trusts. In the first blank, include any other names which you are known by. Do this by adding the phrase: "also known as" after your principal full name. For example:

"John James Smith, also known as Jimmy John Smith."

In the spaces provided for your residence, use the location of your principal residence; that is, where you currently live permanently. Fill in the date when you wish the living trust to take effect.

Name of Trust Clause: Fill in your own name prior to the title of the trust (for example: "The John Smith Living Trust").

Marital and Parental Status Clause: Depending upon your current marital and parental status you will choose one of the following clauses. If you have children, list the appropriate information for each child. This clause should be included in your living trust after the phrase "My marital status is that…:

- "I am single and have no children."

- "I am currently married to [name of spouse] and we have no children."

- "I was previously married to [name of spouse] and that marriage ended on [date] by [death, divorce, or annulment] and we had no children."

- "I am single and have [number] child[ren] currently living. Their names and dates of birth are:"

- "I am currently married to [name of spouse] and we have [number] child[ren] currently living. Their names and dates of birth are:"

- "I was previously married to [name of spouse] and that marriage ended on [date] by [death, divorce, or annulment] and we have [number] child[ren] currently living. Their names and dates of birth are:"

Trusteeship Clause: Under this clause, you declare that you will act as the trustee of the trust and any subtrusts which may be created by the trust (such as a children's trust).

Property Transfer Section: No additional information need be filled-in in this section. This section of your trust provides that you are transferring ownership of all of the property listed on your Schedule of Assets of Living Trust to the trust itself. You are also reserving the right to make any changes to your Schedule of Assets at any time, as long as they are in writing, notarized, and attached to the trust. You are also agreeing to prepare any additional paperwork that may be necessary to complete any such transfers of ownership, such as completing a deed or title transfer if necessary.

Grantor's Rights Section: No additional information need be filled-in for this section. Under this section, you retain full lifetime control of all of the trust's assets that you have transferred in the above section (and by other transfer documents, if necessary). Regarding your home, you specifically state that you retain the right of possession for your entire life and that any transfer to the trust does not interfere with any rights to homestead exemptions that you may have under state law.

Successor Trustee Section: This section is included in every living trust in this book. With this clause, you will make your choice of successor trustee and alternate successor trustee, the persons who will administer and distribute your trust assets upon your death or who will take over the management of your trust upon your incapacitation or death. The various duties of your successor trustee are explained in Chapter 4. You also provide that any such incapacitation be certified by a physician before the successor trustee may assume management of your trust. The chosen alternate successor trustee will assume the powers of the trustee only if the successor trustee that you have chosen is not surviving or is otherwise unable to serve. A spouse, sibling, or other trusted party is usually chosen to act as successor trustee. The person chosen should be a resident of the state in which you currently reside. You also provide that he or she not be required to post a bond in order to be appointed to serve as successor trustee and that he or she will not be compensated for their service as trustee. Finally, you note that any reference to "trustee" in your document also refers to the successor or alternate successor trustee. Be sure to clearly identify the successor trustee and alternate successor trustee by full name and address.

Trustee's Powers Section: In this section, no additional information needs to be filled-in. You grant any trustee broad powers to manage your trust assets. The powers are granted without court supervision and without oversight by anyone else. The powers granted are the same power and authority as an individual person has over their own property.

Additional Trustee Powers Section: No additional information need be filled-in in this section. This section provides a detailed enumeration of the powers that are granted to the trustee. Although in the previous section you granted any powers granted by law, many businesses and financial institutions require that a trustee's actual power to perform a specific act be spelled-out in a trust document. As you can see, the powers granted to the trustee are very extensive and approximate the power that an individual would have over his or her property.

Incapacitation Section: No additional information needs to be filled-in for this section. This section goes into effect in the event that a grantor becomes incapacitated during his or her lifetime. This incapacitation must be certified by a physician, as noted in the successor trustee section above. In this event, the successor trustee is bound to manage the trust solely for the benefit of the grantor and in accordance with the grantor's accustomed manner of living. Thus, any beneficiaries of the trust cannot demand that the successor trustee stop spending trust assets to care for an incapacitated grantor and save the trust assets for them. Please note that the power and authority that a successor trustee has over the assets of a living trust when the original trustee is incapacitated is similar to the power and authority that an attorney-in-fact appointed under a durable power of attorney has over a person's assets when that person becomes incapacitated. If you are also intending on appointing an attorney-in-fact under a durable power of attorney in your estate plan, you should appoint the same person as successor trustee of your trust and as attorney-in-fact under your durable power of attorney. If you do not wish to appoint the same person for both roles, you will need to consult an attorney to be certain that the powers and authority that you provide to each separate person do not overlap and create a situation in which a court will have to intervene to determine which person has authority over which of your property.

Children's Trust Fund Section: This clause is only present in the living trust in which a parent with children wishes to set up a children's trust fund (within the main living trust) for any gifts to be made to their minor children. The form in this book that contains this children's trust immediately follows these instructions. The second following trust is designed for individuals either without children or those who have children but do not wish to restrict their children's access to the gifts under the trust (generally parents with children above the age of 21). Under this children's trust, you also may delay the time when they will actually have unrestricted control over your gift. It is not recommended, however, to attempt to delay receipt of control beyond the age of 35 .In this section, you will fill in two ages. First, you will select an age that a child must be under for the children's trust section to take effect. You may desire the gifts under the main trust to be held in the children's trust for any child under the age of, say, 30 years of age. Then you will also select an age when the children's trust will terminate and the then-adult will receive the property with no restrictions, for example, 35 years of age. The ages that you select may be any reasonable age. The terms of the trust provide that the trustee may distribute any or all of the income or principal to the children as he or she deems necessary to provide for their health, support, and education. The trust will terminate when either the specific age is reached, all of the money is spent prior to that age, or the child dies prematurely. Upon termination, any remaining trust funds will be distributed to the child (beneficiary), if surviving. If the child is not surviving at the age when the trust is to terminate, the trust funds will be distributed to the heirs of the beneficiary (if there are any). If there are none, then the trust funds remaining will revert back to the residue of your trust (as noted on your Schedule of Beneficiaries of Living Trust) and be distributed accordingly. Additionally, since the trustee of the children's trust should be the same person who is successor trustee, you have already granted the trustee broad powers to manage the trust and also provided that he or she not be required to post a bond nor allowed compensation for services rendered.

Termination of Trust Section: This section provides that the trust shall become irrevocable upon the death of the grantor. Upon that event, the successor trustee will then be empowered to pay all of the valid debts, last expenses, and taxes of the grantor and then distribute the trust assets as specified on the Schedule of Beneficiaries of Living Trust. It is also noted in any of the trusts which contain a children's trust that any such distributions to beneficiaries are subject to the terms of the children's trust. This section also provides that the Schedule of Beneficiaries may be amended at any time (before it becomes irrevocable) by a written, notarized amendment which is attached to the trust.

Survivorship Section: This clause is included in every living trust. This clause provides for two possibilities. First, it provides for a required period of survival for any beneficiary to receive a gift under your living trust. The practical effect of this is to be certain that your property passes under your living trust and not that of a beneficiary who dies shortly after receiving your gift. The second portion of this clause provides for a determination of how your property should pass in the eventuality that both you and a beneficiary (most likely your spouse) should die in a manner that makes it impossible to determine who died first. Without this clause in your living trust it would be possible that property would momentarily pass to a beneficiary under your living trust. When that person dies (possibly immediately if a result of a common accident or disaster) your property could wind up being left to the person whom your beneficiary designated, rather than to your alternate beneficiary. If you and your spouse are both preparing individual living trusts, it is a good idea to be certain that each of your living trusts contains identical survivorship clauses. If you are each other's primary beneficiary, it is also wise to attempt to coordinate who your alternate beneficiaries may be in the event of a simultaneous death.

Amendments and Revocations Section: This form of trust reserves the right to allow you to cancel (revoke) or amend this trust or any of the schedules at any time. However, any changes (amendments) must be in writing, notarized, and attached to the original trust document to be valid.

Governing Law Section: You will fill in the number of pages, including all schedules, and the state of your legal residence where indicated after you have properly typed or had your living trust typed. The laws of the state of your principal residence will govern any questions regarding the operation of the trust or the actions of any trustee.

Signature Section: The signature lines of your living trust will be completed in front of a notary public as explained next in the instructions on completing your living trust for signature.

Completing Your Living Trust Forms

1. On the photocopy worksheet version of your living trust and schedules, cross out all of the instructions, circled numbers, and any other extraneous material which is not to become a part of your Living Trust. Carefully re-read the entire worksheet version of your living trust to be certain that it is exactly as you wish.

2. After making any necessary changes, type or print-out the entire living trust and the appropriate schedules on good quality letter-sized (8½" x 11") paper.

3. After you have completed typing or printing out your living trust and schedules, fill in the total number of pages in the line above the signature section. Again, very carefully proofread your entire living trust. Be certain that there are no errors. If there are any errors, retype that particular page. Do not attempt to correct any errors with white-out type correcting fluid or tape or with erasures of any kind. Do not cross out or add anything to the typewritten words using a pen or pencil. The signature and notary acknowledgement spaces should be blank.

4. When you have a perfect original of your living trust and schedules, with no corrections and no additions, staple all of the pages together in the top left-hand corner.

5. Take the original of your living trust and schedules before a Notary Public. Many banks, real estate offices, and government offices have notary services and most will be glad to assist you. In front of the Notary Public, you should sign your living trust and schedules in the places indicated. (Note: unlike a will, the signing of a living trust need not be witnessed by anyone other than a notary public).

6. The final step is for the Notary Public to complete the Notary Acknowledgments, sign in the space indicated, and stamp with his or her Notary Seal. When this step is completed, your living trust is a valid legal document and you may be assured that your wishes will be carried out upon your death.

Safeguarding Your Living Trust

Having completed your living trust according to the foregoing instructions, it is now time to place your living trust in a safe place. Many people keep their important papers in a safe deposit box at a local bank. Although this is an acceptable place for storing a living trust, be advised that there are certain drawbacks. Your living trust should be in a place which is readily accessible to your successor trustee at a moment's notice. Often there are certain unavoidable delays in gaining access to a safe deposit box in an emergency situation. If you are married and your safe deposit box is jointly held, many of these delays can be avoided. However, even in this situation, some states prevent immediate access to the safe deposit box of a deceased married person. If you decide to keep the original in your safe deposit box, it is a good idea to keep a clearly-marked copy of your living trust at home in a safe but easily-located place, with a note as to where the original may be found.

Wherever you decide to store your living trust, you will need to inform your chosen successor trustee of its location. The successor trustee will need to obtain the original of your living trust shortly after your demise to determine if there are any necessary duties which must be looked after without delay, for example: funeral plans or organ donations.

It is also a good practice to store any life insurance policies and a copy of your birth certificate in the same location. Additionally, it is also prudent to store a copy of your property questionnaire, beneficiary questionnaire, and the successor trustee information list with your living trust in order to provide your successor trustee with an inventory and location list of your assets and a list of information regarding your beneficiaries. Any title documents or deeds relating to property which is to be transferred under your living trust may also be stored with your living trust for the convenience of your successor trustee. A final precaution, if you desire, is to allow the successor trustee whom you have named to keep a copy of your living trust. Be careful, however, to be certain that you immediately inform him or her of any amendments to your living trust which you prepare or of any decision to revoke your living trust.

Instructions for Living Trust with a Children's Trust Included

This living trust is appropriate for use by an individual married person or a single person with one or more minor children, who desires to place the property and assets which may be left to the children in a trust fund. In most cases, a married person may desire to choose the other spouse as both successor trustee and trustee for any of their children's trusts, although this is not a legal requirement.

Fill in each of the appropriate blanks in this living trust, a Schedule of Assets of Living Trust, and a Schedule of Beneficiaries of Living Trust using the information which you included in your Property and Beneficiary Questionnaires. Cross out any information that is not appropriate to your situation. You will then complete the preparation of all your forms following the instructions later in this chapter.

To complete this form, you will need the following information:

① The name of the living trust (generally, your full name is the name of the trust, such as the "Gwendolyn Smith Living Trust")
② Your complete name
   The date on which you wish the living trust to take effect
   The name of the living trust
   Your complete name and
   Your marital status and the names of any children
③ No information needed
④ No information needed
⑤ The names and addresses of your chosen Successor Trustee and Alternate Successor Trustee
⑥ No information needed
⑦ No information needed
⑧ No information needed
⑨ The age of your child(ren) under which you wish the Children's Trust to take effect, and the age of each child when the Children's Trust will terminate
⑩ No information needed
⑪ No information needed
⑫ No information needed
⑬ The number of pages of the living trust, including schedules, and the state of your legal residence
⑭ Your signature and printed name (do not sign unless in front of a notary public)
⑮ The notary acknowledgment section (to be completed by notary public)

Living Trust with a Children's Trust Included

① ## Living Trust of _____

② Declaration of Trust

I, _____ , the grantor of this trust, declare and make this Living Trust on _____ (date).

This trust will be known as the _____ Living Trust.

I, _____ , will be trustee of this trust and any subtrusts created under this trust.

My marital status is that _____ .

③ Property Transfer

I transfer ownership to this trust of all of the assets which are listed on the attached Schedule of Assets of Living Trust, which is specifically made a part of this trust. I reserve the right to add or delete any of these assets at any time. In addition, I will prepare a separate Deed, Assignment, or any other documents necessary to carry out such transfers. Any additions or deletions to the Schedule of Assets of Living Trust must be written, notarized, and attached to this document to be valid.

④ Grantor's Rights

Until I die, I retain all rights to all income, profits, and control of the trust property. If my principal residence is transferred to this trust, I retain the right to possess and occupy it for my life, rent-free and without charge. I will remain liable for all taxes, insurance, maintenance, related costs, and expenses. The rights that I retain are intended to give me a beneficial interest in my principal residence such that I do not lose any eligibility that I may have for a state homestead exemption for which I am otherwise qualified.

⑤ Successor Trustee

Upon my death or if it is certified by a licensed physician that I am physically or mentally unable to manage this trust and my financial affairs, then I appoint _____

_____ (name), of _____
_____ (address), as Successor Trustee, to serve without bond and without compensation. If this successor trustee is not surviving or otherwise unable to serve, I appoint _____ (name), of _____
_____ (address), as Alternate Successor Trustee, also to serve without bond and without compensation. The successor trustee or alternate successor trustee shall not be liable for any actions taken in good faith. References to "trustee" in this document shall include any successor or alternate successor trustees.

⑥ Trustee's Powers

In addition to any powers, authority, and discretion granted by law, I grant the trustee any and all powers to perform any acts, in his or her sole discretion and without court approval, for the management and distribution of this trust and any subtrusts created by this trust. I intend the trustee to have the same power and authority to manage and distribute the trust assets as an individual owner has over his or her own wholly-owned property.

⑦ Additional Trustee Powers

The trustee's powers include, but are not limited to: the power to sell trust property, borrow money, and encumber that property, specifically including trust real estate, by mortgage, deed of trust, or other method; the power to manage trust real estate as if the trustee were the absolute owner of it, including the power to lease or grant options to lease the property, make repairs or alterations, and insure against loss; the power to sell or grant options for the sale or exchange of any trust property, including stocks, bonds, and any other form of security; the power to invest trust property in property of any kind, including but not limited to bonds, notes, mortgages, and stocks; the power to receive additional property from any source and add to any trust created by this trust; the power to employ and pay reasonable fees to accountants, lawyers, or investment consultants for information or advice relating to the trust; the power to deposit and hold trust funds in both interest-bearing and non-interest-bearing accounts; the power to deposit funds in bank or other accounts uninsured by FDIC coverage; the power to enter into electronic fund transfer or safe deposit arrangements with financial institutions; the power to continue any business of the grantor; the power to institute or defend legal actions concerning the trust or grantor's affairs; and the power to execute any document necessary to administer any children's trust created in this trust.

⑧ Incapacitation

Should the successor trustee or alternate successor trustee assume management of this trust during the lifetime of the grantor, the successor trustee or alternate successor trustee shall manage the trust solely for the proper health care, support, maintenance, comfort, welfare of the grantor, in accordance with the grantor's accustomed manner of living.

⑨ Children's Trust Fund

A If any of my children who are named as beneficiaries on the attached Schedule of Beneficiaries of Living Trust are under _____ years old on my death, I direct that any property that I give them under this trust be held in an individual children's trust for each child under the following terms, until each shall reach the age of _____ years old.

B In the trustee's sole discretion, the trustee may distribute any or all of the principal, income, or both as deemed necessary for the beneficiary's health, support, welfare, and education. Any income not distributed shall be added to the trust principal. Any such trust shall terminate when the beneficiary reaches the required age, dies prior to reaching the required age, or all trust funds have been distributed. Upon termination, any remaining undistributed principal and income shall pass to the beneficiary; or if not surviving, to the beneficiary's heirs; or if none, to the residue of the main trust created by this document.

⑩ Termination of Trust

Upon my death, this trust shall become irrevocable. The successor trustee shall then pay my valid debts, last expenses, and estate taxes from the assets of this trust. The successor trustee shall then distribute the remaining trust assets in the manner shown on the attached Schedule of Beneficiaries of Living Trust which is specifically made a part of this trust, subject to the provisions of any children's trust which is created by this document. I reserve the right to add and/or delete any beneficiaries at any time. Any additions or deletions to the Schedule of Beneficiaries of Living Trust must be written, notarized, and attached to this document to be valid.

⑪ Survivorship

All beneficiaries named in the Schedule of Beneficiaries of Living Trust must survive me by thirty (30) days to receive any gift under this living trust. If any beneficiary and I should die simultaneously, I shall be conclusively presumed to have survived that beneficiary for purposes of this living trust.

⑫ Amendments and Revocations

I reserve the right to amend any or all of this trust at any time. The amendments must be written, notarized, and attached to this document to be valid. I also reserve the right to this trust at any time. A revocation of this trust must be written, notarized, and attached to this document to be valid.

⑬ Governing Law

This trust, containing _____ pages, was created on the date noted above and will be governed under the laws of the State of _____ .

⑭ Signature

_____
Signature of Grantor

_____
Printed Name of Grantor

⑮ Notary Acknowledgment

State of _____
County of _____

On _____ , _____ came before me personally and, under oath, stated that he or she is the person described in the above document and he or she signed the above document in my presence. I declare under penalty of perjury that the person whose name is subscribed to this instrument appears to be of sound mind and under no duress, fraud, or undue influence.

_____
Notary Public
In and for the County of _____
State of _____
My commission expires _____   Notary Seal

Instructions for Living Trust without a Children's Trust

This living trust is appropriate for use by a single person or an individual married person with or without children. If the person has children, this form is to be used only if the person desires that any assets to be transferred to the children at the grantor's death not be held in a children's trust, but rather be transferred directly to the children upon the death of the grantor. This will normally be used only when any children are already above the legal age of minority.

Fill in each of the appropriate blanks in this living trust, a Schedule of Assets of Living Trust, and a Schedule of Beneficiaries of Living Trust using the information which you included in your Property and Beneficiary Questionnaires. Cross out any information that is not appropriate to your situation. You will then complete the preparation of all your forms following the instructions later in this chapter.

To complete this form, you will need the following information:

① The name of the living trust (generally, your full name is the name of the trust, such as the "Gwendolyn Smith Living Trust")
② Your complete name
  The date on which you wish the living trust to take effect
  The name of the living trust
  Your complete name, and
  Your marital status and the names of any children
③ No information needed
④ No information needed
⑤ The names and addresses of your chosen Successor Trustee and Alternate Successor Trustee
⑥ No information needed
⑦ No information needed
⑧ No information needed
⑨ No information needed
⑩ No information needed
⑪ No information needed
⑫ The number of pages of the living trust, including schedules, and
  The state of your legal residence
⑬ Your signature and printed name (do not sign unless in front of a notary public)
⑭ The notary acknowledgment section (to be completed by notary public)

Living Trust without a Children's Trust

① **Living Trust of** _____

② Declaration of Trust

I, _____ , the grantor of this trust, declare and make this Living Trust on _____ (date).

This trust will be known as the _____ Living Trust.

I, _____ , will be trustee of this trust and any subtrusts created under this trust.

My marital status is that _____ .

③ Property Transfer

I transfer ownership to this trust of all of the assets which are listed on the attached Schedule of Assets of Living Trust, which is specifically made a part of this trust. I reserve the right to add or delete any of these assets at any time. In addition, I will prepare a separate Deed, Assignment, or any other documents necessary to carry out such transfers. Any additions or deletions to the Schedule of Assets of Living Trust must be written, notarized, and attached to this document to be valid.

④ Grantor's Rights

Until I die, I retain all rights to all income, profits, and control of the trust property. If my principal residence is transferred to this trust, I retain the right to possess and occupy it for my life, rent-free and without charge. I will remain liable for all taxes, insurance, maintenance, related costs, and expenses. The rights that I retain are intended to give me a beneficial interest in my principal residence such that I do not lose any eligibility that I may have for a state homestead exemption for which I am otherwise qualified.

⑤ Successor Trustee

Upon my death or if it is certified by a licensed physician that I am physically or mentally unable to manage this trust and my financial affairs, then I appoint _____ (name) of_____ (ad-dress), as Successor Trustee, to serve without bond and without compensation. If this successor trustee is not surviving or otherwise unable to serve, I appoint _____ _____ (name), of _____ _____ (address), as Alternate Successor Trustee, also to serve without bond and without compensation. The successor trustee or alternate successor trustee shall not be liable for any actions taken in good faith. References to "trustee" in this document shall include any successor or alternate successor trustees.

⑥ Trustee's Powers

In addition to any powers, authority, and discretion granted by law, I grant the trustee any and all powers to perform any acts, in his or her sole discretion and without court approval, for the management and distribution of this trust and any subtrusts created by this trust. I intend the trustee to have the same power and authority to manage and distribute the trust assets as an individual owner has over his or her own wholly-owned property.

⑦ Additional Trustee Powers

The trustee's powers include, but are not limited to: the power to sell trust property, borrow money, and encumber that property, specifically including trust real estate, by mortgage, deed of trust, or other method; the power to manage trust real estate as if the trustee were the absolute owner of it, including the power to lease or grant options to lease the property, make repairs or alterations, and insure against loss; the power to sell or grant options for the sale or exchange of any trust property, including stocks, bonds, and any other form of security; the power to invest trust property in property of any kind, including but not limited to bonds, notes, mortgages, and stocks; the power to receive additional property from any source and add to any trust created by this trust; the power to employ and pay reasonable fees to accountants, lawyers, or investment consultants for information or advice relating to the trust; the power to deposit and hold trust funds in both interest-bearing and non-interest-bearing accounts; the power to deposit funds in bank or other accounts uninsured by FDIC coverage; the power to enter into electronic fund transfer or safe deposit arrangements with financial institutions; the power to continue any business of the grantor; the power to institute or defend legal actions concerning the trust or grantor's affairs; and the power to execute any document necessary to administer any children's trust created in this trust.

⑧ Incapacitation

Should the successor trustee or alternate successor trustee assume management of this trust during the lifetime of the grantor, the successor trustee or alternate successor shall manage the trust solely for the proper health care, support, maintenance, comfort, and/or welfare of the grantor, in accordance with the grantor's accustomed manner of living.

⑨ Termination of Trust

Upon my death, this trust shall become irrevocable. The successor trustee shall then pay my valid debts, last expenses, and estate taxes from the assets of this trust. The successor trustee shall then distribute the remaining trust assets in the manner shown on the attached Schedule of Beneficiaries of Living Trust which is specifically made a part of this trust, subject to the provisions of any children's trust which is created by this document. I reserve the right to add and/or delete any beneficiaries at any time. Any additions or deletions to the Schedule of Beneficiaries of Living Trust must be written, notarized, and attached to this document to be valid.

⑩ Survivorship

All beneficiaries named in the Schedule of Beneficiaries of Living Trust must survive me by thirty (30) days to receive any gift under this living trust. If any beneficiary and I should die simultaneously, I shall be conclusively presumed to have survived that beneficiary for purposes of this living trust.

⑪ Amendments and Revocations

I reserve the right to amend any or all of this trust at any time. The amendments must be written, notarized, and attached to this document to be valid. I also reserve the right to revoke this trust at any time. A revocation of this trust must be written, notarized, and attached to this document to be valid.

⑫ Governing Law

This trust, containing _____ pages, was created on the date noted above and will be governed under the laws of the State of _____ .

⑬ Signature

_____
Signature of Grantor

_____
Printed Name of Grantor

⑭ Notary Acknowledgment

State of _____
County of _____

On _____ , _____ came before me personally and, under oath, stated that he or she is the person described in the above document and he or she signed the above document in my presence. I declare under penalty of perjury that the person whose name is subscribed to this instrument appears to be of sound mind and under no duress, fraud, or undue influence.

_____
Notary Public
In and for the County of _____
State of _____
My commission expires _____   Notary Seal

Completing Your Schedule of Assets of Living Trust Form

On this form, you will include a listing of all of the property that you wish to transfer into the trust. It is relatively simple to complete. Simply fill in the title information (name and date of trust) and then carefully list the property that you have chosen to include in the trust. Please refer to the Property Questionnaire (on the CD under the chapter on wills) that you completed to be certain that you include all of the property that you desire to be held in trust. Always describe the property in as detailed and clear a manner as possible. In your description of the property, you should be as specific and precise as possible. For land, it is suggested that you use the description exactly as shown on the deed to the property. For personal property, be certain that your description clearly differentiates your gift from any other property. This Schedule of Assets will become a part of the living trust. It should be stapled to the original of the trust document. Any time that any changes are made to the assets that are to be included in the living trust, this schedule must be changed and an Amendment to living trust form should be filled out as explained in the next section.

Very Important Note: If the particular asset that you list on this Schedule has any type of ownership document, such as a title, deed, stock certificate, or similar document, you must also transfer the ownership of the asset to the trust by completing a new deed, title, or other transfer paperwork. Simply listing the asset on this form does not transfer it to the trust if an ownership document is required. For those items of personal property for which no such ownership document exists (such as a stereo system, appliances, antiques, etc.), the listing on the Schedule of Assets of Living Trust will effectively transfer the ownership to the Trust.

Instructions for Schedule of Assets of Living Trust

This form should be used to list the assets of a single person or an individual spouse who is setting up an individual living trust. Please remember that any assets that have ownership documents must be transferred to the ownership of the trust using the appropriate method of documentary transfer (such as a deed or title). Even if such additional paperwork is necessary, you should list the property on this Schedule of Assets. Please refer to the property instructions in the will chapter for details of how to list the property.

To complete this form, you will need the following information:

①　Date of assignment
　　Full name of grantor
　　Name of living trust, and
　　Date original living trust was created
②　Full description of property to be transferred to the trust
③　Your signature and printed name (do not sign unless in front of a notary public)
④　The notary acknowledgment section (to be completed by notary public)

Schedule of Assets of Living Trust

①   This Schedule of Assets of Living Trust is made on _____ (date),
by _____ , the grantor, to the _____
_____ Living Trust dated _____ .

②   All grantor's right, title, and interest in the following property shall be the property of the trust:

③

_____
Signature of Grantor

_____
Printed Name of Grantor

④   Notary Acknowledgment

State of _____
County of _____

On _____ , _____ came before me personally
and, under oath, stated that he or she is the person described in the above document and he
or she signed the above document in my presence. I declare under penalty of perjury that the
person whose name is subscribed to this instrument appears to be of sound mind and under
no duress, fraud, or undue influence.

_____
Notary Public
In and for the County of _____
State of _____
My commission expires _____   Notary Seal

Completing Your Schedule of Beneficiaries of Living Trust

Using this form, you will direct how your property will be distributed by your Successor Trustee upon your death. You will select your beneficiaries, alternate beneficiaries, and the property that each of them will receive. Please refer to both your Schedule of Assets and complete a beneficiary questionnaire (from the CD) to prepare this form. The information that you compiled for that questionnaire will be your guide for preparing your living trust, both in terms of being certain that you have disposed of all of your Trust assets, and in terms of being certain that you have left gifts to all those persons or organizations that you wished to. Using the clauses in this section, you will be able to prepare a living trust in which you may:

• Make specific gifts of cash, real estate, or personal property to anyone
• Make specific gifts of certain shares of your trust assets
• Make a gift of the rest (residue) of your assets to anyone

Specific Gifts Clause: Use this type of clause to provide specific gifts to your beneficiaries. If chosen, add this clause or clauses after the phrase "Upon the death of the grantor of the trust and the payment of all debts, taxes, and liabilities of the grantor, the Successor Trustee shall then distribute the remaining assets of the trust as follows:

To my [relationship], [name of beneficiary], or if not surviving, to my [relationship], [name of alternate beneficiary], the following trust assets shall be distributed:"

For making specific gifts, use as many of the "To my…" paragraphs as is necessary to complete your chosen gifts. In these paragraphs, you may make any type of gift that you wish, either a cash gift, a gift of a specific piece of personal property or real estate, or a specific share of your total trust estate. If you wish to give some of your trust estate in the form of portions of the total, it is recommended to use fractional portions. For example, if you wish to leave your trust estate in equal shares to two persons, name both parties after "To my…" and state "one-half of my total trust estate to each party."

Although none of the living trusts in this book contain a specific clause which states that you give one person your entire trust estate, you may make such a gift using this clause by simply stating after "The following trust assets shall be distributed:…"

"My entire trust estate"

Be sure that you do not attempt to give any other gifts. However, you should still include the residuary clause in your living trust, which is explained on the following pages.

You may only give away property that the trust itself owns. Be certain that any property included in any of the gift clauses is also included on your Schedule of Assets and has been effectively transferred to the Trust. In your description of the property, you should be as specific and precise as possible. For land, it is suggested that you use the description exactly as shown on the deed to the property. For personal property, be certain that your description clearly differentiates your gift from any other property. Use serial numbers, colors, or any other descriptive words to clearly indicate the exact nature of the gift. For cash gifts, specifically indicate the amount of the gift. For gifts of securities, state the amount of shares and the name of the company. You may add simple conditions to the gifts that you make, if you desire. Complex conditions, however, are not possible in this clause, and immoral or illegal conditions are not acceptable.

Be sure to clearly identify the beneficiary and alternate beneficiary by full name. You can also name joint beneficiaries, such as several children, if you choose. The space provided for an identification of the relationship of the beneficiary can be simply a descriptive phrase like "my wife," "my brother-in-law," or "my best friend." It does not mean that the beneficiary must be related to you personally.

The choice of alternate beneficiary is for the purpose of allowing you to designate someone to receive the gift if your first choice to receive the gift dies before you do (or, in the case of an organization chosen as primary beneficiary, is no longer in business). In this or any of the other gift clauses, your choice for alternate beneficiary may be one or more persons or an organization. It is recommended to always specifically name your beneficiary(s), rather than using a description only, such as "my children." In addition, you may delete the alternate beneficiary choice and substitute the words "*the residue*" instead. The result of this change will be that if your primary beneficiary dies before you do, your gift will pass under your residuary clause, which is discussed below. If additional gifts are desired, simply photocopy an additional page.

Residuary Clause: Although not a technical legal requirement, a residuary clause is included in every living trust in this book. With it, you will choose the person, persons, or organization to receive anything not covered by other clauses of your living trust. Even if you feel that you have given away everything that your trust owns under other clauses of your living trust, this can be a very important clause. If, for any reason, any other gifts under your living trust are not able to completed, this clause goes into effect. For example, if a beneficiary refuses to accept your gift or the chosen beneficiary has died and no alternate was selected or both the beneficiary and alternate has died, the gift is put back into your trust estate and will pass under the residuary clause. If there is no residuary clause included, any property not disposed of could potentially be forfeited to the state.

In addition, you may use this clause to give all of your estate (except your specific gifts) to one or more persons. For example: you make specific gifts of $1,000.00 to a sister and a car to a friend. By then naming your spouse as the residuary clause beneficiary, you will have gifted everything in your trust estate to your spouse—except the $1,000.00 and the car. You could then name your children, in equal shares, as the alternate residuary beneficiaries. In this manner, if your spouse were to die first, your children would then equally share your entire trust estate—except the $1,000.00 and the car.

Be sure to clearly identify the beneficiary by full name. The space provided for an identification of the relationship of the beneficiary can be simply a descriptive phrase like "my wife," or "my brother-in-law," or "my best friend." It does not mean that the beneficiary must be related to you personally.

After you have completed your Schedule of Beneficiaries of Living Trust form, you should revisit your living trust and the Asset and Beneficiary Schedules whenever there is any significant change in your life or circumstances. If you are married, divorced, have or adopt any children, or sell, transfer, or otherwise become dispossessed of any of the assets mentioned in your living trust schedules, you should make certain to make the appropriate changes in the trust itself, any schedules that are impacted, and any ownership documents relating to property that make have been affected.

Instructions for Schedule of Beneficiaries of Living Trust

This form should be used to list the beneficiaries of a single person or an individual spouse who is setting up an individual Living Trust.

Please refer to your Beneficiary Questionnaire to determine which property you desire to leave to which beneficiaries of your Living Trust. Please refer to the property and beneficiary instructions in Chapter 5 for details of how to list the property and beneficiaries.

To complete this form, you will need the following information:

① Date of assignment
   Full name of grantor
   Name of Living Trust, and
   Date original Living Trust was created
② For each item of property, complete the following:
   Name of beneficiary
   Relationship of beneficiary
   Name of alternate beneficiary (if main beneficiary has died first)
   Relationship of alternate beneficiary, and
   Full description of property to be transferred.
③ For your residuary clause, complete the following:
   Name of residuary beneficiary
   Relationship of residuary beneficiary
   Name of alternate residuary beneficiary (if main beneficiary has died first), and relationship
      of alternate residuary beneficiary
④ No information needed
⑤ Your signature and printed name (do not sign unless in front of a notary public)
⑥ The notary acknowledgment section (to be completed by notary public)

Schedule of Beneficiaries of Living Trust

① This Schedule of Beneficiaries is made on _____ (date), by
_____ , the grantor, to the _____
_____ Living Trust dated _____ .

② Upon the death of the grantor of the trust and the payment of all debts, taxes, and liabilities of the grantor, the Successor Trustee shall distribute the remaining assets of the Trust as follows:

To _____ (name), my _____
(relationship), or if not surviving, to _____ (name), my ___
_____ (relationship), the following trust assets shall be distributed:

To _____ (name), my _____
(relationship), or if not surviving, to _____ (name), my ___
_____ (relationship), the following trust assets shall be distributed:

To _____ (name), my _____
(relationship), or if not surviving, to _____ (name), my ___
_____ (relationship), the following trust assets shall be distributed:

To _____ (name), my _____
(relationship), or if not surviving, to _____ (name), my ___
_____ (relationship), the following trust assets shall be distributed:

To _____ (name), my _____
(relationship), or if not surviving, to _____ (name), my ___
_____ (relationship), the following trust assets shall be distributed:

③ All the rest and residue of the trust assets shall be distributed to _____ _____ (name), my _____ (relationship), or if not surviving, to _____ (name), my _____ (relationship).

④ If any Beneficiary named on this Schedule of Beneficiaries is subject to the terms of any children's trust in the main trust document to which this Schedule pertains, then any property distributed to such Beneficiary shall be subject to the terms of any such children's trust.

⑤

_____
Signature of Grantor

_____
Printed Name of Grantor

⑥ Notary Acknowledgment

State of _____
County of _____

On _____, _____ came before me personally and, under oath, stated that he or she is the person described in the above document and he or she signed the above document in my presence. I declare under penalty of perjury that the person whose name is subscribed to this instrument appears to be of sound mind and under no duress, fraud, or undue influence.

_____
Notary Public

In and for the County of _____,

State of _____

My commission expires _____   Notary Seal

Instructions for Assignment to Living Trust

This form may be used if an assignment of ownership of personal property to a living trust is necessary. An assignment of property is used for the transfer of personal property to the trust. Recall that you must complete transfer paperwork if the property in question is real estate, patents, copyrights, trademarks, motor vehicles, boats, stocks, bonds, or some other form of property that has ownership documents (such as a deed or title). For property with no ownership documentation, generally, the listing of property to be held by the trust on the Schedule of Trust Assets effectively transfers ownership of property to the trust. Thus, an assignment of property is not normally a legal necessity. However, some businesses or financial institutions may require this particular document to verify that the property has been technically "assigned" to the trust. In addition, this form is also necessary for assigning patents, copyrights, or trademarks to the trust. If such occasions arise, you may use this document.

To complete this form, you will need the following information:

① Date of assignment
   Full name of grantor
   Name of Living Trust, and
   Date original Living Trust was created
② Full description of property to be assigned to the trust
③ No information needed
④ No information needed
⑤ Your signature and printed name (do not sign unless in front of a notary public)
⑥ The notary acknowledgment section (to be completed by notary public)

Assignment to Living Trust

① This Assignment to Living Trust is made on _____ (date) ,
between _____ , the grantor, and the _____
_____ Living Trust dated _____ .

② The grantor transfers and conveys possession, ownership, and all right, title, and interest in
the following property to the Living Trust:

③ The grantor warrants that he or she owns this property and that he or she has the full authority to transfer and convey the property to the Living Trust. Grantor also warrants that the
property is transferred free and clear of all liens, indebtedness, or liabilities.

④ Signed and delivered to the Living Trust on the above date.

⑤ _____
Signature of Grantor

_____
Printed Name of Grantor

⑥ Notary Acknowledgment

State of _____
County of _____

On _____ , _____ came before me personally
and, under oath, stated that he or she is the person described in the above document and he
or she signed the above document in my presence. I declare under penalty of perjury that the
person whose name is subscribed to this instrument appears to be of sound mind and under no
duress, fraud, or undue influence.

_____
Notary Public
In and for the County of _____ -
State of _____
My commission expires _____   Notary Seal

Instructions for Registration of Living Trust

Residents of a number of states are required to register the main details regarding the existence of a Living Trust with their local courts when a trustee takes authority under the terms of the trust. Please check the Estate Planning Appendix listing (on the CD) for your state to determine if such registration is required in your state. Note also that even though such registration may technically be required for your state, there are generally no penalties or consequences for failing to do so. Note: This form is only provided on the CD.

(1) Full name of trustee
  Name of Living Trust
  Date original Living Trust was created, and
  Full name of grantor of trust
(2) No information needed.
(3) Your signature and printed name (do not sign unless in front of a notary public)
(4) The Notary Acknowledgment section (to be completed by notary public)

Instructions for New York Notice of Assignment of Property to Living Trust

This form may be used by residents of New York to provide notice that real or personal property has been assigned to the trust. You should attach a copy of your completed and notarized Schedule of Assets of Living Trust to this form. Note: This form is only provided on the CD.

To complete this form, you will need the following information:

(1) Full name of grantor
  Name of Living Trust, and
  Date original Living Trust was created
(2) Your signature and printed name (do not sign unless in front of a notary public)
(3) The notary acknowledgment section (to be completed by notary public)

Chapter 7

Living Wills

In this chapter, you will be given instructions on how to prepare a *living will,* a document that states your desires regarding end-of-life medical care. A living will is a relatively new legal document that has been made necessary due to recent technological advances in the field of medicine. These advances can allow for the continued existence of a person on advanced life support systems long after any normal semblance of "life," as many people consider it, has ceased. The inherent problem that is raised by this type of extraordinary medical life support is that the person whose life is being artificially continued by such means may not wish to be kept alive beyond what they may consider to be the proper time for their life to end. However, since a person in such condition has no method of communicating their wishes to the medical or legal authorities in charge, a living will was developed that allows one to make these important decisions in advance of the situation.

The purpose of a living will is to provide doctors and other health care workers with clear directions regarding how you would like your medical care handled toward the end of your life. A living will makes it possible for you to specify, in advance, exactly what your preferences are regarding the use of life-sustaining medical procedures if you are ever in a terminal medical condition or in a vegetative state, and are unable to give such directions yourself. *Terminal* is generally defined as an incurable condition that will cause imminent death such that the use of life-sustaining procedures only serve to prolong the moment of death. Likewise, a *vegetative state* is generally defined as a complete and irreversible loss of cognitive brain function and consciousness. Thus, a living will comes into effect only when there is no medical hope for a recovery from a particular injury or illness which will prove fatal or leave one in a permanent and irreversible coma.

As more and more advances are made in the medical field in terms of the ability to prevent "clinical" death, the difficult situations envisioned by a living will are destined to occur more often. The legal acceptance of a living will is currently at the forefront of law. Living wills are accepted in all states, but they must adhere to certain legal conditions. A few states do not currently have specific legislation providing express statutory recognition of living wills, but courts in those states have ruled that living wills are legally valid. Although a living will does not address all possible contingencies regarding terminally-ill patients, it does provide a written declaration for the individual to make known her or his decisions on life-prolonging procedures. A living will declares your wishes not to be kept alive by artificial or mechanical means if you are suffering from a terminal condition and your death would be imminent without the use of such artificial means. It provides a legally-binding written set of instructions regarding your wishes about this important matter.

In most states, in order to qualify for the use of a living will, you must meet the following criteria:

• You must be at least 19 years of age
• You must be of "sound mind"
• You must be able to comprehend the nature of your action in signing such a document

A living will becomes valid when it has been properly signed and witnessed. However, it is very important to remember that as long as you are capable of making decisions and giving directions regarding your medical care, your stated wishes must be followed–*not* those directions that are contained in your living will. Your living will only comes into force when you are in a terminal or vegetative condition, with no likelihood of recovery, and are unable to provide directions yourself. Until that time, *you*–and not your living will–will provide the directions for your health care. Generally, a licensed physician is required to determine when your condition has become terminal or vegetative with no likelihood of recovering.

There are 2 separate methods for preparing a living will in this book. First, this chapter contains a general, standardized living will (this standard living will is also contained on the CD). Additionally, the next chapter living will forms that are part of state-specific advance health care directives. These forms have been taken directly from the most recent legislation regarding living wills in each state. You may use either the general living will form or the living will that is part of your state-specific advance health care directive. Please compare these forms and select the appropriate form that you feel best expresses your wishes regarding health care if you are in a terminal or vegetative condition.

Typical Living Will Provisions

Nearly all states have passed legislation setting up a statutorily-accepted living will form. Those states that have not expressed a preference for a specific type of living will have, nevertheless, accepted living wills that adhere to general legal requirements. There are many different types of living wills, from very brief statements such as the following from the State of Illinois:

"If at any time I should have an incurable and irreversible injury, disease, or illness judged to be a terminal condition by my attending physician who has personally examined me and has determined that my death is imminent except for death-delaying procedures, I direct that such procedures which would only prolong the dying process be withheld or withdrawn, and that I be permitted to die naturally with only the administration of medication, sustenance, or the performance of any medical procedure deemed necessary by my attending physician to provide me with comfort care."

to lengthy and elaborate multi-page forms with detailed and very specific instructions. All of the various state forms try to assure that a person's own wishes are followed regarding health care decisions. Many states have drafted their legislation with the intention that people prepare both a living will and a health care power of attorney (or similar form) which appoints a person of your choosing to act on your behalf in making health care decisions when you are unable to make such decisions for yourself. It is advisable that you prepare both of these advance health care forms in order to cover most, if not all, eventualities that may arise regarding your health care in difficult situations. Health care powers of attorney are explained in Chapter 3.

In general, the purpose of your living will is to convey your wishes regarding life-prolonging treatment and artificially provided nutrition and hydration if you no longer have the capacity to make your own decisions, and have either a terminal condition, or become permanently unconscious. You should very carefully think about your own personal desires should either of these conditions arise. Please also note that the basic living will included in this book also contains a release of medical information under the federal HIPAA guidelines for privacy of medical information.

You should also read through this statement concerning the importance of the decisions that you make in a living will (This notice is also part of the living will itself):

Notice to the Adult Signing this Document:

This is an important legal document. This document directs the medical treatment you are to receive in the event you are unable to participate in your own medical decisions and you are in a terminal condition. This document may state what kind of treatment you want or do not want to receive. This document can control whether you live or die. Prepare this document carefully. If you use this form, read it completely.

You may want to seek professional help to make sure the form does what you intend and is completed without mistakes. This document will remain valid and in effect until and unless you revoke it. Review this document periodically to make sure it continues to reflect your wishes. You may amend or revoke this document at any time by notifying your physician and other health-care providers. You should give copies of this document to your physician and your family. This form is entirely optional. If you choose to use this form, please note that the form provides signature lines for you, the three witnesses whom you have selected and a notary public.

Finally, the Federal Patient Self-Determination Act encourages all people to make their own decisions about the type of medical care they wish to receive. This act also requires all health care agencies (hospitals, long-term care facilities, and home health agencies) receiving Medicare and Medicaid reimbursement to recognize a living will and/or health care power of attorney as advance directives that indicate the patient's wishes. Under this Act, all health care agencies must ask you if you have advance directives and must give you materials with information about your rights under state law. The living will in this chapter and/or the state-specific living wills on the CD (included in the state-specific advance health care directives) must be recognized by all health care agencies.

Instructions for Preparing and Signing a Living Will

If you desire that your life not be prolonged artificially when there is no reasonable chance for recovery and death is imminent, please follow the instructions below for completion of your living will. The entire following form is should be used if you choose to use this form. It has been adapted to be valid in all states. Courts, health care professionals, members of your family, and physicians will be guided by this expression of your desires concerning life support. Please consult the Estate Planning Appendix on the CD for further information regarding recognition of living wills in your state.

1. Make a photo-copy or printout a copy of the entire living will form from this chapter or the state-specific living will form from the Forms-on-CD. Using the photo-copy as a worksheet, please fill in the correct information in the appropriate blanks as noted below:

    ① Name of person making living will
    ② Name of person making living will
    ③ State whose laws will govern the living will
    ④ Any additional directions, terms or conditions that you wish to add
    ⑤ Number of pages of entire living will (fill in after printing out final copy)
    ⑥ Date of signing of living will (fill in upon signing)
    ⑦ Your signature and printed name (do not sign unless in front of a notary public)
    ⑧ Date, signatures and printed names of witnesses to signing of living will
    ⑨ The notary acknowledgment section (to be completed by notary public)

2. On clean, white, 8 1/2 x 11" paper, printout the entire living will exactly as shown with your information added. Carefully re-read this original living will to be certain that it exactly expresses your desires on this very important matter. When you have a clean, clear original version, staple all of the pages together in the upper left-hand corner. Do not yet sign this document or fill in the date.

3. You should now assemble two or three witnesses and a Notary Public to witness your signature. Note that the standardized living will provides for three witnesses so that it will be legally valid in all states. Most of the state-specific living wills provide for only two witnesses, although some will require three. As noted on the document itself, these witnesses should have no connection with you from a health care or beneficiary standpoint (exception: see note following). Specifically, the witnesses must:

- Be at least 19 years of age
- Not be related to you in any manner: by blood, marriage, or adoption
- Not be your attending physician, or a patient or employee of your attending physician; or a patient, physician, or employee of the health care facility in which you may be a patient. However, please see below.
- Not be entitled to any portion of your estate on your death under any laws of intestate succession, nor under your will or any codicil
- Have no claim against any portion of your estate on your death
- Not be directly financially responsible for your medical care
- Not have signed the living will for you, even at your direction
- Not be paid a fee for acting as a witness

Note: a few states have laws in effect regarding witnesses when the declarant is a patient in a nursing home, boarding facility, hospital, or skilled or intermediate health care facility. In those situation, it is advisable to have a patient ombudsman, patient advocate, or the director of the health care facility to act as the third witness to the signing of a living will. Please check the Estate Planning Appendix on the CD for your state's requirements.

4. In front of all of the witnesses and in front of the Notary Public, the following should take place in the order shown:

- You will then sign your living will at the end, exactly as your name is typewritten on your living will, where indicated, in ink using a pen.

- After you have signed, pass your living will to the first witness, who should sign where indicated and fill in his or her address.

- After the first witness has signed, have the living will passed to the second witness, who should also sign where indicated.

- If you are using a living will that requires a third witness, then after the second witness has signed, have the living will passed to the third and final witness, who also signs where indicated and fills in his or her address. Throughout this ceremony, you and all of the witnesses must remain together.

The final step is for the notary public to sign in the space indicated. When this step is completed, your living will is a valid legal document. Have several copies made and, if appropriate, deliver a copy to your attending physician to have placed in your medical records file. You may also desire to give a copy to the person you have chosen as the executor of your will (or successor trustee of your living trust), a copy to your clergy, and a copy to your spouse or other trusted relative.

Living Will Declaration and Directive to Physicians of

① _____

Notice to Adult Signing This Document: This is an important legal document. This document directs the medical treatment you are to receive in the event you are unable to participate in your own medical decisions and you are in a terminal condition. This document may state what kind of treatment you want or do not want to receive. This document can control whether you live or die. Prepare this document carefully. If you use this form, read it completely. You may want to seek professional help to make sure the form does what you intend and is completed without mistakes. This document will remain valid and in effect until and unless you revoke it. Review this document periodically to make sure it continues to reflect your wishes. You may amend or revoke this document at any time by notifying your physician and other health-care providers. You should give copies of this document to your physician and your family. This form is entirely optional. If you choose to use this form, please note that the form provides signature lines for you, the three witnesses whom you have selected and a notary public.

② I, _____ , being of sound mind, willfully and voluntarily make known my desire that my life not be artificially prolonged under the circumstances set forth below, and, ③ pursuant to any and all applicable laws in the State of _____ , I declare that:

If at any time I should have an incurable injury, disease, or illness which has been certified as a terminal condition by my attending physician and one additional physician, both of whom have personally examined me, and such physicians have determined that there can be no recovery from such condition and my death is imminent, and where the application of life prolonging procedures would serve only to artificially prolong the dying process, then:

I direct that such procedures be withheld or withdrawn, and that I be permitted to die naturally with only the administration of medication, the administration of nutrition and/or hydration, or the performance of any medical procedure deemed necessary to provide me with comfort, care, or to alleviate pain.

If at any time I should have been diagnosed as being in a persistent vegetative state which has been certified as incurable by my attending physician and one additional physician, both of whom have personally examined me, and such physicians have determined that there can be no recovery from such condition, and where the application of life prolonging procedures would serve only to artificially prolong the dying process, then:

I direct that such procedures be withheld or withdrawn, and that I be permitted to die naturally with only the administration of medication, the administration of nutrition and/or hydration, or the performance of any medical procedure deemed necessary to provide me with comfort, care, or to alleviate pain.

In the absence of my ability to give directions regarding my treatment in the above situations, including directions regarding the use of such life prolonging procedures, then:

It is my intention that this declaration shall be honored by my family, my physician, and any court of law, as the final expression of my legal right to refuse medical and surgical treatment. I declare that I fully accept the consequences for such refusal.

④ If I have any additional directions, I will state them here:

If I have also signed a Health Care Power of Attorney, Appointment of Health Care Agent, or Health Care Proxy, I direct the person who I have appointed with such instrument to follow the directions that I have made in this document. I intend for my agent to be treated as I would be with respect to my rights regarding the use and disclosure of my individually identifiable health information or other medical records. This release authority applies to any information governed by the Health Insurance Portability and Accountability Act of 1996 (aka HIPAA), 42 USC 1320d and 45 CFR 160-164.

If I am diagnosed as pregnant, this document shall have no force and effect during my pregnancy.

I understand the full importance of this declaration, and I am emotionally and mentally competent to make this declaration and Living Will. I also understand that I may revoke this document at any time.

⑤ I publish and sign this Living Will and Directive to Physicians, consisting of ⑥ _____ typewritten pages, on _____, 20_____ , and declare that I do so freely, for the purposes expressed, under no constraint or undue influence, and that I am of sound mind and of legal age.

⑦ _____
Declarant's Signature

_____
Printed Name of Declarant

⑧ On _____, 20_____ , in the presence of all of us, the above-named Declarant published and signed this Living Will and Directive to Physicians, and then at the Declarant's request, and in the Declarant's presence, and in each other's presence, we all signed below as witnesses, and we each declare, under penalty of perjury, that, to the best of our knowledge:

1.   The Declarant is personally known to me and, to the best of my knowledge, the Declarant signed this instrument freely, under no constraint or undue influence, and is of sound mind and memory and legal age, and fully aware of the possible consequences of this action.

2.   I am at least 19 years of age and I am not related to the Declarant in any manner: by blood, marriage, or adoption.

3.   I am not the Declarant's attending physician, or a patient or employee of the Declarant's attending physician; or a patient, physician, or employee of the health care facility in which the Declarant is a patient, unless such person is required or allowed to witness the execution of this document by the laws of the state in which this document is executed.

4.   I am not entitled to any portion of the Declarant's estate on the Declarant's death under the laws of intestate succession of any state or country, nor under the Last Will and Testament of the Declarant or any Codicil to such Last Will and Testament.

5.   I have no claim against any portion of the Declarant's estate on the Declarant's death.

6.   I am not directly financially responsible for the Declarant's medical care.

7.   I did not sign the Declarant's signature for the Declarant or on the direction of the Declarant, nor have I been paid any fee for acting as a witness to the execution of this document.

⑨

_____
Signature of Witness #1

_____
Printed name of Witness #1

_____
Address of Witness #1

_____   _____
Signature of Witness #2   Signature of Witness #3

_____   _____
Printed name of Witness #2   Printed name of Witness #3

_____   _____
Address of Witness #2   Address of Witness #3

Notary Acknowledgement

⑪ County of _____
State of _____

On _____ , 20_____, before me personally appeared _____ , the Declarant, and _____ , the first witness, _____ , the second witness, _____ , the third witness, and, being first sworn on oath and under penalty of perjury, state that, in the presence of all the witnesses, the Declarant published and signed the above Living Will Declaration and Directive to Physicians, and then, at Declarant's request, and in the presence of the Declarant and of each other, each of the witnesses signed as witnesses, and stated that, to the best of their knowledge, the Declarant signed said Living Will Declaration and Directive to Physicians freely, under no constraint or undue influence, and is of sound mind and memory and legal age and fully aware of the potential consequences of this action. The witnesses further state that this affidavit is made at the direction of and in the presence of the Declarant.

_____
Signature of Notary Public

_____
Printed name of Notary Public

Notary Public,
In and for the County of _____
State of _____
My commission expires: _____

Notary Seal

Instructions for Revocation of Living Will

All states which have recognized living wills have provided methods for the easy revocation of them. Since they provide authority for medical personnel to withhold life-support technology which will likely result in death to the patient, great care must be taken to insure that a change of mind by the patient is heeded.

If revocation of your living will is an important issue, please consult your state's law directly. The name of your particular state's law relating to living wills is provided in the Estate Planning Appendix on the CD of this book.

For the revocation of a living will, any one of the following methods of revocation is generally acceptable:

- Physical destruction of the living will, such as tearing, burning, or mutilating the document.

- A written revocation of the living will by you or by a person acting at your direction. A form for this is provided at the end of this chapter. You may use two witnesses on this form, although most states do not require the use of witnesses for the written revocation of a living will to be valid.

- An oral revocation in the presence of a witness who signs and dates a writing confirming a revocation. This oral declaration may take any manner. Most states allow for a person to revoke such a document by any indication (even non-verbal) of the intent to revoke a living will, regardless of their physical or mental condition.

To use the Revocation of Living Will form provided on the next page, simply fill in the following information:

① Name of person revoking living will
② Date of original living will
③ Date of signing revocation of living will
④ Signature and printed name of person revoking living will
⑤ Signatures and printed names of two witnesses to signing of revocation

Revocation of Living Will

① I, _____ , am the Declarant and maker of a Living Will and Directive to
② Physicians, dated _____ , 20_____ .

By this written revocation, I hereby entirely revoke such Living Will and Directive to Physicians and intend that it no longer have any force or effect whatsoever.

③ Dated _____ , 20_____ .

④ _____
Declarant's Signature

_____
Printed Name of Declarant

⑤ _____
Signature of Witness

_____
Printed name of Witness

_____
Address of Witness

_____
Signature of Witness

_____
Printed name of Witness

_____
Address of Witness

Chapter 8

Advance Health Care Directive

An advance health care directive is a legal document that may be used in any state and that allows you to provide written directions relating to your future health care should you become incapacitated and unable to speak for yourself. Advance health care directives give you a direct voice in medical decisions in situations when you cannot make those decisions yourself. Your advance health care directive will not be used as long as you are able to express your own decisions. You can always accept or refuse medical treatment and you always have the legal right to revoke your advance health care directive at any time. Instructions regarding revocations are discussed later in these instructions. The Federal Patient Self-Determination Act encourages all people to make their own decisions about the type of medical care they wish to receive. This act also requires all health care agencies (hospitals, long-term care facilities, and home health agencies) receiving Medicare and Medicaid reimbursement to recognize a living will and health care power of attorney as advance directives. Under this Act, all health care agencies must ask you if you have advance directives and must give you materials with information about your rights under state law.

Advance health care directives are not only for senior citizens. Serious life-threatening accidents or disease can strike anyone and leave them unable to communicate their desires. In fact, the rise of the use of advance health care directives can be attributed in part, to legal cases involving medical care to young people, particularly Karen Ann Quinlan and Nancy Cruzan, and most recently, Terry Schiavo. Anyone over the age of 18 (19 in Alabama) who is mentally competent should complete an advance health care directive. Be aware, however, that advance health care directives are intended for non-emergency medical treatment. Most often, there is no time for health care providers to consult and analyze the provisions of an advance health care directive in an emergency situation.

The advance health care directives that are contained on the CD that accompanies this book all contain four separate sections, each dealing with different aspects of potential situations that may arise during a possible period of incapacitation:

- Living will
- Selection of health care agent (generally, by health care power of attorney)
- Designation of primary physician
- Organ donation

In addition, this book also provides (in Chapter 3) a fifth legal form that may be useful in many health care situations if you are unable to handle your own financial affairs: a durable unlimited power of attorney for financial affairs. A brief explanation of each of the forms included in an advance health care directive follows:

Living Will: A *living will* is a document that can be used to state your desire that extraordinary life support means not be used to artificially prolong your life in the event that you are stricken with a terminal disease or injury. Its use has been recognized in all states in recent years. The purpose of a living will is to provide doctors and other health care workers with clear directions regarding how you would like your medical care handled toward the end of your life. A living will makes it possible for you to specify, in advance, exactly what your preferences are regarding the use of life-sustaining medical procedures if you are ever in a terminal medical condition or in a vegetative state, and are unable to give such directions yourself. For instructions and forms for preparing a living will that is not part of an advance health care directive, please see Chapter 7.

Health Care Power of Attorney: This relatively new legal document has been developed to allow a person to appoint another person to make health care decisions on one's behalf, in the event that he or she becomes incapacitated or incompetent. Generally, a *health care power of attorney* will only take effect upon a person becoming unable to manage his or her own affairs, and only after this incapacitation has been certified by an attending physician. The person appointed will then have the authority to view your medical records, consult with your doctors and make any required decisions regarding your health care. This document may be carefully tailored to fit your needs and concerns and can be used in conjunction with a living will. It can be a valuable tool for dealing with difficult healthcare situations. For instructions and forms for preparing an individual durable health care power of attorney that is not part of an advance health care directive, please refer to Chapter 3.

Designation of Primary Physician: Through the use of this document, you will be able to designate your choice for your primary physician in the event you are unable to communicate your wishes after an accident or during an illness. Although your family may know your personal doctor, it may still be a good idea to put this choice in writing so that there is no question regarding who your choice for a doctor may be.

Organ Donation: You may also wish that your vital organs or, indeed, your entire body be used after your death for various medical purposes. Every year, many lives are saved and much medical research is enhanced by organ donations. All states allow for you to personally declare your desires regarding the use of your body and/or organs after death. Please note that you must be certain that any organ donation decisions must be coordinated with any such donation decisions that you may have made in any other manner, such as on your driver's license or with your state motor vehicles department.

The combination of these four forms provides a comprehensive method by which you may provide, in advance, for a situation in which you may be unable to communicate your desires to your family, your friends, and your health care providers. It is an opportunity to carefully plan how you would like various medical situations to be handled should they arise.

If you intend to prepare a living will *and* a health care power of attorney, however, you are encouraged to use the state-specific advance health care directive for your state, which contains a state-specific living will and a state-specific health care power of attorney form as part of that document. This will allow the provisions in your living will and the provisions in your health care power of attorney (both as part of your complete advance health care directive) to complement each other. It is important that these two documents be coordinated so that the actions that your health care agent may be asked to take on your behalf (when you are unable to communicate) are in line with your stated desires as shown in your living will. Keeping these two documents together as part of a comprehensive advance health care directive makes such coordination much more likely. This method also provides a simple compact package that contains your entire advance health care directive with forms using legal language that most health care providers in your state are familiar with. In a few states, the legislatures have not developed specific language for one or more of the forms. These few instances are noted under the state's heading in the appendix of this book. In addition, in such situations, an appropriate and legally-valid form has been added to the directives for those states. Any such forms have been prepared following any guidelines set out by the state's legislature.

When You Should Use an Advance Health Care Directive

The forms explained in this chapter are comprehensive state-specific advance health care directives and are provided on the enclosed CD. Please review your own state's advance health care directive form. A *'state-specific advance health care directive'* is a form that has been taken directly from the laws of your particular state. The legal effects of the language in such a document have been approved by the legislature of the state. This provides an advantage in that the legal language in such a 'statutory' form is generally familiar to health care providers in the particular state and they know that such language has been approved. This does not mean, however, that other 'non-statutory' forms are not legally valid in the state as well. Anyone may use a 'non-statutory' legal form with language that they find appropriate to their own situation, as long as the document meets certain minimum legal standards for a particular state.

You need not necessarily adopt all four sections of the document for your own use. You may select and complete any or all of the four separate sections of the form. For example, if you choose not to select a health care agent, you may use the other three parts of the form and not complete that section. Instructions for filling in the forms are contained later in this chapter. Many people find using a single comprehensive document easier than completing each separate form as an individual document.

Important Note: The state-specific advance health care directive forms *do not* contain a durable unlimited power of attorney for financial affairs. As this form is not directly related to health care decision issues, it is provided only as a separate individual form located in Chapter 3. Should you desire to use this type of document to authorize someone to handle your financial affairs in the event of your disability or incapacitation, you should use one of the forms provided in Chapter 3.

Witness and Notary Requirements

All states have provided protections to ensure the validity of an advance health care directive. They have also provided legal protections against persons using undue influence to force or coerce someone into signing an advance health care directive. There are various requirements regarding who may be a witness to your signing of your advance health care directive. In general, these protections are for the purpose of ensuring that the witnesses have no actual or indirect stake in your death. These witnesses should have no connection with you from a health care or beneficiary standpoint. In most states, the witnesses must:

- Not be under 18 years of age (19 in Alabama)
- Not be related to you in any manner either by blood, marriage, or adoption
- Not be your attending physician
- Not be a patient or employee of your attending physician
- Not be a patient, physician, or employee of the health care facility in which you may be a patient
- Not be entitled to any portion of your estate upon your death under any laws of intestate succession, nor under your will or any codicil
- Not have a claim against any portion of your estate upon your death
- Not be directly financially responsible for your medical care
- Not have signed the advance health care directive for you, even at your direction
- Not be paid a fee for acting as a witness

In addition, please note that several states and the District of Columbia (Washington D.C.) have laws in effect regarding witnesses when the *declarant* (the person signing the advance health care directive) is a patient in a nursing home, boarding facility, hospital, or skilled or intermediate health care facility. In those situations, it is advisable to have a patient ombudsman, patient advocate, or the director of the health care facility act as the third witness to the signing of an advance health care directive. These restrictions on who may be a witness to your signing of an advance health care directive require, in most cases, that the witnesses either be 1) friends who will receive nothing from you under your will, or 2) strangers. Please review the requirements for your own state in the witness statements on your particular state's form.

In addition, all of the advance health care directive forms included on this book's CD are designed to be notarized. This is a requirement in most states for most forms and has been made mandatory on all of the forms in this book. The purpose of notarization in this instance is to add another level of protection against coercion or undue pressure being exerted to force anyone to sign any of these legal forms against their wishes. Sadly, such undue pressure has been applied in some cases to force senior citizens to sign legal documents against their own wishes. The requirement that one sign a document in front of a notary and in front of two additional witnesses can significantly lessen the opportunity for such abuse.

Instructions for Preparing Your Advance Health Care Directive

1. Select the appropriate form from the CD. Carefully read through each section of your Advance Health Care Directive. You may wish to make a copy of the form that you choose. This will allow you to use the copy as a draft copy.

2. Note that you will need to initial your choices in the first section of the form as to which sections of the entire advance health care directive you wish to be effective. The choices are:
    *   Living will
    *   Selection of health care agent
    *   Designation of primary physician
    *   Organ donation

    Please note that you may choose to exclude any of the above portions of your form and the remaining portions will be valid. If you wish to exclude one or more portions, DO NOT place your initials in the space before the section that you wish to exclude. Be careful so that you are certain you are expressing your desires exactly as you wish on these very important matters. If you do not wish to use a particular main section of the entire form, cross out that section of the form clearly and do not initial that section in either the first paragraph of the Directive or in the paragraph directly before your signature near the end of the Directive. If you do not wish to use a particular paragraph within one of the four main sections of the form, cross out that paragraph also.

    Make the appropriate choices in each section where indicated by initialing the designated place or filling in the appropriate information. Depending on which form that you use, you may have many choices to initial or you may have no choices to initial. Please carefully read through the paragraphs and clauses that require choices to be certain that you understand the choices that you will be making. If you wish to add additional instructions or limitations in an area of the form, you should do so within the Adobe Acrobat Reader® program. If you need to add additional pages, please use the form titled "Additional Information for Advance Health Care Directive" which is also provided on the CD. If you need and use additional pages, be certain that you initial and date each added page and that you clearly label each additional page regarding which paragraph or section of the form to which it pertains.

3. In the form or section on organ donations, you may choose to either donate all of your organs or limit your donation to certain specific organs. Likewise, you may provide that the organs be used for any purpose or you may limit their use to certain purposes.

4. Print out (or type) a final copy of your advance health care directive. You will now need to complete the signature and witness/notary sections of your forms. When you have a completed original with no erasures or corrections, staple all of the pages together in the upper left-hand corner. Do not sign this document, initial your choices or fill in the date yet. You should now assemble your witnesses and a notary public to witness your signature. Be certain that your witnesses meet your specific state requirements. In addition, please note that several states and the District of Columbia have laws in effect regarding witnesses when the declarant is a patient in a nursing home, boarding facility, hospital, or skilled or intermediate health care facility. In those situations, it is advisable to have a patient ombudsman, patient advocate, or the director of the health care facility to act as the third witness to the signing of an advance health care directive. In order that your advance health care directive be accepted by all legal and medical authorities with as little difficulty as possible, it is highly recommended that you have your signing of this important document witnessed by both your appropriate witnesses and a notary public.

5. In front of all of the witnesses and the notary public, the following should take place in the order shown:

    (a) There is no requirement that the witnesses know any of the terms of your advance health care directive or other legal forms, or that they read any of your advance health care directive or legal forms. All that is necessary is that they observe you sign your advance health care directive and that they also sign the advance health care directive as witnesses in each other's presence.

    (b) You will sign your legal form at the end where indicated, exactly as your name is shown on the form, in ink using a pen. At this time, you should also again initial your choices as to which sections you have chosen (directly before your signature space). You will also need to fill in the date on the first page of the directive or form, date and initial each additional information page (if you have used any), and fill in your address after your signature. Once you have signed and completed all of the necessary information, pass your advance health care directive or other legal form to the first witness, who should sign and date the acknowledgment where indicated and also print his or her name.

    (c) After the first witness has signed, have the advance health care directive or other legal form passed to the second witness, who should also sign and date the acknowledgment where indicated and print his or her name.

    (d) Throughout this ceremony, you and all of the witnesses must remain together. The final step is for the notary public to sign in the space where indicated and complete the notarization block on the form.

(e) If you have chosen individuals to act as your health care agent (durable power of attorney for health care), you should have them sign the form at the end where shown acknowledging that they accept their appointment.

6. When this step is completed, your advance health care directive or individual legal form that you have signed is a valid legal document. Have several photo-copies made and, if appropriate, deliver a copy to your attending physician to have placed in your medical records file. You should also provide a copy to any person who was selected as either your health care agent or your agent for financial affairs. You may also desire to give a copy to the person you have chosen as the executor of your will (or successor trustee of your living trust), your clergy, and your spouse or other trusted relative.

If you need to add additional pages to your advance health care directive, please use the form titled "Additional Information for Advance Health Care Directive" at the end of this chapter. If you need and use additional pages, be certain that you initial and date each added page and that you clearly label each additional page regarding which paragraph or section of the form to which it pertains. You should also note in the form itself that you are using additional pages by printing or writing "See attached additional page which is incorporated by reference" in the section of the form where you wish to insert additional instructions or information.

Revocation of Advance Health Care Directive

All states have provided methods for the easy revocation of advance health care directives and the forms that they contain. Since such forms provide authority to medical personnel to withhold life-support technology that will likely result in death to the patient, great care must be taken to insure that a change of mind by the patient is heeded. Any one of the following methods of revocation is generally acceptable:

- Physical destruction of the advance health care directive, such as tearing, burning, or mutilating the document.

- A written revocation of the advance health care directive by you or by a person acting at your direction. A form for this is provided later in this chapter and on the CD.

- An oral revocation in the presence of a witness who signs and dates an affidavit confirming a revocation. This oral declaration may take place in any manner (verbal or non-verbal). Most states allow for a person to revoke such a document by any indication (even non-verbal) of the intent to revoke an advance health care directive, regardless of his or her physical or mental condition. A form for this effect is included later in this chapter and on the CD, titled "Witness Affidavit of Oral Revocation of Advance Health Care Directive."

If your revoke your advance health care directive, make sure that you provide a copy (or notice) of this revocation to anyone or any health care facility that has a copy or original of the advance health care directive that you are revoking.

Instructions for Revocation of Advance Health Care Directive

To complete this document, fill in the following information:

1. Name of person who originally signed the advance health care directive (principal or declarant)
2. Date of original advance health care directive
3. State in which original advance health care directive was signed
4. Signature of person revoking advance health care directive
5. Date of revocation of advance health care directive

Revocation of Advance Health Care Directive

① I, _____ , am the maker and signatory of an Advance Health Care Directive which was dated ② _____ , and which was executed by me for use in the State of ③_____ .

By this written revocation, I hereby entirely revoke such Advance Health Care Directive, any Living Will, any Durable Power of Attorney for Health Care, any Organ Donation, or any other appointment or designation of a person to make any health care decisions on my behalf. I intend that all of the above mentioned documents have no force or effect whatsoever.

BY SIGNING HERE I INDICATE THAT I UNDERSTAND THE PURPOSE AND EFFECT OF THIS DOCUMENT.

④ Signature _____

⑤ Date _____

Instructions for Witness Affidavit of Oral Revocation of Advance Health Care Directive

If it is necessary to use the Witness Affidavit of Oral Revocation of Advance Health Care Directive form, the witness should actually observe your indication of an intention to revoke your Advance Health Care Directive. This may take the form of any verbal or non-verbal direction, as long as your intent to revoke is clearly and unmistakably evident to the witness. This form does not need to be notarized to be effective. Make sure that you provide a copy of this revocation to anyone or any health care facility that has a copy or original of the Advance Health Care Directive that you are revoking.

To complete this document, fill in the following information:

① Name of person who originally signed the advance health care directive (principal or declarant)
② Date of original advance health care directive
③ State in which original advance health care directive was signed
④ Printed name of witness
⑤ Date of act of revocation
⑥ Signature of witness to the oral or non-verbal revoking of advance health care directive
⑦ Date of witness signature
⑧ Printed name of witness

Witness Affidavit of Oral Revocation of Advance Health Care Directive

The following person, ① _____ , herein referred to as the declarant, was the maker and signatory of an Advance Health Care Directive which was dated ② _____ , and which was executed by him or her for use in the State of ③ _____ .

By this written affidavit, I, ④ _____ , the witness, hereby affirm that on the date of ⑤ _____ , I personally witnessed the above-named declarant make known to me, through verbal and/or non-verbal methods, their clear and unmistakable intent to entirely revoke such Advance Health Care Directive, any Living Will, any Durable Power of Attorney for Health Care, any Organ Donation, or any other appointment or designation of a person to make any health care decisions on his or her behalf. It is my belief that the above-named declarant fully intended that all of the above-mentioned documents no longer have any force or effect whatsoever.

Witness Acknowledgment

The declarant is personally known to me and I believe him or her to be of sound mind and under no duress, fraud, or undue influence.

Witness Signature ⑥ _____ Date ⑦ _____

Printed Name of Witness ⑧ _____

Instructions for Additional Information for Advance Health Care Directive

If you need to add additional pages to your advance health care directive document, please use the form titled "Additional Information for Advance Health Care Directive" which is provided on the following page and on the CD. If you need to use additional pages, be certain that you initial and date each added page and that you clearly label each additional page regarding which paragraph or section of the form to which it pertains. You should also note in the form itself that you are using additional pages by printing or writing "See attached additional information page, which is incorporated by reference" in the section of the form where you wish to insert additional instructions or information. Note that this form should be attached to the original advance health care directive document prior to the signing and notarization of the original document.

To complete this document, fill in the following information:

1. Date of original advance health care directive
2. Name and address of person who originally signed advance health care directive (declarant)
3. Detailed statement of any additional information or instructions in advance health care directive (Be certain that you note the paragraph or section of the original advance health care directive where the additional information or instructions will apply).
4. Initials of declarant and date of advance health care directive

Additional Information for Advance Health Care Directive

The following information is incorporated by reference and is to be considered as a part of the Advance Health Care Directive, dated ① _____,
which was signed by the following declarant ② _____,

Declarant must initial and date at bottom of form and insert additional information here: ③

④ Initials of Declarant _____   Date _____

Chapter 9

Premarital Agreements

A premarital (or prenuptial) agreement is a specific type of contract between two persons who are intending to marry. This agreement is entered into in order to spell out the effect of the couple's forthcoming marriage on their individual property and financial situations. A premarital agreement is, essentially, an agreement to alter the general legal effect of marriage.

In the United States, there are two general sets of rules that apply to the ownership of marital property. Under the laws of the community property states of Alaska, Arizona, California, Idaho, Louisiana, Nevada, New Mexico, Texas, Washington, and Wisconsin, all property owned by spouses is divided into two distinct classes: *separate* property and *community* property. Separate property is generally described as consisting of three types of property:

- Property that each spouse owned individually prior to their marriage
- Property that each spouse acquired by individual gift, either before or during the marriage (gifts given to both spouses together or gifts given by one spouse to the other are generally considered community property)
- Property that each spouse acquired by inheritance (legally referred to as "by bequest, descent, or devise"), either before or during the marriage

In community property states, all marital property that is not separate property is referred to as community property. This includes anything that is not separate property that either spouse earned or acquired at any time during the marriage. The property acquired during the marriage is considered community property regardless of whose name may be on the title to the property, and regardless of who actually paid for the property (unless it was paid for entirely with one spouse's separate property funds and remains separate). *Note:* Alaska allows spouses to create community property by mutual agreement.

The other 40 states follow what is referred to as the *common-law* method of marital property ownership. This method has distinct similarities to the community property system and yet is different in many respects. In common-law jurisdictions, certain marital property is subject to division by the judge upon divorce. Which property is subject to division varies somewhat from state to state but generally follows two basic patterns. The most common method of classifying property in common-law states closely parallels the method used in community property states. Property is divided into two basic classes: *separate* or *non-marital* property and *marital* property. What constitutes property in each class is very similar to the definitions in community property states. This method of property division is termed *equitable distribution*.

The second method for distribution that is used in several states is to make *all* of a couple's property subject to division upon divorce. Regardless of whether the property was obtained by gift, by inheritance, or was brought into the marriage, and regardless of whose name is on the title or deed, the property may be apportioned to either spouse depending upon the decision of the judge. There is no differentiation between marital, non-marital, or separate property. The property is still divided on a basis which attempts to achieve a general fairness, but all of a couple's property is available for such distribution. Some states use a hybrid of the above two methods.

The use of a premarital agreement can effectively alter the classification of a spouse's property that is brought into a marriage. Thus, with the use of a premarital agreement, the potential spouses can agree that all of their property that they bring into a marriage will remain as their own separate property throughout the marriage and will not be subject to any division upon eventual divorce. A premarital agreement of this type makes a couple's property rights regarding property brought to a marriage similar to that of community property states and those common-law states that follow similar laws regarding separate and marital property.

The premarital agreement in this book also provides that the potential spouses waive forever any and all rights that they may have to alimony or claims of support that would have to be provided out of any property that is in existence as of the date of the premarital agreement. Any property that is acquired during the marriage, however, will remain subject to division in the event of a divorce.

Please use the property questionnaire that is included in Chapter 9: *Marital Settlement Agreements* to specify what property each potential spouse actually owns prior to the marriage. That questionnaire should then be used to fill in the information detailing the property ownership on the premarital agreement. *Note*: If you are at all unsure of the correct use the form in this chapter, please consult a competent attorney.

Instructions for Premarital Agreement

To complete this form, you will need the following information:

1. Date of agreement
2. Name of first party
3. Address of first party
4. Name of second party
5. Address of second party
6. Date of intended marriage
7. County of intended marriage
8. State of intended marriage
9. Name of first party
10. List property that will remain solely the first party's property
11. Name of second party
12. List property that will remain solely second party's property
13. State that agreement is made in
14. Date agreement is signed
15. Signature of first party
16. Printed name of first party
17. Signature of second party
18. Printed name of second party
19. Signature of witness #1
20. Printed name of witness #1
21. Address of witness #1
22. Signature of witness #2
23. Printed name of witness #2
24. Address of witness #2
25. Notary will fill out this portion

Premarital Agreement

This agreement is made on ①_____ , 20 _____ , between ②
_____ ,
address: ③

and ④_____ ,
address: ⑤

We intend to be married on ⑥_____ , 20 _____ , County of ⑦
_____ , State of ⑧ _____ .

We both desire to settle by agreement the ownership rights of all of our property that we currently own and our rights to alimony, spousal support, or maintenance.

THEREFORE, in consideration of our mutual promises, and other good and valuable consideration, we agree as follows:

We agree that the following property of ⑨_____ shall be his or her sole and separate property: ⑩

We agree that the following property of ⑪_____ shall be his or her sole and separate property: ⑫

We agree that the above listed property shall remain their own separate and personal estate, including any rents, interest or profits which may be earned on such property. This property shall forever remain free and clear of any claim by the other person. Each person shall have the right to control, sell, or give away their own separate property as if they were not married. We both agree to waive any rights or claims that we may have now or in the future to receive any distribution of any of the other's separate property in the event of divorce or dissolution of marriage.

However, in the event of divorce or dissolution of marriage, any marital property which is acquired after marriage will be subject to division, either by agreement between us or by a judicial determination.

After careful consideration of our circumstances and all of the other terms of this agreement, we both agree to waive any rights or claims that we may have now or in the future to receive alimony, maintenance, or spousal support from any separate property of the other spouse in the event of divorce or dissolution of marriage. We both fully understand that we are forever giving up any rights that we may have to alimony, maintenance, or spousal support from any separate property of the other spouse in the event of divorce or dissolution of marriage.

We have prepared this agreement cooperatively and each of us has fully and honestly disclosed to the other the extent of our assets.

We each understand that we have the right to representation by independent counsel. We each fully understand our rights and we each consider the terms of this agreement to be fair and reasonable.

Both of us agree to execute and deliver any documents, make any endorsements, and do any and all acts that may be necessary or convenient to carry out all of the terms of this agreement.

We agree that this document is intended to be the full and entire premarital agreement between us and should be interpreted and governed by the laws of the State of ⑬_____ .

We also agree that every provision of this agreement is expressly made binding upon the heirs, assigns, executors, administrators, successors in interest, and representatives of each of us.

Signed and dated this day ⑭_____ , 20 _____

⑮_____
Signature

⑰_____
Signature

⑯_____
Printed Name

⑱_____
Printed Name

⑲_____
Signature of Witness #1

㉒_____
Signature of Witness #2

⑳_____
Printed Name of Witness #1

㉓_____
Printed Name of Witness #2

㉑_____
Address of Witness #1

㉔_____
Address of Witness #2

㉕
State of _____
County of _____

On _____ , 20 _____ , _____ and _____
_____ came before me personally and, under oath, stated that they are the persons described in the above document and they signed the above document in my presence. I declare under penalty of perjury that the persons whose names are subscribed to this instrument appear to be of sound mind and under no duress, fraud, or undue influence.

_____
Signature of Notary Public

Notary Public, In and for the County of _____
State of _____

My commission expires: _____   Notary Seal

Chapter 10

Marital Settlement Agreements

For many people, separation is the first step in the divorce process. You and your spouse may decide to separate under the terms of a separation agreement or you may wish to seek an actual legal separation from a court. A legal court-ordered separation is slightly different than a separation by agreement. Legal court-ordered separations are not provided for in all states. However, a marital separation by mutual agreement is recognized and honored in every state. Check the Appendix for the law in your state. In a legal court-ordered separation, there is actually a court order that specifies that the couple is separated. This court order may set out all of the terms of the separation, or the court order may simply validate all of the terms that the couple have already agreed to in a separation agreement. Neither a legal court-ordered separation nor a separation agreement will legally end the marriage. Only a divorce can do that.

There are some distinct benefits to a separation prior to divorce. First, the period of separation from your spouse begins to prepare you for the emotional impact of divorce. In a separation, you may enter into an agreement covering all of the issues that arise during the course of an actual divorce, and it is much easier to mutually change the terms of this agreement prior to an actual divorce. In some ways, a separation may act as a trial divorce. You can always get back together with your spouse, if you both desire. In addition, some couples who do not wish to divorce decide to live separately for religious or moral reasons.

The marital settlement agreement that you prepare using this book may be used in the same manner as a separation agreement. It will cover all of the same concerns as a separation agreement. Your marital settlement agreement addresses the issue of separation and may be used if you desire to enter into a legal court-ordered separation. Your state's listing in the Divorce Law Appendix on the CD briefly explains the law regarding legal court-ordered separations in your state. In this chapter, you will begin the process of making the decisions necessary to prepare a marital settlement agreement. This agreement will cover all of the terms of your eventual divorce. Included in your agreement will be all of the decisions that you and your spouse make regarding how your property and bills are divided, whether either of you should get alimony, and, if you have any children, who will have custody of them and how their support will be provided. This agreement, when signed by you and your spouse, will become a valid legal contract that will be enforceable in a court of law if either you or your spouse violate its terms. In addition, the agreement that you prepare will be used in your actual divorce proceedings. Judges will not generally change any of the terms in a marital settlement agreement, unless they feel that the terms are obviously unfair, were obtained by force or threats, or are not in the best interests of any children.

The method set out in this chapter for preparing a marital settlement agreement is essentially identical to the method used by the vast majority of lawyers who handle divorces. Upon visiting a lawyer for a divorce, you would be asked to fill out an extensive questionnaire covering all of the aspects that might arise in the course of your divorce proceeding. The lawyer would then determine what you want to achieve in your divorce; what property you wish to retain, which parent you wish to have custody, and whether child support or alimony is desired. Your lawyer and your spouse's lawyer would then attempt to negotiate the various issues, and if possible, put them in the form of a marital settlement. The lawyers would use legal texts that contain clauses very similar to the ones set out in this chapter to prepare your agreement. The only difference is that the language in the agreement that most lawyers would prepare would be unintelligible to most people. You and your spouse, however, are the two people who know the most about your current relationship. You both are the two most qualified people to understand what each wants out of the marriage. If you can both cooperate enough to agree to the terms of your marital settlement agreement, your subsequent divorce should be achieved with far less difficulty and expense than if you use the services of lawyers. If you can't agree to the terms of your agreement without lawyers, it is not likely that you will be able to agree once you both have hired lawyers. If you can't come to an agreement, even with the assistance of lawyers, a judge who knows very little about you and your spouse will make the important decisions that you were unable to make.

Preliminary Questionnaire

The Preliminary Questionnaire (included on the CD only) that you need fill out first covers basic personal information and details the history of your marriage. By filling in this questionnaire and the ones in the next four sections, you will be able to have all of the necessary and relevant information in front of you for preparing your agreement. On the next page, there is a list of important documents that should be assembled and kept on hand for use during the process of your divorce. There will then be a discussion of some of the preliminary matters that must be understood.

Locate the Preliminary Questionnaire on the CD and fill it out first.

Document Checklist

The following is a listing of various documents that may be necessary during your divorce. The list is as comprehensive as possible and many of the documents may not apply to your individual situation. If you have the documents listed in your possession, assemble them into one place and make a note of that fact on this list. If your spouse has the documents, request that he or she do the same. If you know that the document exists, but do not have access to it, make a note to that effect on this list. This checklist is also available on the CD.

Wife's Birth Certificate:
Husband's Birth Certificate:
Immigration and Naturalization Documents:
Marriage License:
Birth Certificates of any Children:
Any Written Agreements between Wife and Husband:
Social Security Cards:
Documents relating to any prior marriage:
All documents relating to income, expenses, and property:
>   **Federal, state, and local income tax returns:**
>   **Payroll stubs and W-2 Forms:**
>   **Records regarding any other income:**
>   **Records regarding monthly living expenses:**
>   **Pension and retirement plan policies and records:**

Stock option and profit-sharing plans and records:
Personal financial statements:
Business tax returns:
Business financial statements:
Deeds to any real estate:
Mortgages or deeds of trust for any real estate:
Copies of any leases:
Checking account statements:
Savings account statements and passbooks:
Certificates of Deposit:
Stock certificates and bonds:
Securities stockbroker account statements:
Titles to cars, boats, motorcycles, etc.:
Any outstanding loan documents:
Credit card records:
Records of any other debts:
Life insurance policies:
Health insurance policies:

Auto insurance policies:
Homeowner's insurance policy:
Other insurance policies:
Inventory of contents of safety deposit boxes:
Appraisals of any property:
Records of any gifts or inheritances:

After you have filled in the Preliminary Questionnaire (available on the CD) and assembled the necessary documents, you are ready to begin the process of preparing your marital settlement agreement and obtaining your divorce. Based on what you have put on your questionnaire, you must make certain preliminary decisions. First, you must determine what the specific grounds for your divorce will be.

What Will be the Grounds for Your Divorce?

Your divorce will be based on the particular no-fault basis that is allowed in your own state. Some states have more than one basis for filing. In general however, there are four basic types of no-fault grounds: (1) irretrievable breakdown of the marriage; (2) irreconcilable differences; (3) incompatibility; and (4) living separate and apart for a certain time period. The grounds for filing for a no-fault divorce in your state are listed in the Appendix. Most states have only one type of available grounds for a no-fault divorce and it is this type that you will use. However, a few states have available a choice of no-fault grounds. You must choose the grounds that most closely fit your particular circumstances. (Residents of Louisiana: Please note that Louisiana has instituted the most liberal system for divorce grounds in the U.S. In Louisiana, it is now grounds for a divorce if one spouse simply "desires" not to be married. In addition, Louisiana has also eliminated all defenses to a divorce requested on such grounds. The only way to prevent such a divorce in Louisiana is to reconcile with the spouse desiring to divorce.)

In states that have "irretrievable breakdown of the marriage," "irreconcilable differences," or "in-compatibility" as grounds, it is generally easy to satisfy the grounds. If either spouse decides that the marriage should be ended, it is very difficult for the other spouse to prevent the divorce. If both spouses agree on the no-fault grounds or if the other spouse does not deny that the marriage is broken, the grounds are generally satisfied. There may be a court-enforced mediation attempt or a counseling session required if the other spouse does deny that the marriage is irretrievably broken or that there are irreconcilable differences. Any such denial of the breakdown of the marriage will only delay the divorce for a specific period of time while an attempt at reconciliation is made. The divorce will proceed after the mediation period is over, usually after about 30 to 90 days. A few states have certain specific ways to prove that the marriage is irretrievably broken. Two states (New York and Tennessee) allow proof of the grounds by use of a written agreement reached between the spouses. One state (Texas) uses a unique type of grounds that is very similar to the other general no-fault grounds. The different states' requirements are listed in the Appendix. In any states with these type of no-fault grounds, the couple may separate prior to the actual divorce. During the time of separation, the spouses can live under the terms of the marital settlement agreement that may be prepared by using this book.

The fourth type of grounds for obtaining a divorce is "living separately and apart" for a specific length of time. This type of grounds is able to be shown by objective evidence and is proven merely by showing that the spouses did not live together or sleep together for the required time limit. There is no requirement that either spouse be at fault for the separation. The necessary time limit for living apart ranges from six months to five years. During the time of separation, the spouses can live under the terms of the marital settlement agreement that may be prepared using this book. Please refer to the Appendix to see if your state requires this type of grounds.

As noted, a few states will show two or more no-fault grounds. Generally, if there is more than one type of no-fault grounds for divorce, there is a general marital breakdown grounds and a separation-based grounds. Which grounds that you and your spouse choose will depend on your individual circumstances and an agreement between you and your spouse.

Tax Consequences of Divorce

There are various tax consequences to your divorce or separation that must be considered as you prepare your marital settlement agreement. Among these are:

- Whether you will file joint or separate returns for the current year
- Who will be liable for any taxes due for the current year
- Who will have a right to any refund due for the current year
- Who will receive the tax exemption for any dependent children

The full details regarding the potential tax aspects of divorce and separation are beyond the scope of this chapter. Tax laws are among the most complex and rapidly changing laws in existence. Detailed information regarding current federal income tax laws may be found in IRS Publication 504: *Divorced or Separated Individuals*. For information on your individual state's treatment of divorce for tax purposes, please consult the instructions or regulations available from your state's department of taxation or revenue. For further information, you should consult a competent accountant, attorney, or other qualified tax professional. There are, however, some general taxation guidelines that may assist you in determining your personal income tax situation before and after your divorce or separation.

Property Transfers
The most important rule regarding federal income taxes relating to property is that any transfers of property between you and your spouse that are related to your divorce or separation are not taxable. There will be no recognition of any gain or loss on the transfer of any property, regardless of who actually owned the property. The transfer of property related to a divorce is considered a gift from

one spouse to the other for tax purposes as long as the property is actually transferred within one year after the date of the actual final divorce. The spouse who receives the property is not required to report any gain or income as the result of the receipt of any such property. However, there may be future tax consequences for a spouse who receives property that has increased in value while it was held during the marriage. In general, the spouse who receives such property in a divorce settlement and later sells the property will be liable for any taxes due on any gain in the value of the property.

For example, as a result of their divorce negotiations, Spouse A agrees to sign a deed transferring full ownership of their jointly-owned home to Spouse B. The original equity in the home at the time of original purchase was $10,000.00 (their down payment). Therefore, the value of Spouse A's one-half share at the time of purchase was $5,000.00. The equity value of the home is now $40,000.00. The current market value of Spouse A's one-half share of the equity value of the home is $20,000.00. Upon transfer of Spouse A's share to Spouse B, Spouse B is not required to report any gain or income related to the transfer. However, if Spouse B later sells the home, the $15,000.00 gain in value that is attributable to Spouse A's share ($20,000.00 - $5,000.00 = $15,000.00) may be considered as taxable gain to Spouse B. Spouse B's own share of the equity may also be taxable as gain on the sale of the home.

Additionally, there are some relatively complex tax regulations that relate to the treatment of community property in the 9 community-property states (Arizona, California, Idaho, Louisiana, Nevada, New Mexico, Texas, Washington, and Wisconsin). (*Note*: Alaska is considered an "equitable distribution state" but allows married couples to designate, by written agreement, which of their property they wish to be considered "community property"). In general, the IRS may choose to disregard community-property rules in certain specific tax situations. Although these situations seldom arise under normal circumstances, IRS Publication 504: *Divorced or Separated Individuals* should be referred to for more information on this aspect of taxation.

Alimony

In general, alimony payments are treated as income to the spouse who receives them. Conversely, the spouse who actually pays the alimony may deduct such payments as an expense. The spouse paying alimony can (at the present time) deduct the alimony payments from income for tax purposes whether or not deductions are itemized on the federal tax forms. In order for alimony payments to qualify for this tax treatment for federal income tax purposes, there are certain conditions. For payments based on agreements, the following requirements must be met:

- The alimony payment must be the result of a written settlement agreement or a divorce decree or judgment
- The payment must be by cash, check, or money order
- The spouses do not live together when the payment is made
- The payment is not for child support
- The payments may not continue after death

The terms of the marital settlement agreement clause included in this chapter relating to the continuing payment of alimony would qualify under current federal tax law as long as: (1) the payments are terminated on the death of the recipient; (2) they are not a one-time lump-sum payment; and (3) all of the other above conditions are met.

A one-time lump-sum alimony payment is treated as a simple transfer of funds from one spouse to the other. Such a lump-sum alimony payment is neither taxable to the spouse receiving it nor deductible by the spouse paying it. Life insurance premium payments that are made by an ex-spouse for a policy that names the other ex-spouse as sole irrevocable beneficiary are also considered to be alimony, as long as the payments also meet the above qualifications. Any other voluntary payments in excess of the amount required under the marital settlement agreement or divorce decree, however, will not qualify as alimony and may not be deducted as alimony expenses for tax purposes. For example, under the terms of their marital settlement agreement, Spouse A has agreed to pay Spouse B $500.00 per month for three years or until Spouse B's death, whichever occurs first. The spouses currently have separated and live apart. Spouse A makes the required payments for a full year. For income tax purposes, Spouse A may deduct the full $6,000.00 from his income, even if other deductions are not itemized. Spouse B must report the entire $6,000.00 as income for federal income tax purposes.

Child Support and Custody
For federal income tax purposes, child support payments are treated differently from alimony payments. In general, any amount that is fixed in your marital settlement agreement or in your final divorce decree as child support will not be treated as income to the parent who receives it. In addition, unlike alimony payments, the parent who makes such child support payments cannot deduct this payment as an expense for federal income tax purposes. For example, Parent A has custody of one child and Parent B has agreed to pay $400.00 per month in child support. The payments are made on time for a full year. Parent B may not deduct any of the amount of the child support payments from income and Parent A is not required to report any of the payments as income for tax purposes. Which parent receives the benefit of the tax exemption for a dependent child is also subject to IRS regulations. In general, the parent with physical custody of the child for over one-half of the year will have the right to the exemption if the following qualifications are also met:

- You are divorced, separated, or live apart for at least the last six months of the current tax year
- You and your spouse together provided over one-half of the total support for the child (as opposed to support being provided by a non-parent)
- You and your spouse had custody of the child, either alone or together for over one-half of the current year (as opposed to a non-parent having custody)
- You have not agreed in writing that your spouse should have the right to claim the dependency exemption and have not filed a written IRS waiver form (IRS Form 8332: *Release of Claim to Exemption for Child of Divorced or Separated Parents*)

Marital Settlement Agreement Instructions

You are now ready to begin preparing a draft copy of your marital settlement agreement. Begin by printing out a blank copy of the marital settlement agreement form that is included the Forms-on-CD. You will begin by filling in the information noted below in the spaces indicated by the numbers on the sample Marital Settlement Agreement that follows. The initial information will lay the legal groundwork that identifies you, your spouse, and any children, and will satisfy the basic minimum legal requirements for a valid contract. The first 15 items to fill in are covered in this section. The following sections will cover filling in information regarding property, alimony, child custody and support, and completing the Agreement form. At the end of this section is a sample Marital Settlement Agreement noting where the numbered choices should be filled in. Note: you may use either the PDF version or the text version of the Marital Settlement Agreement. Both are included on the Forms-on-CD. Using the text version will allow you to cut and paste the various clauses that you select into the form.

① Date of agreement
② Name of wife
③ Address of wife (including county of residence)
④ Name of husband
⑤ Address of husband (including county of residence)
⑥ Date of marriage
⑦ Place of marriage (city and state)

⑧ **Children Identification Clause**: Choose the clause that applies to your particular circumstances. This clause identifies whether or not any children will be involved in the terms of the agreement. Fill in the names and birthdates of any children. One of these clauses is mandatory. If the wife is currently pregnant and there are already children, use both appropriate clauses.

[   ]   There were no children born or adopted into our marriage, and none are expected.
[   ]   The wife is currently pregnant and the expected birthdate is:
[   ]   The following child(ren) was (were) born (or adopted) into our marriage:
          Child's name _____
          Child's birthdate _____
          Child's sex _____
          Child's name _____
          Child's birthdate _____
          Child's sex _____

⑨ **Grounds for Divorce/Separation Clause**: Choose one of the following clauses that most closely fits the divorce grounds that you have chosen in your state and your particular circumstances. Refer to your state's listing in the Appendix to determine the grounds that you will use for your divorce. One of these clauses is mandatory for your agreement. (Texas and Louisiana residents: please check the Appendix for details of the language used as grounds in your respective states.)

[   ] As a result of disputes and serious differences, we sincerely believe that our marriage is irretrievably broken and that there is no possible chance for reconciliation.

[   ] As a result of disputes and serious differences, we sincerely believe that there are irreconcilable differences between us and that there is no possible chance for reconciliation.

[   ] As a result of disputes and serious differences, we sincerely believe that there is a complete incompatibility of temperament between us and that there is no possible chance for reconciliation.

[   ] As a result of disputes and serious differences, we have separated and are now living apart and intend to continue to remain permanently apart.

⑩ and ⑪ **Marital Settlement Agreement Taxation Clause**: The following clause may be used to define your various decisions regarding the tax consequences of your divorce. If you are living apart under the terms of your marital settlement agreement or under the terms of a separation decree, but your divorce is not final by the end of the year, you may choose to file: (1) a joint tax return with your spouse; (2) a separate return; or (3) you may be considered unmarried and file a "head of household" return. You may choose to file a joint income tax return with your spouse for the current tax year *only* if your divorce has not been made final before the end of the year. If your divorce is final by the end of the year, you must file either an individual return or a "head of household" return. In addition, if your divorce is finalized prior to the end of the current tax year, you may not claim your spouse as an exemption, even if you have provided all of the support for your spouse for the year. With this clause, you will decide who will receive any tax refund that may be due for the current year and who will pay any taxes due for the current year. For more information, please refer to the section earlier in this chapter regarding the tax consequences of divorce. Where ⑩ and ⑪ appear, fill in either "Wife" or "Husband."

[   ] We both agree that we will cooperate in the filing of any necessary tax returns. We also agree that any tax refunds for the current year will be the property of the ⑩ and that any taxes due for the current tax year will be paid by the ⑪ .

⑫ and ⑬ **Name Change Clause**: Most states have specific laws that allow a person to request that his or her former name be restored upon divorce. Although many of these laws are now written to make no reference to the sex of the person requesting this type of change, it is generally a wife who desires to use either her maiden name or her former name (if her former name was a previous married name). The restoration of this name may be accomplished by a simple request in the divorce papers and a provision in the divorce decree or judgment. It is useful to have your spouse's agreement to such a name change request. Such an agreement is contained in the following clause that is part of the marital settlement agreement in this book. For ⑫ , generally fill in "Wife" and for ⑬ indicate the desired name upon divorce.

[   ]   We both agree that, in the event of divorce or dissolution of marriage, the ⑫ desires to and shall have the right to be known by the name of ⑬.

Additional Marital Settlement Agreement Clauses: There are various other marital settlement agreement issues that must be dealt with in order for your agreement to have the necessary legal force. These standard legal phrases are included in the basic marital settlement agreement form in this book. They are very important and should not be altered. They cover the following points:

- That you both want the terms of your marital settlement agreement to be the basis for your court order in the event of a divorce
- That you both have prepared complete and honest Financial Statements and they are attached to your agreement
- That you both know that you have the right to see your own lawyers and that you both understand your legal rights
- That you both will sign any necessary documents
- That you both intend that your agreement is the full statement of your rights and responsibilities
- That your agreement will be binding on any of your future representatives

⑭ **Number of pages**: After you have completed your entire marital settlement agreement, fill in the total number of pages of the agreement. Then the husband and wife should initial *each and every one* of the pages of the final copy of the agreement.

The following sections will explain how to complete the remaining portions of your marital settlement agreement:

⑮ to ⑱ Property division (see property section)

⑲ Alimony (see alimony section)

⑳ Child custody (include this page only if you have children [see child custody section])

㉑ Child support (include this page only if you have children [see child support section])

㉒ **Additional page**: If you should need an additional page to include further information for any section of your Marital Settlement Agreement, you may use the form on the last page of this chapter as a template. Simply fill in the appropriate information and be certain to number the page accordingly and have each spouse initial the page where noted.

㉓ Fill in the name of the state that one or both of you currently reside in.

㉔ to ㊹ Completing and signing the form

Marital Settlement Agreement

This agreement is made on _____ , between
_____ , the Wife, who lives at
_____ , and
_____ , the Husband, who lives
at _____ . We
were married on _____ , in
_____ .

Child Identification:

Grounds for Separation:

We both desire to settle by agreement all of our marital affairs,
THEREFORE, in consideration of our mutual promises, and other good and valuable
consideration, we agree as follows:

We both desire and agree to permanently live separate and apart from each other,
as if we were single, according to the terms of this agreement. We each agree not to
annoy, harass, or interfere with the other in any manner.

We both agree that we will cooperate in the filing of any necessary tax returns. We also
agree that any tax refunds for the current year will be the property of the _____
and that any taxes due for the current tax year will be paid by the _____ .

We both agree that, in the event of divorce or dissolution of marriage, the _____
desires to and shall have the right to be known by the name of
_____ .

Page 1 of _____ pages   Husband's initials _____   Wife's initials _____

Division of Property

To settle all issues relating to our property, we both agree that the following property shall be the sole and separate property of the Wife, and the Husband transfers and quit-claims any interest that he may have in this property to the Wife:

We also agree that the following property shall be the sole and separate property of the Husband, and the Wife transfers and quit-claims any interest that she may have in this property to the Husband:

Page 2 of _____ pages   Husband's initials _____   Wife's initials _____

Division of Bills

To settle all issues relating to our debts, we agree that the Wife shall pay and indemnify and hold the Husband harmless from the following debts:

We agree that the Husband shall pay and indemnify and hold the Wife harmless from the following debts:

We also agree not to incur any further debts or obligations for which the other may be liable.

Page 3 of _____ pages   Husband's initials _____   Wife's initials _____

Alimony

To settle any and all issues regarding alimony and maintenance, we both agree that:

Child Custody and Visitation

To settle all issues relating to our child custody and visitation, we both agree that:

Page _____ of _____ pages   Husband's initials _____   Wife's initials _____

Child Support

To settle all issues relating to child support, we both agree that:

Additional Terms

We further agree to the following additional terms:

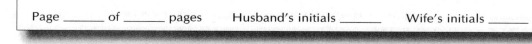

Page _____ of _____ pages   Husband's initials _____   Wife's initials _____

Signature

We each understand that we have the right to representation by separate lawyers. We each fully understand our rights and we each consider the terms of this agreement to be fair and reasonable. Both of us agree to execute and deliver any documents, make any endorsements, and do any and all acts that may be necessary or convenient to carry out all of the terms of this agreement.

We agree that this document is intended to be the full and entire settlement and agreement between us regarding our marital rights and obligations and that this agreement should be interpreted and governed by the laws of the State of _____ .

We also agree that every provision of this agreement is expressly made binding upon the heirs, assigns, executors, administrators, successors in interest, and representatives of each of us.

We both desire that, in the event of our divorce or dissolution of marriage, this marital settlement agreement be approved and merged and incorporated into any subsequent decree or judgment for divorce or dissolution of marriage and that, by the terms of the judgment or decree, we both be ordered to comply with the terms of this agreement, but that this agreement shall survive.

We have prepared this agreement cooperatively and each of us has fully and honestly disclosed to the other the extent of our assets, income, and financial situation. We have each completed Financial Statements that are attached to this agreement and incorporated by reference.

Signed and dated: _____

_____   _____
Signature of Wife   Printed Name of Wife

_____   _____
Signature of Husband   Printed Name of Husband

_____   _____
Signature of Witness #1   Printed Name of Witness #1

_____   _____
Signature of Witness #2   Printed Name of Witness #2

Page _____ of _____ pages   Husband's initials _____   Wife's initials _____

Notary Acknowledgment

State of _____
County of _____

On the _____ ,
_____ and
_____ , husband and
wife, and _____ and
_____ , their witnesses,
personally came before me and, being duly sworn, did state that they are the persons
described in the above document and that they signed the above document in my presence as a free and voluntary act for the purposes stated.

_____
Signature of Notary Public
Notary Public, In and for the County of _____
State of _____
My commission expires:_____   Notary Seal

Page _____ of _____ pages   Husband's initials _____   Wife's initials _____

Property Division

In the course of your attempts to reach a marital settlement agreement with your spouse, the division of your property is one of most likely areas in which arguments may arise. As the change to no-fault divorce has essentially removed the relevance of marital misconduct from consideration, many spouses are unable to vent their hostilities regarding the faults of their spouse during the course of a modern divorce proceeding. Thus, there may often be a tendency to attempt to bring anger and animosity to bear on the other areas left to resolve in a marital settlement. This, however, is not a productive manner in which to approach the division of your and your spouse's property. As much as is possible, you should attempt to keep the discussion of the division of your property on an amicable level. The division of your marital property may be the most important economic event of your lives and should be dealt with in a mature and business-like manner.

Prior to actually making the important decisions regarding the division of your property, it is important to have before you a complete inventory of all of your property. Even if you feel that you have no property to divide, in order to make sure that your marital settlement agreement covers all of your property, you should fill out the Property Questionnaire which is available on the CD. It is very easy to overlook certain types of property. In order to try to list every possible type of property, this questionnaire is very comprehensive. Many of the listings may not apply to your particular situation. Fill in only those areas which apply. Each spouse should fully answer as many of the questions that he or she is able to. You should include on this questionnaire *everything* that you and your spouse own or owe money on. This is a big task but it is crucial in understanding and properly dividing your possessions and obligations in a fair manner.

After the questionnaire there is a discussion of property laws in the individual states and various other matters which are relevant to the division of your property. Next, there is a Property Division Worksheet on which you will list the property that each spouse will retain. Following this are optional property division clauses for selection and inclusion in your marital settlement agreement. Finally there is a Financial Statement that details your and your spouse's employment, monthly income, expenses, assets, and liabilities. Both of you will need to prepare one of these forms for attachment to your completed marital settlement agreement.

Locate the Property Questionnaire on the CD and fill it out now.

The Law of Marital Property Division
As noted earlier, there have been many recent changes in the way that the law deals with each spouse's property upon divorce. Under prior law in most states, the property generally belonged to the person whose name was on the title. This led in many instances to the wife being left with little or no property upon divorce, since it was usually the husband whose name was used to title property. Today, there are two general sets of rules that apply to the division of property upon divorce in the United States. There are 9 *community property* states which essentially view all of the property

obtained during a marriage as being owned equally by the spouses. The community property states are: Arizona, California, Idaho, Louisiana, Nevada, New Mexico, Texas, Washington, and Wisconsin. *Note*: Alaska is considered an "equitable distribution state" but allows married couples to designate, by a written agreement, which of their property they wish to be considered "community property." All of the other states are known as *equitable distribution* states. In these states, upon divorce, a couple's property is subject to being divided on a more or less fair or "equitable" basis. The Appendix will explain which laws apply to your state and will also give some detail as to which property is subject to being shared with your spouse upon divorce.

Bear in mind that these methods of property distribution are what a judge will use if you and your spouse cannot come to an agreement regarding the division in your situation. However, these rules are only guidelines. You and your spouse may legally divide your property in any manner that you choose and can mutually agree on. The only qualification is that the division must be relatively fair. If the division of property by your marital settlement agreement appears inherently unfair to one of the spouses, the judge in most states has the authority and power to change the division upon your ultimate divorce.

What follows is a general discussion of the method by which property is divided in "community property" states and "equitable distribution" states. Check the Appendix to see which method of property division applies to your state and then read that section carefully. The property division rules provided here are general in nature and reflect the modern trends in property division law. However, specific legal rights to particular pieces of property may not always be clear. By following the general rules and applying a sense of fairness in your attempts to reach a settlement, you should be able to reach an equitable agreement. The laws relating to property and property division, however, can get extremely complicated. If either you or your spouse has a great deal of property, your property is owned in complex manners, or you are confused about your rights, it may be wise to seek professional assistance. A lawyer, accountant, or real estate broker may be able to provide enough information for you to understand your property and continue with preparing your own settlement agreement. If you are hesitant about losing any property or feel that you and your spouse cannot agree to a fair division, you should seek the aid of a competent attorney or mediator.

Community Property States

The law in "community property" states generally stems from French or Spanish civil law. Under this type of law, it was felt that all property that a couple obtained while they were married should be shared equally by the spouses. Marriage was viewed essentially as an equal business partnership. Property owned by spouses in these states is divided into two distinct classes: *separate property* and *community property*.

Separate Property
Separate property is generally described as consisting of three types of property:

- Property that each spouse owned individually prior to their marriage

- Property that each spouse acquired by individual gift, either before or during the marriage (gifts given to both spouses together or gifts given by one spouse to the other are generally considered community property)

- Property that each spouse acquired by inheritance (legally referred to as "by bequest, descent, or devise"), either before or during the marriage

Each spouse's separate property is treated as his or her own sole property and is generally not subject to being divided upon divorce. Typically, community property states also provide that if a spouse's particular separate property is exchanged for another piece of property, the new property continues to be separate property. Similarly, in most cases, if separate property is sold and the proceeds are used to purchase different property, this new property is also considered separate property. In order for a piece of property to remain classified as "separate property" however, generally the property must actually be kept separate from any jointly-owned property. It must not be mixed at all with community property: for example, in a joint savings account or in a joint investment. Generally, you must be able to clearly trace the whereabouts of the separate property and show that it has remained separate in order to claim it as separate. In addition, interest or profits earned by separate property and any increases in value of the separate property during the marriage are also generally considered to be separate property. Some states, however, do not classify increase in value or exchanges as separate property. Check the Appendix for your state's specific rules.

Bills and obligations that either spouse incurred prior to their marriage are also considered separate property. The spouse who incurred the debt prior to getting married is solely liable for the payment of the unpaid balance. In addition, you may agree that any debts that either of you incur after your separation are to be considered separate. Be aware, however, that even though you may have a valid legal agreement with your spouse that you will each be responsible only for your own debts, such an agreement does not bind any third party. In other words, even if you have a settlement agreement, if your spouse runs up substantial debts prior to your actual divorce, you may still be liable for payment on these debts. You will, however, generally be able to sue your spouse for reimbursement under the terms of your settlement agreement.

As a rule, if you have a clear record or understanding with your spouse that certain property is your personal separate property, then that property is not to be included in your division of community property. List each of your individual pieces of separate property on the Property Division Worksheet (found on the CD). That property is yours to keep regardless of the division of your community property. Be aware, however, that some community property states do allow a spouse's separate property to be subject to division by a judge under certain circumstances. If there is a very lopsided amount of separate property owned by one of the spouses and it is felt that an equal division of the community property is not at all fair to the other spouse, some states will allow a court to use a spouse's separate property to provide for a more equitable division. Remember, though, that you and your spouse can agree to divide your own property in any manner that you both agree is fair. Please check the Appendix to see how your state deals with this situation. If the Appendix does not contain enough specific information for you to classify a particular piece of property, you may have to consult an attorney for that determination.

Community Property
All marital property that is not separate property is referred to as "community property." This includes anything that either spouse earned or acquired at any time during the marriage that is not separate property. The property acquired during the marriage is considered community property regardless of whose name may be on the title to the property, and regardless of who actually paid for the property (unless it was paid for entirely with one spouse's separate property funds and remains separate). All of a couple's bills and obligations that were incurred during a marriage are also considered community property and are to be divided equally upon divorce. (A few states, however, consider educational loans for one spouse to be a separate debt and not to be shared by the other spouse upon divorce).

Unless there is an agreement otherwise, and unless separate property can be clearly shown, all property that the spouses own at the time of their divorce is generally presumed to be community property. If there is no separation or settlement agreement stating otherwise, this may include any property acquired even after the couple has separated.

Most "community property" states require an equal division of all community property or start with a presumption that an *equal* division is the fairest method, although even these states will allow some leeway from an exact 50/50 division depending on the facts of the case. The remaining "community property" states provide for an *equitable* division of the community property. In this situation, "equitable" is defined to mean fair and just. An exact equal division is not necessarily required. However, in practice, judges generally begin their distribution deliberations from a 50/50 division point, adjusting the balance as the particular circumstances of the case may dictate. To deviate from an equal division of the property, judges are commonly guided by a set of statutory guidelines or factors that are to be considered. A few states, however, have no statutory guidelines to follow. The guidelines available in "community property" states are, in most cases, similar to those available in "equitable distribution" states.

Finally, in California and a few other states, there is a class of property that is referred to as *quasi-community* property. It is simply property that the spouses may have acquired before they moved to the particular state that would have been "community" property if they had lived in the state when they acquired it. This type of property may generally be treated as "community" property.

Equitable Distribution States

There are 41 states that abide by what is known as an "equitable distribution" method of property division. This is a relatively new property law concept which is still evolving. It has distinct similarities to the "community property" system, and yet is different in many respects. There are several versions of this system of property law in effect in various states. Check the Appendix to determine which specific method is used in your state. In "equitable distribution" jurisdictions, certain marital property is subject to division by the judge upon divorce. Which property is subject to division varies somewhat from state to state but generally follows three basic patterns:

• The most common method of classifying property in "equitable distribution" states closely parallels the method used in "community property" states. Property is divided into two basic classes: *separate* or *non-marital* property and *marital* property. What constitutes property in each class is very similar to the definitions in "community property" states.

Separate or *non-marital* property typically consists of property that either spouse brought to the marriage, property acquired by individual gift, and property that was obtained by inheritance (legally known as "by bequest, descent, or devise"). Each spouse's separate non-marital property is treated as his or her own sole property and generally is not subject to being divided upon divorce. Typically, states that use this method of property division also provide that if a spouse's particular separate non-marital property is exchanged for another piece of property, the new property continues to be separate non-marital property. Similarly, in most cases, if separate non-marital property is sold and the proceeds are used to purchase different property, this new property is also considered separate non-marital property. In order for a piece of property to remain classified as "separate non-marital property," generally however, the property must actually be kept separate from any jointly-owned property. It must not be mixed at all with marital property: for example, in a joint savings account or in a joint investment. Generally, you must be able to clearly trace the whereabouts of the separate non-marital property and show that it has remained separate in order to claim that it should not be subject to division. In addition, interest or profits earned by separate non-marital property and any increases in value of the such property during the marriage are also generally considered to be separate non-marital property. Some states, however, do not classify increase in value or exchanges as separate non-marital property. Check the Divorce Appendix on the CD for your state's particular rules.

Similarly to community property states, *marital* property consists of all other property; essentially all property which the spouses acquired, either jointly or individually at any time during the marriage, regardless of whose name is on the title and who actually paid for the property (unless it was paid for entirely with one spouse's separate non-marital property funds and remains separate). All of a couple's bills and obligations that are incurred during a marriage are also generally considered marital property and are to be divided equally upon divorce. Unless there is an agreement otherwise, and unless separate non-marital property can be clearly shown, all property that the spouses own at the time of their divorce is generally presumed to be marital property. If there is no separation or settlement agreement stating otherwise, this may include any property acquired even after the couple has separated.

• The second method for distribution that is used in several states is to make *all* of a couple's property subject to division upon divorce. Regardless of whether it was obtained by gift or by inheritance or was brought into the marriage, and regardless of whose name is on the title or deed, the property may be apportioned to either spouse depending upon the decision of the judge. There is no differentiation between marital, non-marital, or separate property. The property is still divided on a basis that attempts to achieve a general fairness, but all of a couple's property is available for such distribution.

• The third method for distribution is basically a hybrid of the above two methods. In several states, specific property is exempted from distribution. For example, in some states, all property except gifts may be subject to division upon divorce. In other states, only inheritances may be exempted from division. In still other states, marital property may consist of all property owned by the spouses except that property brought to the marriage by either spouse and kept separate. The rules for these states are outlined in the Appendix.

You will need to carefully read the rules in the Divorce Appendix that apply to your state to determine which property is subject to division and distribution in your state. Keep in mind, however, that regardless of what your state law dictates, you and your spouse may divide your property in any manner that you can agree on. If you both feel that it is fair to share in a particular gift, or divide the proceeds of an inheritance, you may accomplish this by use of your marital settlement agreement. If it seems fair for one spouse to use his or her separate funds to purchase the other spouse's share of a particular piece of jointly-held property, this may also be accomplished. The state laws and guidelines are only a starting point for discussions and negotiations.

Bills and obligations that either spouse incurred prior to their marriage are also considered separate or non-marital property (except in the few states which make all property subject to division). The spouse who incurred the debt prior to getting married is solely liable for the payment of the unpaid balance. In addition, you may agree that any debts that either of you incur after your separation are to be considered separate non-marital debts. Be aware, however, that even though you may have a valid legal agreement with your spouse that you will each be responsible only for your own debts, such an agreement does not bind any third party. In other words, even if you have a settlement agreement, if your spouse runs up substantial debts prior to your actual divorce, you may still be liable for payment on these debts. You will, however, generally be able to sue your spouse for reimbursement under the terms of your settlement agreement.

In "equitable distribution" states, you will decide which property is you or your spouse's separate non-marital property and which is marital property. In those few states that allow any property to be subject to division, this step will not be necessary. Once you have determined which of your property is subject to being divided, you must then decide exactly how you will accomplish this task. As in many community property states, a 50/50 division of property is most often the starting point for property division decisions made by courts in equitable distribution jurisdictions. Please note, however, the individual differences in your state's property division laws as shown in the Appendix on the CD.

Factors for Consideration in Property Divisions

In most states, there is a list of factors provided in the statutes for the judge to use in making any property distribution decisions. These factors are present in both "community property" and "equitable distribution" states. Each state is free to allow its judges to consider what has been determined to be relevant factors in dividing the property. Each factor carries no specific weight in the decisions to be made. In no state is a particular preference given to each factor. Rather, the list of factors is to be used as a guideline to balance the contributions of each spouse and to attempt to arrive at a fair division of the couple's property.

Recently, there have been some substantial changes in what factors are considered relevant in dividing a couple's property. Marital fault is no longer a factor for consideration in most states. Adultery, desertion, cruelty, and other marital faults have no bearing on property decisions in a majority of states. However, in many states (even those which do not consider marital fault) economic misconduct continues to be a factor. Economic misconduct is generally viewed as one spouse attempting to hide any property from the other spouse, dissipating joint assets, cleaning out joint bank accounts and keeping the money, running up major joint bills in anticipation of divorce, or other such vengeful acts.

It is wise to close all of your joint bank accounts and cancel all joint credit cards upon your separation. This, however, should be a joint decision. The obligations and proceeds of these joint accounts will then be dealt with in your settlement agreement. If you do not trust your spouse enough to discuss the closing of a joint account, or if you fear that your spouse may attempt to clean out your accounts, you will probably not be able to cooperate enough to reach a marital settlement agreement without the aid of a lawyer or mediator. Do not try to hide or conceal any of the assets that belong to both you and your spouse. If your divorce ends up contested and before a judge, you will be required to account for these assets. Such economic misconduct may influence your right to property and support.

In order to attempt to equalize the treatment of homemakers and spouses who give primary care to a couple's children, the efforts of a spouse in caring for children and homemaking are now specifically being considered as a relevant factor in a majority of states. The career and economic sacrifice that one spouse has made to put the other through school is also increasingly being considered as a factor in property divisions.

The trend is for the consideration of any relevant factors that have accounted for the economic contributions to the marriage, whether such contributions are tangible (wages, salary, etc.) or intangible (homemaking, childcare, career sacrifices, etc.). The tax consequences of your property division may also be an important factor. Refer back to the discussion of taxes earlier in this chapter.

The division of property is generally considered to be interrelated to any provisions for alimony and child support. As you work through your agreement with your spouse, realize that all of the provisions that you discuss relate to each other. For your agreement to be a success in eliminating discord from your divorce, it must be a careful balance of all factors and considerations. In short, it must be fair to both you and your spouse. If the property settlement discussions can be kept on a rational and mature level, you and your spouse are in a far better position to determine how all of these various factors should affect your agreement on the division of property. Please carefully read the factors in your state's Appendix listing on the CD.

Property Division Worksheet Instructions

With the various differences between state laws in mind, you must make certain decisions regarding the division of your property. You and your spouse should use the information that you previously filled in on the Property Questionnaire to examine your total property holdings. The first step in filling in your worksheet should be to list the property that you both agree is the *separate* property of each. For this worksheet, we will use the term "separate" to mean any property that you and your spouse agree is not to be subject to division, either because of your state's law on the matter or simply because of your agreement as such. Generally, this is property that either of you owned prior to your marriage and any property that either of you acquired by gift or inheritance. If you are unclear on this, refer to the specific discussion of your state's laws in the Divorce Appendix located on the CD.

The next step will be to list, in the general areas provided, the type and value of all of your *marital* property. For the purpose of this worksheet, the term "marital" property will be used to refer to all property that you and your spouse agree should be subject to division. This should include all of your property that is not listed in the *separate* property section. Be aware that various states may refer to such property by differing terms, such as "community" property. At this same time, you should make a general listing of all of the bills that you and your spouse have accumulated. These, too, will need to be divided.

The next step will generally be the most difficult. You will need to divide all of the listed marital property and bills into two equal or equitable shares. Your jointly-owed bills will be used as an offset against any property. As a general rule, you should begin with an equal division of the marital property and bills. Most "community property" states require an equal division of property and many "equitable division" states also tend to use an equal division. An equal division is perhaps the easiest and most fair method of division to apply in most cases. Courts have found that the equal division method eliminates much of the confusion that may result from trying to value many of the intangible items that are relevant to the decision, such as the value of homemaking, childrearing, and career sacrifices. If an exact equal division is not possible, attempt to reach agreement on a division that is as close to equal as is reasonably possible.

On a piece-by-piece basis, divide and list the property as being given to that spouse who wishes to retain it. Certain pieces of property will not be easily subject to division. For those pieces, there are various ways to reach a fair settlement. If one spouse truly desires the property, other property or cash may be traded for that particular property in order to essentially equalize the division. If an agreement cannot be reached on a particular piece of property, the property can be sold and the proceeds simply divided in half. If a specific value cannot be readily attached to a particular piece of property, it is wise to have an independent appraisal made of the property.

The next step is to first determine what property you both have. First, take out the separate property that you will each keep and which will not be subject to your marital property division. Then determine the total value of all of your marital property that remains. Finally, agree on a method that apportions approximately one-half of the value of the remaining marital property and bills to each party.

Certain mediators have used a method of equal division to assure that each spouse is satisfied with the conclusion. Simply attempt to reach a division of property settlement in which either spouse would be satisfied with either share of the marital property. If you or your spouse would be content with either share of the divided property, you can be relatively assured that a generally fair division has been achieved.

If at this point you are not clear about what property you own or your rights to that property, or are unable to reach a fair agreement with your spouse regarding the division of your property, it may be wise to consider consulting a mediator or an attorney. Once you are clear on your position, you may still be able to proceed with preparing your own settlement agreement.

Locate the Property Division Worksheet on the CD and fill it out now.

Property and Bills Division Marital Settlement Agreement Clauses

⑮ and ⑯ **Division of Property Clauses**: Once you have reached an agreement on the division of your property and bills that you are both satisfied with, you are ready to fill in your settlement agreement clause relating to property.

Division of Property (Basic): The following two clauses are already included in the Marital Settlement Agreement. In these clauses, you are to specifically list the property that each of you will retain, both each spouse's separate property and his or her individual share of the marital property, as agreed to in your Property Division Worksheet. This clause provides that both of you have transferred the property mentioned and quit-claimed it to the other spouse. For each item of property, provide a complete description. For real estate, list the legal description as shown on the deed to the property. For other property, list the serial number, if available, or a clear description. If either of you has a pension plan or retirement plan, list that plan under the appropriate spouse's clause and describe it fully.

> *To settle all issues relating to our property, we agree that the following property shall be the sole and separate property of the Wife, and the Husband transfers and quit-claims any interest that he may have in this property to the Wife: (Here list Wife's property)*

We also agree that the following property shall be the sole and separate property of the Husband, and the Wife transfers and quit-claims any interest that she may have in this property to the Husband: (Here list Husband's property)

Division of Property (by Sale): This clause should be used *only* if there is marital property that is to be sold and the proceeds of the sale are to be divided between you and your spouse. It may be used for the disposition of anything from items to be sold at a yard sale to the sale of your home. An exact description of the property to be sold should be included. If the property is real estate, the description should be the legal description as shown on the deed to the property. This clause provides for an equal division of the proceeds of the sale after any expenses of the sale are deducted. In the case of the sale of a home, this would allow for any appraisal expenses and real estate broker fees to be deducted from the proceeds of the sale before dividing the profits. This clause may be used in conjunction with the previous clause. *Note*: If used, this clause must be added to the Agreement, on a separate sheet. Please see instructions in Chapter 8.

[   ]   We agree that the following property will be sold as soon as possible and any proceeds from the sale of this property, after the deduction of any expenses of the sale, will be divided equally between us: (Here list a description of the property to be sold)

⑭ Fill in the total number of pages of the agreement and each spouse initials the page space.

⑰ and ⑱ **Division of Bills Clauses**: These two clauses are also in the Marital Settlement Agreement. These clauses are used to specifically divide your bills. It provides that you will each individually assume and pay the bills listed after your name and not hold the other liable for the debts ("hold harmless and indemnify"). It also provides that neither of you will incur any more debts for which the other spouse would be liable. For each bill, list to whom the bill is owed and the amount to be paid.

We agree that the Wife shall pay and indemnify and hold the Husband harmless from the following debts: (Here list debts that Wife will pay. If none, state "None.")

We agree that the Husband shall pay and indemnify and hold the Wife harmless from the following debts: (Here list debts that Husband will pay. If none, state "None.")

⑭ Fill in the total number of pages of the agreement and each spouse initials the page.

Financial Statement Instructions

The following Financial Statement will be your record of the disclosures that you and your spouse have made to each other regarding your joint and individual economic situations. Each spouse will complete a separate Financial Statement that will detail each individual spouse's monthly income and expenses and his or her overall net worth (assets and liabilities). The information that you include on this form should be current and should be based upon your economic situation immediately *after* your settlement agreement takes effect. The monthly income that you list should be based on your current job and sources of income, but should not include any income derived from child support payments or alimony from your current spouse. The expenses that you include on this statement should be based on your estimated or actual expenses while you are living separate from your spouse. If you have physical custody of any children, any expenses related to their care should also be included. The assets and liabilities listed should be your separate and marital property and bills as you and your spouse have agreed to in your Marital Settlement Agreement. Fill in only those items that apply to your circumstances. The Financial Statement of each of you will become a permanent part of your Marital Settlement Agreement and will also become a part of your final divorce papers. Both you and your spouse will need to prepare an individual copy of this statement. This Financial Statement is mandatory for you to fill out and is required, in some form, in most states. Some states have similar mandatory Financial Statement forms and you should use such forms. Check the Divorce Law Appendix on the CD. This form assures that both you and your spouse are fully aware of each other's economic circumstances and that you have made your decisions and agreements based on full knowledge of all of the facts relating to your property and income. The method for preparation is as follows:

1. Make two photocopies of the entire blank Financial Statement.

2. Each spouse should then take a copy of the Financial Statement and fill in all of the items that apply to his or her personal situation. Use information that will apply on the day that you sign your Marital Settlement Agreement. In other words, describe your employment, ownership of property, and debts, as of the day that you and your spouse sign your agreement.

3. Each filled-in Financial Statement should then be typed neatly and double-spaced on one side of white 8 ½" x 11" paper. You should then make two photocopies of each of the completed, but unsigned, original Financial Statements. Note: If you are using the Forms-on-CD, you may complete your financial statements on your computer and print them out. (References to "originals" in this book refer to any *unsigned* documents, even if they are photocopies. "Copies" refer to photocopies of *signed* documents).

4. You and your spouse will then sign all three original copies of your own individual Financial Statement in front of a notary public and have the final Financial Statements notarized at the same time that you sign your final Marital Settlement Agreement as explained later in this chapter.

Financial Statement of _____

Employment

Occupation: _____
Employed by: _____
Address of Employer:

Pay period: _____
Next pay day: _____
Rate of pay .... $ _____

Average Monthly Income

Gross monthly salary or wages .... $ _____
   Deductions from paycheck on monthly basis
      Social Security .... $ _____
      Income tax .... $ _____
      Insurance .... $ _____
      Credit Union .... $ _____
      Union dues .... $ _____
      Other deductions .... $ _____
   Total Deductions .... $ _____
Net monthly salary or wages (gross minus [-] total deductions) .... $ _____

Monthly income from other sources
      Commissions, bonuses, etc. .... $ _____
      Unemployment, welfare, etc. .... $ _____
      Dividends, interest, etc. .... $ _____
      Business income .... $ _____
      Rents, royalties .... $ _____
      Other monthly income .... $ _____
Net monthly income from other sources................................ $ _____

Total Average Monthly Income .... (A) $ _____

227

Average Monthly Expenses

Mortgage or rental payment .... $ _____
Property taxes .... $ _____
Homeowner's insurance .... $ _____
Electricity .... $ _____
Water, garbage, sewer .... $ _____
Cable television .... $ _____
Telephone .... $ _____
Fuel oil and natural gas .... $ _____
Cleaning and laundry .... $ _____
Repairs and maintenance .... $ _____
Pest control .... $ _____
Housewares .... $ _____
Food and grocery items .... $ _____
Meals outside home .... $ _____
Clothing .... $ _____
Medical, dental, prescriptions .... $ _____
Education .... $ _____
Childcare/babysitter .... $ _____
Entertainment .... $ _____
Gifts or donations .... $ _____
Vacation expenses .... $ _____
Public transportation .... $ _____
Automobile
   Gasoline and oil .... $ _____
   Repairs .... $ _____
   License .... $ _____
   Insurance .... $ _____
   Payments .... $ _____
Insurance
   Health .... $ _____
   Disability .... $ _____
   Life .... $ _____
   Other .... $ _____
Any other expenses (list)

_____ $ _____
_____ $ _____
_____ $ _____
_____ $ _____

Fixed debts on a monthly basis
   Creditor _____ Monthly payment $ _____
   Creditor _____ Monthly payment $ _____
   Creditor _____ Monthly payment $ _____

Creditor _____ Monthly payment $ _____
Creditor _____ Monthly payment $ _____
Creditor _____ Monthly payment $ _____
Creditor _____ Monthly payment $ _____

Any other debts
Creditor _____ Monthly payment $ _____
Creditor _____ Monthly payment $ _____
Creditor _____ Monthly payment $ _____
Creditor _____ Monthly payment $ _____
Creditor _____ Monthly payment $ _____

Total Average Monthly Expenses .... (B) $ _____

Assets

Cash .... $ _____
Stocks .... $ _____
Bonds .... $ _____
Real estate .... $ _____
Automobiles .... $ _____
Contents of home or apartment .... $ _____
Jewelry .... $ _____
Any other assets (list)
_____ $ _____
_____ $ _____
_____ $ _____
_____ $ _____
_____ $ _____

Total Assets .... (C) $ _____

Liabilities

Creditor _____ Total balance due $ _____
Creditor _____ Total balance due $ _____
Creditor _____ Total balance due $ _____
Creditor _____ Total balance due $ _____
Creditor _____ Total balance due $ _____
Creditor _____ Total balance due $ _____
Creditor _____ Total balance due $ _____

Total Liabilities .... (D) $ _____

Summary of Income and Expenses

Total Average Monthly Income .... (A) $ _____
Total Average Monthly Expenses .... (B) $ _____

Summary Of Assets And Liabilities

Total Assets .... (C) $ _____
Total Liabilities .... (D) $ _____

Signed and dated: _____ .

_____
Signature

_____
Printed Name

State of _____
County of _____

On this day, before me, the undersigned authority, in and for and residing in the above county and state, personally appeared _____ , who is personally known to me to be the same person whose name is subscribed to the foregoing document, and, being duly sworn, verified that the information contained in the foregoing document is true and correct on personal knowledge and acknowledged that said document was signed as a free and voluntary act.

Subscribed and sworn to before me on _____ .

_____
Signature of Notary Public
Notary Public, In and for the County of _____
State of _____
My commission expires: _____   Notary Seal

Alimony, Maintenance, and Spousal Support

Alimony has been a subject of both fear and confusion for many people considering divorce. For some, there is an unfounded fear that they will be forced to make exorbitant alimony payments to their former spouse for the rest of their life. For others approaching divorce, there is a fear that they will be left stranded without any income, job skills, or support. For most people, confusion is the likely response to questions regarding alimony. The best way to approach a consideration of alimony is to try and forget all of your preconceived notions about it. The laws regarding alimony have changed drastically in the last few years and the common understandings regarding alimony no longer apply.

Alimony Questionnaire Instructions

Before the general discussion of alimony, however, please complete the Alimony Questionnaire that is available on the CD regarding the desirability and need for alimony in your divorce situation. A copy should be filled out by each spouse. The comparison of the answers on the two forms will form the basis for the beginning of your discussions regarding alimony. The responses to the questions should be openly and honestly discussed by both spouses during the conversations relating to alimony. The purpose of this questionnaire is to isolate and present the facts relating to your circumstances that are relevant to alimony. This will give both you and your spouse the information necessary to reach a rational decision on this difficult subject. Please note that all of the information that is listed on both the Property Questionnaire and the Financial Statement in the previous section is relevant to any discussion of alimony and may be necessary for filling in this alimony questionnaire. Please refer to those previous forms when necessary.

Locate the Alimony Questionnaire on the CD and fill it out now.

The Law of Alimony

The laws relating to alimony have undergone enormous changes in recent years. Most of these changes have been in response to the phenomenal changes in our society in the last few decades. Much of prior alimony law was based on the stereotypical subservient role of the wife in a marriage. This traditional role pattern has been irrevocably altered. As more women are seeking and finding employment outside of the home during a marriage, the role of alimony in a divorce has shifted. In the past, alimony was paid almost exclusively to the wife and was used, in many cases, to enable the wife to continue to live in the lifestyle to which she had become accustomed to during the marriage.

Alimony has evolved from this traditional pattern to a modern method that enables the spouse in the least secure economic position to become self-supporting. The right to alimony in a modern divorce setting is no longer the sole province of the wife. Both spouses are considered to be equally eligible to receive alimony under the laws in all states. Although it is still far more common for a husband to provide alimony to the wife, in some cases, husbands have been awarded alimony. In situations where the wife is the sole support of the family or the husband is incapable of self-support, the law ignores the gender of each spouse and awards alimony on the basis of need.

Alimony awards are not commonly awarded to either spouse, however. Such awards are only made in approximately 15 percent of all divorces. Thus, only in about one out of every seven divorces is alimony even considered necessary. Spousal support after marriage is definitely not common, and you should approach your discussion of alimony with this fact firmly in mind. In certain situations, however, alimony is an important and valuable right. The length of time during which alimony payments are typically paid after a divorce has also been decreasing in recent years. The average duration of alimony payments is now approximately two to five years. This is because the emphasis for economic support has been shifting away from providing periodic alimony payments toward awarding the non-working spouse a larger share of the marital assets. By providing a larger lump-sum share of marital assets as a form of alimony rather than periodic payments, the continued involvement between the spouses is terminated much sooner.

Misconduct by either spouse during the marriage is also no longer an important factor in alimony awards. It is the economic and not the moral aspects of divorce that have achieved prominence in the legal process. Although most states no longer consider marital fault relevant to the awarding of alimony, a few states continue to allow misconduct to play a role in alimony decisions. Please check the Appendix on the CD to determine how the laws of your state approach this aspect of alimony.

Alimony is not generally favored when the marriage has been of short duration. If you have not been married for at least two years, it is very unlikely that a court would award any alimony. Where there are no children and both spouses are healthy and have the ability to be self-sufficient, there is also far less chance that a court will order either spouse to provide alimony to the other. If the marriage has been of long duration (at least ten years), however, and one spouse is essentially without the ability to become self-sufficient in a reasonable length of time, alimony of long duration may be necessary to prevent injustice. If one spouse has been a homemaker or has provided full-time childcare for the couple's children, there is a likelihood that he or she will have difficulty in making the transition from a position as a supported married person to that of a self-sufficient single person.

Somewhat related to alimony is the problem of a divorced spouse obtaining health insurance protection. For those spouses who were formerly covered by the other spouse's employer-sponsored group health insurance, obtaining sufficient health insurance coverage at a reasonable rate may be a serious problem. This is particularly true if the spouse who will lose the coverage is not presently employed in a job that provides health insurance. In an effort to alleviate this problem, recent federal legislation now requires that employer-sponsored group health plans must offer the option to continue health insurance coverage at group rates for up to three years after divorce to divorced spouses of employees with coverage. If you are in this situation, contact the office of the insurance company that provides the group coverage for your spouse.

If your marriage has been of long duration and one of you will be reasonably incapable of self-support in the future, it is recommended that you seek the assistance of a competent attorney. In such cases, alimony may be the most important economic factor in the divorce and may be the only method by which a spouse who is not self-sufficient will be able to achieve a secure life. In cases where alimony will be a major factor and will constitute the primary economic support for one spouse, many other factors (for example: cost-of-living adjustments and long-term tax consequences) become important. The advice of a lawyer is highly recommended in such situations.

Alimony Marital Settlement Agreement Clauses

⑲ **Clauses for Alimony**: One of the following clauses should be selected for inclusion in every marital settlement agreement. There are clauses for use if: (1) neither spouse is to receive alimony; (2) one spouse is to receive monthly alimony payments for a set period of time; or (3) one spouse is to receive a one-time lump-sum payment of alimony. Choose the clause that most closely fits your particular situation:

No Alimony to Either Spouse Clause: This clause should be used only if, after careful consideration, both you and your spouse agree that neither of you should be required to pay any alimony to the other. You are also agreeing that neither of you will remain as beneficiaries of any life insurance policies held by the other spouse. By using this clause, you will be giving up forever any rights that you may have to alimony. However, if this is what you have both decided is fair, then you should use this clause.

[   ]   We both agree to waive any rights or claims that we may have now or in the future to receive alimony, maintenance, or spousal support from the other. We both also agree that neither of us shall remain as the beneficiary on any insurance policy carried by the other. We both fully understand that we are forever giving up any rights that we may have to alimony, maintenance, or spousal support.

Alimony Payable in Monthly Payments Clause: This clause should be used if you and your spouse have agreed that one of you should receive alimony and one of you should pay alimony to the other in the form of periodic monthly payments. You will need to decide the amount of each payment, the day of the month that each payment will be due, and the date on which the payments should begin. You will also need to decide when the payments are to end. You may wish the payments to end upon remarriage, death, or on a particular date. Or you may decide that the alimony payments should end upon the first happening of any one of these events. In addition, in this clause you agree that your decisions may be modifiable by a court in the future. This allows for a court to alter the alimony arrangements if there is a change in circumstances that makes the agreement unfair in the future.

Finally, if using this clause, you will need to choose a method by which the payments should be made. Some states have enacted legislation that allows or requires any support payments to be made through the court or certain state agencies and then be passed on to the spouse who is to receive the payment. This indirect method of payment, although generally slower, has the benefit of allowing for immediate action to be taken if any payments are missed. There is a clear record of payment in the hands of the appropriate state authorities. In fact, some states automatically take direct action against any spouse who is late with a payment. That action may include garnishing wages, requiring a bond or deposit, or actually seizing a delinquent spouse's property. However, in virtually all states that allow this indirect method of payment, there are provisions that allow the spouses to opt out of the state requirement. In this clause, you and your spouse agree that the payments may be made directly to the spouse who is to receive them, but that the arrangement may be modifiable by a court at a later date. By making the clause subject to court modification, the spouse receiving the payments will retain the right to have the payments made through the court or state at a later date should any problems in late or delinquent payments arise.

In addition, this clause specifies that you and your spouse have agreed that one of you will remain as a beneficiary on a life insurance policy of the other. Retaining a position as beneficiary on the other's life insurance is generally a good idea if there are continuing support payments to be paid. The spouse who pays the alimony will be the spouse who maintains the insurance. The spouse who receives the alimony will be the spouse who is designated as beneficiary. In the event of the supporting spouse's death, this allows the spouse to whom the support is due to collect the benefits of any insurance and apply it to the continuing maintenance or child support obligations.

[   ]   We both agree that, as alimony and maintenance, the (Husband or Wife) shall pay to the other spouse, the sum of $ (amount of payment) per month, payable on the (date when due each month) day of each month. The first payment will be due on (date first payment due) and the payments shall continue until the first of the following occurrences: (Select two or more of the following phrases: [1] the date that either of us dies; [2] the date that the spouse receiving alimony remarries; or [3] any specific date that you both agree upon [for example: May 5, 2009].)

We both intend that the amount and the duration of the payments may be modified by a court in the future. We also both agree that these payments should be made directly to the spouse to whom they are due, but that this payment method may be modified by a court in the future and that, if appropriate and in the event of divorce or dissolution of marriage, the payments may be made through the appropriate court or state agency for payment to the spouse by such court or state agency.

The life of the (Husband or Wife) is currently insured by (name of insurance company) in the amount of $ (amount of coverage) and the (Husband or Wife) agrees to keep this policy in full force until the first of the following occurrences: (Select two or more of the following phrases: [1] the date that either of us dies; [2] the date that the spouse receiving alimony remarries; or [3] any specific date that you both agree upon [for example: May 5, 2008]. Note: This date should correspond to the date in the first paragraph of this clause.) We agree that the [Husband or Wife] shall be designated as irrevocable sole beneficiary of this policy. The spouse obligated to provide such insurance will provide the other spouse with annual proof of such coverage.

Alimony Payable in a Lump-Sum Payment Clause: This clause should be used if you and your spouse agree that the fairest method of dealing with the payment of alimony is for one spouse to pay the other a one-time lump-sum payment. The funds may then be used by the spouse who receives the payment to obtain education, job skills, or training to become self-supporting. This lump-sum payment is separate from and in addition to any shift in funds or property under the terms of your property settlement. To be fair, this alimony lump-sum payment should be taken out of a spouse's share of separate and marital property after all of the couple's property has been equally or equitably divided. This method of spousal support has the benefit of lessening the future ties between you and your spouse and, thus, lessening the opportunities for problems to develop. It also has the benefit of not leaving one spouse subject to overdue payments from the other spouse. This method, however, is not workable if the spouse who is to pay the lump-sum payment does not currently have the assets by which to pay. In this clause, you are also agreeing that neither of you will remain as beneficiary of any life insurance policy held by the other spouse.

[   ]   We both agree that in full payment of any claims or rights to alimony, spousal support, or maintenance, the [Husband or Wife] shall pay to the other the sum of $ [amount of lump sum payment], which shall be paid on or before [date payment due]. We both also agree that neither of us shall remain as the beneficiary on any insurance policy carried by the other.

⑭ Fill in the total number of pages and each spouse initial the page.

Child Custody Questionnaire Instructions

If you have the issue of child custody, you need to fill out the Child Custody Questionnaire which is located on the CD. Two copies should be made of this form, one for each spouse to complete. This form is designed to assist you in understanding what factors are pertinent to your discussions regarding custody and visitation. Each of you should complete your questionnaire by honestly and completely answering the questions. Although the questions relate to one child, if you have more than one child please include answers on the form relating to each child. Many of the questions relate to which parent in general currently provides the primary care for the children. Your answers will be the basis for your custody discussions with your spouse and will allow both of you to focus on the relevant issues. After each of you have completed the questionnaire and read this section, you will then confer with your spouse and jointly complete a Custody and Visitation Worksheet that is explained later in this chapter.

Locate the Child Custody Questionnaire on the CD and fill it out now.

Child Custody and Visitation

Determining which parent is to have custody of a minor child is one of the most difficult decisions that you will encounter in your divorce. Judges and legislators have also grappled extensively with the difficulty of this decision. In recent years, certain legal trends have emerged regarding how an impartial judge might decide which parent is to be awarded custody of a minor child. These relatively new legal doctrines are a clear break with many of the traditional methods that were previously used to determine custody. In the past, there were several legal doctrines that governed child custody decisions. Most notably, there was a very strong presumption that a mother should be awarded custody of any child. This presumption stemmed directly from the traditional, though not universal, role of the mother as homemaker in our society at that time. The younger the child was, the stronger the presumption that custody should be given to the mother. This doctrine was known as the "tender years doctrine" and carried very considerable weight in legal custody decisions. If the child in question was a girl, the presumption that custody be awarded to the mother was almost insurmountable. Effectively, the only method by which a father could get custody of a minor child was to prove in open court that the mother was totally unfit to care for the child. This required, in most instances, that the father and his attorney attempt to paint as negative a picture as possible of the mother for the court. Innocent past actions and harmless present circumstances were often distorted and misrepresented to the court in attempts to have a mother declared unfit. This type of custody battle provided a forum for some of the most psychologically and emotionally damaging court proceedings in our society's history. The traumatic effects on the children involved in these proceedings were particularly tragic.

In an attempt to overcome the type of proceeding that encouraged the dredging up of irrelevant details of each parent's private life, a doctrine known as the "best interests of the child" was developed. Under this legal theory, the mental, physical, and emotional well-being of the child was considered paramount in any legal proceeding regarding custody. Theoretically, a parent's actions were pertinent only to the extent that they had an impact on the child. In practice, however, much irrelevant testimony and evidence were still allowed in custody battles. Detailed lists of factors were also developed to guide a court in determining what was actually important in making decisions regarding the custody of a child. Most states continue to provide these guidelines for custody decisions.

In the 1970s, extensive legal battles were waged in attempts to overturn the "tender years" doctrine and allow fathers an equal footing in custody disputes. For the most part, the battles were successful. Fathers do have an equal legal ability now to obtain custody of any minor children. However, despite the changes in the law that provide that both parents have an equal right to custody, mothers are still overwhelmingly the parent who retains custody. In over 90 percent of all custody cases, it is the mother who is awarded custody of the children. There is also an unhappy consequence of the legal changes that make it easier for fathers to request custody. Some fathers and their attorneys have unscrupulously used this right as a weapon to pressure the mother into trading her property, alimony, or child support rights for uncontested custody of a child. Fathers who have no desire at all

236

to actually have custody have used this manipulative tactic to prey upon the maternal fear of losing a child. In order to be certain that they do not lose custody of their child, many mothers have given up their rights to substantial property and support. Any attempts to engage in this tactic are highly disfavored by courts. If you feel that this tactic is being used in your situation, you should immediately consult an attorney for legal guidance.

Another legal doctrine has emerged recently however, that allows both parents much greater flexibility in sharing parental responsibility. Joint or shared custody has been developed in an effort to allow a child reasonable access to both parents while growing up. Some confusion has resulted from the use of this phrase and it is important to understand exactly what joint custody is and is not. Some definitions are offered here in an attempt to clear up this confusion. Unfortunately, some people (lawyers and judges included) will use some of these terms interchangeably or incorrectly. Be certain in your discussions regarding custody that you both agree on exactly what you are taking about.

Types of Custody Arrangements

In the past, *sole custody* by one parent was the standard form of custody. Under sole custody, one parent was awarded both the *physical* custody of the child (the right to have the child live with the custodial parent) and the *legal* custody (the right to make all of the major decisions relating to the upbringing of the child). Decisions regarding which school the child should attend, whether the child should have medical attention, what religion the child should be taught, and all decisions regarding the child's activities, conduct, and well-being are the responsibility of the parent with sole custody. In most sole custody arrangements, the non-custodial parent is afforded some type of reasonable visitation rights unless there is a danger of harm to the child. This form of custody arrangement, with sole custody to one parent and liberal visitation for the other parent, is still the predominant method used in the majority of divorce situations involving children.

Joint or *shared custody*, on the other hand, is an attempt to allow both parents a voice in the major decisions involved in the raising of a child. Joint custody is generally divided into two separate rights: joint *physical* custody (actual custody of the child), and joint *legal* custody (rights to share in important decisions regarding the child). While both parents may be awarded joint physical custody of a child, generally one parent is still awarded sole physical custody of the child, with the other parent being allowed reasonable visitation privileges. However, both parents are awarded joint legal custody of the child. This rather confusing terminology simply means that both parents will continue to share the rights and responsibilities that come with parenthood. They will both have a right to jointly make the major decisions that will affect the child's life: religious, educational, medical, and social decisions. Naturally, the parent with actual physical custody for the majority of the time is allowed individual control over the minor day-to-day decisions that must be made. In many joint custody situations, the actual physical custody time a child spends with each parent mirrors sole custody situations. It is the decision-making process affecting the child that is the responsibility shared by the parents.

Divided or *alternating custody* is another form of custody (in some areas this is referred to as *split custody*; in others, as *joint physical custody*). Under this form of custody, each parent is awarded actual physical and legal custody for alternating periods of time. A child may be awarded to each parent for six months out of a year, or for alternating months or weeks. This type of custody arrangement is not generally favored by either the courts or child psychologists. It is seen as emotionally difficult for a child to be continually shifted back and forth between each parent, without a sense of where his or her "home" is truly located. In some situations, however, it may be appropriate.

Another alternative that has also proved to be difficult for the children involved is also known as *split custody*. This type of custody has been used in the past to attempt to achieve a technical fairness when there is more than one child by giving each parent physical custody of one or more of the children. For the children involved, however, this constitutes not only a splitting up of one's parents, but also a forced separation from one's siblings. Arrangements of this type are not favored by courts.

Currently, there seems to be a general national trend towards approval of joint custody arrangements. The encouragement of frequent and continuing contact with both parents is clearly preferable to fostering single-parent childhoods for children of divorce. These types of arrangements work well and are a benefit to the child, however, only if both parents can cooperate maturely in the necessary decision-making. For joint custody to be successful, both parents must be willing to compromise for the sake of the child and to consider the well-being of the child as the most important factor. In situations where there is genuine hostility between the parents, however, one parent should generally be granted sole physical and legal custody. This is often the clearest and most definite method to establish which parent has the necessary authority to make the major decisions. Some states have established a legal preference for joint custody, while others clearly state that there is no preference for one particular type of custody. Most states specifically allow for joint custody, while others have no particular statutory authorization for any type of shared custody. In all states, however, there is legal precedent to allow custody arrangements that are most beneficial to the children involved.

The most recent trend in custody legislation and court decisions provides one of the most common-sense approaches to the problem. Increasingly, courts are looking at a child's day-to-day circumstances in an effort to determine which parent has been the primary caregiver of the child. The parent who has provided most of the day-to-day care for the child during the marriage is then considered to be the most likely candidate to continue on as the primary custodian of the child after the divorce. The preference is given to the parent who has actively participated in caring for the child and performed the majority of the parenting activities: preparing meals, readying the child for sleep, sharing in his or her playtime, dealing with medical problems, participating in the child's education, etc. This method does not presuppose that either parent has an entitlement to being awarded custody, but rather is based on an examination of the reality of the burdens of parenthood. The decision is based on the practical considerations of which parent has provided the most time, care, and guidance to the child prior to the actual divorce. It allows each parent an equal right to earn the custody of a child by providing care for the child before the divorce proceeding begins. This method of selection of the parent to have physical custody places the greatest emphasis on which one has been providing the most parental care for the child prior to the divorce. Selection of the primary caregiver as continuing custodian generally fosters a home life of stability and continuity for the child. In the family upheaval caused by divorce, this factor deserves considerable attention.

Visitation

In any custody arrangement, and in all states, the parent who is not awarded actual physical custody of a child has a legal right to reasonable and frequent visitation with the child. Unless there is a genuine and substantiated fear of emotional or physical harm to the child, such visitation is generally allowed on an unsupervised basis and in the non-custodial parent's home. A court does have the authority to completely deny any visitation to a parent who has abused a child. In most cases, however, reasonable visitation is standard. When, where, and how long such visitation should be is one of the major decisions that you and your spouse will have to work out as you discuss your children's future. Visitation should be structured to allow frequent contact between the non-custodial parent and the child and should attempt to fit into the child's normal schedule. The schedule should be firm enough to allow for a degree of long-term planning, but flexible enough to allow for reasonable changes. Remember that any visitation schedule is only a starting point. Reasonable adjustments can be made as you and your spouse become more comfortable in your roles as divorced parents. Visitation is as much the child's right as it is the parents'. As you approach the decisions on visitation, you should remember certain points. You should keep in mind that:

- Visitation with the other parent is necessary and helpful for your child's normal development and future welfare
- Visitation should be a pleasant and positive experience for both the parents and the child
- Visitation is a time for the parent and child to be with each other and enjoy each other's company and should be maintained on a clear schedule and without interference
- Visitation exchanges may be the only time that you see your spouse after the divorce. Both of you should show mutual respect for the other while in the child's presence

As you and your spouse discuss specific visitation terms, you should make every effort to insure that both of you are treated fairly regarding visitation. As you discuss the amount of visitation, put yourself in the other's place. Imagine that your only contact with your child will be the visitation that is agreed upon. You would want it to be as liberal and as frequent as possible. An agreement that is fair and reasonable for both parents will generally be the best for your child.

Modification of Custody and Visitation Terms

Finally, in all states, any custody and visitation agreements that are reached between parents remain subject to court modification. Of all the terms of your Marital Settlement Agreement, the terms that relate to the care and custody of your children will receive the closest scrutiny by a court. The court has total authority in this area and has the power to totally disregard any agreement that is felt to be harmful to the children. In fact, in many states the court has the authority to appoint a lawyer who will represent the interests of the child in a contested custody situation. This court-appointed legal guardian of a child's legal rights is generally referred to as a *guardian ad litem*. In the vast majority of cases, however, a court will accept reasonable custody and visitation provisions contained in marital settlement agreements, particularly if it appears that such agreements were obtained through thoughtful and mature negotiation. Most judges, however, are conservative when it comes to the rights of children and will not favor any unusual custody arrangements that fall outside of the traditional boundaries. Recognize also that although the court that handles your divorce will have the right to modify your custody agreement at any time in the future, it is much more difficult to have such modifications made after your divorce is finalized. For the sake of promoting a sense of stability in a child's life, courts are somewhat reluctant to make changes in settled custody arrangements. For this reason, you and your spouse should work diligently to attempt to initially fashion a fair agreement for custody and visitation. As you examine your own lives and consider the realities of custody and visitation, keep these legal trends in mind. They are what guide most courts in their deliberations of custody disputes. Decisions on custody and visitation, however, are best made by both parents in a cooperative manner without the involvement of courts and lawyers. Cooperating parents can adopt any practical arrangement that provides a reasonable resolution to the difficult problems of dividing a child's time between two parents who no longer desire to live together.

Both parents deserve an opportunity to interact with their child during childhood. More importantly, your child deserves to have both of you available for love, affection, and guidance as he or she grows up. You should make every possible attempt to work out a reasonable child custody arrangement that is satisfactory to both of you and your child. However, if you and your spouse are unable to reach an agreement, the use of an impartial mediator may be useful. In child custody disputes, mediation is the preferred first alternative for providing a solution. If personal negotiation and mediation both fail to help you achieve an agreement, a resort to the legal process may be necessary. However, keep in mind the tremendous psychological and emotional toll that a bitter court battle over custody can have on both you and your child. If your spouse hires a lawyer to engage in a custody battle, you should, however, seek legal assistance immediately.

As you examine your particular situation, you should attempt to realistically assess what type of child custody and visitation arrangements would be best suited to your family. Remember that you and your spouse are in the best position to clearly understand the particular circumstances that influence your lives and the life of your child. Although a judge will make custody decisions in contested cases, a court decision will never be as meaningful to a child as one that his or her parents have worked out in an amicable and loving manner.

Child Custody Jurisdiction

Related to the actual custody decisions is the issue of which specific state has the proper authority and jurisdiction to hear a child custody case. All 50 states and Washington D.C. have now enacted a uniform law relating to jurisdiction in custody matters: The Uniform Child Custody Jurisdiction Act. This legislation was passed in an effort to create a uniform nationwide system for determining which individual state should be the proper forum for custody decisions in every situation. It is an attempt to deal with the problems of child-snatching by parents who are dissatisfied with a particular state's custody decision. In the past, some parents who have lost custody battles have taken their children across state lines in an attempt to have another state's court award custody to them. This new uniform legislation provides a set of standardized guidelines to determine which single state should have the sole power and authority to decide the custody of a child in all situations. The decision as to which state will have jurisdiction is based on a variety of factors, such as: the length of time the child has resided in the state, whether there have been any previous court proceedings concerning the child's custody, the residency of both parents, etc. If you and your spouse: (1) have never before been involved in any child custody proceedings concerning your children; (2) are both able to agree upon the arrangements regarding your child's care; and (3) both live in the same state; then you may assume that the state that you both live in presently is the state with the proper jurisdiction to decide your child's custody. If, however, you, your spouse, or your child have previously been involved in child custody litigation in another state, you will need to consult a lawyer for advice relating to the court with proper jurisdiction in your particular situation.

Custody and Visitation Worksheet Instructions

With all of the various factors that influence the decisions regarding child custody firmly in mind, you and your spouse should be ready to approach the actual mechanics of custody and visitation arrangements. The Child Custody Worksheet (found on the CD) sets out the most common questions that arise in custody situations. You and your spouse should fill in this Worksheet together as the decisions that are made regarding custody and visitation must be arrived at in as amicable a manner as possible. As parents, you will both spend the rest of your lives under the terms of the agreement that you reach regarding custody and visitation rights. After completing the worksheet, various clauses are listed outlining custody and visitation arrangements. Several are provided, ranging from very simple statements of general rights to detailed provisions regarding times and dates. You and your spouse may not wish to make as detailed an arrangement as this worksheet provides. In such case, you may choose to use the simplified version of the custody and visitation clause.

Locate the Custody and Visitation Worksheet on the CD and fill it out now.

Child Custody and Visitation Marital Settlement Agreement Clauses

⑳ **Marital Settlement Agreement Clauses for Child Custody and Visitation**: On the following pages are various clauses that may be used for completing your Marital Settlement Agreement. There are many possible arrangements that may be made for custody and visitation. They can range from very brief to extremely complex and lengthy statements. Listed below are four separate child custody and visitation clauses. The first is a very simplified clause, the second moderately-detailed, and the third and fourth are very comprehensive. According to your particular situation, you and your spouse should read through each of these clauses and choose the one with which you feel most comfortable. In each of the two more detailed clauses, you will be given various choices regarding specific provisions of your arrangements. You may wish to add other specific provisions to these clauses that you both agree are important. You may do so if you use simple straightforward language that you both agree clearly states your agreements. The particular child custody and visitation clause that you choose will be used when you prepare your actual Marital Settlement Agreement. Please refer back to this section at that time. Fill in the appropriate choices for the clause that you have chosen and type (or cut and paste from the text clauses) this clause into your Agreement where indicated on the sample agreement form.

Sole Custody and Visitation Clause (Basic Agreement): The following clause is a very simplified and straightforward agreement relating to your child's custody arrangements. It provides for sole custody to be given to one parent. It should be used only if both you and your spouse are cooperative and amicable in your relationship and it is likely that you will remain that way in the future. This approach allows a wide range of flexibility in setting up visitation and vacation arrangements. Such arrangements are not spelled out at all in this clause, but are left for you and your spouse to structure as they arise. The very flexibility of this approach has some inherent dangers, however. Since there are no definite details or dates and times of visitation provided, there is a danger that arguments may erupt regarding interpretation of this clause. This clause should, therefore, be used only if you both feel that you have a clear understanding of each other's views and feelings regarding custody and visitation and have complete faith that you and your spouse will be able to agree on the details of visitation in the future. Even if you and your spouse are currently on friendly terms, it may be wise to use a clause with a more detailed schedule of visitation terms. Then you can always mutually agree after the divorce to allow different visitation, but you will at least have a written base of minimum terms. If you wish to provide for joint custody, you will need to use one of the more detailed clauses later in this section.

[   ]   We both agree that it is in the best interests of our child(ren) that the (Wife or Husband) have sole physical and legal custody of our child(ren). We also agree that the other parent has the right to be with our child(ren) on a frequent and liberal basis through reasonable visitation, at such times as we and the child(ren) can agree upon. We agree that we will share as equally as possible the right to be with our child(ren) on holidays, birthdays, and during the child(ren)'s school vacations. We agree that our child(ren)'s time with either of us should not interfere with his or her (their) attendance at school. We also agree that the parent with custody should have the right to make the major decisions regarding the care and upbringing of the child(ren), but that the other parent has the right to be notified of any major decisions. We both also agree that, in the event of divorce or dissolution of marriage, our child(ren) will be known by the last name of (desired name).

Sole Custody and Visitation Clause (with Visitation Schedule): This clause is somewhat more detailed than the above clause. In particular, it allows for provisions to be made for specific times and dates for visitation with the non-custodial parent. This detailed schedule has the advantage of putting your agreements in writing as to how to deal with visitation. This will generally lessen the opportunity for future disagreements to arise over what was actually agreed upon during your discussions. This clause also provides for sole physical and legal custody to be given to one parent with reasonable visitation rights for the non-custodial parent. If you and your spouse have agreed that joint custody is preferable, you should use one of the more detailed clauses that follow later in this section.

[   ]   We both agree that it is in the best interests of our child(ren) that the (Wife or Husband) have sole physical and legal custody of our child(ren). We also agree that the other parent has the right to be with our child(ren) on a frequent and liberal basis through reasonable visitation, at such times as we and the child(ren) can agree upon. If in the future we are unable to agree upon visitation, the (Wife or Husband) will have the right to be with our child(ren) as follows:

1. On the following holidays during even-numbered years:
2. On the following holidays during odd-numbered years:
3. On the following dates and times each (every other) weekend:
4. On the following dates and times during each (every other) week:
5. For the following vacation periods each year:

We agree that our child(ren)'s time with either of us should not interfere with attendance at school. We also agree that the parent with custody should have the right to make the major decisions regarding the care and upbringing of our child(ren), but that the other parent should have the right to be notified of any major decisions. We both also agree that, in the event of divorce or dissolution of marriage, our child(ren) will be known by the last name of (desired name).

Custody and Visitation Clause (Joint Legal and Sole Physical Custody): The following clause provides a very detailed and comprehensive agreement for joint custody. It should be used in all situations in which both you and your spouse have decided that joint decision-making but sole physical custody with one parent is the best alternative. In some states, a detailed agreement of this nature is a requirement for both parents being awarded joint or shared custody. This agreement provides for both parents to share in the major decisions and lists the general categories of such decisions. It provides that the home of one parent shall be the primary residence of the child, but that the other parent be allowed frequent and liberal visitation and contact with the child. Specific visitation provisions are also included. In addition, various other rights and responsibilities of the parents are spelled out in detail in this clause.

[   ]   We both agree that it is in the best interests of our child(ren) that we both have joint legal custody of our child(ren). We also agree that it is in the best interests of our child(ren) that

the (Wife or Husband) have sole physical custody of our child(ren). We acknowledge that our child(ren) presently live(s) with the (Wife or Husband) and that the actual physical residence of our child(ren) may be changed at any time as we may mutually agree. All decisions pertaining to the education, discipline, health, extracurricular and summer activities, religious training, medical and dental care, and welfare of our child(ren) will be decided by both of us after reasonable and adequate discussion. We also agree that the parent with physical custody shall have control over the minor day-to-day decisions affecting the child(ren), including any medical or dental emergencies. We agree that if, after reasonable attempts, we are unable to reach an agreement on any of the decisions affecting our child(ren), we will jointly seek professional mediation to resolve our differences. We also agree that each of us has the right to know of any circumstances or decisions that affect our child(ren) and that each of us has the right to any medical, dental, or school records of our child(ren). Neither of us will do anything to hamper or interfere with the natural and continuing relationship between our child(ren) and the other parent. We both also agree that, in the event of divorce or dissolution of marriage, our child(ren) will be known by the last name of (desired name). We both realize that the well-being of our child(ren) is of paramount importance and, therefore, we agree that our child(ren) should have as much contact as possible with the parent who does not have physical custody and that our child(ren) may visit that parent as often as may be agreed upon. We additionally agree to use our very best efforts to insure that our child(ren) receive(s) the most care, love, and affection possible from both parents throughout his or her (their) entire childhood. Although visitation may be scheduled more often, the parent who does not have physical custody will have the right to be with our child(ren) at least as follows:

1. On the following holidays during even-numbered years:
2. On the following holidays during odd-numbered years:
3. On the following dates and times each (every other) weekend:
4. On the following dates and times during each (every other) week:
5. For the following vacation periods each year:

Custody and Visitation Clause (Joint Legal and Physical Custody): This clause is the most detailed and comprehensive provided. This does not necessarily mean that this is the most appropriate clause in all situations. The following clause provides for both parents to share the physical and legal custody of their child. This clause still designates one parent's home as the primary residence of the child and provides for visitation with the other parent. Most of the other terms of this clause are identical to the preceding clause. For practical purposes, the day-to-day lives of parents and children under this clause would be very similar to their lives under the terms of the preceding clause. Legally, however, there are slight differences between these clauses. Under this clause, both parents have the right to retain the actual physical custody of the child. For this reason, there is an agreement included in this clause regarding taking the child out of the state in which you both live. Where there is a genuine and honest joint effort and agreement to cooperate in raising a child, this clause may provide the most even and equal division of the rights to the upbringing and custody of the child.

[   ]   We both agree that it is in the best interests of our child(ren) that we both have joint legal and physical custody of our child(ren). We also agree that it is in the best interests of our child(ren) that the home of the (Wife or Husband) be the primary residence of the child(ren). We acknowledge that our child(ren) presently live(s) with the (Wife or Husband) and that the actual physical residence of our child(ren) may be changed at any time as we may mutually agree. All decisions pertaining to the place of residence, discipline, education, health, extracurricular and summer activities, vacations, religious training, medical and dental care, and welfare of our child(ren) will be decided by both of us after reasonable and adequate discussion. We also agree that the parent with physical custody shall have control over the minor day-to-day decisions affecting the child(ren), including any medical or dental emergencies. We agree that if, after reasonable attempts, we are unable to reach an agreement on any of the decisions affecting our child(ren), we will jointly seek professional mediation to resolve our differences. We also agree that each of us has the right to know of any circumstances or decisions that affect our child(ren) and that each of us has the right to any medical, dental, or school records of our child(ren). Neither of us will do anything to hamper or interfere with the natural and continuing relationship between our child(ren) and the other parent. We both also agree that, in the event of divorce or dissolution of marriage, our child(ren) will be known by the last name of (desired name). We both agree that frequent and continuing contact with both parents is vital to our child(ren), and therefore we both agree that neither of us will permanently remove our child(ren) from this state without the express written permission of the other parent. We additionally agree to use our very best efforts to insure that our child(ren) receive(s) the most care, love, and affection possible from both parents throughout his or her (their) entire childhood. We both realize that the well-being of our child(ren) is of paramount importance and, therefore, we agree that our child(ren) should have as much contact as possible with the parent who does not have physical custody and that our child(ren) may visit that parent as often as may be agreed upon. Although contact may be scheduled more often, the parent who does not live in the primary physical residence of the child(ren) will have the right to be with our child(ren) at least as follows:

1. On the following holidays during even-numbered years:
2. On the following holidays during odd-numbered years:
3. On the following dates and times each (every other) weekend:
4. On the following dates and times during each (every other) week:
5. For the following vacation periods each year:

⑭ Fill in the total number of pages and have each spouse initial the page.

Child Support

Each year, over one million children experience the divorce of their parents. Too often, when children are part of a divorcing family, a devastating legal battle is waged over the right to retain custody. The emotional and psychological scars that children receive in these fierce custody wars are perhaps the most tragic results of divorce. Unfortunately, in too many instances, children become pawns in a destructive game of revenge and vindictiveness between their divorcing parents. If you and your spouse have children, the decisions that you will face regarding their custody and visitation will perhaps be the most difficult of the entire divorce process. But in many respects, they may also be the most important. Your children's future well-being will depend directly on your ability to come to a reasonable agreement with your spouse regarding custody and visitation. If you have children, you must understand that your divorce will not end the relationship between you and your spouse. You will both still continue to be parents, even though you will no longer be wife and husband. Because of the necessity for this ongoing relationship, it is very important to keep your settlement discussions regarding your children on a calm and peaceful level. In many cases there is a temptation to allow personal animosity toward your spouse to enter into the discussions regarding your children. If you personally no longer wish to live with your spouse, you may feel that you don't want your children to live with him or her either. There may also be a tendency to attempt to vent your frustration at the prospect of divorce through a battle over custody. For your children's sake, you must make every effort to keep your discussions about custody on a reasonable and mature basis. Your children will have to live the rest of their lives with the results of you and your spouse's custody decisions.

Closely related to the decisions that must be made regarding child custody are those decisions relating to the support of a child. In most instances, the parent who does not have physical custody of a child must provide child support to the parent who has custody. Child support agreements are essentially financial in nature. Much of the information that you and your spouse have already provided each other in the Financial Statements will be used in determining the proper support amounts. However, a Child Support Worksheet is provided on the CD to allow you to gather the necessary information for these decisions.

Before you and your spouse consider the legal aspects of child support, you should both understand that child support terms are the provisions of marital settlement agreements and divorce orders that are most often defaulted upon or ignored. Tragically, this has resulted in the creation of a new class of poverty-level individuals: children of divorced parents. The majority of court-ordered child support payments are neither paid in full nor on time. Nearly one-third of the children entitled to child support receive no support at all. The reasons for this tragedy are many, but perhaps the most important stems from the frustration of the non-custodial parent having to pay for the support for children that he or she does not live with or raise. If you and your spouse can come to a reasonable and workable agreement regarding the custody and visitation arrangements for your child, there will be a far greater chance that your child support agreement will also be seen as reasonable. As you approach your child support discussions, please keep these tragic statistics firmly in mind.

The Law of Child Support

Both natural parents of a minor child have a legal obligation to provide adequate support for the child until the child reaches 18 years of age (21 in some states). This legal duty includes providing food, clothing, shelter, medical care, and education for a child. This is the law in every state. Parents of adopted children also have this same obligation. Child support, however, is not merely the delivery of a monthly support payment. It is a legal, moral, and ethical obligation to provide full care and support for your offspring. Divorce does not end this legal obligation for support. It merely complicates the duty. Both parents have an equal duty to support their children. In the vast majority of divorces that involve children however, the mother is awarded physical custody of those children. Also, in the majority of family situations, it is the mother who earns a disproportionately lower income than the father. Thus, in most divorce situations involving children, there will be an immediate and definite need for considerable child support to be provided by the father. Regardless of which parent has physical custody and even when the incomes of both parents are equal, both parents still need to provide their fair share of support for the child. A child should not be forced to suffer economically because of the divorce of his or her parents. When a single family unit is divided into two households upon divorce, the total living costs will naturally escalate. Two homes must be maintained instead of one. Two sets of furniture, appliances, and housewares must be provided. Two cars, two televisions, two of almost every household item will need to be purchased and maintained. Unfortunately, the income of the divorced family will not increase. In many cases, in fact, it may actually decrease as the parent with custody may find it more difficult to maintain a full-time job. Because both parents are no longer able to share their time with the child as easily, child care costs may also increase. The goals of child support laws are to achieve a fair division of the income of both parents in order to provide for the satisfactory support of the children of a marriage. As much as is possible, a child should be entitled to share in the income of both parents, despite their divorce.

Federal legislation (the Family Support Act of 1988) requires each state to provide some type of formula or guidelines for the determination of child support awards. In the attempt to provide specific financial guidelines for child support provisions, many states have adopted detailed legislation and rules regarding how to arrive at a fair support amount. Some states have provided only simple formulas. Included in this book is a general set of guidelines for determining child support. In recent years, these child support guidelines have tended to become more detailed, specific, and mathematical. The newest versions of child support legislation are full of various charts and financial formulas for determining the correct amount of support. These detailed guidelines are an attempt to take the mystery out of the manner in which a court determines how much child support to award. In most states that have such guidelines, however, the rules are only to be used to provide a structure for determining a minimum amount of child support. A court has the authority to order more or less child support if necessary.

While each state's guidelines may be somewhat different, they all generally require that if the non-custodial parent has sufficient income, he or she must provide a specific level of monthly support to the parent who has custody of the child. Increasingly, states are adopting legislation that goes beyond simply providing a monthly payment for child support. Some of these recent laws may require various non-monetary forms of support: that a parent provide health insurance, dental insurance, and life insurance for the parent with the child as sole beneficiary, or that the family home not be sold for a particular period of time. All of these provisions are an attempt to provide sufficient security for a child of divorce to prevent the child from requiring welfare or other social service support from the state. Please check the Appendix for information on your state's specific statutory child support guidelines.

You and your spouse must take into consideration that the court always has absolute authority over child support decisions. This power is retained regardless of any agreement that you may reach. The obligation for child support cannot be bargained away in your negotiations. Courts are very protective of the rights of a child to be supported by both parents and will not accept the terms of any settlement agreement that does not provide for reasonable levels of support. Although courts will often accept the child support terms to which parents agree in settlement negotiations, the courts can and will ignore any agreements they find unreasonable. Ultimately, it is the court that has final authority to issue support orders for dependent children and they take that power very seriously. Much as you cannot trade away the custody of your child for monetary rewards, you cannot bargain away your child's rights to support. The marital settlement agreement that you and your spouse sign will bind the two of you, but will not bind your children. Their rights to reasonable support may be enforced by a court if necessary, despite your and your spouse's agreement.

Enforcement and Modification of Child Support

Of all the provisions of a final divorce, child support obligations are, unfortunately, the ones that are most often ignored. Over one-half of court-ordered child support payments are not paid in full or on time. Nearly one-third of qualifying children receive no child support at all. Recent studies have shown that the income level of the divorced parents has no bearing on whether a child will receive adequate child support. Unfortunately, wealthy parents are just as likely to default on child support payments as poor parents. There is now a concerted national effort to collect and enforce overdue child support payments. This effort is backed by very comprehensive and powerful laws that are beginning to turn the tide of non-payment of child support. In recent years, all 50 states have enacted legislation to deal with this problem: the Uniform Reciprocal Enforcement of Support Act. Many states have also enacted other strict laws dealing with methods to enforce child support obligations. In addition, the federal government has enacted very tough child support enforcement legislation. Child support provisions in a marital settlement agreement or final divorce order are always subject to modification, regardless of any attempt to limit such future modification. The courts always have the authority to increase or decrease the amount of the support. However, modifying a child support order in the future involves a showing of changed circumstances and an often lengthy lawsuit and court hearing. It is far easier to attempt to anticipate any lifestyle and income changes in advance than to resort to the courts to keep changing the amount of child support.

General Child Support Guidelines

The guidelines provided here are just that: guidelines. They are not intended to be an ultimate method for determining support payments in all cases. They should be reviewed and used while considering all of the other relevant factors in your particular situation. The determination of the proper amount of child support in each case will always be difficult. A careful balance must be obtained between providing an adequate level of support and overburdening the parent who must pay the support. If the support payments are set at a level that becomes a tremendous financial burden to the paying parent, there will be a tendency and temptation to default on the payments. On the other hand, if the payments are too low, the child will suffer the consequences. Both parents must work together carefully to actually determine a fair and reasonable amount of support. Care must be taken to keep the negotiations on a mature and rational basis. Discussions involving child support have the very real potential of deteriorating into hostile arguments. Of all the aspects of divorce, child support obligations have spawned more post-divorce lawsuits than any other.

Many different methods of determining the amount of child support payments have been utilized around the country. A mathematical formula method of determining child support has been adopted recently in many states. Generally, this method consists of determining the actual monthly needs of the child based on the particular circumstances of the family and the ability of the parents to pay. Other methods rely upon charts of child support amounts. The method of determining the proper amount of child support that is provided in this book was adapted from the guidelines used in many different states and is a combination of the most common methods in use. It attempts to take both parents' economic situations into account. Your particular state may use a similar method or a variation. You should refer to the Appendix for information regarding your state's specific requirements. In addition, you may wish to check with the clerk of the court in the county where you live to see if there are any local child support guidelines or rules in effect. In addition, many states have specific child support worksheets that are to be used. Check the Divorce Appendix on the CD and with your court clerk.

Child Support Worksheet and Child Support Guidelines Instructions

To determine the figures necessary for the calculations on the Child Support Worksheet, please refer back to the Financial Statement that you and your spouse prepared when you negotiated the division of your property. The Child Support Guidelines Chart is provided on the CD as an example of how various states have decided to calculate minimum child support amounts. You should use the highest amount provided by the calculations as a starting point for your discussions. Other factors, in addition to income and deductions, may then be used to adjust the amount accordingly. To use this method, you must first determine the monthly net income of each parent. To obtain this figure, combine all of the income of each parent from any source. Then, subtract the mandatory deductions from this income as shown on the child support worksheet (found on the CD). This will give you the monthly net income of each parent for child support purposes. If there are seasonal or monthly fluctuations in the parent's income or deductions, you may wish to determine the income and deductions on an annual basis and then divide that amount by 12 for the net monthly income.

Next, combine the two monthly net income amounts for a total net family income. Using this combined net monthly family income, consult the child support chart to determine the total minimum amount of child support that is necessary. Always go to the next higher level if your combined monthly income falls in between the amounts shown. As with all decisions concerning children, the courts will always favor the decision that benefits the children the most. Remember, the amount shown is only the general minimum amount necessary and the actual amount of support required may be higher (or even lower) than this amount, depending on the particular circumstances of your situation. Federal law requires that if a judge decides to award less child support than is warranted by a state's guidelines, the specific reasons must be stated. Also remember that your particular state may have a slightly different set of guidelines or various other charts for determining support. Note also that the amount shown on the chart is the amount of support required by *both* parents together. The amount of the non-custodial parent's individual share is determined as explained in the next paragraph.

After the amount on the chart is determined, the non-custodial parent's share must be determined. Divide the net monthly income of the parent without custody by the total net monthly family income to determine the fractional or percentage share of the total child support. This figure multiplied times the figure from the support guideline chart will be the minimum monthly support required to be paid by the non-custodial parent. To this amount should then be added any childcare costs that are required to enable the parent with custody to obtain employment. This final general minimum figure should be adjusted up or down based on the following factors and any other relevant information:

- Any extraordinary medical, dental, or health expenses
- Any independent income of the child
- Any seasonal variations in a parent's income
- The age of the child, taking into consideration the greater needs of older children
- Any special needs that have previously been met by the family budget
- The total assets available to the parents and the child
- The custody arrangements for the child

In situations where there is joint physical custody, the actual amount of time the child spends with each parent may be particularly relevant. The amount of the actual payment as calculated using this method depends upon the income, deductions, and childcare expenses of both parents. If the income of the parent with custody is very low, the non-custodial parent will be required to pay all or the bulk of the amount of child support shown on the chart. On the other hand, if the income of the parent with custody is very high and that of the non-custodial parent is low, the required child support payment may be very low.

Locate the Child Support Worksheet on the CD and fill it out now.

Child Support Marital Settlement Agreement Clauses

㉑ **Clauses for Child Support**: Once you have determined the specific amount that the monthly child support payments should be, it is a relatively simple matter to include that provision in a clause for your Marital Settlement Agreement. A standard clause for this purpose is set out below. There is also a provision regarding insurance that requires that, as additional child support, the parent who is to pay the support must maintain a life insurance policy naming the children as beneficiaries and health insurance coverage for the children. This provision is highly recommended and is required in some states. Federal law mandates that states require a parent responsible for child support to include any children under a health and dental insurance plan if such a plan is available to the parent through their place of employment or otherwise at a relatively low cost. The life insurance provision provides some measure of security and insurance protection for the children in the event of death of the paying parent. The health insurance protection provides the child with protection in case of illness or injury. Fill in the appropriate choices and then type this clause into your Agreement where indicated on the sample form.

[   ]   We both agree that the (Wife or Husband) will pay to the other spouse, for child support, the amount of $ (amount of each child's support payment) per child per month, for a total monthly payment of $ (total monthly combined child support payment amount). The payments will begin on the (date of first payment) and will continue for each child until that child has reached the age of majority, died, become self-supporting, or married. We both agree that this obligation is subject to modification by a court at any time. We both further agree that should the parent obligated to pay the support receive a salary or income increase in the future, the amount of child support due per child per month shall be increased proportionately. The parent obligated to pay support agrees to notify the other parent immediately of any salary or income increase. As additional child support, we both agree that as long as support payments are due, the (Wife or Husband) will carry and maintain life insurance in the amount of $ (amount of life insurance coverage), naming our child(ren) as sole irrevocable beneficiary(ies). The parent obligated to provide such insurance will provide the other parent with annual proof of such coverage. As additional child support, we both agree that as long as support payments are due, the (Wife or Husband) will carry and maintain adequate health, dental, and hospitalization insurance for the child(ren)'s benefit, pay any required deductible amount, and pay for any necessary medical or dental expenses of the child(ren) that are not covered by such insurance. The parent obligated to provide such insurance will provide the other parent with annual proof of such coverage.

In addition to selecting the amount of the payment, another child support issue must be addressed. A decision must be reached on how the payment is to be made. In response to the enormous rate of default on child support payments, all states in recent years and in response to federal legislation have adopted various methods to attempt to insure that the payments will continue to be paid and paid on time. These methods range from automatic wage assignments and withholding of wages, to having the support payments made through the clerk of the court or some other government agency. The most common arrangement is for the paying parent to be required to make the payments directly to the clerk of the court. Once the payment is received, the clerk then pays the parent to whom the payment is due. There are several benefits to having the payments made in this indirect way. By having the payment made through an official government body instead of directly to the other parent, there is an official documented record of the amount and date the payment is made. Furthermore, many states have programs to collect past due payments that will automatically go into effect when a payment is missed. This takes much of the burden of enforcement off the parent who is to be paid the support.

This book offers two alternatives for this situation. The first alternative is for the payments, in the event of a divorce, to be made to an official state agency or court official for disbursement to the other parent. The other alternative is for the payments to be made directly to the other parent. Most courts will allow a couple to waive any requirement that the payments be made through the state if the agreement to make the child support payments directly to the parent is in the form of a marital settlement agreement. To allow the payments to be made directly to the parent, there must be valid reason why the parents wish to avoid the indirect payment method. Good reasons might be that the parent who is to make the payments is very reliable or has established a clear record of making the payments on time while the parents were separated. However, if there is any doubt as to whether the payments may be paid late or not at all after a divorce, you should choose the alternative that requires the payments to be made through an official state agency or court official. The clause that provides for direct payment to the other spouse also allows the payments to be switched to collection by the court or state if problems arise in the future. Remember that there is a definite tendency for child support payments to be paid late or not at all in the majority of cases. Choose the clause below that you and your spouse agree would be most appropriate in your circumstances:

[   ]   We agree that the required child support payments should be made directly to the parent to whom they are due. However, in the event of a divorce or dissolution of marriage, we agree that the required child support payments are to be paid directly to the court or state official or agency so designated by the laws of this state to receive and disburse such payments. We both further agree that, in the event of a divorce or dissolution of marriage, we will cooperate in obtaining any necessary income withholding orders or income assignments if required to guarantee this obligation.

[   ]   We agree that the required child support payments should be made directly to the parent to whom they are due and should not be required to be paid through any court or state agency or official. The parent receiving the payments, however, does not waive the right to request, at any time and in his or her sole discretion, that such payments be made directly through a court or state agency or official in the future. We both further agree that, in the event of a divorce or dissolution of marriage, we will cooperate in obtaining any necessary income withholding orders or income assignments if required to guarantee this obligation.

Additional Child Support Clause: Finally, a general clause is provided for those parents who wish to provide a written agreement on any other provisions regarding the support of their children. This clause may be used, for example, to indicate that the non-custodial parent will contribute additional amounts for the college education of the child. Generally, a parent's legal support obligation ends when the child reaches the age of majority (usually 18 years old). However, parents may legally agree to provide support beyond this minimum cutoff date. You and your spouse may also desire to use this clause to provide additional sums for other needs of your children, such as summer camp fees, special educational costs, or religious training. For any such additional support provisions, use clear explanatory language to define the obligations that you have agreed upon.

[   ]   As additional child support, we both agree that the (Wife or Husband) will provide: (here include the terms of the agreed upon provision [for example: one-half of the amount necessary for the child's college education]).

Federal Income Tax Dependency Exemption: You and your spouse will also have an opportunity to choose which of you will receive the federal income tax dependency exemption. Generally, the parent with custody should receive the exemption. This is true even if the non-custodial parent provides over one-half of the actual monetary support for the child. If the non-custodial parent is given the right to claim the exemption, IRS Form 8332: *Release of Claim to Exemption for Child of Divorced or Separated Parents* must be signed by the custodial parent and filed with the non-custodial parent's tax return in order to officially waive the right to the exemption.

[   ]   We also agree that the (Wife or Husband) may claim the federal dependency tax exemption for the child(ren).

⑭ Fill in the total number of pages and have each spouse initial the page.

Completing Your Marital Settlement Agreement

After you and your spouse have reached all of the necessary decisions and have chosen the appropriate clauses in the preceding sections, you are ready to assemble your final Marital Settlement Agreement. After it is assembled, you will be given instructions on signing and having your agreement notarized. Once you have reached this step in your divorce process, you may relax somewhat with the knowledge that the most difficult decisions in your divorce are behind you. You and your spouse have essentially worked out all of the matters relating to your marriage that require agreement. The divorce procedure now becomes the rather routine matter of preparing and processing the necessary paperwork.

Before you begin to actually assemble your agreement, you should both carefully review each clause that you and your spouse have chosen and be certain that it embodies your complete agreement.

Preparing Your Marital Settlement Agreement

If you are both satisfied that your choices are complete, you are ready to complete and finalize the agreement. The actual preparation of your Marital Settlement Agreement will be accomplished in four easy steps. These steps are as follows:

1. Using a word processor (or Adobe Acrobat Reader®), carefully type or prepare each page of the Marital Settlement Agreement, being certain to include the proper words or clauses where indicated by the numbers (① to ㊹) on the sample form. The only blank lines that should appear on your typed Agreement should be:

   - the date of the agreement
   - the spaces for each spouse's initials at the bottom of each page
   - the spaces for the signatures on the signature page
   - the Notary Acknowledgment information

Both you and your spouse should then carefully proofread your entire Marital Settlement Agreement when it is completed. If any corrections are necessary, you will need to redo the entire page that requires the correction. Make sure that, on each page of the Agreement, you have indicated the correct page number and the total number of pages of the Agreement.

2. When you are satisfied that the Agreement is complete, make two photocopies of the unsigned original, so that you will have three original unsigned Agreements. Using a pen, each spouse should then initial each page at the bottom in the space provided.

3. Attach to each of the three unsigned Agreements an unsigned version of each of your Financial Statements that you prepared earlier. Staple the upper left-hand corner of all of the pages of each original together. (References to *originals* in this book refer to any *unsigned* documents, even if they are photocopies. *Copies* refer to photocopies of *signed* documents). You should now have three identical unsigned "original" documents. Each document will consist of a complete Marital Settlement Agreement, a Financial Statement completed by you, and a Financial Statement completed by your spouse.

4. Take all three original Agreement documents along with two witnesses to the office of a local notary public or other similar authority for signing. The witnesses may be family or friends, as long as they are over 18 years old. There may also be acceptable people available to use as witnesses at the office of the notary. Call in advance and check. In front of the notary public, both you and your spouse should complete all three versions of your Marital Settlement Agreement as follows:

㉔ Fill in the date on which the Agreement is actually being signed
㉕ Wife should sign in front of the notary public and witnesses
㉖ Print the Wife's name
㉗ Husband should sign in front of the notary public and witnesses
㉘ Print the Husband's name
㉙ Witness #1 should sign in front of the notary public
㉚ Print Witness #1's name
㉛ Witness # 2 should sign in front of the notary public
㉜ Print Witness #2's name
㉝ to ㊹ The notary public should complete these items and sign where indicated

5. Additionally, each spouse should also sign the last page of his or her individual Financial Statement where indicated and the notary public should also complete, sign, and notarize these documents that have been stapled to each of the three original Marital Settlement Agreements.

Thus each spouse will have signed each of the three full sets of documents in two places, for a total of six signatures each (once on each Marital Settlement Agreement and once on each Financial Statement times three).

After Signing Your Martial Settlement Agreement

You should each retain one of the complete signed originals of your agreement. The third original signed Agreement will be filed with your divorce papers when and if you should file for divorce. You will also need to make at least three photocopies of the already-signed original for later use when you file for your divorce. Place the original agreement and the photocopies in a safe place.

The final signed and notarized Marital Settlement Agreement (with its attached Financial Statements) will be a valid legal contract between you and your spouse that is enforceable in a court of law if either of you break your promises in the agreement. Under the terms of your agreement, you may proceed to fulfill the promises that you made to each other. You may begin to live separately. You may divide your property and sell any property that you have agreed to sell. Any necessary papers for transferring property may be signed (for example: car titles, quit-claim deeds, etc.). The custody and visitation provisions of your agreement should go into effect and you may begin to make and receive any alimony or child support payments. Essentially, under the terms of your Marital Settlement Agreement, you may begin to live your life as a single person again. However, you are not yet free to remarry and you cannot yet legally have sexual relations with other people. You are not yet divorced.

Chapter 11

Releases

Releases are a method of acknowledging the satisfaction of an obligation or of releasing parties from liability or claims. Releases are used in various situations in the business world, from releasing a person or company from liability after an accident to a release of liens or claims against property. Releases can be very powerful documents. The various releases contained in this chapter are tailored to meet the most common situations in which a release is used. For a release to be valid, there must be some type of consideration received by the person who is granting the release. Releases should be used carefully as they may prevent any future claims against the party to whom it is granted. In general, a release from claims relating to an accident which causes personal injury should not be signed without a prior examination by a doctor. Also note that a release relating to damage to community property in a "community property" state must be signed by both spouses. Study the various forms provided to determine which one is proper for the use intended.

Instructions for Releases

General Release: This release serves as a full blanket-release from one party to another. It should only be used when all obligations of one party are to be released. The party signing this release is discharging the other party from all of their obligations to the other party stemming from a specific incident or transaction. This form can be used when one party has a claim against another and the other agrees to waive the claim for payment. To complete this form, fill in the following information:

① Name of person granting release
② Address of person granting release
③ Name of person granted release
④ Address of person granted release
⑤ Transaction or incident for which release is being granted

⑥ Date of release
⑦ Signature of person granting release
⑧ Printed name of person granting release

Mutual Release: The mutual release form provides a method for two parties to jointly release each other from their mutual obligations or claims. This form should be used when both parties intend to discharge each other from all of their mutual obligations. It essentially serves the purpose of two reciprocal General Releases.

① Name of first person granting release
② Address of first person granting release
③ Name of second person granting release
④ Address of second person granting release
⑤ Transaction or incident for which release is being granted
⑥ Date of release
⑦ Signature of first person granting release
⑧ Printed name of first person granting release
⑨ Signature of second person granting release
⑩ Printed name of second person granting release

Specific Release: This release form should be used only when a particular claim or obligation is being released, while allowing other liabilities to continue. The obligation being released should be spelled out in careful and precise terms to prevent confusion with any other obligation or claim. In addition, the liabilities or obligations which are not being released, but will survive, should also be carefully noted.

① Name of person granting release
② Address of person granting release
③ Name of person granted release
④ Address of person granted release
⑤ Claim or obligation for which release is being granted (Also note any claims, liabilites, or obligations that are not being released)
⑥ Transaction or incident for which release is being granted
⑦ Date of release
⑧ Signature of person granting release
⑨ Printed name of person granting release

General Release

For consideration, I, (1)_____ ,
address: (2)

release (3)_____ ,
address: (4)

from all claims and obligations, known or unknown, to this date arising from the following transaction or incident: (5)

The party signing this release has not assigned any claims or obligations covered by this release to any other party.

The party signing this release intends that it both bind and benefit itself and any successors.

Dated (6)_____ , 20 _____

(7)_____
Signature of person granting release

(8)_____
Printed name of person granting release

Mutual Release

For consideration, ①_____ ,
address: ②

and ③_____ ,
address: ④

release each other from all claims and obligations, known or unknown, that they may have against each other arising from the following transaction or incident: ⑤

Neither party has assigned any claims or obligations covered by this release to any other party.

Both parties signing this release intend that it both bind and benefit themselves and any successors.

Dated ⑥_____ , 20 _____

⑦_____
Signature of 1st person

⑨_____
Signature of 2nd person

⑧_____
Printed name of 1st person

⑩_____
Printed name of 2nd person

Specific Release

For consideration, I, ①_____ ,
address: ②

release ③_____ ,
address: ④

from the following specific claims and obligations: ⑤

arising from the following transaction or incident: ⑥

Any claims or obligations that are not specifically mentioned are not released by this Specific Release.

The party signing this release has not assigned any claims or obligations covered by this release to any other party.

The party signing this release intends that it both bind and benefit itself and any successors.

Dated ⑦_____ , 20 _____

⑧_____
Signature of person granting release

⑨_____
Printed name of person granting release

Chapter 12

Receipts

In this chapter, various receipt forms are provided. In general, receipts are a formal acknowledgment of having received something, whether it is money or property. These forms do not have to be notarized. Please note that Chapter 13: *Leases of Real Estate* contains a Receipt for Lease Security Deposit and a Rent Receipt to be used in conjunction with leases of real estate. The following receipt forms are included in this chapter:

Receipt in Full: This form should be used as a receipt for a payment that completely pays off a debt. You will need to include the amount paid, the name of the person who paid it, the date when paid, and a description of the obligation that is paid off (for example: an invoice, statement, or bill of sale). The original receipt should go to the person making the payment, but a copy should be retained.

1. Amount paid
2. Name of person paying
3. Identify what is being paid for
4. Date
5. Signature
6. Printed name

Receipt on Account: This form should be used as a receipt for a payment that does not fully pay off a debt, but, rather, is a payment on account and is credited to the total balance due. You will need to include the amount paid, the name of the person who paid it, the date when paid, and a description of the account to which the payment is to be applied. The original receipt should go to the person making the payment, but a copy should be kept by you.

① Amount paid
② Name of person paying
③ Identify what account
④ Date
⑤ Signature
⑥ Printed name

Receipt for Goods: This form should be used as a receipt for the acceptance of goods. It is intended to be used in conjunction with a delivery order or purchase order. It also states that the goods have been inspected and found to be in conformance with the order. The original of this receipt should be retained by the person delivering the goods and a copy should go to the person accepting delivery.

① Date
② Signature
③ Printed name

Note: If you are at all unsure of the correct use of any forms in this chapter, please consult a competent attorney.

Receipt in Full

The undersigned acknowledges receipt of the sum of $ ①_____ paid by

②_____ .

This payment constitutes full payment and satisfaction of the following obligation: ③

Dated ④_____ , 20 _____

⑤_____
Signature of Person Receiving Payment

⑥_____
Printed Name of Person Receiving Payment

Receipt on Account

The undersigned acknowledges receipt of the sum of $ ①_____ paid by

②_____ .

This payment will be applied and credited to the following account: ③

Dated ④_____ , 20 _____

⑤_____
Signature of Person Receiving Payment

⑥_____
Printed Name of Person Receiving Payment

Receipt for Goods

The undersigned acknowledges receipt of the goods which are described on the attached purchase order. The undersigned also acknowledges that these goods have been inspected and found to be in conformance with the purchase order specifications.

Dated (1)_____ , 20 _____

(2)_____
Signature of Person Receiving Goods

(3)_____
Printed Name of Person Receiving Goods

Chapter 13

Leases of Real Estate

A lease of real estate is simply a written contract for one party to rent a specific property from another for a certain amount and certain time period. As such, all of the general legal ramifications that relate to contracts also relate to leases. However, all states have additional requirements which pertain only to leases. If the rental period is to be for one year or more, most states require that leases be in writing. Leases can be prepared for *periodic tenancies* (that is, for example, month-to-month or week-to-week) or they can be for a fixed period. There are leases contained in this chapter that provide for both fixed-period tenancies and for month-to-month tenancies.

There are also general guidelines for security deposits in most states. These most often follow a reasonable pattern and should be adhered to. Most states provide for the following with regard to lease security deposits:

- Should be no greater than one month's rent and should be fully refundable
- Should be used for the repair of damages only, and not applied for the nonpayment of rent (an additional month's rent may be requested to cover potential nonpayment of rent situations)
- Should be kept in a separate, interest-bearing account and returned, with interest, to the tenant within 10 days of termination of a lease (minus, of course, any deductions for damages)

In addition to state laws regarding security deposits, many states have requirements relating to the time periods required prior to terminating a lease. These rules have evolved over time to prevent both the landlord or the tenant from being harmed by early termination of a lease. In general, if the lease is for a fixed time period, the termination of the lease is governed by the lease itself. Early termination of a fixed-period lease may, however, be governed by individual state law. For periodic leases (month-to-month, etc.), there are normally state rules as to how much advance notice must be given prior to termination of a lease. If early lease termination is anticipated you should check your state law in the Real Estate Appendix, located on the CD, regarding this issue. This Appendix provides a state-by-state listing of the main provisions of landlord-tenant law for all 50 states and Washington D.C., including details of state laws regarding security deposits, entry into leased premises, and other rental issues. Please see the Real Estate Appendix on the CD for information on the requirements in your state. In addition, be advised that there may also be specific local laws that pertain to landlord and tenant relationships that may be applicable. You are advised to check any local ordinances or state laws for any possible additional requirements. You will also need to supply your tenant with a copy of the enclosed federal form: "Protect Your Family from Lead in Your Home," if the rental unit was built before 1978.

Instructions

Credit/Rental Application: This form is the basis of a check into the credit history of a potential tenant (or customer). With this form, an applicant furnishes various information which may be checked further to ascertain the reliability and background of the credit or tenant applicant. The applicant is requested to furnish personal information, two credit references, two bank references, two personal references, and answer a few basic questions. The form also provides for information to be entered regarding the verification of the references.

The Applicant will furnish the following information:

① Name, address, phone number, fax number, and e-mail address of applicant
② Creditor #1- Name, account number, phone, and address of creditor #1
③ Creditor #2- Name, account number, phone, and address of creditor #2
④ Bank #1- Name, account number, phone, and address of bank #1
⑤ Bank #2- Name, account number, phone, and address of bank #2
⑥ Personal Reference #1- Name, relationship, phone, and address of personal reference #1
⑦ Personal Reference #2- Name, relationship, phone, and address of personal reference #2
⑧ Other informations (bankruptcy, felony, eviction, etc.)
⑨ Applicant's driver's license number and state issuing driver's license
⑩ Date of Application
⑪ Signature of Applicant
⑫ Printed Name of Applicant

Landlord (or Creditor) to fill in the following information:

⑬ Person at Credit reference #1 contacted
⑭ Remarks
⑮ Person at Credit reference #2 contacted
⑯ Remarks

⑰ Person at Bank reference #1 contacted
⑱ Remarks
⑲ Person at Bank reference #2 contacted
⑳ Remarks
㉑ Person at Personal reference #1 contacted
㉒ Remarks
㉓ Person at Personal reference #2 contacted
㉔ Remarks
㉕ Person contacting references
㉖ Date references contacted
㉗ Applicant approval
㉘ Person making approval
㉙ Date of approval

Move-in/Move-out Checklist and Acknowledgment: This form is to be used to catalog and note the condition of all of the furniture, furnishings, appliances, and personal property that are present at the leased property. The tenant is responsible for returning all of the following property in as good a condition as is noted on the Move-in section of this form, except for normal wear and tear. Landlord should complete this form prior to move-in and Tenant should check this form upon move-in, noting any disagreements with landlord's assessment. Both Tenant and Landlord should sign the form at move-in. When the Tenant moves out, the Landlord should again check the presence and condition of the items listed on this form and note the condition of such items on the form. The Tenant should then check the items and note any disagreements with the Landlord's assessment of the condition or presence of any of the items listed. Both the Tenant and Landlord should sign this form again at the moving out of the Tenant. This form may be used to determine any deductions from the security deposit of the Tenant. Both the Landlord and the Tenant should get a copy of this form. To complete this form, enter the following information:

① Name of landlord
② Name of tenant
③ Address of leased property
④ Term of the lease
⑤ Date tenant moves into property
⑥ Date tenant moves out of property
⑦ Listing of all items and their condition (Complete at time of move-in and again at move-out)
⑧ Date of landlord signature for move-in condition
⑨ Signature of landlord for move-in condition
⑩ Date of tenant signature for move-in condition
⑪ Signature of tenant for move-in condition
⑫ Date of landlord signature for move-out condition
⑬ Signature of landlord for move-out condition
⑭ Date of tenant signature for move-out condition
⑮ Signature of tenant for move-out condition

Residential Lease: This form should be used when renting a residential property for a fixed period. Although the landlord and tenant can agree to any terms they desire, this particular lease provides for the following basic terms to be included:

- A fixed-period term for the lease
- A security deposit for damages, which will be returned within 10 days after the termination of the lease, but without interest unless required by state law
- An additional month's rent as security for payment of the rent, which will be returned within 10 days after the termination of the lease, but without interest unless required by state law
- That the tenant agrees to keep the property in good repair and not make any alterations without consent
- Tenant agrees not to conduct any business without permission of the landlord
- Tenant agrees not to have any pets without permission of the landlord
- That landlord and tenant agree on who will pay utilities
- That the tenant agrees not to assign the lease or sublet the property without the landlord's consent
- That the landlord has the right to inspect the property on a reasonable basis, and that the tenant has already inspected it and found it satisfactory
- That the landlord has the right to re-enter and take possession upon breach of the lease (as long as it is in accordance with state law)
- Once the lease term has expired, any continued occupancy will be as a month-to month tenancy
- That the landlord will provide tenant with the U.S. EPA lead pamphlet: "Protect Your Family from Lead in Your Home." *Note*: This document is provided on the Forms-on-CD and is necessary *only* if the rental dwelling was built prior to 1978
- Any other additional terms that the parties agree upon

You will also need to supply your tenant with a copy of the enclosed federal form: "Protect Your Family from Lead in Your Home" if the property was built prior to 1978. (Note: Residents of California will need to include the California Addendum to Lease form that is included on the Forms-on-CD. Residents of Chicago will need to include the Chicago Addendum to Lease and other required Chicago forms that are included on the Forms-on-CD).

To prepare this form, fill in the following information:

① Date of lease
② Name of landlord
③ Address of landlord
④ Name of tenant
⑤ Address of tenant
⑥ Complete address of leased property
⑦ Beginning date of lease

⑧ End date of lease
⑨ Amount of the rental payment
⑩ Day of the period when rent will be due and length of period (usually, month)
⑪ Due date of first rental payment
⑫ Amount of security deposit for damages
⑬ Which state's laws will be used
⑭ Amount of additional rent held as rental default deposit
⑮ Which state's laws will be used
⑯ Maximum number of tenants
⑰ Which state's laws will be used
⑱ Utilities that landlord will supply
⑲ Utilities that tenant will provide
⑳ Which state's laws will be used
㉑ Landlord's initials on presence of lead paint disclosure
㉒ Landlord's initials on records and/or reports of lead paint
㉓ Tenant's initials on lead paint acknowledgment
㉔ Any other additional terms
㉕ Which state's laws will be used to interpret lease
㉖ Signature of landlord
㉗ Printed name of landlord
㉘ Signature of tenant
㉙ Printed name of tenant

Month-to-Month Rental Agreement: This rental agreement provides for a month-to-month tenancy: one that continues each month indefinitely or until terminated by either party. For a fixed tenancy lease, please see the Residential Lease, explained above. Although the landlord and tenant can agree to any terms they desire, this particular lease provides for the following basic terms to be included:

- A month-to-month tenancy for the agreement
- A security deposit for damages, to be returned within 10 days after the termination of the agreement, but without interest unless required by state law
- An additional month's rent as security for payment of the rent, which will be returned within 10 days after the termination of the agreement, but without interest unless required by state law
- That the tenant agrees to keep the property in good repair and not make any alterations without consent
- Tenant agrees not to conduct any business without permission of the landlord
- Tenant agrees not to have any pets without permission of the landlord
- That landlord and tenant agree on who will pay utilities
- That the tenant agrees not to assign or sublet the property without the landlord's consent
- That the landlord has the right to inspect the property on a reasonable basis, and that the tenant has already inspected it and found it satisfactory

- That the landlord has the right to re-enter and take possession upon breach of the agreement (as long as it is in accordance with state law)
- That the landlord will provide tenant with the U.S. EPA lead pamphlet: "Protect Your Family from Lead in Your Home." *Note*: This document is provided on the Forms-on-CD and is necessary *only* if the rental dwelling was built prior to 1978
- Any other additional terms that the parties agree upon

You will also need to supply your tenant with a copy of the enclosed federal form: "Protect Your Family from Lead in Your Home" if the property was built prior to 1978. (Note: Residents of California will need to include the California Addendum to Lease form that is included on the Forms-on-CD. Residents of Chicago will need to include the Chicago Addendum to Lease and other required Chicago forms that are included on the Forms-on-CD).

To prepare this form, fill in the following information:

1. Date of rental agreement
2. Name of landlord
3. Address of landlord
4. Name of tenant
5. Address of tenant
6. Complete address of rental property
7. Beginning date of rental agreement
8. Number of days required for termination of rental agreement
9. Amount of rental payment
10. Day of the month when rent will be due and period of tenancy
11. Due date of first rent payment
12. Amount of security deposit for damages
13. Which state's laws will be used
14. Amount of additional rent held as rental default deposit
15. Which state's laws will be used
16. Maximum number of tenants
17. Which state's laws will be used
18. Utilities that landlord will supply
19. Utilities that tenant will provide
20. Which state's laws will be used
21. Landlord's initials on presence of lead paint disclosure
22. Tenant's initials on lead paint acknowledgment
23. Any other additional terms
24. Which state's laws will be used to interpret agreement
25. Signature of landlord
26. Printed name of landlord
27. Signature of tenant
28. Printed name of tenant

Commercial Lease: This form should be used when renting a commercial property. Although the landlord and tenant can agree to any terms they desire, this particular lease provides for the following basic terms to be included:

- An initial fixed-period term for the lease, with the lease continuing on after this term as a month-to-month lease
- A five percent late charge for rent payments over five days late
- A limitation on what business the tenant may conduct on the property
- A security deposit for damages, which will be returned within 10 days after the termination of the lease
- An additional month's rent as security for payment of the rent, which will be returned within 10 days after the termination of the lease
- That the tenant agrees to keep the property in good repair and not make any alterations without consent
- That the tenant agrees not to assign the lease or sublet the property without the landlord's consent
- That the landlord has the right to inspect the property on a reasonable basis, and that the tenant has already inspected it and found it satisfactory
- That the landlord has the right to re-enter and take possession upon breach of the lease (as long as it is in accordance with state law)
- That the landlord is responsible for the upkeep of the exterior and the tenant for the upkeep of the interior of the property
- That the landlord will carry fire and casualty insurance on the property, and that the tenant will carry casualty insurance on their own equipment and fixtures and also carry general business liability insurance
- That the lease is subject to any mortgage or deed of trust and that the tenant agrees to sign any future subordination documents
- Any other additional terms that the parties agree upon

To prepare this form, fill in the following information:

① Date of lease
② Name of landlord
③ Address of landlord
④ City of landlord
⑤ State of landlord
⑥ Name of tenant
⑦ Address of tenant
⑧ City of tenant
⑨ State of tenant
⑩ Complete address and description of leased property
⑪ Amount of rental payment

⑫ Day of the month when rent will be due
⑬ Due date of first rent payment
⑭ Beginning date of lease
⑮ End date of lease
⑯ Additional lease term upon renewal of lease
⑰ Amount of rent upon renewal
⑱ Amount of rent if tenancy is extended as month-to-month
⑲ Amount of security deposit for damages
⑳ Amount of additional rent held as rental default deposit
㉑ Description of tenant's business
㉒ Description of equipment or fixtures tenant will install
㉓ Number of days tenant allowed to correct violation or rent default
㉔ Number of days required for termination of lease if violation or default
㉕ Minimum amount of business liability insurance tenant will carry
㉖ Number of days required for termination of lease for other than violation or default
㉗ Any other additional terms
㉘ Any attachments to lease
㉙ Which state's laws will be used to interpret lease
㉚ Signature of landlord
㉛ Printed name of landlord
㉜ Signature of tenant
㉝ Printed name of tenant

Lease with Purchase Option: This lease provides for a fixed-period tenancy and contains a "purchase option" which offers the tenant a time period in which to have an exclusive option to purchase a parcel of real estate. Through the use of this agreement, the landlord can offer the tenant a time period with which to consider the purchase without concern of a sale to another party. This option provides that in exchange for a percentage of the rent (which will be applied to the purchase price if the option is exercised), the tenant is given a period of time to exercise the option and accept the terms of a completed real estate contract. If the tenant accepts the terms and exercises the option in writing, the landlord agrees to complete the sale. If the option is not exercised, the landlord is then free to sell the property on the market and retain the money paid for the option as rent. You will also need to supply your tenant with a copy of the enclosed federal form: "Protect Your Family from Lead in Your Home," if the rental unit was built before 1978. (Note: Residents of California will need to include the California Addendum to Lease form that is included on the Forms-on-CD. Residents of Chicago will need to include the Chicago Addendum to Lease and other required Chicago forms that are included on the Forms-on-CD).

To prepare this form, fill in the following information:

① Date of lease
② Name of landlord

③ Address of landlord
④ City of landlord
⑤ State of landlord
⑥ Name of tenant
⑦ Address of tenant
⑧ City of tenant
⑨ State of tenant
⑩ Complete address of leased property
⑪ Beginning date of lease
⑫ End date of lease
⑬ Amount of rental payment
⑭ Period of time between payments
⑮ Day of the month when rent will be due
⑯ Due date of first rental payment
⑰ Percentage of each rental payment which will be applied to purchase price if option exercised
⑱ Date option period expires
⑲ Anticipated purchase price of property
⑳ Anticipated rental payment deposit held in trust for option (use full term of lease amount)
㉑ Type of any other deposit
㉒ Amount of any other deposit
㉓ Balance of purchase price due at closing
㉔ Total purchase price
㉕ Amount of mortgage commitment required
㉖ Number of monthly payments of mortgage commitment
㉗ Annual interest rate of mortgage commitment
㉘ Amount of security deposit for damages
㉙ Amount of additional rent held as rental default deposit
㉚ Maximum number of tenants
㉛ Utilities that landlord will supply
㉜ Utilities that tenant will provide
㉝ Landlord's initials on presence of lead paint disclosure
㉞ Landlord's initials on records and/or reports of lead paint
㉟ Tenant's initials on lead paint acknowledgment
㊱ Any other additional terms
㊲ State where property is located
㊳ Signature of landlord
㊴ Printed name of landlord
㊵ Signature of tenant
㊶ Printed name of tenant

Amendment of Lease: Use this form to modify any terms of a lease. A copy of the original lease should be attached to this form. The amendment can be used to change any portion of the lease.

Simply note what changes are being made in the appropriate place on this form. If a portion of the lease is being deleted, make note of the deletion. If certain language is being substituted, state the substitution clearly. If additional language is being added, make this clear. For example, you may wish to use language as follows:

"Paragraph _____ is deleted from this lease."

"Paragraph _____ is deleted from this lease and the following paragraph is substituted in its place:

"The following new paragraph is added to this lease:"

In order to prepare this Amendment, please fill in the following information:

① Date of amendment
② Name of landlord and address
③ Name of tenant and address
④ Description of original lease (including date of lease and description of property involved)
⑤ Terms of amendment
⑥ Signature of landlord
⑦ Printed name of landlord
⑧ Signature of tenant
⑨ Printed name of tenant

Extension of Lease: This document should be used to extend the effective time period during which a lease is in force. The use of this form allows the time limit to be extended without having to entirely re-draft the lease. Under this document, all of the other terms of the lease will remain the same, with only the expiration date changing. A copy of the original lease should be attached to this form.

To complete this form, fill in the following information:

① Date of extension
② Name of landlord and address
③ Name of tenant and address
④ Description of original lease (including date of lease and description of property involved)
⑤ Date on which original lease will end
⑥ Date on which extension of lease will end
⑦ Signature of landlord
⑧ Printed name of landlord
⑨ Signature of tenant
⑩ Printed name of tenant

Mutual Termination of Lease: This form should be used when both the landlord and tenant desire to terminate a lease. This document releases both parties from any claims that the other may have against them for any actions under the lease. It also states that the landlord agrees that the rent has been paid in full and that the property has been delivered in good condition.

To complete this form, fill in the following information:

① Date of termination
② Name of landlord and address
③ Name of tenant and address
④ Description of original lease (including date of lease and description of property involved)
⑤ Signature of landlord
⑥ Printed name of landlord
⑦ Signature of tenant
⑧ Printed name of tenant

Assignment of Lease: This form is for use if one party to a lease is assigning its full interest in the lease to another party. This effectively substitutes one party for another under a lease. This particular assignment form has both of the parties agreeing to indemnify and hold each other harmless for any failures to perform under the lease while they were the party liable under it. This Assignment of Lease may be used by a seller of real estate to assign their interest in any lease that covers the property for sale to the new buyer. This *indemnify and hold harmless* clause simply means that if a claim arises for failure to perform, each party agrees to be responsible for the period of their own performance obligations. A description of the lease which is assigned should include the parties to the lease, a description of the property, and the date of the lease. Other information that is necessary to complete the assignment is the name and address of the *assignor* (the party who is assigning the lease), the name and address of the *assignee* (the party to whom the lease is being assigned), and the date of the assignment. A copy of the original lease should be attached to this form.

In order to prepare this Assignment, please fill in the following information:

① Date of assignment
② Name of assignor
③ Address of assignor
④ Name of assignee
⑤ Address of assignee
⑥ Description of original lease (including date of lease and description of property involved)
⑦ Signature of assignor
⑧ Printed name of assignor
⑨ Signature of assignee
⑩ Printed name of assignee

Consent to Assignment of Lease: This form is used if the original lease states that the consent of the landlord is necessary for the assignment of the lease to be valid. A landlord may wish to supply a copy of this form to a tenant if a tenant requests the landlord's consent for an assignment of the lease to another party. A copy of the original lease should be attached to this form.

To complete this form, the following information is needed:

① Date of consent to assignment
② Name of tenant requesting consent
③ Address of tenant requesting consent
④ Name of tenant requesting consent
⑤ Description of lease, including date of lease and location of leased premises
⑥ Signature of landlord
⑦ Printed name of landlord

Sublease: This form is used if the tenant subleases the property covered by an original lease. This particular sublease form has both of the parties agreeing to indemnify and hold each other harmless for any failures to perform under the lease while they were the party liable under it. This *indemnify and hold harmless* clause simply means that if a claim arises for failure to perform, each party agrees to be responsible for the period of their own performance obligations. A description of the lease which is subleased should include the parties to the lease, a description of the property, and the date of the lease. Note that the *subtenant* is the party to whom the property is being subleased. A copy of the original lease should be attached to this form. A copy of a Consent to Sublease of Lease should also be attached, if necessary.

To complete this form, enter the following information:

① Date of sublease
② Name of tenant
③ Address of tenant
④ Name of subtenant
⑤ Address of subtenant
⑥ Description of property covered by lease
⑦ Description of original lease (including date of lease and name and address of landlord)
⑧ Beginning date of sublease
⑨ Ending date of sublease
⑩ Amount of subrental payments
⑪ Period for each subrental payment (generally, per month)
⑫ Day of month each subrental payment is due
⑬ Beginning date for first subrental payment ·
⑭ Any additional terms of sublease
⑮ State law which will govern the sublease

⑯ Signature of tenant
⑰ Printed name of tenant
⑱ Signature of subtenant
⑲ Printed name of subtenant

Consent to Sublease: This form is used if the original lease states that the consent of the landlord is necessary for a sublease to be valid. A landlord may wish to supply a copy of this form to a tenant if a tenant requests the landlord's consent for a sublease of the lease to another party. A copy of the original lease should be attached to this form and a copy should be attached to any sublease of a property.

To complete this form, the following information is needed:

① Date of consent to sublease
② Name of tenant requesting consent
③ Address of tenant requesting consent
④ Name of tenant requesting consent
⑤ Description of lease, including date of lease and location of leased premises
⑥ Signature of landlord
⑦ Printed name of landlord

Notice of Rent Default: This form allows for notice to a tenant of default in the payment of rent. It provides for the amount of the defaulted payments to be specified and for a time limit to be placed on payment before further action is taken. Most states have laws relating to the time limits that must be allowed to a tenant to pay the late rent after the landlord's notice of a rent default. You should check your state's listing in the Real Estate Appendix on the CD for the time limit that you should use in this form. If the breach is not taken care of within the time period allowed, you may send the tenant a Notice to Pay Rent or Vacate (shown later in this kit). In addition, a lawyer should be consulted for further action, which may involve a lawsuit to enforce the lease terms. A copy of the original lease should be attached to this form.

To complete this form, fill in the following information:

① Date of notice
② Name of tenant
③ Address of tenant
④ Name of tenat
⑤ Description of lease (address of property, dates covered, etc.)
⑥ Date of this notice
⑦ Exact amount of rent past due
⑧ Number of days allowed to pay rent (Check the Appendix for your state's requirements)
⑨ Signature of landlord
⑩ Printed Name of landlord

Notice of Breach of Lease: This form should be used to notify a party to a lease of the violation of a term of the lease or of an instance of failure to perform a required duty under the lease, other than the failure to pay rent. Such violation might be having a pet if the lease prohibits this, or perhaps having too many people living in the rental property, or any other violation of the terms of the lease. This notice provides for a description of the alleged violation of the lease and for a time period in which the party is instructed to cure the breach of the lease. If the breach is not taken care of within the time period allowed, you may send the tenant a Final Notice Before Legal Action. In any event, a lawyer should be consulted for further action, which may entail a lawsuit to enforce the lease terms. A copy of the original lease should be attached to this form.

To complete this form, fill in the following information:

① Date of notice
② Name of tenant
③ Address of tenant
④ Name of tenat
⑤ Description of lease (address of property, dates covered, etc.)
⑥ Date of this notice
⑦ Exact description of breach of lease
⑧ Number of days allowed to correct the breach
⑨ Signature of landlord
⑩ Printed Name of landlord

Notice to Pay Rent or Vacate: This form allows for notice to be given to a tenant who is in default of the payment of rent. It provides for the amount of the defaulted payments to be specified and for a time limit to be placed on payment before further action is taken. It provides notice to either pay the rent or to vacate the property by a certain date. If the defaulted rent is not paid or the property is not vacated by the tenant within the time period allowed, a Landlord's Notice to Terminate Lease may be delivered to the tenant which demands that possession of the property be relinquished. Most states have laws relating to the time limits that must be allowed to a tenant to pay the late rent after the landlord's notice of a rent default. You should check your state's listing in the Appendix of this book for the time limit that you should use in this form. A lawyer should be consulted for further action, which may involve a lawsuit to enforce the lease terms, a lawsuit for collection of the past due rent, or legal proceedings for eviction of the tenant. A copy of the original lease should be attached to this form.

To complete this form, fill in the following information:

① Date of notice
② Name of tenant
③ Address of tenant
④ Name of tenant

⑤ Description of lease (address of property, dates covered, etc.)
⑥ Date of this notice
⑦ Exact amount of rent past due
⑧ Date on which tenant must pay rent or vacate the property (Check state's listing in the Appendix)
⑨ Signature of landlord
⑩ Printed Name of landlord

Landlord's Notice to Terminate Lease: By this notice, a landlord may inform a tenant of the termination of a lease for breach of the lease. This action may be taken under a lease, provided that there are specific lease provisions that allow this action and the tenant has agreed to these provisions by signing the lease. This notice is generally sent to a tenant after the tenant has first been notified that the rent is past due or that the lease has been breached for other reasons and the tenant has been given a time period in which to pay. This notice is not an eviction notice. It is a notice to demand that the tenant surrender possession of the property back to the landlord. Some states have time limits that must be complied with before a lease can be terminated and you should check your state's listing in the Appendix to determine if your state has such requirements. A lawyer should be consulted for further action, which may involve a lawsuit to enforce the lease terms, a lawsuit for collection of the past-due rent, or legal proceedings for eviction of the tenant. A copy of the original lease should be attached to this form. This form should be delivered to the tenant by certified first-class mail and the Proof of Service portion of this form should be completed by the person actually mailing the notice.

To complete this form, fill in the following information:

① Date of notice
② Name and address of tenant
③ Name of tenant
④ Description of lease (address of property, dates covered, etc.)
⑤ Date of this Notice
⑥ Exact nature of breach of lease (amount rent past due, etc.)
⑦ Date of the original Notice to Pay Rent or Vacate or Notice of Breach of Lease
⑧ Number of days allowed in original Notice to Pay Rent or Vacate or Notice of Breach of Lease
⑨ Date on which possession of property is demanded
⑩ Signature of landlord
⑪ Printed Name of landlord
⑫ Address of landlord
⑬ City, state, and zip code of landlord
⑭ Date of mailing of Notice
⑮ Date of signature on Proof of Service
⑯ Signature of person mailing Notice
⑰ Name of person mailing Notice

Final Notice Before Legal Action: This form allows for a final notice to be given to a person who is in default with a rent payment or other breach of a lease. It provides for the amount of the defaulted payments to be specified and for a time limit to be placed on payment before immediate legal action is taken. If the defaulted amount is not paid within the time period allowed, a lawyer should be consulted for further action, Further action may involve a lawsuit for collection of the past due amount, a lawsuit for possession of any collateral (if involved) or other legal proceedings. A copy of the original account statement or invoice should be attached to this form.

To complete this form, fill in the following information:
1. Date of notice
2. Name of person in default
3. Address of person in default
4. Description of lease which has been breached
5. Date of this notice
6. Exact amount of past due rent
7. Date on which payment must be made
8. Date of this notice
9. Signature of landlord
10. Printed name of landlord
11. Address of landlord
12. City, state, and zip code of landlord

Notice of Lease: This document should be used to record notice that a parcel of real estate has a current lease in effect on it. This may be necessary if the property is on the market for sale or it may be required by a bank or mortgage company at the closing of a real estate sale in order for the seller to verify to the buyer the existence of a lease covering the property. This form should be notarized.

In order to complete this document, the following information is required:

1. Description of lease
2. Name of landlord
3. Address of landlord
4. Name of tenant
5. Address of tenant
6. Description of property leased
7. Term of lease
8. Any extensions of lease
9. Signature of landlord
10. Printed name of landlord
11. The following should be completed by a notary public:

Receipt for Lease Security Deposit: This form is to be used for receipt of a lease security deposit. To complete this form, insert the following information:.

1. Amount of security deposit paid
2. Description of lease
3. Date of receipt
4. Signature of landlord
5. Printed name of landlord

Rent Receipt: This form may be used as a receipt for the periodic payment of rent. To complete this form, insert the following information:

1. Amount of rent paid
2. Name of Tenant
3. Time period
4. Description of property for which rent is due
5. Date of receipt
6. Signature of landlord
7. Printed Name of landlord

CREDIT/RENTAL APPLICATION

Name ①
Address
City
State   Zip
Phone
Fax
e-mail Address

CREDIT REFERENCES

Creditor Name ②
Account Number
Phone
Address
City
State   Zip

Creditor Name ③
Account Number
Phone
Address
City
State   Zip

BANK REFERENCES

Bank Name ④
Account Number
Phone
Address
City
State   Zip

Bank Name ⑤
Account Number
Phone
Address
City
State   Zip

PERSONAL REFERENCES

Name ⑥
Relationship
Phone
Address
City
State   Zip

Name ⑦
Relationship
Phone
Address
City
State   Zip

OTHER INFORMATION ⑧

Have you ever filed for bankruptcy?

Have you ever been convicted of a felony?

Have you ever been evicted from or asked to leave a property you were renting?

Have you ever intentionally refused to pay rent when due?

How were you referred to us?

Driver's License Number: ⑨   State:

The Applicant accepts the above terms and states that all information contained in this application is true and correct. Applicant authorizes creditor to contact all references, inquire as to credit information, and receive any confidential information relevant to approving credit.

Dated: ⑩_____

⑪_____
Signature of Applicant

⑫_____
Printed Name of Applicant

FOR OFFICE USE ONLY

References Contacted	Person Contacted	Remarks
Creditor #1	⑬	⑭
Creditor #2	⑮	⑯
Bank #1	⑰	⑱
Bank #2	⑲	⑳
Personal #1	㉑	㉒
Personal #2	㉓	㉔

References Contacted by: ㉕
Date References Contacted: ㉖

Applicant Approved: ㉗

Approval by: ㉘
Date Approved: ㉙

Move-in/Move-out Checklist and Acknowledgment

Landlord Name: ①

Tenant Name: ②

Address of leased property: ③

Term of Lease: ④

Date of Move-in: ⑤

Date of Move-out: ⑥

This form is to catalog and note the condition of all of the furniture, furnishing, appliances, and personal property that is present at the leased property. The tenant is responsible for returning all of the following property upon moving out in as good a condition as is noted on the Move-in section of this form, except for normal wear and tear. Landlord should complete this form prior to move-in and Tenant should check this form upon move-in, noting any disagreements with landlord's assessment.

Item Description	Move-in Condition	Landlord Comments	Tenant Comments	Move-out Condition	Landlord Comments	Tenant Comments
⑦						

Move-in Acknowledgment

Landlord has reviewed this document and agrees with the items listed and their condition on the date of the Tenant's moving into the leased property.

Date: ⑧_____

⑨_____
Landlord Signature

Tenant has inspected all of the listed items and found them to be present on the leased property and to be in the condition indicated on the date of the Tenant's moving in to the leased property (or else has noted any discrepancy on this form). Tenant agrees to return all of the listed property on the date of moving out of the leased property in the same condition as indicated on this form, except for normal wear and tear. By signing this form, Tenant agrees with Landlord's assessment or notes his or her disagreement with the Landlord.

Date: ⑩_____

⑪_____
Tenant Signature

Move-out Acknowledgment

Landlord has inspected the listed items and compared them to the move-in condition. If any property differs from its move-in condition, other than normal wear and tear, any differences have been listed on this form.

Date: ⑫_____

⑬_____
Landlord Signature

Tenant has inspected the listed items and compared them to the move-in condition. If any property differs from its move-in condition, other than normal wear and tear, any differences have been listed on this form. If Tenant disagrees with Landlord's assessment of any differences in condition upon moving out, those discrepancies have been listed on this form. By signing this form, Tenant agrees with Landlord's assessment or notes his or her disagreement with the Landlord.

Date: ⑭_____

⑮_____
Tenant Signature

RESIDENTIAL LEASE

This lease is made on ①_____ , 20 _____ , between
②_____ , landlord,
address:③_____

and ④_____ , tenant,
address:⑤_____

1. The landlord agrees to rent to the tenant and the tenant agrees to rent from the landlord the following residence:
    ⑥

2. The term of this lease will be from ⑦_____ , 20 _____ , until
    ⑧_____ , 20 _____ .

3. The rental payments will be $ ⑨_____ per ⑩_____ and will be payable by the tenant to
    the landlord on the ⑪_____ day of each month, beginning on _____ , 20 _____ .

4. The tenant has paid the landlord a security deposit of $ ⑫_____ . This security deposit will be held
    as security for the repair of any damages to the residence by the tenant. This deposit will be returned to the tenant
    within ten (10) days of the termination of this lease, minus any amounts needed to repair the residence, but without
    interest, except as required by law in the State of ⑬_____ .

5. The Tenant has paid the Landlord an additional month's rent in the amount of $ ⑭_____ . This rent
    deposit will be held as security for the payment of rent by the tenant. This rent payment deposit will be returned to the
    tenant within ten (10) days of the termination of this lease, minus any rent still due upon termination but without inter-
    est, except as required by law in the State of ⑮_____ .

6. Tenant agrees to maintain the residence in a clean and sanitary manner and not to make any alterations to the
    residence without the landlord's written consent. Tenant also agrees not to conduct any business in the residence. At
    the termination of this lease, the tenant agrees to leave the residence in the same condition as when it was received,
    except for normal wear and tear.

7. Tenant also agrees not to conduct any type of business in the residence, nor store or use any dangerous or hazard-
    ous materials. Tenant agrees that the residence is to be used only as a single family residence, with a maximum of
    ⑯_____ tenants. Tenant also agrees to comply with all rules, laws, and ordinances affecting the residence, including
    all laws of the State of ⑰_____ . Tenant agrees that no pets or other animals are allowed in the resi-
    dence without the written permission of the Landlord.

8. The landlord agrees to supply the following utilities to the tenant:⑱

9. The tenant agrees to obtain and pay for the following utilities:⑲

10. Tenant agrees not to sublet the residence or assign this lease without the landlord's written consent. Tenant agrees to allow
    the landlord reasonable access to the residence for inspection and repair. Landlord agrees to enter the residence only after
    notifying the tenant in advance, except in an emergency, and according to the laws of the State of ⑳_____ .

11. The tenant has inspected the residence and has found it satisfactory.

12. If the tenant fails to pay the rent on time or violates any other terms of this lease, the landlord will have the right to terminate
    this lease in accordance with state law. The landlord will also have the right to re-enter the residence and take possession
    of it and to take advantage of any other legal remedies available under the laws of the State of ㉑_____ .

13. If the Tenant remains as tenant after the expiration of this lease without signing a new lease, a month-to-month tenancy will be created with the same terms and conditions as this lease, except that such new tenancy may be terminated by thirty (30) days written notice from either the Tenant or the Landlord.

14. As required by law, the landlord makes the following statement: "Radon gas is a naturally occurring radioactive gas that, when accumulated in sufficient quantities in a building, may present health risks to persons exposed to it. Levels of radon gas that exceed federal and state guidelines have been found in buildings in this state. Additional information regarding radon gas and radon gas testing may be obtained from your county health department."

15. As required by law, the landlord makes the following LEAD WARNING STATEMENT:
"Every purchaser or lessee of any interest in residential real property on which a residential dwelling was built prior to 1978 is notified that such property may present exposure to lead from lead-based paint that may place young children at risk of developing lead poisoning. Lead poisoning in young children may produce permanent neurological damage, including learning disabilities, reduced intelligence quotient, behavioral problems, and impaired memory. Lead poisoning also poses a particular threat to pregnant women. The seller or lessor of any interest in residential real estate is required to provide the buyer with any information on lead-based paint hazards from risk assessments or inspection in the seller's or lessor's possession and notify the buyer or lessee of any known lead-based paint hazards. A risk assessment or inspection for possible lead-based paint hazards is recommended prior to purchase."

Landlord's Disclosure

Presence of lead-based paint and/or lead-based paint hazards: (Landlord to initial one). ㉒

_____ Known lead-based paint and/or lead-based paint hazards are present in building (explain):

_____ Landlord has no knowledge of lead-based paint and/or lead-based paint hazards in building.

Records and reports available to landlord: (Landlord to initial one).
_____ Landlord has provided tenant with all available records and reports pertaining to lead-based paint and/or lead-based paint hazards are present in building (list documents):

_____ Landlord has no records and reports pertaining to lead-based paint and/or lead-based paint hazards in building.

Tenant's Acknowledgment

(Tenant to initial all applicable). ㉓

_____ Tenant has received copies of all information listed above.

_____ Tenant has received the pamphlet "Protect Your Family from Lead in Your Home."

_____ Tenant has received a ten (10)-day opportunity (or mutually agreed on period) to conduct a risk assessment or inspection for the presence of lead-based paint and/or lead-based paint hazards in building.

_____ Tenant has waived the opportunity to conduct a risk assessment or inspection for the presence of lead-based paint and/or lead-based paint hazards in building.

The landlord and tenant have reviewed the information above and certify, by their signatures at the end of this lease, to the best of their knowledge, that the information they have provided is true and accurate.

16. The following are additional terms of this lease: ㉔

17. The parties agree that this lease is the entire agreement between them. This lease binds and benefits both the landlord and tenant and any successors. This Lease is governed by the laws of the State of ㉕_____ .

㉖_____
Signature of Landlord

㉘_____
Signature of Tenant

㉗_____
Printed Name of Landlord

㉙_____
Printed Name of Tenant

MONTH TO MONTH RENTAL AGREEMENT

This Agreement is made on ①_____ , 20 _____ , between
②_____ , landlord,
address:③

and④ _____ , tenant,
address:⑤

1. The Landlord agrees to rent to the Tenant and the Tenant agrees to rent from the Landlord on a month-to-month ba-
    sis, the following residence: ⑥

2. This Agreement will begin on ⑦_____ and will continue on a month-to-month basis until
    terminated. This agreement may only be terminated by ⑧_____ days written notice from either party.

3. The rental payments will be $ ⑨_____ per ⑩_____ and will be payable by the tenant to
    the landlord on the ⑪_____ day of each month, beginning on _____ , 20 _____ .

4. The tenant has paid the landlord a security deposit of $ ⑫_____ . This security deposit will be held
    as security for the repair of any damages to the residence by the tenant. This deposit will be returned to the tenant
    within ten (10) days of the termination of this agreement, minus any amounts needed to repair the residence, but with-
    out interest, except as required by law in the State of ⑬_____ .

5. The Tenant has paid the Landlord an additional month's rent in the amount of $ ⑭_____ . This rent
    deposit will be held as security for the payment of rent by the tenant. This rent payment deposit will be returned to the
    tenant within ten (10) days of the termination of this agreement, minus any rent still due upon termination but without
    interest, except as required by law in the State of ⑮_____ .

6. Tenant agrees to maintain the residence in a clean and sanitary manner and not to make any alterations to the
    residence without the landlord's written consent. Tenant also agrees not to conduct any business in the residence.
    At the termination of this agreement, the tenant agrees to leave the residence in the same condition as when it was
    received, except for normal wear and tear.

7. Tenant also agrees not to conduct any type of business in the residence, nor store or use any dangerous or hazardous
    materials. Tenant agrees that the residence is to be used only as a single family residence, with a maximum of
    ⑯_____ tenants. Tenant also agrees to comply with all rules, laws, and ordinances affecting the residence, in-
    cluding all the laws of the State of ⑰_____ . Tenant agrees that no pets or other animals are allowed
    in the residence without the written permission of the Landlord.

8. The landlord agrees to supply the following utilities to the tenant:⑱

9. The tenant agrees to obtain and pay for the following utilities:⑲

10. Tenant agrees not to sublet the residence or assign this agreement without the landlord's written consent. Tenant
    agrees to allow the landlord reasonable access to the residence for inspection and repair. Landlord agrees to enter
    the residence only after notifying the tenant in advance, except in an emergency, and according to the laws of the
    State of ⑳_____ .

11. The tenant has inspected the residence and has found it satisfactory.

12. If the tenant fails to pay the rent on time or violates any other terms of this agreement, the landlord will have the right
    to terminate this agreement in accordance with state law. The landlord will also have the right to re-enter the resi-
    dence and take possession of it and to take advantage of any other legal remedies available.

13. As required by law, the landlord makes the following statement: "Radon gas is a naturally occurring radioactive gas that, when accumulated in sufficient quantities in a building, may present health risks to persons exposed to it. Levels of radon gas that exceed federal and state guidelines have been found in buildings in this state. Additional information regarding radon gas and radon gas testing may be obtained from your county health department."

14. As required by law, the landlord makes the following LEAD WARNING STATEMENT: "Every purchaser or lessee of any interest in residential real property on which a residential dwelling was built prior to 1978 is notified that such property may present exposure to lead from lead-based paint that may place young children at risk of developing lead poisoning. Lead poisoning in young children may produce permanent neurological damage, including learning disabilities, reduced intelligence quotient, behavioral problems, and impaired memory. Lead poisoning also poses a particular threat to pregnant women. The seller or lessor of any interest in residential real estate is required to provide the buyer or lessee with any information on lead-based paint hazards from risk assessments or inspection in the seller's or lessor's possession and notify the buyer or lessee of any known lead-based paint hazards. A risk assessment or inspection for possible lead-based paint hazards is recommended prior to purchase."

Landlord's Disclosure

Presence of lead-based paint and/or lead-based paint hazards: (Landlord to initial one).㉑

_____ Known lead-based paint and/or lead-based paint hazards are present in building (explain):
_____ Landlord has no knowledge of lead-based paint and/or lead-based paint hazards in building.

Records and reports available to landlord: (Landlord to initial one).

_____ Landlord has provided tenant with all available records and reports pertaining to lead-based paint and/or lead-based paint hazards are present in building (list documents):
_____ Landlord has no records and reports pertaining to lead-based paint and/or lead-based paint hazards in building.

Tenant's Acknowledgment

(Tenant to initial all applicable).㉒

_____ Tenant has received copies of all information listed above.
_____ Tenant has received the pamphlet "Protect Your Family from Lead in Your Home."
_____ Tenant has received a ten (10)-day opportunity (or mutually agreed on period) to conduct a risk assessment or inspection for the presence of lead-based paint and/or lead-based paint hazards in building.
_____ Tenant has waived the opportunity to conduct a risk assessment or inspection for the presence of lead-based paint and/or lead-based paint hazards in building.

The landlord and tenant have reviewed the information above and certify, by their signatures at the end of this agreement, to the best of their knowledge, that the information they have provided is true and accurate.

15. The following are additional terms of this agreement: ㉓

16. The parties agree that this agreement is the entire agreement between them. This Agreement binds and benefits both the landlord and tenant and any successors. This Agreement is governed by the laws of the State of ㉔ _____ .

㉕_____
Signature of Landlord

㉗_____
Signature of Tenant

㉖_____
Printed Name of Landlord

㉘_____
Printed Name of Tenant

COMMERCIAL LEASE

This lease is made on ①_____ , 20 _____ , between
②_____ , landlord,
address:③④⑤

and ⑥_____ , tenant,
address:⑦⑧⑨

1. The Landlord agrees to rent to the Tenant and the Tenant agrees to rent from the Landlord the following property: ⑩

2. The rental payments will be $ ⑪ _____ per month and will be payable by the Tenant to the Landlord on the
⑫_____ day of each month, beginning on _____ . If any rental
payment is not paid within 5 (five) days of its due date, the Tenant agrees to pay an additional late charge of 5% (five
percent) of the rental due.

3. The term of this Lease will be from⑬ _____ , until ⑭_____
_____ . If Tenant is in full compliance with all of the terms of this Lease at the expiration of this term, Tenant
shall have the option to renew this Lease for an additional term of ⑮ _____ , with
all terms and conditions of this Lease remaining the same, except that the rent shall be $⑯_____ If the
Tenant remains as tenant after the expiration of this Lease with the consent of the Landlord but without signing a new
lease, a month-to-month tenancy will be created with the same terms and conditions as this Lease, except that such
new tenancy may be terminated by ninety (90) days written notice from either the Tenant or the Landlord, and that the
rent shall be $ ⑰_____ .

4. The Tenant has paid the Landlord a security deposit of $⑱ _____ . This security deposit will be held
as security for the repair of any damages to the property by the Tenant. This deposit will be returned to the Tenant within
10 (ten) days of the termination of this Lease, minus any amounts needed to repair the property, but without interest.,
unless required by state law.

5. The Tenant has paid the Landlord an additional month's rent in the amount of $⑲_____ . This rent deposit will be held as
security for the payment of rent by the Tenant. This rent payment deposit will be returned to the Tenant within 10 (ten) days of
the termination of this Lease, minus any rent still due upon termination, but without interest, unless required by state law.

6. The Tenant agrees to use the property only for the purpose of carrying on the following lawful business: ⑳

7. The Landlord agrees that the Tenant may install the following equipment and fixtures for the purpose of operating the
Tenant's business and that such equipment and fixtures shall remain the property of the Tenant: ㉑

8. The Tenant has inspected the property and has found it satisfactory for its intended purposes. The Landlord shall be
responsible for the repair and upkeep of the exterior of the property, including the roof, exterior walls, parking areas,
landscaping, and building foundation. The Tenant shall be responsible for the repair and upkeep of the interior of the
property, including all electrical, mechanical, plumbing, heating, cooling, or any other system or equipment on the
property. Tenant agrees to maintain the interior of the property and the surrounding outside area in a clean, safe,
and sanitary manner and not to make any alterations to the property without the Landlord's written consent. At the
termination of this Lease, the Tenant agrees to leave the property in the same condition as when it was received, except
for normal wear and tear. Tenant also agrees to comply with all rules, laws, regulations, and ordinances affecting the
property or the business activities of the Tenant.

9. The Tenant agrees to obtain and pay for all necessary utilities for the property.

10. The Tenant agrees not to sub-let the property or assign this Lease without the Landlord's written consent, which shall
not be unreasonably withheld. Tenant agrees to allow the Landlord reasonable access to the property for inspection and
repair. Landlord agrees to enter the property only after notifying the Tenant in advance, except in an emergency.

11. If the Tenant fails to pay the rent on time or violates any other terms of this Lease, the Landlord will provide written notice of the violation or default, allowing ㉓ _____ days to correct the violation or default. If the violation or default is not completely corrected within the time prescribed, the Landlord will have the right to terminate this Lease with ㉔ _____ days notice and in accordance with state law. Upon termination of this Lease, the Tenant agrees to surrender possession of the property. The Landlord will also have the right to re-enter the property and take possession of it, remove Tenant and any equipment or possessions of Tenant, and to take advantage of any other legal remedies available.

12. The Landlord agrees to carry fire and casualty insurance on the property, but shall have no liability for the operation of the Tenant's business. The Tenant agrees not to do anything that will increase the Landlord's insurance premiums and, further agrees to indemnify and hold the Landlord harmless from any liability or damage, whether caused by Tenant's operations or otherwise. The Tenant agrees to carry and pay all premiums for casualty insurance on any equipment or fixtures that Tenant installs at the property. In addition, the Tenant agrees to carry business liability insurance, including bodily injury and property damage coverage, covering all Tenant's business operations in the amount of $ ㉕ _____ with the Landlord named as a co-insured party. Tenant agrees to furnish Landlord copies of the insurance policies and to not cancel the policies without notifying the Landlord in advance. Tenant agrees to provide Landlord with a Certificate of Insurance which indicates that Landlord is a co-insured party and that Landlord shall be provided with a minimum of ten (10) days written notice prior to cancellation or change of coverage.

13. This Lease is subject to any mortgage or deed of trust currently on the property or which may be made against the property at any time in the future. The Tenant agrees to sign any documents necessary to subordinate this Lease to a mortgage or deed of trust for the Landlord.

14. This Lease may only be terminated by ㉖_____ days written notice from either party, except in the event of a violation of any terms or default of any payments or responsibilities due under this Lease, which are governed by the terms in Paragraph 11 of this Lease.

15. Tenant agrees that if any legal action is necessary to recover the property, collect any amounts due under this Lease, or correct a violation of any term of this Lease, Tenant shall be responsible for all costs incurred by Landlord in connection with such action, including any reasonable attorney's fees.

16. As required by law, the Landlord makes the following statement: "Radon gas is a naturally-occurring radioactive gas that, when accumulated in sufficient quantities in a building, may present health risks to persons exposed to it. Levels of radon gas that exceed federal and state guidelines have been found in buildings in this state. Additional information regarding radon gas and radon gas testing may be obtained from your county health department."

17. The following are additional terms of this Lease: ㉗

18. The parties agree that this Lease, including the following attachments: ㉘

is the entire agreement between them and that no terms of this Lease may be changed except by written agreement of both parties. This Lease is intended to comply with any and all applicable laws relating to landlord and tenant relationships in this state. This Lease binds and benefits both the Landlord and Tenant and any heirs, successors, representatives, or assigns. This Lease is governed by the laws of the State of ㉙_____ .

㉚_____
Signature of Landlord

㉛_____
Printed Name of Landlord

㉜_____
Signature of Tenant

㉝_____
Printed Name of Tenant

LEASE WITH PURCHASE OPTION

This lease is made on ①_____ , 20 _____ , between
②_____ , landlord,
address:③④⑤

and ⑥_____ , tenant,
address:⑦⑧⑨

1. The Landlord agrees to rent to the Tenant and the Tenant agrees to rent from the Landlord the following residence: ⑩

2. The term of this lease will be from ⑪_____ , until ⑫_____ .

3. The rental payments will be $ ⑬_____ per ⑭_____ and will be payable by the Tenant to the Landlord on the ⑮_____ day of each month, beginning on ⑯_____ .

4. The Landlord agrees to give the Tenant an exclusive option to buy this property for the following price and terms:

   A. ⑰_____ percent of the amount that the Tenant pays the Landlord as rent under this Lease will be held as a deposit and credited against the purchase price of this property if this option is exercised by the Tenant. If the option is not exercised, the Seller will retain all of these payments as rent under this Lease.

   B. The option period will be from the beginning date of this Lease until ⑱_____ , at which time it will expire unless exercised.

   C. During this period, the Tenant has the exclusive option and right to buy the leased property for the purchase price of $ ⑲_____ . The Tenant must notify the Landlord, in writing, of the decision to exercise this option. The purchase price will be paid as follows:

Rental payment deposit, to be held in trust by Landlord	$ ⑳_____
Other deposit: ㉑_____	$ ㉒_____
Cash or certified check for balance on closing	$ ㉓_____
(subject to any adjustments or prorations on closing)	
Total Purchase Price	$ ㉔_____

   D. Should the Tenant exercise this Option in writing, Landlord and Tenant agree to enter into a standard Agreement for the Sale of Real Estate. The Agreement will be conditional upon the Tenant being able to arrange suitable financing on the following terms at least thirty (30) days prior to the closing date specified in the Agreement for the Sale of Real Estate: a mortgage in the amount of ㉕_____ , payable in ㉖ _____ monthly payments, with an annual interest rate of ㉗_____ percent.

5. The Tenant has paid the Landlord a security deposit of $ ㉘_____ . This security deposit will be held as security for the repair of any damages to the residence by the Tenant. This deposit will be returned to the Tenant within ten (10) days of the termination of this lease, minus any amounts needed to repair the residence, but without interest, unless required by state law.

6. The Tenant has paid the Landlord an additional month's rent in the amount of $ ㉙_____ . This rent deposit will be held as security for the payment of rent by the Tenant. This rent payment deposit will be returned to the Tenant within ten (10) days of the termination of this lease, minus any rent still due upon termination, but without interest unless required by state law.

7. The Tenant has inspected the residence and has found it satisfactory. Tenant agrees to maintain the residence and the surrounding outside area in a clean and sanitary manner and not to make any alterations to the residence without the Landlord's written consent. At the termination of this lease, the Tenant agrees to leave the residence in the same condition as when it was received, except for normal wear and tear.

8. Tenant also agrees not to conduct any type of business in the residence, nor store or use any dangerous or hazardous materials. Tenant agrees that the residence is to be used only as a single family residence, with a maximum of _____ ___㉚____ tenants. Tenant also agrees to comply with all rules, laws, and ordinances affecting the residence. Tenant agrees that no pets or other animals are allowed in the residence without the written permission of the Landlord.

9. The Landlord agrees to supply the following utilities to the Tenant: ㉛

10. The Tenant agrees to obtain and pay for the following utilities: ㉜

11. Tenant agrees not to sub-let the residence or assign this lease without the Landlord's written consent. Tenant agrees to allow the Landlord reasonable access to the residence for inspection and repair. Landlord agrees to enter the residence only after notifying the Tenant in advance, except in an emergency.

12. If the Tenant fails to pay the rent on time or violates any other terms of this lease, the Landlord will provide written notice of the violation or default. If the violation or default is not corrected, the Landlord will have the right to terminate this lease in accordance with state law. The Landlord will also have the right to re-enter the residence and take possession of it and to take advantage of any other legal remedies available.

13. If the Tenant remains as tenant after the expiration of this lease without signing a new lease, a month-to-month tenancy will be created with the same terms and conditions as this lease, except that such new tenancy may be terminated by thirty (30) days written notice from either the Tenant or the Landlord.

14. As required by law, the Landlord makes the following statement: "Radon gas is a naturally-occurring radioactive gas that, when accumulated in sufficient quantities in a building, may present health risks to persons exposed to it. Levels of radon gas that exceed federal and state guidelines have been found in buildings in this state. Additional information regarding radon gas and radon gas testing may be obtained from your county health department."

15. As required by law, the Landlord makes the following LEAD WARNING STATEMENT: "Every purchaser or lessee of any interest in residential real property on which a residential dwelling was built prior to 1978 is notified that such property may present exposure to lead from lead-based paint that may place young children at risk of developing lead poisoning. Lead poisoning in young children may produce permanent neurological damage, including learning disabilities, reduced intelligence quotient, behavioral problems, and impaired memory. Lead poisoning also poses a particular threat to pregnant women. The seller of any interest in residential real estate is required to provide the buyer with any information on lead-based paint hazards from risk assessments or inspection in the seller's possession and notify the buyer of any known lead-based paint hazards. A risk assessment or inspection for possible lead-based paint hazards is recommended prior to purchase."

LANDLORD'S DISCLOSURE

Presence of lead-based paint and/or lead-based paint hazards: (Landlord to initial one). ㉝
_____ Known lead-based paint and/or lead-based paint hazards are present in building (explain).
_____ Landlord has no knowledge of lead-based paint and/or lead-based paint hazards in building.

RECORDS AND REPORTS AVAILABLE TO LANDLORD: (Landlord to initial one). ㉞
_____ Landlord has provided Tenant with all available records and reports pertaining to lead-based paint and/or lead-based paint hazards are present in building (list documents).
_____ Landlord has no records and reports pertaining to lead-based paint and/or lead-based paint hazards in building.

TENANT'S ACKNOWLEDGMENT (Tenant to initial all applicable). ㉟
_____ Tenant has received copies of all information listed above.
_____ Tenant has received the pamphlet "Protect Your Family from Lead in Your Home."
_____ Tenant has received a 10-day opportunity (or mutually-agreed on period) to conduct a risk assessment or inspection for the presence of lead-based paint and/or lead-based paint hazards in building.
_____ Tenant has waived the opportunity to conduct a risk assessment or inspection for the presence of lead-based paint and/or lead-based paint hazards in building.

The Landlord and Tenant have reviewed the information above and certify, by their signatures at the end of this Lease, to the best of their knowledge, that the information they have provided is true and accurate.

16. The following are additional terms of this Lease: ㊱

17. The parties agree that this Lease with Option is the entire agreement between them and that no terms of this Lease with Option may be changed except by written agreement of both parties. This Lease is intended to comply with any and all applicable laws relating to landlord and tenant relationships in this state. This Lease binds and benefits both the Landlord and Tenant and any successors, representatives, or assigns. Time is of the essence of this agreement. This Lease is governed by the laws of the State of ㊲_____ .

㊳_____
Signature of Landlord

㊴_____
Printed Name of Landlord

㊵_____
Signature of Tenant

㊶_____
Printed Name of Tenant

AMENDMENT OF LEASE

This amendment of lease is made on ①_____ , 20 _____ , between
②_____ , landlord,
address:

and ③_____ , tenant,
address:

For valuable consideration, the parties agree as follows:

1. The following described lease is attached to this amendment and is made a part of this amendment: ④

2. The parties agree to amend this lease as follows:⑤

3. All other terms and conditions of the original lease remain in effect without modification. This amendment binds and benefits both parties and any successors. This document, including the attached lease, is the entire agreement between the parties.

The parties have signed this amendment on the date specified at the beginning of this amendment.

⑥_____   ⑧_____
Signature of Landlord   Signature of Tenant

⑦_____   ⑨_____
Printed Name of Landlord   Printed Name of Tenant

EXTENSION OF LEASE

This extension of lease is made on ①_____ , 20 _____ , between
②_____ , landlord,
address:

and ③_____ , tenant,
address:

For valuable consideration, the parties agree as follows: ④

1. The following described lease will end on ⑤_____ , 20 _____ :

    This lease is attached to this extension and is a part of this extension.

2. The parties agree to extend this lease for an additional period, which will begin
    immediately on the expiration of the original time period and will end on
    ⑥_____ , 20 _____ .

3. The extension of this lease will be on the same terms and conditions as the original lease. This extension binds and
    benefits both parties and any successors. This document, including the attached lease, is the entire agreement between
    the parties.

The parties have signed this extension on the date specified at the beginning of this extension.

⑦_____   ⑨_____
Signature of Landlord   Signature of Tenant

⑧_____   ⑩_____
Printed Name of Landlord   Printed Name of Tenant

MUTUAL TERMINATION OF LEASE

This termination of lease is made on ①_____ , 20 _____ , between
②_____ , landlord,
address:

and ③_____ , tenant,
address:

For valuable consideration, the parties agree as follows:

1. The parties are currently bound under the terms of the following described lease: ④

2. They agree to mutually terminate and cancel this lease effective on this date. This termination agreement will act as a mutual release of all obligations under this lease for both parties, as if the lease has not been entered into in the first place. Landlord agrees that all rent due has been paid and that the possession of the property has been returned in satisfactory condition.

3. This termination binds and benefits both parties and any successors. This document, including the attached lease being terminated, is the entire agreement between the parties.

The parties have signed this termination on the date specified at the beginning of this termination.

⑤_____
Signature of Landlord

⑥_____
Printed Name of Landlord

⑦_____
Signature of Tenant

⑧_____
Printed Name of Tenant

ASSIGNMENT OF LEASE

This assignment is made on ①_____ , 20 _____ , between
②_____ , assignor,
address: ③

and ④_____ , assignee,
address: ⑤

For valuable consideration, the parties agree to the following terms and conditions:

1. The assignor assigns all interest, burdens, and benefits in the following described lease to the assignee: ⑥

    This lease is attached to this assignment and is a part of this assignment.

2. The assignor warrants that this lease is in effect, has not been modified, and is fully assignable. If the consent of the landlord is necessary for this assignment to be effective, such consent is attached to this assignment and is a part of this assignment. Assignor agrees to indemnify and hold the assignee harmless from any claim which may result from the assignor's failure to perform under this lease prior to the date of this assignment.

3. The assignee agrees to perform all of the obligations of the assignor and receive all of the benefits of the assignor under this lease. Assignee agrees to indemnify and hold the assignor harmless from anyclaim which may result from the assignee's failure to perform under this lease after the date of this assignment.

4. This assignment binds and benefits both parties and any successors. This document, including any attachments, is the entire agreement between the parties.

⑦_____
Signature of Assignor

⑨_____
Signature of Assignee

⑧_____
Printed Name of Assignor

⑩_____
Printed Name of Assignee

CONSENT TO ASSIGNMENT OF LEASE

Date: ①_____ , 20 _____

To: ②③

RE: Assignment of Lease

Dear ④_____ :

I am the landlord under the following described lease: ⑤

This lease is the subject of the attached assignment of lease.

I consent to the assignment of this lease as described in the attached assignment, which provides that the assignee is fully substituted for the assignor.

⑥_____
Signature of Landlord

⑦_____
Printed Name of Landlord

SUBLEASE

This sublease is made on ①_____ , 20 _____ , between
②_____ , tenant,
address:③

and ④_____ , subtenant,
address:⑤

For valuable consideration, the parties agree to the following terms and conditions:

1. The tenant subleases to the subtenant the following described property: ⑥

2. This property is currently leased to the tenant under the terms of the following described lease: ⑦

   This lease is attached to this sublease and is a part of this sublease.

3. This sublease will be for the period from ⑧_____ , 20 _____ , to
   ⑨_____ , 20 _____ .

4. The subrental payments will be $ ⑩_____ per ⑪_____ and will be payable by the subtenant
   to the landlord on the ⑫_____ day of each month, beginning on ⑬ _____ , 20 _____ .

5. The tenant warrants that the underlying lease is in effect, has not been modified, and that the property may be sublet. If
   the consent of the landlord is necessary for his sublease to be effective, such consent is attached to this sublease and
   is a part of this sublease. Tenant agrees to indemnify and hold the subtenant harmless from any claim which may result
   from the tenant's failure to perform under this lease prior to the date of this sublease.

6. The subtenant agrees to perform all of the obligations of the tenant under the original lease and receive all of the benefits
   of the tenant under this lease. Subtenant agrees to indemnify and hold the tenant harmless from any claim which may
   result from the subtenant's failure to perform under this lease after the date of this sublease.

7. The tenant agrees to remain primarily liable to the landlord for the obligations under the lease.

8. The parties agree to the following additional terms:⑭

9. This sublease binds and benefits both parties and any successors. This document, including any attachments, is the entire agreement between the parties. This sublease is subject to the laws of the State of ⑮_____ .

⑯_____   ⑱_____
Signature of Tenant   Signature of Subtenant

⑰_____   ⑲_____
Printed Name of Tenant   Printed Name of Subtenant

CONSENT TO SUBLEASE

Date: ①_____ , 20 _____

To ②③

RE: Sublease of Lease

Dear ④_____ :

I am the landlord under the following described lease: ⑤

This lease is the subject of the attached sublease.

I consent to the sublease of this lease as described in the attached sublease, which provides that the subtenant is substituted for the tenant for the period indicated in the sublease. This consent does not release the tenant from any obligations under the lease and the tenant remains fully bound under the lease.

⑥_____
Signature of Landlord

⑦_____
Printed Name of Landlord

NOTICE OF RENT DEFAULT

Date: ①_____ , 20 _____

To:②③

RE: Notice of Rent Default

Dear ④_____ :

This notice is in reference to the following described lease: ⑤

Please be advised that as of ⑥_____ , 20 _____ , you are in
DEFAULT IN YOUR PAYMENT OF RENT in the amount of $⑦ _____ .

If this breach of lease is not corrected within ⑧_____ days of this notice, we will take further action to
protect our rights, which may include termination of this lease and collection proceedings. This notice is made under all
applicable laws. All of our rights are reserved under this notice.

⑨_____
Signature of Landlord

⑩_____
Printed Name of Landlord

NOTICE OF BREACH OF LEASE

Date: ①_____ , 20 _____

To:②③

RE: Breach of Lease

Dear ④_____ :

This notice is in reference to the following described lease: ⑤

Please be advised that as of ⑥_____ , 20 _____ , we are holding you in BREACH OF LEASE for the following reasons:⑦

If this breach of lease is not corrected within ⑧_____ days of this notice, we will take further action to protect our rights, which may include termination of this lease. This notice is made under all applicable laws. All of our rights are reserved under this notice.

⑨_____
Signature of Landlord

⑩_____
Printed Name of Landlord

NOTICE TO PAY RENT OR VACATE

Date: ①_____ , 20 ____

To: ②③

RE: Notice to Vacate Property

Dear ④_____ :

This notice is in reference to the following described lease: ⑤

Please be advised that as of ⑥_____ , you are in DEFAULT OF YOUR PAYMENT OF RENT in the amount of $ ⑦_____ , which is immediately payable.

THEREFORE, YOU ARE HEREBY GIVEN NOTICE:

To immediately pay the amount of rent that is in default as noted above or to immediately vacate the property and deliver possession to the Landlord on or before ⑧_____ . If you fail to pay the rent in default or vacate the property by this date, we will take further action to protect our rights, which may include termination of this lease, collection, and eviction proceedings. Be also advised that any legal costs involved in the collection of rent in default or in obtaining possession of this property will also be recovered from you as may be allowed by law. This notice is made under all applicable laws of this state. All of our rights are reserved under this notice. Regardless of your vacating the property, you are still responsible for all rent due under the lease.

THIS IS NOT AN EVICTION NOTICE.

⑨_____
Signature of Landlord

⑩_____
Printed Name of Landlord

LANDLORD'S NOTICE TO TERMINATE LEASE

Date: ①_____ , 20 _____

To: ②

RE: Notice to Terminate Lease

Dear ③_____ :

This notice is in reference to the following described lease: ④

Please be advised that as of ⑤_____ , 20 _____ , you have been in BREACH OF LEASE for the following reasons: ⑥

You were previously notified of this breach in the NOTICE dated ⑦_____ , 20 _____ . At that time you were given ⑧_____ days to correct the breach of the lease and you have not complied.

THEREFORE, YOU ARE HEREBY GIVEN NOTICE:

The lease is immediately terminated and you are directed to deliver possession of the property to the landlord on or before ⑨_____ , 20 _____ . If you fail to deliver the property by this date, legal action to evict you from the property will be taken. Regardless of your deliverance of the property, you are still responsible for all rent due under the lease.

⑩_____
Signature of Landlord

⑪_____
Printed Name of Landlord

⑫_____
Address of Landlord

⑬_____
City, State, Zip code of Landlord

PROOF OF SERVICE

I, the undersigned, being of legal age, declare under penalty of perjury that I served the above Notice to Terminate Lease on the above-named tenant by mailing an exact copy to the tenant by certified mail on ⑭_____ .

Signed on: ⑮_____

By: ⑯_____
Signature of person mailing notice

⑰_____
Printed name of person mailing notice

FINAL NOTICE BEFORE LEGAL ACTION

Date: ①_____ , 20 _____

To: ②③

This notice is in reference to the following Lease: ④

Please be advised that as of ⑤_____ , you are in DEFAULT ON THIS LEASE in the amount of $ ⑥_____ , which is immediately due and payable. You have previously been repeatedly notified of your delinquency regarding this Lease.

THEREFORE, YOU ARE HEREBY GIVEN FINAL NOTICE:

That you must immediately pay the full amount that is in default as noted above on or before ⑦_____ . If you fail to pay the full amount in default by this date, we will take immediate action to protect our rights by proceeding with legal action. Be also advised that any and all legal costs associated with such legal action will also be recovered from you to the fullest extent allowed by law and that such legal proceedings may impair your credit rating. This notice is made under all applicable laws of this state. All of our rights are reserved under this notice.

THIS IS YOUR FINAL OPPORTUNITY TO RESOLVE MATTERS WITHOUT THE EXPENSE OF COURT PROCEED-INGS.

Dated: ⑧ _____

⑨_____
Signature

⑩_____
Printed Name

⑪_____
Address

⑫_____
City, State, Zip Code

NOTICE OF LEASE

NOTICE is given of the existence of the following lease:①

Name of landlord:②
Address:③

Name of tenant:④
Address:⑤

Description of property leased:⑥

Term of lease: From ⑦_____ , 20 _____ , to _____ , 20 _____ .

Any options to extend lease:⑧

⑨_____   ⑩_____
Signature   Printed Name

⑪
State of _____
County of _____

On _____ , 20 _____ , _____
personally came before me and, being duly sworn, did state that he or she is the person described in the above document and that he or she signed the above document in my presence.

_____
Signature of Notary Public

Notary Public, In and for the County of _____
State of _____

My commission expires: _____ Notary Seal

RECEIPT FOR LEASE SECURITY DEPOSIT

The landlord acknowledges receipt of the sum of $ ① _____ paid by the tenant under the following described lease: ②

This security deposit payment will be held by the landlord under the terms of this lease, and unless required by law, will not bear any interest. This security deposit will be repaid when due under the terms of the lease.

Dated: ③ _____ , 20 _____

④ _____
Signature of Landlord

⑤ _____
Printed Name of Landlord

RENT RECEIPT

The landlord acknowledges receipt of the sum of $ ① _____ paid by
② _____ , the tenant, for rent during the time period of ③ _____ to
_____ for the property located at: ④ _____ .

Dated: ⑤ _____ , 20 _____

⑥ _____
Signature of Landlord

⑦ _____
Printed Name of Landlord

Chapter 14

Rental and Sale of Personal Property

Instructions for Rental of Personal Property

Leases of personal property are often undertaken for the use of tools, equipment, or property necessary to perform a certain task. Other situations where such an agreement is often used is in the rental of property for recreational purposes. The needs of the parties for a personal property rental agreement depend a great deal on the type of property involved and the value of the property.

Personal Property Rental Agreement:
To prepare this form, fill in the following information:
① Date of rental agreement
② Name of Owner
③ Address of Owner
④ Name of Renter
⑤ Address of Renter
⑥ Complete description of rental property
⑦ Beginning and ending date and time of rental agreement
⑧ Amount being charged for rental
⑨ period of time for payment (usally a month or day)
⑩ Describe payment details
⑪ Amount of late fee
⑫ Number of days the rental not paid to make it in default
⑬ Amount of security deposit
⑭ Amount of insurance coverage required
⑮ Additional terms
⑯ Which state's laws will be used
⑰ Signature of Owner

⑱ Printed name of Owner
⑲ Signature of Renter
⑳ Printed name of Renter

Instructions for Sale of Personal Property

Contract for Sale of Personal Property: This form may be used for documenting the sale of any type of personal property. It may be used for vehicles, business assets, or any other personal property. The information necessary to complete this form are the names and addresses of the seller and the buyer, a complete description of the property being sold, the total purchase price, and the terms of the payment of this price.

To prepare this form, fill in the following information:
① Date of Contract
② Name of Seller
③ Address of Seller
④ Name of Buyer
⑤ Address of Buyer
⑥ Describe personal property being sold
⑦ Amount personal property being sold for
⑧ Payment description
⑨ The date that the buyer takes ownership of property
⑩ State where transaction occurs
⑪ Signature of Seller
⑫ Printed nmae of Seller
⑬ Signature of Buyer
⑭ Printed name of Buyer

Bill of Sale, with Warranties: This document is used as a receipt of the sale of personal property. It is, in many respects, often used to operate as a *title* (or ownership document) to items of personal property. It verifies that the person noted in the bill of sale has obtained legal title to the property from the previous owner. This particular version also provides that the seller *warrants* (or guarantees) that he or she has the authority to transfer legal title to the buyer and that there are no outstanding debts or liabilities for the property. In addition, this form provides that the seller warrants that the property is in good working condition on the date of the sale. To complete this form, simply fill in the names and addresses of the seller and buyer, the purchase price of the item, and a description of the property.

To prepare this form, fill in the following information:
① Date of Bill of Sale
② Name of Seller
③ Address of Seller

④ Name of Buyer
⑤ Address of Buyer
⑥ Amount received for property
⑦ Describe property being purchased
⑧ Signature of Seller
⑨ Printed name of Seller

Bill of Sale, without Warranties: This form also provides a receipt to the buyer for the purchase of an item of personal property. However, in this form, the seller makes no warranties at all, either regarding the authority to sell the item or the condition of the item. It is sold to the buyer in "as is" condition. The buyer takes it regardless of any defects. To complete this form, fill in the names and addresses of the seller and buyer, the purchase price of the item, and a description of the property.

To prepare this form, fill in the following information:
① Date of Bill of Sale
② Name of Seller
③ Address of Seller
④ Name of Buyer
⑤ Address of Buyer
⑥ Amount received for property
⑦ Describe property being purchased
⑧ Signature of Seller
⑨ Printed name of Seller

Bill of Sale, Subject to Debt: This form also provides a receipt to the buyer for the purchase of an item of personal property. This form, however, provides that the property sold is subject to a certain prior debt. It verifies that the seller has obtained legal title to the property from the previous owner, but that the seller specifies that the property is sold subject to a certain debt which the buyer is to pay off. In addition, the buyer agrees to indemnify the seller regarding any liability on the debt. This particular bill of sale version also provides that the seller warrants that he or she has authority to transfer legal title to the buyer. In addition, this form provides that the owner warrants that the property is in good working condition on the date of the sale. To complete this form, fill in the names and addresses of the seller and buyer, the purchase price of the item, a description of the property, and a description of the debt.

To prepare this form, fill in the following information:
① Date of Bill of Sale
② Name of Seller
③ Address of Seller
④ Name of Buyer

⑤ Address of Buyer
⑥ Amount received for property
⑦ Describe property being purchased
⑧ Describe debt
⑨ Signature of Seller
⑩ Printed name of Seller
⑪ Signature of Buyer
⑫ Printed name of Buyer

PERSONAL PROPERTY RENTAL AGREEMENT

This Agreement is made on ①_____ , 20 _____ , between
②_____ , Owner,
address:③

and ④_____ , Renter,
address:⑤

1. The Owner agrees to rent to the Renter and the Renter agrees to rent from the Owner the following property: ⑥

2. The term of this agreement will be from ⑦_____ o'clock _____ .m.,
    _____ , 20 _____ , until _____ o'clock _____ . m., _____
    _____ , 20 _____ .

3. The rental payments will be $ ⑧_____ per ⑨_____ and will be payable by the Renter to the Owner as
    follows:⑩

4. The Renter agrees to pay a late fee of $ ⑪_____ per day that the rental payment is late. If the rental payments
    are in default for over ⑫_____ days, the Owner may immediately demand possession of the property
    without advance notice to the Renter.

5. The Owner warrants that the property is free of any known faults which would affect its safe operation under normal
    usage and is in good working condition.

6. The Renter states that the property has been inspected and is in good working condition. The Renter agrees to use the
    property in a safe manner and in normal usage and to maintain the property in good repair. The Renter further agrees
    not to use the property in a negligent manner or for any illegal purpose.

7. The Renter agrees to fully indemnify the Owner for any damage to or loss of the property during the term of this agree-
    ment, unless such loss or damage is caused by a defect of the rented property.

8. The Owner shall not be liable for any injury, loss, or damage caused by any use of the property.

9. The Renter has paid the Owner a security deposit of $ ⑬_____ . This security deposit will be held as security for
    payments of the rent and for the repair of any damages to the property by the Renter. This deposit will be returned to the
    Renter upon the termination of this agreement, minus any rent still owed to the Owner and minus any amounts needed
    to repair the property, beyond normal wear and tear.

10. The Renter may not assign or transfer any rights under this agreement to any other person, nor allow the property to be
    used by any other person, without the written consent of the Owner.

11. Renter agrees to obtain insurance coverage for the property during the term of this rental agreement in the amount of
    $ ⑭_____ . Renter agrees to provide the Owner with a copy of the insurance policy and to not cancel the policy
    during the term of this rental agreement.

12. This agreement may be terminated by either party by giving twenty-four (24) hours written notice to the other party.

13. Any dispute related to this agreement will be settled by voluntary mediation. If mediation is unsuccessful, the dispute will be settled by binding arbitration using an arbitrator of the American Arbitration Association.

14. The following are additional terms of this agreement:⑮

15. The parties agree that this agreement is the entire agreement between them. This agreement binds and benefits both the Owner and Renter and any successors. Time is of the essence of this agreement.

16. This agreement is governed by the laws of the State of ⑯_____ .

⑰_____
Signature of Owner

⑲_____
Signature of Renter

⑱_____
Printed Name of Owner

⑳_____
Printed Name of Renter

CONTRACT FOR SALE OF PERSONAL PROPERTY

This Contract is made on ①_____ , 20 _____ , between
②_____ , Seller,
address:③

and ④_____ , Buyer,
address:⑤

1. The Seller agrees to sell to the Buyer, and the Buyer agrees to buy the following personal property:⑥

2. The Buyer agrees to pay the Seller $ ⑦_____ for the property. The Buyer agrees to pay this purchase price in the following manner:⑧

3. The Buyer will be entitled to possession of this property on
    ⑨_____ , 20 _____ .

4. The Seller represents that it has legal title to the property and full authority to sell the property. Seller also represents that the property is sold free and clear of all liens, indebtedness, or liabilities. Seller agrees to provide Buyer with a Bill of Sale for the property.

5. This Contract binds and benefits both the Buyer and Seller and any successors. This document, including any attachments, is the entire agreement between the Buyer and Seller. This agreement is governed by the laws of the State of
    ⑩_____ .

⑪_____   ⑬_____
Signature of Seller   Signature of Buyer

⑫_____   ⑭_____
Printed Name of Seller   Printed Name of Buyer

BILL OF SALE, WITH WARRANTIES

This Bill of Sale is made on ①_____ , 20 _____ , between

②_____ , Seller,

address:③

and ④_____ , Buyer,

address:⑤

In exchange for the payment of $ ⑥_____ , received from the Buyer, the Seller sells and transfers possession of the following property to the Buyer:⑦

The Seller warrants that it owns this property and that it has the authority to sell the property to the Buyer. Seller also warrants that the property is sold free and clear of all liens, indebtedness, or liabilities.

The Seller also warrants that the property is in good working condition as of this date.

Signed and delivered to the Buyer on the above date.

⑧_____

Signature of Seller

⑨_____

Printed Name of Seller

BILL OF SALE, WITHOUT WARRANTIES

This Bill of Sale is made on ①_____ , 20 _____ , between
②_____ , Seller,
address:③

and ④_____ , Buyer,
address:⑤

In exchange for the payment of $ ⑥_____ , received from the Buyer, the Seller sells and transfers possession of the following property to the Buyer:⑦

The Seller disclaims any implied warranty of merchantability or fitness and the property is sold in its present condition, "as is."

Signed and delivered to the Buyer on the above date.

⑧_____
Signature of Seller

⑨_____
Printed Name of Seller

BILL OF SALE, SUBJECT TO DEBT

This Bill of Sale is made on ①_____ , 20 _____ , between
②_____ , Seller,
address:③

and ④_____ , Buyer,
address:⑤

In exchange for the payment of $ ⑥_____ , received from the Buyer, the Seller sells and transfers possession of the following property to the Buyer:⑦

The Seller warrants that it owns this property and that it has the authority to sell the property to the Buyer. Seller also states that the property is sold subject to the following debt:⑧

The Buyer buys the property subject to the above debt and agrees to pay the debt. Buyer also agrees to indemnify and hold the Seller harmless from any claim based on failure to pay off this debt.

The Seller also warrants that the property is in good working condition as of this date.

Signed and delivered to the Buyer on the above date.

⑨_____
Signature of Seller

⑪_____
Signature of Buyer

⑩_____
Printed Name of Seller

⑫_____
Printed Name of Buyer

Chapter 15

Sale of Real Estate

In this chapter

are various forms for the sale and transfer of real estate. Although most real estate sales today are handled by real estate professionals, it is still perfectly legal to buy and sell property without the use of a real estate broker or lawyer. The forms provided in this chapter allow anyone to prepare the necessary forms for many basic real estate transactions. Please note, however, that there may be various state and local variations on sales contracts, mortgages, or other real estate documents. If in doubt, check with a local real estate professional or an attorney. Please read the description of what each form provides and also what information is necessary to complete each form. Also, carefully read through each form itself so that you understand the meaning of each of the terms of the documents.

Instructions for Sale of Real Estate

Agreement to Sell Real Estate: This form can be used for setting down an agreement to buy and sell property. It contains the basic clauses to cover situations that will arise in most typical real estate transaction. The various items that are covered in this contract are

- That the sale is conditioned on the buyer being able to obtain financing 30 days prior to the closing
- That if the sale is not completed, the buyer will be given back the earnest money deposit, without interest or penalty
- That the seller will provide a Warranty Deed for the real estate and a Bill of Sale for any personal property included in the sale
- That certain items will be pro-rated and adjusted as of the closing date
- That the buyer and the seller may split the various closing costs
- That the seller represents that it has good title to the property and that the personal property included is in good working order

- That the title to the property will be evidenced by either title insurance or an abstract of title
- That the buyer has the right to a termite inspection
- That the buyer has a right to a complete home inspection at least 30 days prior to closing
- That the seller provide a radon statement and lead paint disclosure
- That the seller will provide the buyer with the U.S. EPA pamphlet: "Protect Your Family from Lead in Your Home." *Note*: This document is necessary *only* if the residential dwelling was built prior to 1978
- That the seller will provide a Real Estate Disclosure Statement to the buyer within 5 days and that the buyer has the right to rescind the agreement within 5 days after the receipt of the disclosure statement

In order to prepare this agreement, please fill in the following information:

① Date of Agreement
② Name of seller
③ Address of seller
④ City of seller
⑤ State of seller
⑥ Name of buyer
⑦ Address of buyer
⑧ City of buyer
⑨ State of buyer
⑩ Address of property
⑪ City of property
⑫ State of property
⑬ A legal description of the property involved
⑭ A description of any personal property to be included in the sale
⑮ The purchase price of the property
⑯ The amount of any mortgage which will be arranged 30 days prior to closing
⑰ Number of monthly payments of this mortgage
⑱ Annual interest rate of this mortgage
⑲ Amount of earnest money deposit
⑳ Description of any other deposit
㉑ Amount of any other deposits
㉒ Amount of balance due at closing
㉓ Total purchase price of the property
㉔ Amount of earnest money paid upon signing the contract
㉕ Date for closing sale
㉖ Time for closing
㉗ Address of closing
㉘ City of closing
㉙ State of closing

㉚ Any other documents to be provided to buyer at closing
㉛ Any other items that will be adjusted and pro-rated at closing
㉜ Closing costs which will be paid for by seller
㉝ Closing costs which will be paid for by buyer
㉞ Whether there are any outstanding claims, liabilities, indebtedness and/or restrictions pertaining to the property
㉟ Seller's initials on 'presence of lead paint' disclosure
㊱ Seller's initials on records or reports of lead paint
㊲ Buyer's initials on lead paint acknowledgment
㊳ Whether there are any additional terms
㊴ Which state's laws will be used to interpret contract
㊵ Signature of seller
㊶ Printed Name of seller
㊷ Signatures of witnesses for seller
㊸ Printed names of witnesses for seller
㊹ Signature of buyer
㊺ Printed name of buyer
㊻ Signatures of witnesses for buyer
㊼ Printed names of witnesses for buyer

Title insurance or an abstract of title will need to be obtained from a local title company or attorney. A Bill of Sale for any personal property (Chapter 14) and a Warranty Deed (later in this chapter) will need to be prepared for use at the closing of the sale. Finally, a federal lead brochure will need to be provided to the buyer if the dwelling was built before 1978 (also later in this chapter). Both the seller's and buyer's signatures should be witnessed by two witnesses. Note: California residents will need to include the California Addendum to Contract that is included on the Forms-on-CD as well as the appropriate disclosure forms.

Contract for Deed: This form is also known in some localities as an Installment Real Estate Sales Contract, a Land Contract, or a Conditional Sales Contract. This form is used in real estate situations where it is desired that the Buyer receives possession of the property, but does not receive actual title to the property until the entire sales price has been paid to the Seller. Under this type of contract, the Buyer agrees to make periodic installment payments until the sales price of the property has been paid in full. The reason that some real estate transactions are handled in this manner is that it is much easier for the property to be returned to the Seller in the case of a *default* (failure to make an installment payment when due) by the Buyer. Most Contracts for Deed (as does the one provided in this book) provide for the complete forfeiture of all money paid if the Buyer misses even one payment. This harsh remedy also precludes the need for any foreclosure proceedings against a defaulting Buyer in order to regain possession of the property, as the Buyer does not have legal title to the property until all payments have been made. This type of real estate transaction is generally only used for the sale of undeveloped vacant land. Although a Contract for Deed can be used for the sale of improved property as well, the lack of the legal protections that a mortgage provides make this type of real estate contract a bad choice for a Buyer of residential or commercial property that has a home or business already erected on the property.

This contract provides that a Buyer pay a down payment of some amount and that the remaining balance due for the sale of the real estate be paid in equal monthly installment payments, which include principal and interest at a certain percentage rate. The Buyer also has the right to pay off part of or the entire balance due at any time, without penalty. The Buyer and Seller will need to determine a sales price, what the annual interest rate will be, the amount of a down payment, and also how many monthly payments will be required. For example, the Buyer and Seller agree that the property will be sold for $50,000.00 and that this total amount includes an annual interest rate of 6%. They also agree that there will be 60 monthly payments (five years) and that the Buyer will make a $2,000.00 down payment, leaving $48,000.00 remaining to be paid. Thus, the Buyer will be required to make 60 monthly installment payments of $800.00 per payment for a total of $48,000.00.

The contract also provides that the Buyer agrees to forfeit all of the payments made if any payment has been missed for a period of 30 days and another 30-day period has elapsed after the Buyer has received from the Seller, via Certified U.S. Mail, a Declaration of Intent to Forfeit and Terminate Contact for Deed (explained below). The forfeited payments will be then retained by the Seller as accumulated rent for the property. The Buyer also agrees to immediately vacate the property if the Contract for Deed is terminated. The Buyer agrees to pay all real estate property taxes and assessments on the property when due. The contract allows for the Buyer to build new construction on the property as long as the building complies with all applicable zoning laws and health and building codes. Finally, the Buyer has the right, under this contract, to examine an abstract of title to the property to determine that the Seller actually has title to the property. If and when the Buyer has made all payments and is up-to-date on payment of all taxes and assessments on the property, the Seller agrees to transfer full title to the Buyer by the use of a Warranty Deed. A Bill of Sale for any personal property (Chapter 13) and a Warranty Deed (later in this chapter) will need to be prepared for use at the closing of the sale. Finally, a federal lead brochure will need to be provided to the buyer if the dwelling was built before 1978 (explained later in this chapter). Both the seller's and buyer's signatures should be witnessed by two witnesses. Note: California residents will need to include the California Addendum to Contract that is included on the Forms-on-CD as well as the appropriate disclosure forms. To complete this form, you will need the following information:

1. Date of Contract for Deed
2. Name of seller
3. Address of seller
4. City of seller
5. State of seller
6. Name of buyer
7. Address of buyer
8. City of buyer

⑨ State of buyer
⑩ Address of property
⑪ City of property
⑫ State of property
⑬ A legal description of the property involved
⑭ A description of any personal property to be included in the sale
⑮ The purchase price of the property
⑯ The total purchase price of the property
⑰ Amount of the down payment
⑱ Balance due from the buyer
⑲ Number of monthly payment
⑳ Amount of each monthly payments
㉑ Day of the month on which payment will be due
㉒ Due date of first monthly payment
㉓ Percent of interest rate
㉔ Amount of down payment paid upon signing the contract
㉕ Any other documents to be provided to buyer at closing
㉖ Tax year for which buyer will begin paying taxes
㉗ Whether there are any outstanding claims, liabilities, indebtedness and/or restrictions pertaining to the property
㉘ Seller's initials on presence of lead paint disclosure
㉙ Seller's initials on records or reports of lead paint
㉚ Buyer's initials on lead paint acknowledgment
㉛ Whether there are any additional terms
㉜ Which state's laws will be used to interpret contract
㉝ Signature of seller
㉞ Printed Name of seller
㉟ Signatures of witnesses for seller
㊱ Printed names of witnesses for seller
㊲ Signature of buyer
㊳ Printed name of buyer
㊴ Signatures of witnesses for buyer
㊵ Printed names of witnesses for buyer

Declaration of Intent to Forfeit and Terminate Contract for Deed: This form is to be used by a Seller under a Contract for Deed to notify the Buyer that they are in default of a term of the contract and that the Seller is declaring that the Buyer's payments under the contract thus far are forfeited and that the Contract will be terminated by the Seller for non-compliance by the Buyer. Under the terms of the above Contract for Deed, the Seller must provide this Declaration to the Buyer by Certified U.S. Mail. The Buyer then has 30 days to become current with their payments under the contract. If the Buyer does not make the past-due payments within 30 of receipt of this Declaration, the Buyer's prior payments will be forfeited to the Seller, the Contract for Deed will be terminated, and the Buyer will be required to vacate the property immediately. To complete this document, you will need the following information:

① Date of original Contract for Deed
② Name of seller
③ Address of seller
④ Name of buyer
⑤ Address of buyer
⑥ Address of property
⑦ A legal description of the property involved
⑧ Date of Declaration
⑨ Reason buyer is in default on Contract for Deed (if buyer has missed a payment or payments, you will need to specify the due date of the payment(s) and the exact amount of any past due amounts)
⑩ Date of mailing of this Declaration
⑪ Date of this Declaration
⑫ Signature of seller
⑬ Printed name of seller

Option to Buy Real Estate: This form is designed to be used to offer an interested buyer a time period in which to have an exclusive option to purchase a parcel of real estate. It should be used in conjunction with a filled-in but unsigned copy of the above Agreement to Sell Real Estate. Through the use of this option agreement, the seller can offer the buyer a time during which he or she can consider the purchase without concern of a sale to another party.

This agreement provides that in exchange for a payment (which will be applied to the purchase price if the option is exercised), the buyer is given a period of time to accept the terms of a completed real estate contract. If the buyer accepts the terms and exercises the option in writing, the seller agrees to complete the sale. If the option is not exercised, the seller is then free to sell the property on the market and to retain the money that the potential buyer paid for the option. To complete this form, please fill in the following information:

① Date of Option
② Name of seller
③ Address of seller
④ City of seller
⑤ State of seller
⑥ Name of buyer
⑦ Address of buyer
⑧ City of buyer
⑨ State of buyer
⑩ Address of property

⑪ City of property
⑫ State of property
⑬ Legal description of property
⑭ Price buyer will pay for option
⑮ Date that option period will end
⑯ Price buyer will pay seller for property if option is exercised
⑰ State whose laws will govern the agreement
⑱ Date of option agreement
⑲ Signature of seller
⑳ Printed name of seller
㉑ Signature of buyer
㉒ Printed name of buyer

In addition, an Agreement to Sell Real Estate covering the property subject to the option to buy should be completed and attached to the option agreement. This contract will provide all of the essential terms of the actual agreement to sell the property.

Offer to Purchase Real Estate: This document is used by a potential buyer of real estate to make an offer to purchase the property. It is *not* a contract or agreement for the purchase of the real estate. It is an offer to pay a certain price for a parcel of real estate, based on the meeting of certain conditions. The conditions that must be met are as follows: The buyer must be able to arrange for suitable financing prior to closing. The buyer must receive a satisfactory termite inspection report. The property to be purchased will be transferred to the buyer free of any debts or liabilities. The parties agree to sign a standard Agreement to Sell Real Estate. The date of the closing is set forth in the Offer. Any other terms that the buyer would like should be included. The Offer is only open for acceptance by the Owner until the time and date set in the Offer. To complete this form, please fill in the following information:

① Date of Offer
② Name of buyer
③ Address of buyer
④ City of buyer
⑤ State of buyer
⑥ Name of owner
⑦ Address of owner
⑧ City of owner
⑨ State of owner
⑩ Address of property
⑪ City of property
⑫ State of property
⑬ Legal description of property
⑭ Purchase price offered for property

⑮ Escrow deposit included with Offer
⑯ Any additional deposit anticipated
⑰ Balance of price due to owner at closing
⑱ Total purchase price
⑲ Amount of mortgage commitment required within 90 days
⑳ Number of monthly payments of mortgage commitment
㉑ Annual interest rate percentage of mortgage commitment
㉒ Date for closing
㉓ Time for closing
㉔ Address for closing
㉕ City for closing
㉖ State for closing
㉗ Any other terms
㉘ Expiration time of Offer
㉙ Expiration date of Offer
㉚ Signature of buyer
㉛ Printed name of buyer
㉜ Date of buyer's signature
㉝ Signature of owner
㉞ Printed name of owner
㉟ Date of owner's signature

Lead Warning Statement: Under the Federal Real Estate Disclosure and Notification Rule, if you are a seller of a residential property that has a home built before 1978, you are required to notify the buyer of the risk of lead exposure and provide them with a copy of the enclosed brochure: "Protect Your Family from Lead in Your Home." In addition, you must disclose your knowledge of any risk of lead hazards in the home. Clauses in the Agreement to Purchase Real Estate, the Contract for Deed, and the Residential Lease forms that are included in this book satisfy the federal requirement. The Lead Warning Statement form included in this chapter is for use in any real estate transaction for residential property built prior to 1978, for which the main sale or lease document does not already contain the required Lead Warning Statement. To complete this form, the following must be done:

① Seller should initial the appropriate choices regarding knowledge of lead paint and/or hazards in the building
② If available, seller should also provide buyer with any records or reports pertaining to lead paint and/or hazards
③ Buyer should initial the appropriate choices regarding receipt of copies of any seller-provided information, receipt of the Federal Lead Brochure (Protect Your Family From Lead in Your Home).
④ Buyer either accepts or waives the right to conduct an inspection of the building within the following 10 days (or any other agreed upon period).
⑤ Date of signing of statement

⑥ Signature of seller (change to Landlord if using this Statement with a lease)
⑦ Printed name of seller (change to Landlord if using this Statement with a lease)
⑧ Signature of buyer (change to Tenant if using this Statement with a lease)
⑨ Printed name of buyer (change to Tenant if using this Statement with a lease)

Federal Lead Brochure: A PDF-format copy of the U.S. EPA's pamphlet, "Protect Your Family from Lead in Your Home," is provided *only* on the included Forms-on-CD. A copy of this brochure must be provided to every potential buyer (or renter) of any residential dwelling that was built prior to 1978.

Appraisal Report: An appraisal of real estate is an impartial evaluation of real estate by a knowledgeable and qualified person after they have performed a careful inspection and study of the property and have used certain techniques to compare the property to other properties. There are three generally-accepted approaches to estimating real estate values. The 'Cost' approach arrives at a value by estimating the replacement value of the property. The 'Market' approach compares the property with similar properties and uses the comparison to determine what the property would sell for on the open market. The 'Income' approach looks at what the net return for a piece of property would be. This approach is generally used for commercial property. Appraisers will use various combinations of these approaches to come to a reasonable estimate of a property's value. Real estate brokers are qualified to perform appraisals and there are professional appraisers who are also qualified. An appraisal report can range from a short 1 or 2 page opinion to a detailed bound document with a survey, photos, plot plans, etc.

The form provided is a simple version of an Appraisal Report and provides that the appraiser certifies that he or she has investigated a certain piece of property and has determined the market value of the property to be a certain amount. The report then provides a list of conditions which the appraiser has used to limit the market determination. To complete this form, an appraiser will need to insert the following:

① Date of appraisal
② Name of appraiser
③ Address of appraiser
④ Name of person requesting appraisal
⑤ Address of property appraised
⑥ Legal description of property appraised
⑦ Market value of land only
⑧ Market value of improvements to land
⑨ Total market value
⑩ Qualifications of appraiser
⑪ Signature of appraiser
⑫ Printed name of appraiser

Appraisal Affidavit: An appraisal affidavit provides the basic details of an appraisal that is signed and sworn to before a notary public. This type of document is often required by financing institutions at the closing of a real estate transaction. This documents supplies essentially the same information as the basic Appraisal Report, but in a more formal affidavit. To complete this form, the following needs to be completed:

① Date of appraisal
② Name of appraiser
③ Address of appraiser
④ Name of person requesting appraisal
⑤ Address of property appraised
⑥ Legal description of property appraised
⑦ Market value of land only
⑧ Market value of improvements to land
⑨ Total market value
⑩ Qualifications of appraiser
⑪ Signature of appraiser
⑫ Printed name of appraiser
⑬ The following must be completed by a Notary Public

Quitclaim Deed: This form is used to transfer property from the seller (called the '*grantor*' on the deed) to the buyer (called the '*grantee*' on the deed) without any warranties that he or she actually owns the property involved. Any transfers of real estate must be in writing. This type of Quitclaim Deed is intended to be used when the seller is merely selling whatever interest she or he may have in the property. By using a Quitclaim Deed, a seller is not, in any way, guaranteeing that she or he actually owns any interest in the property. This type of Deed may be used to settle any claims that a person may have to a piece of real estate, to settle disputes over property, or to transfer property between co-owners. For this deed form to be recorded, it must be properly notarized. To prepare this Deed, simply fill in the following information:

① Name of person requesting recording of deed (generally, you)
② Name and address of person who prepared the deed
③ Name and address of person to whom the recorded deed should be mailed by the recorder's office (not necessary if you bring the deed to the recorder's office personally)
④ Property Tax Parcel number or Tax account number (generally found on latest tax bill)
⑤ Date of signing deed
⑥ Name of grantor (the one transferring the property)
⑦ Address of grantor
⑧ Name of grantee (the one receiving the property)
⑨ Address of grantee
⑩ Street address of property itself
⑪ Legal description of property (should be taken from current deed)

⑫ Current year for property taxes (taxes will be prorated between grantor and grantee for the portion of the tax year that each party owned the property)
⑬ Date of signing of deed by grantor
⑭ Signature of grantor (signed in the front of notary public)
⑮ Printed Name of grantor
⑯ Signatures and printed names of two witnesses (signed in front of notary public)
⑰ Notary Acknowledgement to be completed by notary public

Warranty Deed: This form is used to transfer property from the seller (called the '*grantor*' in the deed) to a buyer (called the '*grantee*' in the deed) with various standard warranties that he or she actually owns the property involved. Any transfers of real estate must be in writing. This type of Warranty Deed is intended to be used when the seller is selling his or her entire legal interest in the property. By using a Warranty Deed, a seller is guaranteeing that she or he actually owns any interest in the property. This type of deed is used in most real estate situations. It provides that the seller is conveying to the buyer a full and complete title to the land without any restrictions or debts. If the property will be subject to any restrictions or debts, these should be noted in the legal description area provided. For the transfer to actually take place, the grantor must give the actual deed to the grantee. In addition, in order for this document to be recorded, this form should be properly notarized. To prepare this Deed, simply fill in the following information:

① Name of person requesting recording of deed (generally, you)
② Name and address of person who prepared the deed
③ Name and address of person to whom the recorded deed should be mailed by the recorder's office (not necessary if you bring the deed to the recorder's office personally)
④ Property Tax Parcel number or Tax account number (generally found on latest tax bill)
⑤ Date of signing deed
⑥ Name of grantor (the one transferring the property)
⑦ Address of grantor
⑧ Name of grantee (the one receiving the property)
⑨ Address of grantee
⑩ Street address of property itself
⑪ Legal description of property (should be taken from current deed)
⑫ Current year for property taxes (taxes will be prorated between grantor and grantee for the portion of the tax year that each party owned the property)
⑬ Date of signing of deed by grantor
⑭ Signature of grantor (signed in the front of notary public)
⑮ Printed Name of grantor
⑯ Signatures and printed names of two witnesses (signed in front of notary public)
⑰ Notary Acknowledgment to be completed by notary public

AGREEMENT TO SELL REAL ESTATE

This agreement is made on ① _____ , 20 _____ , between
② _____ , seller,
address: ③ ④ ⑤

and ⑥ _____ , buyer,
address: ⑦ ⑧ ⑨

The seller now owns the following described real estate, located at
⑩ _____ ,
City of ⑪ _____ , State of ⑫ _____ , and legally described as follows: ⑬

For valuable consideration, the seller agrees to sell and the buyer agrees to buy this property for the following price and on the following terms:

1. The seller will sell this property to the buyer, free from all claims, liabilities, and indebtedness, unless noted in this agreement.

2. The following personal property is also included in this sale: ⑭

3. The buyer agrees to pay the seller the sum of $ ⑮ _____ , which the seller agrees to accept as full payment. This agreement, however, is conditional upon the buyer being able to arrange suitable financing on the following terms at least thirty (30) days prior to the closing date for this agreement: A mortgage in the amount of $ ⑯ _____ , payable in ⑰ _____ monthly payments, with an annual interest rate of ⑱ _____ % (_____ percent) .

4. The purchase price will be paid as follows:
    Earnest deposit .... $ ⑲ _____
    Other deposit: ⑳ .... $ ㉑ _____
    Cash or certified check on closing .... $ ㉒ _____
    (subject to any adjustments or prorations on closing)
    Total Purchase Price .... $ ㉓ _____

5. The seller acknowledges receiving the earnest money deposit of $ ㉔ _____ from the buyer. If buyer fails to perform this agreement, the seller shall retain this money. If seller fails to perform this agreement, this money shall be returned to the buyer or the buyer may have the right of specific performance. If buyer is unable to obtain suitable financing at least thirty (30) days prior to closing, then this money will be returned to the buyer without penalty or interest.

6. This agreement will close on ㉕ _____ , 20 _____ , at ㉖ _____ o'clock ___ . m., at ㉗ _____
    _____ , City of ㉘ _____ , State of ㉙ _____ . At that time, and upon payment by the buyer of the portion of the purchase price then due, the seller will deliver to buyer the following documents: ㉚

    (a) A Bill of Sale for all personal property
    (b) A Warranty Deed for the real estate
    (c) A Seller's Affidavit of Title
    (d) A closing statement
    (e) Other documents:

7. At closing, pro-rated adjustments to the purchase price will be made for the following items: ㉛

    (a) Utilities
    (b) Property taxes
    (c) The following other items:

8. The following closing costs will be paid by the seller: ㉜

9. The following closing costs will be paid by the buyer: ㉝

10. Seller represents that it has good and marketable title to the property and will supply the buyer with either an abstract of title or a standard policy of title insurance. Seller further represents that the property is free and clear of any restrictions on transfer, claims, indebtedness, or liabilities except the following: ㉞

   (a) Zoning, restrictions, prohibitions, or requirements imposed by any governmental authority
   (b) Any restrictions appearing on the plat of record of the property
   (c) Public utility easements of record
   (d) Other:

   Seller warrants that there shall be no violations of zoning or building codes as of the date of closing. Seller also warrants that all personal property included in this sale will be delivered in working order on the date of closing.

11. At least thirty (30) days prior to closing, buyer shall have the right to obtain a written report from a licensed termite inspector stating that there is no termite infestation or termite damage to the property. If there is such evidence, seller shall remedy such infestation and/or repair such damage, up to a maximum cost of two (2) percent of the purchase price of the property. If the costs exceed two (2) percent of the purchase price and seller elects not to pay for the costs over two (2) percent, buyer may cancel this agreement and the escrow shall be returned to buyer without penalty or interest.

12. At least thirty (30) days prior to closing, buyer or their agent shall have the right to inspect all heating, air conditioning, electrical, and mechanical systems of the property, the roof and all structural components of the property, and any personal property included in this agreement. If any such systems or equipment are not in working order, seller shall pay for the cost of placing them in working order prior to closing. Buyer or their agent may again inspect the property within forty-eight (48) hours of closing to determine if all systems and equipment are in working order.

13. Between the date of this agreement and the date for closing, the property shall be maintained in the condition as existed on the date of this agreement. If there is any damage by fire, casualty, or otherwise, prior to closing, seller shall restore the property to the condition as existed on the date of this agreement. If seller fails to do so, buyer may:

   (a) accept the property, as is, along with any insurance proceeds due seller, *or*
   (b) cancel this agreement and have the escrow deposit returned, without penalty or interest.

14. As required by law, the seller makes the following statement: "Radon gas is a naturally occurring radioactive gas that, when accumulated in sufficient quantities in a building, may present health risks to persons exposed to it. Levels of radon gas that exceed federal and state guidelines have been found in buildings in this state. Additional information regarding radon gas and radon gas testing may be obtained from your county health department."

15. As required by law, the seller makes the following Lead Warning Statement: "Every purchaser of any interest in residential real property on which a residential dwelling was built prior to 1978 is notified that such property may present exposure to lead from lead-based paint that may place young children at risk of developing lead poisoning. Lead poisoning in young children may produce permanent neurological damage, including learning disabilities, reduced intelligence quotient, behavioral problems, and impaired memory. Lead poisoning also poses a particular threat to pregnant women. The seller of any interest in residential real estate is required to provide the buyer with any information on lead-based paint hazards from risk assessments or inspection in the seller's possession and notify the buyer of any known lead-based paint hazards. A risk assessment or inspection for possible lead-based paint hazards is recommended prior to purchase."

Seller's Disclosure
Presence of lead-based paint and/or lead-based paint hazards: (Seller to initial one). ㉟

_____ Known lead-based paint and/or lead-based paint hazards are present in building (explain):
_____ Seller has no knowledge of lead-based paint and/or lead-based paint hazards in building.

Records and reports available to seller: (Seller to initial one). ㊱

_____ Seller has provided buyer with all available records and reports pertaining to lead-based paint and/or lead-based paint hazards are present in building (list documents):
_____ Seller has no records and reports pertaining to lead-based paint and/or lead-based paint hazards in building.

Buyer's Acknowledgment
(Buyer to initial all applicable). ㊲

_____ Buyer has received copies of all information listed above.
_____ Buyer has received the pamphlet "Protect Your Family From Lead in Your Home."
_____ Buyer has received a ten (10)-day opportunity (or mutually agreed-on period) to conduct a risk assessment or inspection for the presence of lead-based paint and/or lead-based paint hazards in building.
_____ Buyer has waived the opportunity to conduct a risk assessment or inspection for the presence of lead-based paint and/or lead-based paint hazards in building.

The seller and buyer have reviewed the information above and certify, by their signatures at the end of this agreement, that to the best of their knowledge, the information they have provided is true and accurate.

16. Seller agrees to provide Buyer with a Real Estate Disclosure Statement (or its equivalent that is acceptable in the State in which the property is located) within five (5) days of the signing of this Agreement. Upon receipt of the Real Estate Disclosure Statement from Seller, Buyer shall have five (5) business days within which to rescind this Agreement by providing Seller with a written and signed statement rescinding this Agreement. The disclosures in the Real Estate Disclosure Statement are made by the seller concerning the condition of the property and are provided on the basis of the seller's actual knowledge of the property on the date of this disclosure. These disclosures are not the representations of any real estate agent or other party. The disclosures themselves are not intended to be a part of any written agreement between the buyer and seller. In addition, the disclosure shall not, in any way, be construed to be a warranty of any kind by the seller.

17. The parties also agree to the following additional terms: ㊳

18. No modification of this agreement will be effective unless it is in writing and is signed by both the buyer and seller. This agreement binds and benefits both the buyer and seller and any successors. Time is of the essence of this agreement. This document, including any attachments, is the entire agreement between the buyer and seller. This agreement is governed by the laws of the State of ㊴_____ .

㊵_____
Signature of Seller

㊶_____
Printed Name of Seller

㊷_____
Signature of Witness for Seller

㊸_____
Printed Name of Witness for Seller

㊷_____
Signature of Witness for Seller

㊸_____
Printed Name of Witness for Seller

㊹_____
Signature of Buyer

㊺_____
Printed Name of Buyer

㊻_____
Signature of Witness for Buyer

㊼_____
Printed Name of Witness for Buyer

㊻_____
Signature of Witness for Buyer

㊼_____
Printed Name of Witness for Buyer

CONTRACT FOR DEED

This contract is made on ①_____ , 20 _____ , between
②_____ , seller,
address:③④⑤

and ⑥_____ , buyer,
address:⑦⑧⑨

The seller now owns the following described real estate, located at
⑩_____ ,
City of ⑪_____ , State of ⑫_____ : and legally described as follows:⑬

For valuable consideration, the seller agrees to sell and the buyer agrees to buy this property for the following price and on the following terms:

1. The seller agrees to sell this property to the buyer, free from all claims, liabilities, and indebtedness, unless noted in this contract.

2. The following personal property is also included in this sale: ⑭

3. The buyer agrees to pay the seller the sum of $ ⑮_____ , which the seller agrees to accept as full payment, such total purchase price includes interest as noted below in Paragraph #4.

4. The purchase price will be paid as follows:
   Total Purchase Price .... $ ⑯_____
   Less Down Payment .... $ ⑰_____
   Balance Due .... $ ⑱_____
   (subject to any adjustments or prorations on closing)
   Balance Due will be paid in ⑲_____ equal monthly payments of $⑳_____ each, until the Balance is paid in full. The monthly payments will be due and payable on the ㉑_____ day of each month, beginning on ㉒____ , 20____. The total purchase price includes principal and interest of ㉓_____ % (percent) per year on the unpaid balance. The balance due under this contract is prepayable at any time, in whole or in part, without penalty

5. The seller acknowledges receiving the down payment of $ ㉔_____ from the buyer.

6. If buyer fails to perform any duties under this contract, including the failure to make any of the required payments within 30 days of when such payment is due, this contact shall be forfeited and terminated 30 days after the receipt by the buyer of a Declaration of Intent to Forfeit and Terminate Contract for Deed, which shall be sent to the buyer via Certified U.S. Mail. During the 30-day period after the receipt of this Declaration, Buyer shall have the right to cure the default. If the default is not satisfied within the 30-day period, then on the 31st day after receipt of the Declaration, Buyer shall forfeit all monies paid to the Seller under the Contract for Deed and Buyer shall immediately vacate the property. Seller shall, on that date, have the right to reenter and take full possession of the property, without being liable for any action or any costs incurred by the Buyer. Upon termination of this contract by the seller, the seller shall retain all money paid by the buyer to the seller as accumulated rent for the property.

7. If seller fails to perform this contract, all money paid to the seller by the buyer shall be returned to the buyer or, at buyer's option, the buyer may have the right of specific performance, including the performance by the seller of delivering a warranty deed to the buyer for full title to the property.

8. All closing costs will be paid by the buyer: Upon payment by the buyer of the entire purchase price when due and the fulfillment of all other contracts under this contract by the buyer, the seller will deliver to buyer the following documents:
   ㉕
   (a) A Bill of Sale for all personal property included in this sale
   (b) A Warranty Deed for the real estate
   (c) A Seller's Affidavit of Title
   (d) A closing statement
   (e) Other documents:

9. The buyer agrees to pay all property taxes and assessments against the property beginning with the tax year of ㉖___.

10. Seller represents that it has good and marketable title to the property and, on request, will supply the buyer with an abstract of title. Seller further represents that the property is free and clear of any restrictions on transfer, claims, indebtedness, or liabilities except the following: ㉗

    (a) Zoning, restrictions, prohibitions, or requirements imposed by any governmental authority
    (b) Any restrictions appearing on the plat of record of the property
    (c) Public utility easements of record
    (d) Other:

    Seller warrants that there shall be no violations of zoning or building codes as of the date of this contract. Seller also warrants that all personal property included in this sale has been delivered to the buyer in working order.

11. Between the date of this contract and the date for closing, the property shall be maintained by the buyer in the condition as existed on the date of this contract. In addition, if there is a structure on this property as of the date of this contract, the buyer agrees to maintain both general liability insurance and property insurance in the amount of the balance due under this contract, as specified in Paragraph #4 of this contract, naming the seller as owner of the property and recipient of all insurance settlements, If there is any damage by fire, casualty, or otherwise, prior to closing, buyer shall restore the property to the condition as existed on the date of this contract, and buyer shall be have the right to use any casualty or fire insurance proceeds for such restoration. If buyer fails to do so within a reasonable time, seller may declare this contract forfeit and terminated.

12. As required by law, the seller makes the following statement: "Radon gas is a naturally occurring radioactive gas that, when accumulated in sufficient quantities in a building, may present health risks to persons exposed to it. Levels of radon gas that exceed federal and state guidelines have been found in buildings in this state. Additional information regarding radon gas and radon gas testing may be obtained from your county health department."

13. As required by law, the seller makes the following Lead Warning Statement: "Every purchaser of any interest in residential real property on which a residential dwelling was built prior to 1978 is notified that such property may present exposure to lead from lead-based paint that may place young children at risk of developing lead poisoning. Lead poisoning in young children may produce permanent neurological damage, including learning disabilities, reduced intelligence quotient, behavioral problems, and impaired memory. Lead poisoning also poses a particular threat to pregnant women. The seller of any interest in residential real estate is required to provide the buyer with any information on lead-based paint hazards from risk assessments or inspection in the seller's possession and notify the buyer of any known lead-based paint hazards. A risk assessment or inspection for possible lead-based paint hazards is recommended prior to purchase."

Seller's Disclosure
Presence of lead-based paint and/or lead-based paint hazards: (Seller to initial one). ㉘

_____ Known lead-based paint and/or lead-based paint hazards are present in building (explain):
_____ Seller has no knowledge of lead-based paint and/or lead-based paint hazards in building.

Records and reports available to seller: (Seller to initial one). ㉙

_____ Seller has provided buyer with all available records and reports pertaining to lead-based paint and/or lead-based paint hazards are present in building (list documents):
_____ Seller has no records and reports pertaining to lead-based paint and/or lead-based paint hazards in building.

Buyer's Acknowledgment
(Buyer to initial all applicable). ㉚

_____ Buyer has received copies of all information listed above.
_____ Buyer has received the pamphlet "Protect Your Family From Lead in Your Home."
_____ Buyer has received a ten (10)-day opportunity (or mutually agreed-on period) to conduct a risk assessment or inspection for the presence of lead-based paint and/or lead-based paint hazards in building.
_____ Buyer has waived the opportunity to conduct a risk assessment or inspection for the presence of lead-based paint and/or lead-based paint hazards in building.

The seller and buyer have reviewed the information above and certify, by their signatures at the end of this contract, that to the best of their knowledge, the information they have provided is true and accurate.

14. Seller agrees to provide Buyer with a Real Estate Disclosure Statement (or its equivalent that is acceptable in the State in which the property is located) within five (5) days of the signing of this Agreement. Upon receipt of the Real Estate Disclosure Statement from Seller, Buyer shall have five (5) business days within which to rescind this Agreement by providing Seller with a written and signed statement rescinding this Agreement. The disclosures in the Real Estate Disclosure Statement are made by the seller concerning the condition of the property and are provided on the basis of the seller's actual knowledge of the property on the date of this disclosure. These disclosures are not the representations of any real estate agent or other party. The disclosures themselves are not intended to be a part of any written agreement between the buyer and seller. In addition, the disclosure shall not, in any way, be construed to be a warranty of any kind by the seller

15. The parties also agree to the following additional terms: ㉛

16. The buyer and seller agree that this contract or any assignment of this contract may not be recorded without the express written permission of the seller. If this contract is recorded contrary to the above provision, then any existing balance shall become immediately due and payable.

17. Buyer agrees that any construction on this property be limited to residences built of new materials and that all construction comply with all applicable building, health and zoning codes and laws.

18. No modification of this contract will be effective unless it is in writing and is signed by both the buyer and seller. No assignment of this contract by buyer will be effective without the written permission of the seller. This contract binds and benefits both the buyer and seller and any successors. Time is of the essence of this contract. This document, including any attachments, is the entire contract between the buyer and seller. This contract is governed by the laws of the State of ㉜_____ .

㉝_____
Signature of Seller

㉞_____
Printed Name of Seller

㉟_____
Signature of Witness for Seller

㊱_____
Printed Name of Witness for Seller

㉟_____
Signature of Witness for Seller

㊱_____
Printed Name of Witness for Seller

㊲_____
Signature of Buyer

㊳_____
Printed Name of Buyer

㊴_____
Signature of Witness for Buyer

㊵_____
Printed Name of Witness for Buyer

㊴_____
Signature of Witness for Buyer

㊵_____
Printed Name of Witness for Buyer

DECLARATION OF INTENT TO FORFEIT AND TERMINATE CONTRACT FOR DEED

Under the terms of the Contract for Deed, dated ①_____, 20_____ which exists between
② _____, seller
address:③

and ④_____ , buyer,
address:⑤

The seller now owns the following described real estate, located at
⑥_____ ,
City of _____ , State of _____: and legally described as follows:⑦

The seller declares that as of the date of ⑧_____, 20 _____,
Buyer is in default of this Contract for Deed for the following reasons:⑨

Due to this default, Seller declares the existing Contract for Deed between Seller and Buyer to be forfeit and terminated 30 days after the receipt of this Declaration by the Buyer. Seller shall send a copy of this Declaration to Buyer at the above address, via Certified U.S. Mail, on the date of ⑩_____, 20 _____.

During the 30-day period after the receipt of this Declaration, Buyer shall have the right to cure the default noted above. If the default is not satisfied within the 30-day period, then on the 31st day after receipt of this Declaration, Buyer shall forfeit all monies paid to the Seller under the Contract for Deed and shall immediately vacate the property. Seller shall, on that date, have the right to reenter and take full possession of the property, without being liable for any action or any costs incurred by the Buyer.

Dated: ⑪_____

⑫_____
Signature of Seller

⑬_____
Printed Name of Seller

OPTION TO BUY REAL ESTATE

This option agreement is made on ①_____ , 20 _____ , between
②_____ , seller,
address:③④⑤

and ⑥_____ , buyer,
address:⑦⑧⑨

The seller now owns the following described real estate, located at
⑩_____ ,
City of ⑪_____ , State of ⑫_____ , and legally described as follows: ⑬

For valuable consideration, the seller agrees to give the buyer an exclusive option to buy this property for the following price and on the following terms:

1. The buyer will pay the seller $ ⑭_____ for this option. This amount will be credited against the purchase price of the property if this option is exercised by the buyer. If the option is not exercised, the seller will retain this payment.

2. The option period will be from the date of this agreement until ⑮_____ , 20 _____ , at which time it will expire unless exercised.

3. During this period, the buyer has the option and exclusive right to buy the seller's property mentioned above for the purchase price of $ ⑯_____ . The buyer must notify the seller, in writing, of the decision to exercise this option.

4. Attached to this Option Agreement is a completed Agreement to Sell Real Estate. If the buyer notifies the seller, in writing, of the decision to exercise the option within the option period, the seller and buyer agree to sign the Agreement to Sell Real Estate and complete the sale on the terms contained in the Agreement.

5. No modification of this Option Agreement will be effective unless it is in writing and is signed by both the buyer and seller. This Option Agreement binds and benefits both the buyer and seller and any successors. Time is of the essence of this Option Agreement. This document, including any attachments, is the entire agreement between the buyer and seller. This Option Agreement is governed by the laws of the State of ⑰_____ .

Dated ⑱_____

⑲_____

Signature of Seller

⑳_____

Printed Name of Seller

㉑_____

Signature of Buyer

㉒_____

Printed Name of Buyer

OFFER TO PURCHASE REAL ESTATE

This offer is made on ①_____ , 20 _____ , by
②_____ , buyer,
address:③④⑤

to ⑥_____ , owner,
address:⑦⑧⑨

The owner now owns the following described real estate, located at
⑩_____ ,
City of ⑪_____ , State of ⑫_____ , and legally described as follows: ⑬

The buyer offers to purchase the above property under the following terms:

The following price is offered for the property: $ ⑭_____
Escrow deposit paid to the Owner with this Offer: $ ⑮_____
Further deposit to Owner upon signing of Sales Agreement: $ ⑯_____
Balance due at closing: $ ⑰_____
Total purchase price: $ ⑱_____

This Offer is conditioned on the following terms:

1. This Offer is conditional upon the Buyer being able to arrange a firm commitment for suitable financing on the following terms within ninety (90) days of acceptance of this Offer by the Owner:

Mortgage amount: $⑲_____
Term of Mortgage: ⑳_____ monthly payments
Interest rate of Mortgage: ㉑_____% (percent) per annum

2. This offer is conditional upon the Buyer obtaining a satisfactory termite report and upon a satisfactory inspection of the property by Buyer within ninety (90) days of acceptance of this Offer by the Owner.

3. Property will be sold free and clear of all encumbrances and with good and marketable title.

4. The parties agree to execute a standard Agreement to Sell Real Estate within ninety (90) days of acceptance of this Offer by the Owner.

5. The closing for this sale shall occur on or before ㉒_____ , at ㉓____m. , at ㉔_____ _____ , City of ㉕_____ , State of ㉖_____ .

6. Other terms: ㉗

7. This Offer shall remain open until ㉘____m. , on ㉙_____ . If not accepted by the Owner by this time, this Offer is rescinded and the deposit money shall be returned.

㉚_____   ㉜_____
Signature of Buyer   Date signed
㉛_____
Printed Name of Buyer

㉝_____   ㉟_____
Signature of Owner   Date Signed
㉞_____
Printed Name of Owner

LEAD WARNING STATEMENT

Every purchaser of any interest in residential real property on which a residential dwelling was built prior to 1978 is notified that such property may present exposure to lead from lead-based paint that may place young children at risk of developing lead poisoning. Lead poisoning in young children may produce permanent neurological damage, including learning disabilities, reduced intelligence quotient, behavioral problems, and impaired memory. Lead poisoning also poses a particular threat to pregnant women. The seller of any interest in residential real estate is required to provide the buyer with any information on lead-based paint hazards from risk assessments or inspection in the seller's possession and notify the buyer of any known lead-based paint hazards. A risk assessment or inspection for possible lead-based paint hazards is recommended prior to purchase. Initial your correct choices.

SELLER'S DISCLOSURE

Presence of lead-based paint and/or lead-based paint hazards: (Seller to initial one).①

_____ Known lead-based paint and/or lead-based paint hazards are present in building (explain).

_____ Seller has no knowledge of lead-based paint and/or lead-based paint hazards in building.

RECORDS AND REPORTS AVAILABLE TO SELLER: (Seller to initial one). ②

_____ Seller has provided Buyer with all available records and reports pertaining to lead-based paint and/or lead-based paint hazards that are present in building (list documents).

_____ Seller has no records and reports pertaining to lead-based paint and/or lead-based paint hazards in building.

BUYER'S ACKNOWLEDGMENT (Buyer to initial all applicable). ③

_____ Buyer has received copies of all information listed above.

_____ Buyer has received the pamphlet "Protect Your Family From Lead in Your Home."

_____ Buyer has received a 10-day opportunity (or mutually-agreed on period) to conduct a risk assessment or inspection for the presence of lead-based paint and/or lead-based paint hazards in building.④

_____ Buyer has waived the opportunity to conduct a risk assessment or inspection for the presence of lead-based paint and/or lead-based paint hazards in building.④

Dated: ⑤_____

⑥_____
Signature of Seller

⑧_____
Signature of Buyer

⑦_____
Printed Name of Seller

⑨_____
Printed Name of Buyer

APPRAISAL REPORT

This Appraisal Report is made on ① _____ , 20 _____ ,
by② _____ , Appraiser,
address:③ _____ .

Appraiser states that at the request of ④ _____ , who employed him/her to appraise the
property commonly known as ⑤ _____ , and whose legal description is: ⑥

and after a careful and thorough inspection of the property and to the best of his or her knowledge, it is the professional
opinion of the Appraiser that the market value of the property is as follows:

Land	$⑦ _____
Improvements	$⑧ _____
Total Market Value	$⑨ _____

The physical conditions of the improvements are based on a visual inspection only and no liability is assumed for the sound-
ness of the structure as no engineering test were done or requested. Appraiser also states that he or she has no financial
interest whatsoever in the property, and that his or her findings are in no way contingent upon the payment that he or she is
to receive for making the appraisal, and that he or she is qualified to make the appraisal for the following reasons: ⑩

⑪ _____
Signature of Appraiser

⑫ _____
Printed Name of Appraiser

APPRAISAL AFFIDAVIT

This Appraisal Affidavit is made on ①_____ , 20 _____ , by
②_____ , Appraiser,
address:③_____ .

Appraiser states that, at the request of ④_____ , who employed him/her to appraise
the property commonly known as⑤_____ , and whose legal description is:⑥

and that after a careful and thorough inspection of the property and to the best of his or her knowledge, it is the professional
opinion of the Appraiser that the market value of the property is as follows:

Land	$⑦_____
Improvements	$⑧_____
Total Market Value	$⑨ _____

Appraiser also states that he or she has no financial interest whatsoever in the property, and that his or her findings are in
no way contingent upon the payment that he or she is to receive for making the appraisal, and that he or she is qualified to
make the appraisal for the following reasons:⑩

⑪_____
Signature of Appraiser

⑫_____
Printed Name of Appraiser

⑬
State of _____
County of _____

On _____ , 20 _____ , _____ personally came before me and, being duly
sworn, did state that he or she is the person described in the above document and that he or she signed the above document
in my presence.

_____
Signature of Notary Public

Notary Public, In and for the County of _____
State of _____

My commission expires: _____   Notary Seal

Recording requested by: ① _____
Document prepared by:
Name ② _____
Address _____

Space above reserved for Recorder
When recorded, mail to:
Name ③ _____
Address _____

Quitclaim Deed

Property Tax Parcel/Account Number: ④ _____

This Quitclaim Deed is made on ⑤ _____ , 20 _____ , between
⑥ _____, grantor, address: ⑦ _____
_____

and ⑧_____ , grantee, address: ⑨ _____
_____.

For valuable consideration, the grantor hereby quitclaims and transfers all right, title, and interest held by the Grantor in the following described real estate to the grantee, and his or her heirs or assigns, to have and hold forever, located at ⑩ _____, City of _____ , State of _____ , and described as follows: ⑪

Subject to all easements, rights of way, protective covenants, and mineral reservations of record, if any. Taxes for the Tax year of ⑫ _____ shall be prorated between the Grantor and Grantee as of the date of recording this deed.

Dated:⑬ _____ , 20 _____

⑭_____
Signature of Grantor

⑮_____
Printed Name of Grantor

⑯_____
Signature of Witness 1

⑯_____
Printed Name of Witness 1

⑯_____
Signature of Witness 2

⑯_____
Printed Name of Witness 2

⑰ Notary Acknowledgement

State of _____
County of _____

On _____ , 20 _____ , _____ personally came before me, is personally known to me or has proved his or her identity to me on the basis of satisfactory evidence, and, being duly sworn, did state that he or she is the person described in the above document and that he or she signed the above document in my presence.

_____
Signature of Notary Public
Notary Public, In and for the County of _____
State of _____
My commission expires: _____   Notary Seal

Recording requested by: ① _____
Document prepared by:
Name ② _____
Address _____

Space above reserved for Recorder
When recorded, mail to:
Name ③ _____
Address _____

Warranty Deed

Property Tax Parcel/Account Number: ④ _____

This Warranty Deed is made on ⑤ _____ , 20 _____ , between
⑥ _____ , grantor, address: ⑦ _____
_____

and ⑧_____ , grantee, address: ⑨ _____
_____.

For valuable consideration, the Grantor hereby sells, grants, and conveys the following described real estate, in fee simple, to the Grantee to have and hold forever, along with all easements, rights, and buildings belonging to the described property, located at ⑩ _____ , City of _____ , State of _____ , and described as follows: ⑪

The Grantor warrants that it is lawful owner and has full right to convey the property, and that the property is free from all claims, liabilities, or indebtedness, and that the Grantor and its successors will warrant and defend title to the Grantee against the lawful claims of all persons. Taxes for the tax year of ⑫_____ shall be prorated between the Grantor and Grantee as of the date of recording of this deed.

Dated: ⑬ _____ , 20 _____

⑭_____
Signature of Grantor

⑮_____
Printed Name of Grantor

⑯_____
Signature of Witness 1

⑯_____
Printed Name of Witness 1

⑯_____
Signature of Witness 2

⑯_____
Printed Name of Witness 2

⑰ **Notary Acknowledgement**

State of _____
County of _____

On _____ , 20 _____ , _____ personally came before me, is personally known to me or has proved his or her identity to me on the basis of satisfactory evidence, and, being duly sworn, did state that he or she is the person described in the above document and that he or she signed the above document in my presence.

_____
Signature of Notary Public
Notary Public, In and for the County of _____
State of _____
My commission expires: _____   Notary Seal

Chapter 16

Promissory Notes

Contained in this chapter are various promissory notes. A *promissory note* is a document by which a borrower promises to pay the holder of the note a certain amount of money under specific terms. In the forms in this chapter, the person who borrows the money is referred to as the *borrower* and the person whom the borrower is to pay is referred to as the *noteholder*. The noteholder is generally also the lender, but this need not be so. The forms in this chapter are intended for use only by individuals who are not regularly in the business of lending money. Complex state and federal regulations apply to lending institutions and such rules are beyond the scope of this book. This chapter also contains various forms for demanding payments on a promissory note. *Note*: If you are at all unsure of the correct use of any forms in this chapter, please consult a competent attorney.

Promissory Note Instructions

Promissory Note (Installment Repayment): This type of promissory note is a standard unsecured note. Being *unsecured* means that the noteholder has no collateral or specific property to foreclose against should the borrower default on the note. If the borrower doesn't pay, the noteholder must sue and get a general judgment against the borrower. Collection of the judgment may then be made against the borrower's assets.

This particular note calls for the borrower to pay a certain annual interest rate on the note and to make periodic payments to the noteholder. It also has certain general terms:

- The borrower may prepay any amount on the note without penalty
- If the borrower is in default, the noteholder may demand full payment on the note
- The note is not assumable by anyone other than the borrower
- The borrower waives certain formalities relating to demands for payment
- The borrower agrees to pay any of the costs of collection after a default

In order to complete this form, the following information is necessary:

① Amount of Note
② Date of Note
③ Name of borrower
④ Address of borrower
⑤ Name of noteholder
⑥ Address of noteholder
⑦ Principle amount
⑧ Interest rate
⑨ Number of installments
⑩ Amount of payments
⑪ What day of the "payment period" payment is due
⑫ The period for the installments (for example, monthly or weekly)
⑬ Payment in full by this date
⑭ The number of days a payment may be late before it is considered a default
⑮ Signature of borrower
⑯ Printed name of borrower

Promissory Note (Lump Sum Repayment): This note is also an unsecured promise to pay. However, this version of a promissory note calls for the payment, including accrued interest, to be paid in one lump sum at a certain date in the future. This note has the same general conditions relating to prepayment, defaults, and assumability as the Promissory Note with Installment Payments discussed on the previous page.

To prepare this form, use the following information:

① Amount of Note
② Date of Note
③ Name of borrower
④ Address of borrower
⑤ Name of noteholder
⑥ Address of noteholder
⑦ Principle amount
⑧ Interest rate
⑨ Date that lump sum is due
⑩ The number of days a payment may be late before it is considered a default
⑪ Signature of borrower
⑫ Printed name of borrower

Promissory Note (on Demand): This also is an unsecured note. This type of promissory note, however, is immediately payable in full at any time upon the demand of the noteholder. This note has the same general conditions relating to prepayment, defaults, and assumability as the Promissory Note with Installment Payments discussed previously.

The following information is necessary to complete this form:

① Amount of Note
② Date of Note
③ Name of borrower
④ Address of borrower
⑤ Name of noteholder
⑥ Address of noteholder
⑦ Principle amount
⑧ Interest rate
⑨ The number of days past the demand date that payment may be made before the note is in default
⑩ Signature of borrower
⑪ Printed name of borrower

Release of Promissory Note: This release is intended to be used to release a party from obligations under a Promissory Note. There are several other methods by which to accomplish this same objective. The return of the original note to the maker, clearly marked "Paid in Full" will serve the same purpose. A Receipt in Full will also accomplish this goal (see Chapter 10: *Releases*). The Release of Promissory Note may, however, be used in those situations when the release is based on something other than payment in full of the underlying note. For example, the note may be satisfied by a gift from the bearer of the note of release from the obligation. Another situation may involve a release of the note based on a concurrent release of a claim that the maker of the note holds against the holder of the note.

The following information is needed to complete this form:

① Date of original promissory note
② Amount of promissory note
③ Name of noteholder
④ Address of noteholder
⑤ Name of borrower
⑥ Address of borrower
⑦ Date of release signed
⑧ Signature of noteholder
⑨ Printed name of noteholder

Demand and Notice of Default on Installment Promissory Note: This form will be used to notify the maker of a promissory note of his or her default on an installment payment on a promissory note. Notice of default should be sent promptly to any account that falls behind in its payments on a note. This promissory note provides a legal basis for a suit for breach of the promissory note.

The following information is needed to complete this form:

① Date of demand
② Name and address of borrower
③ Name of borrower
④ Date of original note
⑤ Amount of original note
⑥ Date of default payment
⑦ Amount of default payment
⑧ Signature of noteholder
⑨ Printed name of noteholder

PROMISSORY NOTE (INSTALLMENT REPAYMENT)

$ ①_____

Dated: ②_____ , 20 _____

For value received, ③_____ , Borrower, address: ④

promises to pay ⑤_____ , Noteholder, address: ⑥

the principal amount of $ ⑦_____ , with interest at the annual rate of ⑧_____ percent, on any unpaid balance.

Payments are payable to the Noteholder in ⑨_____ consecutive installments of $ ⑩_____ , including interest, and continuing on the ⑪____ day of each ⑫____ until paid in full. If not paid off sooner, this note is due and payable in full on ⑬____ , 20 ____ .

This note may be prepaid in whole or in part at any time without penalty. If the Borrower is in default more than ⑭_____ days with any payment, this note is payable upon demand of any Noteholder. This note is not assumable without the written consent of the Noteholder. The Borrower waives demand, presentment for payment, protest, and notice. In the event of any default, the Borrower will be responsible for any costs of collection on this note, including court costs and attorney fees.

⑮_____
Signature of Borrower

⑯_____
Printed Name of Borrower

PROMISSORY NOTE (LUMP SUM REPAYMENT)

$ ①_____

Dated: ②_____ , 20 _____

For value received, ③_____ , Borrower, address: ④

promises to pay ⑤_____ , Noteholder, address: ⑥

the principal amount of $ ⑦_____ , with interest at the annual rate of ⑧_____ percent, on any unpaid balance.

Payment on this note is due and payable to the Noteholder in full on or before ⑨_____ , 20 _____ .

This note may be prepaid in whole or in part at any time without penalty. If the Borrower is in default more than ⑩_____ days with any payment, this note is payable upon demand of any Noteholder. This note is not assumable without the written consent of the Noteholder. The Borrower waives demand, presentment for payment, protest, and notice. In the event of any default, the Borrower will be responsible for any costs of collection on this note, including court costs and attorney fees.

⑪_____
Signature of Borrower

⑫_____
Printed Name of Borrower

PROMISSORY NOTE (ON DEMAND)

$ ① _____

Dated: ② _____ , 20 _____

For value received, ③ _____ , Borrower,
address:④

promises to pay ON DEMAND to
⑤ _____ , Noteholder,
address:⑥

the principal amount of $ ⑦ _____ , with interest at the annual rate of ⑧ _____ percent, on any unpaid balance.

This note may be prepaid in whole or in part at any time without penalty. This note is not assumable without the written consent of the Noteholder. The Borrower waives demand, presentment for payment, protest, and notice. In the event of such default of over ⑨ _____ days in making payment, the Borrower will be also be responsible for any costs of collection on this note, including court costs and attorney fees.

⑩ _____
Signature of Borrower

⑪ _____
Printed Name of Borrower

RELEASE OF PROMISSORY NOTE

In consideration of full payment of the promissory note dated ①_____ , 20 __ , in the face amount of $ ②_____ ,
③_____ , Noteholder,
address:④

releases and discharges
⑤_____ , Borrower(s),
address:⑥

from any claims or obligations on account of this note.

The party signing this release intends that it bind and benefit both itself and any successors.

Dated: ⑦_____ , 20 _____

⑧_____
Signature of Noteholder

⑨_____
Printed Name of Noteholder

DEMAND AND NOTICE OF DEFAULT ON INSTALLMENT PROMISSORY NOTE

Date: ①_____ , 20 _____

To:②_____

RE: Default on Installment Promissory Note

Dear ③_____ :

Regarding the promissory note dated ④_____ , 20 _____ , in the original amount of $ ⑤_____ , of which you are the maker, you have defaulted on the installment payment due on ⑥_____ , 20 _____ , in the amount of $ ⑦_____ .

Demand is made upon you for payment of this past-due installment payment. If payment is not received by us within ten (10) days from the date of this notice, we will proceed to enforce our rights under the promissory note for collection of the entire balance.

Very truly,

⑧_____
Signature of Noteholder

⑨_____
Printed Name of Noteholder

Chapter 17

Business Operations

One of the first decisions that a potential business owner must confront is how the business should be structured and operated. This crucial decision must be made even before the business has actually begun operations. The legal documents which will generally accompany the formation of a business can follow many different patterns, depending on the particular situation and the type of business to be undertaken. There are two initial decisions which must be made in order to begin a business operation: the type of business entity to be used and from where the business assets will come.

First, the type of business entity to be used must be selected. There are many basic forms of business operating entities. The five most common forms are:

- Sole proprietorship
- Partnership
- Corporation
- S-corporation
- Limited liability company

The choice of entity for a particular business depends on many factors. Which of these forms of business organization is chosen can have a great impact on the success of the business. The structure chosen will have an effect on how easy it is to obtain financing, how taxes are paid, how accounting records are kept, whether personal assets are at risk in the venture, the amount of control the "owner" has over the business, and many other aspects of the business.

Keep in mind that the initial choice of business organization need not be the final choice. It is often wise to begin with the most simple form, the sole proprietorship, until the business progresses to a point where another form is clearly indicated. This allows the business to begin in the least complicated manner and allows the owner to retain total control in the important formative period of the business. As the business grows and the potential for liability and tax burdens increase, circumstances may dictate a re-examination of the business structure.

Sole Proprietorship

A sole proprietorship is both the simplest and the most prevalent form of business organization. An important reason for this is that it is the least regulated of all types of business structures. Technically, the *sole proprietorship* is the traditional unincorporated one-person business. For legal and tax purposes, the business is the owner. It has no existence outside the owner. The liabilities of the business are personal to the owner and the business ends when the owner dies. On the other hand, all of the profits are also personal to the owner and the sole owner has full control of the business. For more information on sole proprietorships, please see Nova Publishing Company's *Sole Proprietorship: Small Business Start-Up Kit*.

Partnership

A *partnership* is a relationship existing between two or more persons who join together to carry on a trade or business. Each partner contributes money, property, labor, or skill to the partnership and, in return, expects to share in the profits or losses of the business. A partnership is usually based on a partnership agreement of some type, although the agreement need not be a formal document. It may simply be an oral understanding between the partners, although this is not recommended.

A simple joint undertaking to share expenses is not considered a partnership, nor is a mere co-ownership of property that is maintained and leased or rented. For more detailed information, please see Nova Publishing Company's *Partnership: Small Business Start-Up Kit*. To be considered a partnership for legal and tax purposes, the following factors are usually considered:

- The partner's conduct in carrying out the provisions of the partnership agreement
- The relationship of the parties
- The abilities and contributions of each party to the partnership
- The control each partner has over the partnership income and the purposes for which the income is used

Corporation

A *corporation* is a creation of law. It is governed by the laws of the state of incorporation and the state or states in which it does business. In recent years it has become the business structure of choice for many small businesses. Corporations are, generally, a more complex form of business operation than either a sole proprietorship or partnership. They are also subject to far more state regulations regarding both their formation and operation. Because of this, legal documents for the formation of a corporation are beyond the scope of this book and are not included. Legal forms for the formation and operation of a corporation are contained in Nova Publishing's *Corporation: Small Business Start-up Kit*. The following discussion is provided in order to allow the potential business owner an understanding of this type of business operation.

The corporation is an artificial entity. It is created by filing Articles of Incorporation with the proper state authorities. This gives the corporation its legal existence and the right to carry on business. Adoption of *corporate bylaws*, or internal rules of operation, is often the first business of the corporation. In its simplest form, the corporate organizational structure consists of the following levels:

- **Shareholders:** who own shares of the business but do not contribute to the direct management of the corporation, other than by electing the directors of the corporation

- **Directors:** who may be shareholders, but as directors do not own any of the business. They are responsible, jointly as members of the board of directors of the corporation, for making the major business decisions of the corporation, including appointing the officers of the corporation

- **Officers:** who may be shareholders and/or directors, but, as officers, do not own any of the business. The officers (generally the president, vice president, secretary, and treasurer) are responsible for the day-to-day operation of the business

S-Corporation

The *S-corporation* is a certain type of corporation that is available for specific tax purposes. It is a creature of the Internal Revenue Service. Its purpose is to allow small corporations to choose to be taxed like a partnership, but to also enjoy many of the benefits of a corporation. Formation of an S-corporation is beyond the scope of this book. Legal forms for the formation and operation of an S-corporation are contained in Nova Publishing's *S-Corporation: The Small Business Start-Up Kit*. The following discussion is provided in order to allow the potential business owner an understanding of this type of business operation.

In general, to qualify as an S-corporation under current IRS rules, a corporation must have no more than 100 shareholders, all of whom must be individuals; it must only have one class of stock; and each of the shareholders must consent to the choice of S-corporation status.

The S-corporation retains all of the advantages and disadvantages of the traditional corporation except in the area of taxation. For tax purposes, S-corporation shareholders are treated similarly to partners in a partnership. The income, losses, and deductions generated by an S-corporation are "passed through" the corporate entity to the individual shareholders. Thus, there is no "double" taxation of an S-type corporation. In addition, unlike a standard corporation, shareholders of S-corporations can deduct personally any corporate losses.

Limited Liability Company

A relatively new business form is the *limited liability company*. This business form has been adopted in some manner in all states. It is, essentially, a non-incorporated business form which has been given limited legal liability by legislative mandate. Thus, this hybrid type of business has the pass-through taxation advantages of a partnership and the limited legal liability of a corporation. This type of company consists of one or more members/owners who manage the company. There may also be non-member managers employed to handle the business. As a hybrid-type business structure, this form has many of the same advantages and disadvantages as both corporations (particularly S-corporations) and partnerships. One unique advantage that the limited liability company has over standard corporations is the increased flexibility to allocate profits and losses to its members. As this is a new form of business, you are advised to consult a competent business lawyer for assistance in operating as a limited liability company or check out Nova Publishing Company's *Limited Liability Company: Small Business Start-up Kit.*

Instructions for Business Operations Forms

In addition to selecting the type of structure that the business will take, the other important factor in the initial start-up of a business is where the basic assets of the business will come from. From the point of view of someone who is starting a business, the equipment and supplies needed to begin a business are often purchased from an on-going concern. A purchase of business assets for the purpose of beginning an enterprise will generally take two forms: the purchase of an entire business or the purchase of specific assets and equipment only. There are two legal agreements included in this chapter for these situations. Their use is outlined below.

The following documents are included in this chapter for use in purchasing, selling, or forming a business:

Agreement for Sale of Business: This form should be used when one party is purchasing an entire business from another party. The form, as shown in this book, is set up for use in the sale of a sole proprietorship to an individual. This structure can be easily adapted to fit other particular situations if necessary. For example, if the business being sold is a partnership and the buyer is a corporation, a few simple substitutions will be necessary to change the document to the appropriate form. Simply substitute the name and address of the partnership for the seller's name wherever indicated and substitute the name and address of the corporate buyer where necessary. If changes are made in the type of entity doing the buying or selling on this form, the appropriate notarization and signature line from Chapter 4 must be used also. *Note:* The notarization on this form is only necessary if the sale of the business includes the sale of real estate. A notarization will be needed in order to record this document with the appropriate county office.

The following information will have to be used to fill in this form:

1. Date of agreement
2. Name of seller
3. Address of seller with name of city and state
4. Name of buyer
5. Address of buyer with name of city and state
6. Type of business
7. Name of business
8. Adress of business with name of city and state
9. Address of business premises with name of city and state
10. Amount of full purchase
11. Amount for premises
12. Amount for equipment/furniture
13. Amount for goodwill
14. Amount for stock-in-trade/inventory
15. Amount for notes/accounts receivable
16. Amount for any outstanding contracts
17. Breakdown of purchase price : amount of earnest money
18. Amount of cash down payment
19. Amount of promissory note
20. Amount of total price
21. Amount of promissory note
22. Interest rate of promissory note
23. Number of years to pay on note
24. Amount of payment per month of note
25. Amount of earnest money
26. Date of closing
27. Time of closing
28. Address of closing with name of city and state
29. List all other documents provided to buyer
30. State where sale takes place
31. Date of balance sheet
32. Radius from business that seller cannot compete
33. Number of years that seller cannot compete
34. Amount of insurance
35. Any additional terms
36. State where business is sold
37. Date of signatures

㊳ Signature of seller
㊴ Printed name of seller
㊵ Name of Business (Doing Business As)
㊶ Type of business
㊷ State where business will operate
㊸ Signature of buyer
㊹ Printed name of buyer
㊺ Notary will complete this section

The sale of a complete and ongoing business is one of the most complex business transactions that a small businessperson will encounter. It may incorporate many other the legal documents.

Agreement for Sale of Business Assets: This form should be used when one party is purchasing only certain business assets from another party. As in the previous form, this form, as it is shown in this book, is set up for use in the sale of sole proprietorship assets to an individual. This structure may be easily adapted to fit other particular situations if necessary. For example, if the business assets are being sold by a partnership and the buyer is a corporation, a few simple substitutions will be necessary to change the document to the appropriate form. Simply substitute the name and address of the partnership for the seller's name wherever indicated, substitute the name and address of the corporate buyer where necessary, and provide the proper signature lines as shown in Chapter 4. *Note*: Notarization is not provided for this form. Notarization of this form is only necessary if the sale of the business assets includes the sale of real estate. In that case, a notarization will be needed in order to record this document with the appropriate county real estate records office.

The following information will have to be used to fill in this form:

① Date of agreement
② Name of seller
③ Address of seller with name of city and state
④ Name of buyer
⑤ Address of buyer with name of city and state
⑥ Type of business
⑦ Name of business
⑧ Adress of business with name of city and state
⑨ Amount of full purchase
⑩ Breakdown of purchase price : amount of earnest money
⑪ Amount of cash down payment
⑫ Amount of promissory note
⑬ Amount of total price
⑭ Amount of promissory note
⑮ Interest rate of promissory note
⑯ Number of years to pay on note

⑰ Amount of payment per month of note
⑱ Amount of earnest money
⑲ Date of closing
⑳ Time of closing
㉑ Address of closing with name of city and state
㉒ List all other documents provided to buyer
㉓ Other adjustments to purchase price
㉔ Amount of insurance
㉕ Any additional terms
㉖ State where business assets are sold
㉗ Date of signatures
㉘ Signature of seller
㉙ Printed name of seller
㉚ Name of Business (Doing Business As)
㉛ Type of business
㉜ State where business will operate
㉝ Signature of buyer
㉞ Printed name of buyer

Note that you may also need additional documents in conjunction with the basic Agreement for Sale of Business Assets form.

Notice of Intention to Use Fictitious Name: As noted above, this form is merely a notice to be published in a local newspaper a certain number of times which publicly declares the intention of using a fictitious name in a business. This form is completed by filling in the address of the business, the fictitious name of the business, and the name and percent of interest of all owners of the business.

The general method of registration follows two steps. First, a legal notice (Notice of Intention to Use Fictitious Name) containing the information in the filed document must, generally, be run in a local newspaper for a specified number of times. Second, the Affidavit, or registration form, is actually filed with the appropriate county records office. The legal affidavit provided for this registration should be valid in virtually all jurisdictions. However, certain locales may have slightly differing forms which must be used. Check with your local newspaper and with your county records office to see if the form provided is acceptable in your area.

The following information will have to be used to fill in this form:

① Address of business
② Fictitious name
③ Name of all owners with interest in business
④ Percent of business

⑤ Date of signatures
⑥ Signatures of all owners
⑦ Printed names of all owners

Affidavit of Use of Fictitious Business Name: The registration of the use of a fictitious name is, in most jurisdictions, one of the only documents that needs to be completed prior to operating a business as a sole proprietorship. The purpose of this document is to place on a public record a statement verifying the actual name of the owner of a business that operates under a fictitious name. For example: if Ms. Jill Smith operates Golden Scissors Hair Styling Salon as a sole proprietorship, she would need to register her use of the fictitious name "Golden Scissors Hair Styling." This registration will allow any third party to check the public records and determine who is actually responsible for the business liabilities and debts. The rationale for this registration is to provide a public record of the name of the owner for the purpose of lawsuits.

The following information will have to be used to fill in this form:

① State of Affidavit
② County of Affidavit
③ Address of business
④ Fictitious name
⑤ Name of all owners with interest in business
⑥ Percent of business
⑦ Date of signatures
⑧ Signatures of all owners
⑨ Printed names of all owners
⑩ Notary will complete the following section

Partnership Agreement: This legal agreement is for use in beginning a partnership. This particular agreement provides for three partners to join into a partnership. Any number of partners, however, can be used with this agreement by simple addition or deletion of names and signature lines.

The information necessary to complete this form is as follows:

① Date of agreement
② Name of seller
③ Address of seller with name of city and state
④ Name of buyer
⑤ Address of buyer with name of city and state
⑥ Partnership purpose
⑦ Date of partnership
⑧ Name of partnership

⑨ Total start-up capital
⑩ Breakdown of start-up capital : name all partners
⑪ List partners contribution (cash, service or property) to the partnership
⑫ Value of partners contribution
⑬ Date by which contribution must be made
⑭ Whether the accounting for the partnership will be on an accrual or cash basis
⑮ Name of partner
⑯ The proportionate shares of the profits and losses of the partnership that each partner will be entitled to
⑰ Any additional terms
⑱ State where partnership will operate
⑲ Date of signatures
⑳ Signatures of all partners
㉑ Printed names of all partners

Note that certain basic terms have been provided for the operation of the partnership under this agreement. These terms are general in nature and can be modified if all of the partners agree. The agreement terms which are provided are as follows:

- That additional contributions to capital may be made at any time by unanimous vote of the partners
- That each partner has equal management and control power
- That all decisions will be made by unanimous vote
- That the partners may select a partner to manage the day-to-day operations
- That bank checks may be signed by all of the partners or by the managing partner
- That the accounting will include income and capital accounts for each partner
- That partners can withdraw money from their income accounts only on unanimous agreement of the partners
- That a proportionate share of profits and losses is provided for
- That the partnership can be continued if a partner withdraws (or dies)
- That a withdrawing partner's interest must be sold to the remaining partners after an independent appraisal
- That a partner may not transfer any of his partnership interest to anyone else
- That the assets will be applied in a certain order to partnership obligations upon termination
- That mediation and arbitration will be used to settle disputes among the partners

AGREEMENT FOR SALE OF BUSINESS

This agreement is made on ①_____ , 20 _____ , between ②_____ , seller, of ③
_____ , City of _____ , State of _____ , and ④_____
_____ , buyer, of ⑤_____ , City of _____ , State of _____ .

The seller now owns and conducts a ⑥_____ business, under the name of ⑦_____
_____ , located at ⑧_____ , City of _____ , State of _____ .

For valuable consideration, the seller agrees to sell and the buyer agrees to buy this business for the following price and on the following terms:

1. The seller will sell to the buyer, free from all liabilities, claims, and indebtedness, the seller's business, including the premises located at ⑨_____ , City of _____ , State of _____ , and all other assets of the business as listed on Exhibit A, which is attached and is a part of this agreement.

2. The buyer agrees to pay the seller the sum of $ ⑩_____ , which the seller agrees to accept as full payment. The purchase price will be allocated to the assets of the business as follows:

    a. The premises $ ⑪_____
    b. Equipment/furniture $ ⑫_____
    c. Goodwill $ ⑬_____
    d. Stock-in-trade/inventory $ ⑭_____
    e. Notes/accounts receivable $ ⑮_____
    f. Outstanding contracts $ ⑯_____

3. The purchase price will be paid as follows:

    Earnest money $ ⑰_____
    Cash down payment $ ⑱_____
    Promissory note payable $ ⑲_____

    TOTAL Price $ ⑳_____

The $ ㉑_____ Promissory Note will bear interest at ㉒_____ % (_____ percent) per year, payable monthly for ㉓_____ years at $ ㉔_____ per month with the first payment due one (1) month after the date of closing. The Promissory Note will be secured by a U.C.C. Financing Statement and a Security Agreement in the usual commercial form. The Promissory Note will be prepayable without limitation or penalty.

4. The seller acknowledges receiving the earnest money deposit of $ ㉕_____ from the buyer. If this sale is not completed for any valid reason, this money will be returned to the buyer without penalty or interest.

5. This agreement will close on ㉖_____ , 20 _____ , at ㉗_____ o'clock ____ . m., at ㉘_____ , City of _____ , State of _____ .

At that time, and upon payment by the buyer of the portion of the purchase price then due, the seller will deliver to buyer the following documents:

    a. A Bill of Sale for all personal property (equipment, inventory, parts, supplies, and any other personal property)
    b. A Warranty Deed for any real estate
    c. All accounting books and records
    d. All customer and supplier lists
    e. A valid assignment of any lease
    f. All other documents of transfer as listed below: ㉙

At closing, adjustments to the purchase price will be made for the following items:

    a. Changes in inventory since this agreement was made
    b. Insurance premiums

    c.   Payroll and payroll taxes
    d.   Rental payments
    e.   Utilities
    f.   Property taxes
    g.   The following other items:

6.   The seller represents and warrants that it is duly qualified under the laws of the State of ㉚_____ to carry on the business being sold, and has complied with and is not in violation of any laws or regulations affecting the seller's business, including any laws governing bulk sales or transfers.

7.   Attached as part of this agreement as Exhibit B is a Balance Sheet of the seller as of ㉛_____ , 20 _____ , which has been prepared according to generally accepted accounting principles. The seller warrants that this Balance Sheet fairly represents the financial position of the seller as of that date and sets out any contractual obligations of the seller. If this sale includes the sale of inventory of the business, the seller has provided the buyer with a completed Bulk Transfer Affidavit containing a complete list of all creditors of the seller, together with the amount claimed to be due to each creditor.

8.   Seller represents that it has good and marketable title to all of the assets shown on Exhibit A, and that those assets are free and clear of any restrictions on transfer and all claims, taxes, indebtedness, or liabilities except those specified on the Exhibit B Balance Sheet. The seller also warrants that all equipment will be delivered in working order on the date of closing.

9.   Seller agrees not to participate in any way, either directly or indirectly, in a business similar to that being sold to the buyer, within a radius of ㉜_____ miles from this business, for a period of ㉝_____ years from the date of closing.

10. Between the date of this agreement and the date of closing of the sale, the seller agrees to carry on the business in the usual manner and agrees not to enter into any unusual contract or other agreement affecting the operation of the business without the consent of the buyer.

11. The buyer represents that it is financially capable of completing the purchase of this business and fully understands its obligations under this agreement.

12. Buyer agrees to carry hazard and liability insurance on the assets of the business in the amount of $ ㉞_____ and to provide the seller with proof of this coverage until the Promissory Note is paid in full. However, the risk of any loss or damage to any assets being sold remain with the seller until the date of closing.

13. Any additional terms: ㉟

14. No modification of this agreement will be effective unless it is in writing and is signed by both the buyer and seller. This agreement binds and benefits both the buyer and seller and any successors. Time is of the essence of this agreement. This document, including any attachments, is the entire agreement between the buyer and seller. This agreement is governed by the laws of the State of ㊱_____ .

Dated: ㊲_____ , 20 _____

㊳_____
Signature of Seller

㊴_____
Printed Name of Seller

DBA
㊵_____
Name of Business

A(n) ㊶_____ (type of business)

State of Operation ㊷_____

⑬_____
Signature of Buyer

⑭_____
Printed Name of Buyer

⑮
State of _____
County of _____

On _____ , 20 _____ , _____ personally came before me and, being duly sworn, did state that he or she is the person who owns the business described in the above document and that he or she signed the above document in my presence on behalf of the business and on his or her own behalf.

_____
Signature of Notary Public

Notary Public, In and for the County of _____
State of _____

My commission expires: _____ , 20 _____   Notary Seal

⑮
State of _____
County of _____

On _____ , 20 _____ , _____ personally came before me and, being duly sworn, did state that he or she is the person described in the above document as the buyer and that he or she signed the above document in my presence.

_____
Signature of Notary Public

Notary Public, In and for the County of _____
State of _____

My commission expires: _____ , 20 _____   Notary Seal

AGREEMENT FOR SALE OF BUSINESS ASSETS

This agreement is made on ①_____ , 20 _____ , between ②_____ , seller, of③
_____ , City of _____ , State of _____ , and④
_____ , buyer, of ⑤_____ , City of _____ , State of _____ .

The seller now owns and conducts a ⑥_____ business, under the name of ⑦_____ , located
at ⑧_____ , City of _____ , State of _____ .

For valuable consideration, the seller agrees to sell and the buyer agrees to buy certain assets of this business for the following price and on the following terms:

1. The seller will sell to the buyer certain assets of the business as listed on Exhibit A, which is attached and is a part of this
   agreement. The assets will be transferred free from all liabilities, claims, and indebtedness, unless listed on Exhibit A.

2. The buyer agrees to pay the seller the sum of $ ⑨_____ , which the seller agrees to accept as full pay-
   ment.

3. The purchase price will be paid as follows:

   Earnest money $ ⑩_____
   Cash down payment $ ⑪_____
   Promissory note payable $ ⑫_____

   TOTAL Price $ ⑬_____

   The $ ⑭_____ Promissory Note will bear interest at ⑮_____ % (_____ percent) per
   year, payable monthly for ⑯_____ years at $ ⑰_____ per month with the first payment due one
   (1) month after the date of closing. The Promissory Note will be secured by a UCC Financing Statement and a Security
   Agreement in the usual commercial form. The Promissory Note will be prepayable without limitation or penalty.

4. The seller acknowledges receiving the earnest money deposit of $ ⑱_____ from the buyer. If this sale is not com-
   pleted for any valid reason, this money will be returned to the buyer without penalty or interest.

5. This agreement will close on ⑲_____ , 20 _____ , at ⑳_____ o'clock ____ . m., at ㉑_____ ,City
   of _____ , State of _____ .

   At that time, and upon payment by buyer of the portion of the purchase price then due, the seller will deliver to buyer
   the following documents:

   a. A Bill of Sale for all personal property (equipment, inventory, parts, supplies, and any other personal property)
   b. All other documents of transfer as listed below:㉒

   At closing, adjustments to the purchase price will be made for changes in inventory since this agreement was made,
   and for the following other items: ㉓

6. The seller represents and warrants that it is in full compliance with and is not in violation of any laws or regulations
   affecting the seller's business, including any laws governing bulk sales or transfers.

7. Seller represents that it has good and marketable title to all of the assets shown on Exhibit A, and that those assets
   are free and clear of any restrictions on transfer, claims, taxes, indebtedness, or liabilities except those specified on the
   Exhibit A. If this sale includes the sale of inventory of the business, the seller has provided the buyer with a completed
   Bulk Transfer Affidavit containing a complete list of all creditors of the seller, together with the amount claimed to be
   due to each creditor. Seller also warrants that all equipment will be delivered in working order on the date of closing.

8. Between the date of this agreement and the date of closing of the sale, the seller agrees to carry on the business in the usual manner and agrees not to enter into any unusual contract or other agreement affecting the business assets being sold without the consent of the buyer.

9. The buyer represents that it is financially capable of completing the purchase of these business assets and fully understands its obligations under this agreement.

10. Buyer agrees to carry hazard and liability insurance on the assets of the business in the amount of $ ㉔_____ and to provide the seller with proof of this coverage until the Promissory Note is paid in full. However, the risk of any loss or damage to any assets being sold remain with the seller until the date of closing.

11. Any additional terms:㉕

12. No modification of this agreement will be effective unless it is in writing and is signed by both the buyer and seller. This agreement binds and benefits both the buyer and seller and any successors. Time is of the essence of this agreement. This document, including any attachments, is the entire agreement between the buyer and seller. This agreement is governed by the laws of the State of ㉖_____ .

Dated: ㉗_____ , 20 _____

㉘_____
Signature of Seller

㉙_____
Printed Name of Seller

DBA
㉚_____
Name of Business

A(n) ㉛_____ (type of business)

State of Operation ㉜_____

㉝_____
Signature of Buyer

㉞_____
Printed Name of Buyer

NOTICE OF INTENTION TO USE FICTITIOUS BUSINESS NAME

NOTICE is hereby given that the undersigned intends to engage in business at the following address:①

under the fictitious business name of:②

The full and true name of every person with an interest in this business and the ownership interest of each person is as follows:

③*Name*   ④*Percent of Interest*

_____   _____

_____   _____

_____   _____

_____   _____

Dated: ⑤_____ , 20 _____

⑥*Signature of Owner(s)*   ⑦*Printed Name of Owner(s)*

_____   _____

_____   _____

_____   _____

_____   _____

AFFIDAVIT OF USE OF FICTITIOUS BUSINESS NAME

State of ①_____
County of ②_____

It is hereby stated, under oath, that pursuant to law:

1. The undersigned intends to engage in business at the following address:③

   under the fictitious name of:④

2. The full and true name of every person with an interest in this business and the ownership interest of each person is as follows:

⑤Name	⑥Percent of Interest
_____	_____
_____	_____
_____	_____

3. A Proof of Publication of a Notice of Intention to Use a Fictitious Name is filed with this affidavit.

Dated: ⑦_____ , 20 _____

⑧Signature of Owner(s)	⑨Printed Name of Owner(s)
_____	_____
_____	_____
_____	_____
_____	_____

⑩
State of _____
County of _____

On _____ , 20 _____ , _____ personally came before me and, being duly sworn, did state that he, she, or they is or are the person(s) who own(s) the business described in the above document and that he, she, or they signed the above document in my presence.

_____
Signature of Notary Public

Notary Public, In and for the County of _____
State of _____

My commission expires: _____ , 20 _____   Notary Seal

PARTNERSHIP AGREEMENT

This agreement is made on ①_____ , 20 _____ , between ②_____ , of ③_____
_____ , City of _____ , State of _____ , and
④_____ , of ⑤_____ , City of _____
, State of _____ .

The parties to this agreement agree to carry on a partnership for the following purpose:⑥

and under the following terms and conditions:

1. The partnership will begin on ⑦_____ , 20 _____ , and will continue indefinitely until terminated.

2. The name of the partnership will be ⑧_____ .

3. The start-up capital of the partnership will be a total of $ ⑨_____ . Each partner of the partnership
   will contribute the following property, services, or cash to this total amount:

⑩Name	⑪Cash/Services/Property		⑫Value
_____	_____	$	_____
_____	_____	$	_____
_____	_____	$	_____
_____	_____	$	_____

These contributions must be made by ⑬_____ , 20 _____ . The partners may decide, by unanimous vote, to contribute additional capital to the partnership at any time.

4. Each partner will have an equal right to manage and control the partnership. Partnership decisions will be
   made by unanimous vote. The partners can select one of the partners to carry on the day-to-day operations
   of the partnership.

5. The partnership will maintain a bank account. Checks may be signed by either all of the partners together or by a
   partner selected to carry on the day-to-day operations of the partnership.

6. The partnership will maintain accounting records which will be open to any partner for inspection. These records will
   include separate income and capital accounts for each partner. The accounting will be on the ⑭_____
   basis and on a calendar-year basis. The capital account of each partner will consist of no less than the value of the
   property, services, or cash contributed under paragraph 3 of this agreement. Partners may withdraw money from
   their income accounts upon unanimous agreement of the partners.

7. The profits and losses of the partnership will be shared by all partners in the following proportions:

⑮Name	⑯Percent of Share
_____	_____
_____	_____
_____	_____
_____	_____

8. If any partner withdraws from the partnership for any reason (including death), the partnership can continue and be operated by the remaining partners. However, the withdrawing partner (or his or her representative) will be obligated to sell his or her interest in the partnership to the remaining partners and the remaining partners will be obligated to buy that interest. The value of the withdrawing partner's interest will be his or her proportionate share of the total value of the partnership. The total value of the partnership will be determined by an independent appraisal made within ninety (90) days of the partner's withdrawal. All partners of the partnership (including the partner withdrawing) will equally share the cost of the appraisal.

9. A partner may not transfer all or part of his or her interest in the partnership to any other party.

10. The partnership may be terminated at any time by unanimous agreement among the partners. Upon termination, the partners agree to apply the assets and money of the partnership in the following order:

   a. to pay all the debts of the partnership

   b. to distribute the partner's income accounts to the partners in their proportionate share

   c. to distribute the partner's capital accounts to the partners in their proportionate share

   d. to distribute any remaining assets to the partners in their proportionate share

11. Any dispute between the partners related to this agreement will be settled by voluntary mediation. If mediation is unsuccessful, the dispute will be settled by binding arbitration using an arbitrator of the American Arbitration Association.

12. Any additional terms:⑰

13. No modification of this agreement will be effective unless it is in writing and is signed by all partners. This agreement binds and benefits all partners and any successors. Time is of the essence of this agreement. This document is the entire agreement between the partners. This agreement is governed by the laws of the State of ⑱_____ .

Dated: ⑲_____ , 20 _____

⑳Signature of Partner(s)   ㉑Printed Name of Partner(s)

_____   _____

_____   _____

_____   _____

_____   _____

Chapter 18

Employment Documents

The legal forms in this chapter cover two situations that arise in the area of employment. Written documents that outline each person's responsibilities and duties are important for keeping an employment situation on an even keel. The employment contract contained in this chapter may be used and adapted for virtually any employment situation. As job skills and salaries rise and employees are allowed access to sensitive and confidential business information, written employment contracts are often a prudent business practice. An independent contractor may also be hired to perform a particular task. As opposed to an employee, this type of worker is defined as one who maintains his or her own independent business, uses his or her own tools, and does not work under the direct supervision of the person who has hired him or her. A contract for hiring an independent contractor is provided in this chapter.

Employment Document Instructions

General Employment Contract: This form may be used for any situation in which an employee is hired for a specific job. The issues addressed by this contract are as follows:

- That the employee will perform a certain job and any incidental further duties
- That the employee will be hired for a certain period and for a certain salary
- That the employee will be given certain job benefits (for example: sick pay, vacations, etc.)
- That the employee agrees to abide by the employer's rules and regulations
- That the employee agrees to sign agreements regarding confidentiality and inventions
- That the employee agrees to submit any employment disputes to mediation and arbitration

The information necessary to complete this form is as follows:

① Date of the contract
② Name of employer
③ Address of employer including city and state
④ Name of employee
⑤ Address of employee including city and state
⑥ A complete description of the job
⑦ Date employee to start work
⑧ Length of time job to continue (can be 'indefinite')
⑨ Pay per week for employee
⑩ Amount of sick pay
⑪ Amount of vacations
⑫ Amount of bonuses
⑬ Amount of retirement
⑭ Amount of insurance benefits
⑮ Terms of termination
⑯ Number of days employee can be incapacitated before termination
⑰ Additional documents signed by employee
⑱ Additional terms of the contract
⑲ The state whose laws will govern the contract
⑳ Date of signatures
㉑ Signature of employer
㉒ Printed name of employer
㉓ Signature of employee
㉔ Printed name of employee

Independent Contractor Agreement: This form should be used when hiring an independent contractor. It provides a standard form for the hiring out of specific work to be performed within a set time period for a particular payment. It also provides a method for authorizing extra work under the contract. Finally, this document provides that the contractor agrees to indemnify (reimburse or compensate) the owner against any claims or liabilities arising from the performance of the work. To complete this form, fill in a detailed description of the work; dates by which certain portions of the job are to be completed; the pay for the job; the terms and dates of payment; and the state whose laws will govern the contract.

The information necessary to complete this form is as follows:

① Date of the agreement
② Name of owner
③ Address of owner including city and state
④ Name of contractor
⑤ Address of contractor including city and state
⑥ A complete description of the job that the contractor is performing including all labor and materials

⑦ Describe portion of work being done
⑧ Date that above portion will be completed by
⑨ Amount of full payment
⑩ Specific work description to be completed before owner makes payment
⑪ Dates that work should be completed by before owner makes payment
⑫ The state whose laws will govern the agreement
⑬ Date of signatures
⑭ Signature of owner
⑮ Printed name of owner
⑯ signature of contractor
⑰ Printed name of contractor

General Employment Contract

This contract is made on ①_____ , 20 _____ , between
②_____ , employer, of ③_____
_____ , City of _____ , State of _____
, and ④_____ , employee, of ⑤_____
_____ , City of _____ , State of _____ .

For valuable consideration, the employer and employee agree as follows:

1. The employee agrees to perform the following duties and job description:⑥

    The employee also agrees to perform further duties incidental to the general job descrip-
    tion. This is considered a full-time position.

2. The employee will begin work on ⑦_____ , 20 _____ .

    This position shall continue for a period of ⑧_____ .

3. The employee will be paid the following:

    Weekly salary: $ ⑨_____

    The employee will also be given the following benefits:

    Sick pay: $ ⑩_____
    Vacations: $ ⑪_____
    Bonuses: $ ⑫_____
    Retirement benefits: $ ⑬_____
    Insurance benefits: $ ⑭_____

4. The employee agrees to abide by all rules and regulations of the employer at all times
    while employed.

5. This contract may be terminated by: ⑮

(a) Breach of this contract by the employee

(b) The expiration of this contract without renewal

(c) Death of the employee

(d) Incapacitation of the employee for over ⑯_____ days in any one (1) year

6. The employee agrees to sign the following additional documents as a condition to obtaining employment:⑰

7. Any dispute between the employer and employee related to this contract will be settled by voluntary mediation. If mediation is unsuccessful, the dispute will be settled by binding arbitration using an arbitrator of the American Arbitration Association.

8. Any additional terms of this contract: ⑱

9. No modification of this contract will be effective unless it is in writing and is signed by both the employer and employee. This contract binds and benefits both parties and any successors. Time is of the essence of this contract. This document is the entire agreement between the parties. This contract is governed by the laws of the State of ⑲_____ .

Dated: ⑳_____ , 20 _____

㉑_____
Signature of Employer

㉒_____
Printed Name of Employer

㉓_____
Signature of Employee

㉔_____
Printed Name of Employee

Independent Contractor Agreement

This agreement is made on ① _____ , 20 _____ , between ② _____
_____ , owner, of ③ _____ , City of _____
_____ , State of _____ , and ④ _____
, contractor, of ⑤ _____ , City of _____
_____ , State of _____ .

For valuable consideration, the owner and contractor agree as follows:

1. The contractor agrees to furnish all of the labor and materials to do the following work
   for the owner as an independent contractor:⑥

2. The contractor agrees that the following portions of the total work will be completed by
   the dates specified:

   Work: ⑦

   Dates: ⑧ _____

3. The contractor agrees to perform this work in a workmanlike manner according to standard practices. If any plans or specifications are part of this job, they are attached to
   and are part of this agreement.

4. The owner agrees to pay the contractor as full payment $ ⑨ _____ , for doing the
   work outlined above. This price will be paid to the contractor on satisfactory completion
   of the work in the following manner and on the following dates:

   Work: ⑩

   Dates: ⑪ _____

5. The contractor and the owner may agree to extra services and work, but any such extras must be set out and agreed to in writing by both the contractor and the owner.

6. The contractor agrees to indemnify and hold the owner harmless from any claims or liability arising from the contractor's work under this agreement.

7. No modification of this agreement will be effective unless it is in writing and is signed by both parties. This agreement binds and benefits both parties and any successors. Time is of the essence of this agreement. This document, including any attachments, is the entire agreement between the parties. This agreement is governed by the laws of the State of ⑫ _____.

Dated: ⑬_____ , 20 _____

⑭_____
Signature of Owner

⑮_____
Printed Name of Owner

⑯_____
Signature of Contractor

⑰_____
Printed Name of Contractor

Index of Forms

Addendum to Contract (Real estate)
(California)
    -form (on CD only)
    -instructions 324
Addendum to Lease (California)
    -form (on CD only)
    -instructions 269
Addendum to Lease (Chicago)
    -form (on CD only)
    -instructions 269
Additional Information for Advance Health Care
Directive
    -form 191
    -instructions 190
Advance Health Care Directives-State-Specific
    -forms (on CD only)
    -instructions 179
Affidavit of Use of Fictitious Business Name
    -form 370
    -instructions 362
Agreement for Sale of Business Assets
    -form 367
    -instructions 360
Agreement for Sale of Business
    -form 364
    -instructions 358
Agreement to Sell Real Estate
    -form 332
    -instructions 321
Alimony Questionnaire
    -form (CD only)
    -instructions 231
Amendment of Lease
    -form 297
    -instructions 274
Appraisal Affidavit
    -form 343
    -instructions 330
Appraisal Report
    -form 342
    -instructions 329
Assignment of Contract
    -form 28
    -instructions 23
Assignment of Lease
    -form 300
    -instructions 276

Assignment to Living Trust
    -form 166
    -instructions 165
Beneficiary Questionnaire (Will/Living Trust)
    -form (on CD only)
    -instructions 109
Bill of Sale, Subject to Debt
    -form 320
    -instructions 313
Bill of Sale, without Warranties
    -form 319
    -instructions 313
Bill of Sale, with Warranties
    -form 318
    -instructions 312
California Addendum to Contract (Real Estate)
    -form (on CD only)
    -instructions 324
California Addendum to Lease
    -form (on CD only)
    -instructions 269
California Notary Acknowledgment
    -form (on CD only)
    -instructions 31
Chicago Addendum to Lease
    -form (on CD only)
    -instructions 269
Chicago Heating Disclosure Form
    -form (on CD only)
    -instructions 269
Chicago Residential Landlord and Tenant
Ordinance Summary
    -form (on CD only)
    -instructions 269
Child Custody Questionnaire
    -form (on CD only)
    -instructions 235
Child Support Worksheet and Guidelines
    -form (on CD only)
    -instructions 249
Commercial Lease
    -form 292
    -instructions 272
Consent to Assignment of Contract
    -form 29
    -instructions 23

Consent to Assignment of Lease
  -form 301
  -instructions 277
Consent to Sublease
  -form 303
  -instructions 278
Contract for Sale of Personal Property
  -form 317
  -instructions 312
Contract for Deed
  -form 335
  -instructions 323
Corporate Signature Line
  -form 34
  -instructions 31
Corporate Acknowledgment
  -form 35
  -instructions 32
Credit/Rental Application
  -form 283
  -instructions 267
Custody and Visitation Worksheet
  -form (on CD only)
  -instructions 241
Declaration of Intent to Forfeit and Terminate
Contract for Deed
  -form 338
  -instructions 325
Demand and Notice of Default on Installment
Promissory Note
  -form 354
  -instructions 351
Document Checklist (Marital Settlement
Agreement)
  -form 199
  -instructions 199
Durable Health Care Power of Attorney
  -form 79
  -instructions 78
Durable Powers of Attorney - State Specific
  -forms (on CD only)
  -instructions 43, 66
Durable Unlimited Power of Attorney for
Financial Affairs (Effective Immediately)
  -form 68
  -instructions 67
Durable Unlimited Power of Attorney for
Financial Affairs (Effective on Incapacity or
Disability)
  -form 72
  -instructions 71

Extension of Lease
  -form 298
  -instructions 275
Extension of Contract
  -form 25
  -instructions 21
Federal Lead Brochure
  -form (on CD only)
  -instructions 269, 329
Final Notice Before Legal Action
  -form 308
  -instructions 281
Financial Statement (Marital Settlement
Agreement)
  -form 227
  -instructions 281
General Employment Contract
  -form 276
  -instructions 373
General Contract
  -form 24
  -instructions 20
General Power of Attorney
  -form 45
  -instructions 44
General Release
  -form 258
  -instructions 256
Husband and Wife Acknowledgment
  -form 40
  -instructions 33
Husband and Wife Signature Line
  -form 40
  -instructions 33
Independent Contractor Agreement
  -form 378
  -instructions 374
Individual Acknowledgment
  -form 39
  -instructions 33
Individual Signature Line
  -form 39
  -instructions 33
Landlord's Notice to Terminate Lease
  -form 307
  -instructions 280
Lead Warning Statement
  -form 341
  -instructions 328
Lease with Purchase Option
  -form 294
  -instructions 293

Limited Liability Company Signature Line
  -form 36
  -instructions 32
Limited Liability Company Acknowledgment
  -form 36
  -instructions 32
Limited Power of Attorney
  -form 61
  -instructions 60
Living Will Declaration and Directive to
Physicians
  -form 173
  -instructions 171
Living Trust with Children's Trust
  -form 149
  -instructions 148
Living Trust without Children's Trust
  -form 154
  -instructions 153
Marital Settlement Agreement
  -form 207
  -instructions 204
Modification of Contract
  -form 26
  -instructions 21
Month-to-Month Rental Agreement
  -form 290
  -instructions 270
Move-in/Move-out Checklist and
Acknowledgment
  -form 285
  -instructions 268
Mutual Release
  -form 259
  -instructions 257
Mutual Termination of Lease
  -form 299
  -instructions 276
New York Notice of Assignment of Property to
Living Trust
  -form (on CD only)
  -instructions 167
Notice of Breach of Lease
  -form 305
  -instructions 281
Notice of Intention to Use Fictitious Name
  -form 369
  -instructions 361
Notice of Lease
  -form 309
  -instructions 281

Notice to Pay Rent or Vacate
  -form 306
  -instructions 279
Notice of Rent Default
  -form 304
  -instructions 278
Offer to Purchase Real Estate
  -form 340
  -instructions 327
Option to Buy Real Estate
  -form 339
  -instructions 326
Partnership Acknowledgment
  -form 35
  -instructions 32
Partnership Agreement
  -form 371
  -instructions 362
Partnership Signature Line
  -form 35
  -instructions 32
Personal Property Rental Agreement
  -form 315
  -instructions 311
Power of Attorney Acknowledgment
  -form 38
  -instructions 32
Power of Attorney Signature Line
  -form 38
  -instructions 32
Preliminary Questionnaire (Marital Settlement
Agreement)
  -form (on CD only)
  -instructions 198
Premarital Agreement
  -form 195
  -instructions 194
Promissory Note (Installment Repayment)
  -form 352
  -instructions 348
Promissory Note (Lump Sum Repayment)
  -form 352
  -instructions 349
Promissory Note (on Demand)
  -form 353
  -instructions 350
Property Division Worksheet (Marital
Settlement Agreement)
  -form (on CD only)
  -instructions 223

Property Questionnaire (Marital Settlement Agreement)
 -form (on CD only)
 -instructions 216
Property Questionnaire (Will/Living Trust)
 -form (on CD only)
 -instructions 105
Quitclaim Deed
 -form 344
 -instructions 330
Receipt for Goods
 -form 265
 -instructions 262
Receipt for Lease Security Deposit
 -form 310
 -instructions 282
Receipt in Full
 -form 263
 -instructions 261
Receipt on Account
 -form 264
 -instructions 261
Registration of Living Trust
 -form (on CD only)
 -instructions 167
Release of Promissory Note
 -form 354
 -instructions 350
Rent Receipt
 -form 310
 -instructions 282
Residential Lease
 -form 287
 -instructions 269
Revocation of Advance Health Care Directive
 -form 187
 -instructions 186
Revocation of Durable Health Care Power of Attorney
 -form 85
 -instructions 80
Revocation of Living Will
 -form 178
 -instructions 177
Revocation of Power of Attorney
 -form 89
 -instructions 88
Schedule of Beneficiaries of Living Trust
 -form 163
 -instructions 162

Schedule of Assets of Living Trust
 -form 159
 -instructions 158
Sole Proprietorship Acknowledgment
 -form 37
 -instructions 32
Sole Proprietorship Signature Line
 -form 37
 -instructions 32
Specific Release
 -form 260
 -instructions 257
Sublease
 -form 302
 -instructions 277
Successor Trustee/Executor Information List
 -form (on CD only)
 -instructions 96
Successor Trustee/Executor Duties Checklist
 -form 93
 -instructions 93
Termination of Contract
 -form 29
 -instructions 22
Unlimited Power of Attorney
 -form 50
 -instructions 49
Warranty Deed
 -form 346
 -instructions 331
Will For Married Person Without Children
 -form 128
 -instructions 126
Will For Married Person With Children
 -form 121
 -instructions 118
Will For Single Person Without Children
 -form 134
 -instructions 132
Witness Affidavit of Oral Revocation of Advance Health Care Directive
 -form 189
 -instructions 188
Witness Affidavit of Oral Revocation of Durable Health Care Power of Attorney
 -form 87
 -instructions 86

Nova Publishing Company

Small Business and Consumer Legal Books and Software

Legal Toolkit Series

Estate Planning Toolkit	ISBN 13: 978-1-892949-44-8	Book w/CD	$39.95
Business Start-Up Toolkit	ISBN 13: 978-1-892949-43-1	Book w/CD	$39.95
Legal Forms Toolkit	ISBN 13: 978-1-892949-48-6	Book w/CD	$39.95
No-Fault Divorce Toolkit	ISBN 13: 978-1-892949-35-6	Book w/CD	$39.95
Personal Bankruptcy Toolkit	ISBN 13: 978-1-892949-42-4	Book w/CD	$29.95
Will and Living Will Toolkit (available October 2009)	ISBN 13: 978-1-892949-47-9	Book w/CD	$29.95

Law Made Simple Series

Advance Health Care Directives Simplified	ISBN 13: 978-1-892949-23-3	Book w/CD	$24.95
Living Trusts Simplified	ISBN 0-935755-51-9	Book w/CD	$28.95
Personal Legal Forms Simplified (3rd Edition)	ISBN 0-935755-97-7	Book w/CD	$28.95
Powers of Attorney Simplified	ISBN 13: 978-1-892949-40-0	Book w/CD	$24.95

Small Business Made Simple Series

Corporation: Small Business Start-up Kit (2nd Edition)	ISBN 1-892949-06-7	Book w/CD	$29.95
Employer Legal Forms	ISBN 13: 978-1-892949-26-4	Book w/CD	$24.95
Landlord Legal Forms	ISBN 13: 978-1-892949-24-0	Book w/CD	$24.95
Limited Liability Company: Start-up Kit (3rd Edition)	ISBN 13: 978-1-892949-37-0	Book w/CD	$29.95
Partnership: Start-up Kit (2nd Edition)	ISBN 1-892949-07-5	Book w/CD	$29.95
Real Estate Forms Simplified	ISBN 0-935755-09-1	Book w/CD	$29.95
S-Corporation: Small Business Start-up Kit (3rd Edition)	ISBN 13: 978-1-892949-36-3	Book w/CD	$29.95
Small Business Accounting Simplified (4th Edition)	ISBN 1-892949-17-2	Book only	$24.95
Small Business Bookkeeping System Simplified	ISBN 0-935755-74-8	Book only	$14.95
Small Business Legal Forms Simplified (4th Edition)	ISBN 0-935755-98-5	Book w/CD	$29.95
Small Business Payroll System Simplified	ISBN 0-935755-55-1	Book only	$14.95
Sole Proprietorship: Start-up Kit (2nd Edition)	ISBN 1-892949-08-3	Book w/CD	$29.95

Legal Self-Help Series

Divorce Yourself: The National Divorce Kit (6th Edition)	ISBN 1-892949-12-1	Book w/CD	$39.95
Prepare Your Own Will: The National Will Kit (6th Edition)	ISBN 1-892949-15-6	Book w/CD	$29.95

National Legal Kits

Simplified Divorce Kit (3 rd Edition)	ISBN 13: 978-1-892949-39-4	Book w/CD	$24.95
Simplified Family Legal Forms Kit (2nd Edition)	ISBN 13: 978-1-892949-41-7	Book w/CD	$19.95
Simplified Incorporation Kit	ISBN 1-892949-33-4	Book w/CD	$19.95
Simplified Limited Liability Company Kit	ISBN 1-892949-32-6	Book w/CD	$19.95
Simplified Living Will Kit (2nd Edition)	ISBN 13: 978-1-892949-45-5	Book w/CD	$19.95
Simplified S-Corporation Kit	ISBN 1-892949-31-8	Book w/CD	$19.95
Simplified Will Kit (3rd Edition)	ISBN 1-892949-38-5	Book w/CD	$19.95

Ordering Information

Distributed by:
National Book Network
4501 Forbes Blvd. Suite 200
Lanham MD 20706

Shipping: $4.50 for first & $.75 for additional
Phone orders with Visa/MC: (800) 462-6420
Fax orders with Visa/MC: (800) 338-4550
Internet: www.novapublishing.com
Free shipping on all internet orders (within in the U.S.)